THE
SILENCE
OF
SHIVA

MOHANJI

Gurulight

The Silence of Shiva

Acknowledgments & Credits
Cover Design & Book Layout Design: Mirko Trbusić
Language, Proof Reading and Review:
    Hein Adamson
    K. S. Geetha
    Lata Ganesh
    Shyama Jayaseelan
Editing: Rajesh Kamath

First edition published by Gurulight, 2021
Email: info@gurulight.com
Web: www.gurulight.com

Gurulight

This Book

is offered as flowers of gratitude at the Lotus Feet of Mata, Pita, Guru, Daivam

Mata, Pita: My biological parents and the ancestors of my lineage to whom I owe this physical body

Guru: All the Grand Traditions of Bharat that have been leading mankind to liberation (freedom while living and freedom while leaving) since the beginning of time

Daivam: The Divine Parents, the silent Shiva (the Supreme Consciousness) who defines my essence and the active Shakti (the Divine Play of Consciousness) who defines my purpose

NOTE TO READERS

This book, a follow-up to the book 'The Power of Purity: Essential Essays and Answers About Spiritual Paths and Liberation', is a compilation of questions and answers from Mohanji's discourses as well as Mohanji's literature from 2011 until December 31st 2015. The book reveals the constantly changing flavours of Mohanji as we go through his words from the next five years from where the previous book left off.

An important point that the readers should bear in mind when reading the book. By Shiva, we refer to the state of Supreme Consciousness and the term should not be confused with a person or personification. Shiva is that presence which permeates and activates everything yet has nothing to do with any of it. The book talks about the various aspects of Shiva but these aspects are not Shiva. In essence, the chapters, the explanations, and the questions and answers reflect upon what Shiva is not.

It is an individual journey to attain the state of Shiva. This book is about that journey, not the destination, because the destination is beyond description. None can take us there, not even a spiritual Master who has reached that State. Yet, each one of us has the potential to reach that State and when we reach that State, we become the State: we become Shiva.

— Editor

FOREWORD

Vishwa Kalyanananda Bharathi is the name suggested by a great spiritual Master belonging to a great Tradition of Masters of enlightenment for Shri Mohanji. The physical features and enthusiasm to love and lead the followers have made him an essential part of every devotee. Every valley of aeons has showers of wisdom from Masters to bless and enlighten the path. Here is a fountain of wisdom flowing from Mohanji. It is not an effort but a happening, in response to the thirsty souls after him.

"More than the calf wishes to suck does the cow yearn to suckle". Rabbi Achiba put this feeling to his favourite disciple Ben Yochai in Roman captivity and it is the same with Mohanji. The collected pearls from the valleys of divine Masters wrapped in the syrup of his learning and experience make the work delicious and an eye-opener. Shri Mohanji is an incarnation and embodiment of love which is the prime requirement for this emotional turmoil of the fourth root race of humanity.

Crores (tens of millions) of words and millions of books on spirituality can be summarised in two words, the seer and the scenes. The seer is not at all affected by the scenes and therefore free to enjoy the scenes. The marvels of creation are meant for enjoying.

The purpose of creation is mentioned in the Vedas. The will of the Almighty resulted in two principles and later innumerable principles and resulted in the marvels of creation. If we identify as body, mind and intellect, our lifetime will be just sufficient to fight against hunger, disease, emotional conflicts and ignorance. When we identify with the Soul, we are unaffected by the scenes, and we will be free to enjoy the marvels of creation, which is considered the aim of life. Until we recognise ourselves as the Soul, we will be suffering our life. Once we recognise ourselves as the self, we start enjoying our life.

Mohanji has gracefully dedicated one chapter to enlighten us towards our true nature. which will alleviate all our miseries of misunderstanding about ourselves. The *Yugavatar* of *Kaliyuga* is Shri Krishna, and the unique message is the *Bhagavad Gita*. The gist of both is given to reinforce our steps in the walk to eternity.

I pray that all the devotees be blessed by reading this great work of the time.

Dr. Raman
Retired Asst. Professor,
Calicut Medical College
Dept of Dermatology
December 2015

PREFACE

Be yourself. Be your original self. Be what you originally are. This is the core of spirituality. Your habits, your past, your acquired memories, concepts, education and learnings, your possessions, positions and relations, are not you. They are just your attributes, the attachments of this life. That is not being yourself.

Spirituality is not a journey. In fact, there is no journey. There is nowhere to go and nothing to do. There is only to be; just to be what you originally are. Deep contemplation and a mind dwelling in the Truth that is unchangeable and indivisible. There is neither a teaching good enough nor a teacher that can give you that. A teacher can guide you, but it is finally your consistent state, attained beyond the mind, that helps this awareness. A teacher can be a road sign, a benchmark or a living example of the attainment of Truth. When one attains a state, one becomes that. The teacher is essentially the state that one has attained.

Truth is Awareness. Awareness of the energy that sustains everything, and there is no space without it. The energy that has no boundaries, past, present or future. The energy that is both intelligent and unattached. The energy that does not need replenishment.

To find yourself, all you need is silence. Deep contemplation. Single pointed concentration. Deep silence. Silence from the external and, most importantly, the internal sounds; the sounds of myriad external temptations and their corresponding inner responses. The highest and the truest can be found only through silence. This is the deep and meaningful silence. The silence of Shiva. This is the silence of the Source.

The beginning is the segregation of what you are and what you are not. You are the essence. You are the Presence. You are not your situations. You are not your emotions. You are not your physical and psychological attributes. What you essentially are is what activates all this as a fleeting experience bound by time. Second, comes concentration on this essence. When concentration deepens, the silence deepens. When silence deepens, realisation happens, a realisation of the essence, a realisation of the self. Realisation brings perpetual stillness. This is the state of Shiva, the state of stillness.

Practices and external factors cannot guarantee this communion. To a great extent, focus, concentration, consistent contemplation, patience and perseverance can. What precedes silence is fearlessness and 'needing nothing-ness', in other words, zero dependency on the world of noises. Deep, unshakeable contentment with the inner state. Shiva cannot be practised. The state cannot be practised. Since it is a permanent state, it has to be attained.

Shiva does not do anything. God does not do anything. Silence by itself does not do anything. The Soul does not do anything. The Source just remains the Source, and its Presence activates life in materials. Life in materials is not the responsibility of the Source. But Source is essential for that. There is no spontaneous life in materials. Life happens with association to the Source. But the Source is not 'involved' with life.

There are no additions or subtractions, including desires or entertaining inclinations that the Source holds. There are no expectations or temptations. There are no dos and don'ts. There is no mind, intellect and ego. There are no forms to identify with. There are no *gunas*, states and flavours. There is no past, present and future. There is no birth or death to the Source. There is no expectation, disappointment and suffering. There is nothing except deep, profound, unfathomable Presence. That's it.

Apart from that grand, invisible Presence, there is no sign of its existence. Intelligent beings searched for it. Some found it. Some thought they found it. Those who found it dissolved in it.

Those who thought they found it created names and forms for it and even detached from its innate nature due to that exercise. They even created paths and methods to attain the Truth as per their belief and understanding. Some believed in some dimensions of the wholesome Source as everything and propagated it as the ultimate. The blind led the blind.

The few who attained the Truth never led, never claimed, never spoke. How did they reach it? Through silence. How do you reach silence? Through deep contemplation, concentration, discipline and determination.

It is within you, and outside of you, the same Source. It is in all beings. It is difficult not to see it if we train our eyes towards it, looking for it. If it is your only passion, it is right here for you to experience. When even the experience dissolves, you will become That. Then there is no separation. It is the only unity. Everything else is duality. Unless we detach from the life of duality, we cannot attain unity. That is the silence of Shiva.

Shiva is Presence. The self-glowing, self-illuminated Presence that illumines all divisions while remaining undivided. When living within a divided world of materials and ownership, we cannot recognise Shiva. Shiva is freedom as it has no boundaries, highs or lows, ups or downs. It is immovable. It has no gender or preferences towards anything. It is a witness.

Boundaries are cages. The created universe is a huge cage. Earth is a cage for our species. Moving within this cage is our reality, and the ability of movement within this cage is what our mind calls freedom; the relative movement within birth and death as well, which also means exercising our likes and dislikes, inclination, tendencies and desires, is what we consider freedom.

With our limited vision and illusion of ownership, we even glorify our cages. All our ownerships are just glorified cages. The karmic boundaries of our desire, fulfilment and satisfaction are also well within our cages. In other words, what we consider freedom is the freedom of the senses and the mind to roam over sensory objects. This is not freedom. Freedom is being unbound by any cages, including dependency on the body, birth and death, as well as the associated fulfilments.

Shiva is this freedom. Shiva is the state of being free, unbound and totally independent. Shiva is free and unbound. A person operating in that state can be called Shiva. Since Shiva is not a person but a state, those who live in that state can also be called Shiva. This state has no boundaries, and no name or form can bind the state at all.

It is essential to have a body to know this freedom called Shiva. It takes binding to experience liberation. To consider binding as natural is foolishness. Positions, possessions and relations, and the instincts that bind human existence, are to be understood as unnatural. Being Shiva is natural. Being unbound is natural. This awareness is essential to walk the path towards it.

One who is liberated is the one who is constantly aware. Aware of the bindings of the body, emotions, instincts and materials, which we consider natural. Bindings of sensory pleasures, their dependencies and demands. Constant awareness will lead to detachment. That detached state is close to the state of Shiva, the Presence. When Presence attains purpose, we call that birth an *Avatar* (an incarnation of Divinity in a human form).

Shiva is perpetual and detached as a Presence. It is in everything, unbound and unaffected. It is our soul, too, unbound and unattached to our positions, possessions and emotions. Suppression, imagining and pretending that we are living liberation is foolishness because it prolongs the process of detachment from mind matter, its purpose and demands. Silence, unbiased, unattached witness-hood and eternal is Shiva.

Shiva is not movement, but is within all movements. Shiva cannot be bound by any movement, time or space, name, form or flavour, while it is the Presence within all of these. Shiva is desireless-ness. Even if there is one desire, it is mind. Shiva is a mindless state. Bound by identifications, name, form and position, man suffers from non-understanding of the subtle eternal. When he starts to meditate to the subtle within, Shiva will start revealing itself. Only through the Shiva within can we experience the Shiva everywhere. This is an individual journey. This is a journey without path, progress or destination. This journey is beyond time. Material temptations delay it. Habits, flavours and identifications delay it too. Shiva stays revealed always. All that a seeker needs is to redefine his priorities from the habitual excursions of the senses and the mind, to the ultimate Truth, the infinite Shiva.

With all my love,

Mohanji

Table of Contents

Section 1:

THE DIVINE *LILA* OF SHIVA

~~~~~~~~

Higher than the highest. Larger than the largest. Bigger than the biggest. Harder than the hardest. Deeper than the deepest. Smoother than the smoothest. Heavier than the heaviest. Lighter than the lightest. Still beyond stillness. Bliss beyond happiness. Detached beyond perfection. Unknown and unknowable to human mind-matter (mind, ego, intellect), eternally liberated exists the real One, the unfathomable Shiva.

CHAPTER 1:

The Dance of Shiva...

A Window into Shiva's World

Gam witnessing the glorious egg, brighter than a thousand suns, in the middle of the oceans of galaxies, through my huge eyes, spanning galaxies. I am made to feel unity and diversity. I am made to feel action and inaction at the same time. I feel... I feel... I feel... I feel... I am the galaxy. I am the glorious egg, the firstborn *lingam*. The first and the only. The first and the last. The only One!

Through my cosmic eyes, I witness the grand vastness of existence. The luminous egg in the centre, brighter than a thousand suns, providing nourishment, fire, and life to numerous suns, across galaxies, rising and setting in the horizons of the galaxies, rising and setting over the suns of the universe, nourishing life in them, invisible to many planes of existence. Beyond elements, beyond matter.

I see that the beyond is invisible yet immensely perceivable. I feel the glorious egg, the first and the permanent, linking up the universe through unseen threads of energy, keeping the universe together, united to itself. Every bit of the universe is its expression. Everything formed out of this One Creation. It is the expression of the Supreme Unmanifested on which it and the universe collectively coexist. All manifestations are from the Unmanifested Supreme. All will dissolve back into the Supreme Unmanifested too.

The glorious strings of unity – the wires of energy, the umbilical cord from the glorious *lingam* to numerous suns and planets unite the universe together. Various manifestations thrive on this connectivity. A huge tent of brightness! A huge network linked by unseen cords.

Earth is a small stone – a pebble in the ocean of the suns. Earth is new. Earth is fragile. Earthlings are fragile too. Those who source from the Source are immortal. Those who source from pebbles are mortals. Energy is immortal. Matter is mortal. Those who know will experience the silence of creation. Those who are ignorant will experience the sound of mortality.

I think, "Oh, Man! What have you seen? What have you not seen? What do you perceive beyond the dualities of existence? What is the cosmos to you? What is Truth? Oh, Man! See beyond your eyes. See the glorious *lingam*, the eternal One. The One which is the Sun of all suns. The One, which is the Supreme Source, which the Supreme has provided for the creation, preservation, and dissolution of the universe. The One which is brighter than a thousand suns. The One which is invisible as well as visible. The One which radiates blinding, soothing, and loving brilliance. The One!"

I see the Sun brimming with fire inside. I see all the suns of the universe, managing its galaxies with the fire of dissolution. The Sun in the middle has no fire. It is the source of all fires. It is the ignition, the energy, that causes all fire. It is the soul of all fires. It never burns and depletes itself. It remains as the Source. It is the consciousness of the Creator. It is the creation that is the source of all creations. It is the source of all elements. It maintains the elements to experience its creativity. It maintains the cosmos. It dissolves the cosmos. It wills without willing. It sustains without sustaining. It manages without interfering. It leaves lives to *karma*. It manages the universe through the rules of *dharma*. It is water, air, fire, and space but none of these. It is the soul of all these. It lives in the atoms of creation.

When I climbed the ladder of my spine, I 'saw' the galaxies within me. When I climbed the spine of the galaxies, I 'saw' the universe. When I climbed the spine of the universe, I 'saw' the Sun of all suns. I feel, I felt– I exist. I am not apart from it – as it is the source of me. I am projected outside of it so that it can see itself through me. I am not apart from it. I am it. The Sun of all suns is invisible because of its brilliance. It is unconditional, pure, and brighter than a million suns. Its brilliance has no heat. It is not fire. It is the soul of fire. It is the energy that makes the fire.

I am the spine. I am the source. I am the projection. I am everything. I only exist. Creation is its play. Everything is *lila*. Divine play. A play created by the Supreme Unmanifested just to feel itself. Just bubbles, existing out of emptiness to be bubbles. Nothing else. Being bubbles is the only reason. In order to be bubbles, the attributes of bubbles are worn unconditionally. When clothed, illusion happens. Illusion masks the Truth. Then the bubble bursts and sinks back into the brilliance of creation. There is no room for darkness in the Source. Darkness is only when the created distances itself from the creation.

The Play of Consciousness

If there are eight billion people on Earth, there are as many personalities, with concepts, ideas, fears, conditionings, and all other flavours of life that one could possibly think about. As I have always mentioned, constitution-wise, we are 'hand-made' and not a factory product that looks and feels alike. Whenever man tried to create evenness among his subjects, serious tragedies took place; wars, death and displacements happened. Look into the history of mankind; you will understand what I am talking about.

Each being on Earth is unique, irrespective of the species. This also implies one's free will. We create our destiny. We ourselves, through our own thoughts, words, emotions, and actions, have created our own destiny. We are the creator or scriptwriter of our own life. Soul is only the aiding factor or the fuel that fulfils the journey – the energy that put the script into action. Nobody else is responsible for our life or our experience, even though, many a time, we need co-actors to bring forth effects in experience. Many actors sequentially join and leave the play and each actor has their relevance in the play. None is less or more important. Everyone added their flavour.

In your life story, you are certainly the hero and the rest are the supporting actors. But each supporting actor is the hero of their own script. Comedy, tragedy, drama, action, horror, satire and all its variations are usually part of every script. Each actor represents different flavours of life. They join hands and spice up the drama of your life. They make it worth it. Sometimes the show makes you cry, sometimes it makes you laugh, sometimes it creates fear, sometimes love. The story continues. Many characters happen in the play.

Concepts and questions such as, "Why cannot God remove evil from Earth?" make no sense when we understand how the Infinite Power operates. God is neutral, just like our own soul. It is objective, non-interfering and in perfect detachment from the actor or the action. God allows all characters to come and perform on the stage, or it never interferes, at least. Since each player is also the scriptwriter of their own drama, God allows the experience of the play, irrespective of its theme and reason. There is no good and bad in God's realm. There is only Truth and experience.

Man goes through many relative truths before he understands and attains the absolute Truth. This 'trial and error' is part of every being's life. God shall not take away this experience of existing in duality until one finds his unity. Duality is indeed the state as well as experience that leads one to unity. This Truth cannot be underestimated. Without duality, there is no creativity. When I and my Father become one, there is nothing to experience anymore. There is an experience only when the object and the experiencer are separate from one another. When eyes become one with sight, there is nothing to see. When tongue becomes taste, there is nothing to taste. When ego and all identities dissolve and man becomes one with God, there is no more search. There is only being-ness.

This state can be achieved only at the end of the drama. The chosen script should be acted and completed before the merger can happen. The audience or the operator cannot interfere and change the script or duration. Sometimes, some characters suddenly die and disappear from the drama. Even this is part of the original script, though it may seem quite dramatic to the audience. This is the effect chosen by the script writer. If a 'Wow!' happens from the lips of the audience, the script writer attains fulfilment, even if it means a tragedy.

What is Creation?

ꙮ **Question:** Can you speak on creation?

Mohanji: Creation has happened at various levels. There are 'beings' of various levels of consciousness in the universe. All these beings are not created by the same consciousness. For e.g., you give clay to a fourth-grade child and also to a master architect. The child will create to the best of his ability, but what will the master architect create? He will create something completely different. Same clay, same material but different expressions! Even the same clay in the hands of two people will attain different forms. How is that happening? This is because the consciousness of the creators of these clay models is different. Similarly, Universal Consciousness has different expressions. The material of creation is the same. Energy is the clay. From a unicellular being to reptiles, birds, animals, to humans, all have happened with different levels of consciousness. Hence, expressions are different; the quality and texture of creation are different.

Your perspective or understanding of the higher consciousness may not be true. For e.g., whales or dolphins are creations of a higher consciousness and are beings of higher consciousness. Scientific proof says that they contribute to the oxygen levels of the universe. What is their relevance in the universe? They are not just heavy beings floating in the ocean; they are contributing to the ecosystem. A creature that contributes to the ecosystem of Earth is definitely a creation of a higher consciousness, with a much larger awareness than ours, as we humans have only destroyed the ecosystem. If we are given the same energy, what will we create? Our creation will be a reflection of our consciousness. Indeed, we are creating our destiny every moment through every thought, every word and every action.

We are pretending that we are great, which we are not. Say I am a postgraduate student, so I feel that my neighbourhood graduate student is not great. This is my ego and nothing else. If one feels, "I am better because I have a degree and a higher level of awareness", it is absolute nonsense! Each entity has a purpose. Each one has value. Every animate and inanimate object has consciousness. Each fulfils its role. Some are tangible. We may feel that a stone lying on the road has no value. But tomorrow, when the same stone is used to build a wall, it gets a value, that it is used to construct a house! Everything has had a value, has a value and will always have a value. This is the way the world was created. This has been the way of expression of various levels of consciousness.

Human beings are of a different level of consciousness because we have the ability to realise the highest. We have the ability to liberate ourselves from the birth-death cycle. Some other beings might have the same capacity as ours; we do not know. We cannot say that we are higher just because we created these cities! We are definitely higher because we are expressing our creativity at our level with tangible material! Because we are using our intellect for our survival. Other higher beings are creating things or matter from energy. They created matter which is recyclable. We spill the Earth's guts and we cannot recycle it. This is our level of consciousness! The same situation given to two different people creates two different feelings! With a knife, someone may cut a vegetable and someone may stab a person!

✤ **Question:** Is the universe still expanding?

Mohanji: The universe is infinite. The universe is alive. It is expandable and contractible. The universe exists within God. His will can spontaneously change its dimensions. Just like huge stars disappear into nothingness, just like huge new stars are created, the universe is dynamic. This is a live, pulsating universe. It is infinite and infinitely alive. It can grow or shrink. It is a flexible universe.

Are we familiar with our symbol *Ananta*[1], the snake whose head and tail cannot be traced? Lord *Mahavishnu* sleeps on *Ananta*. *Ananta* signifies infinity. That is the stature of God, *Parabrahma* or *Allah* – whatever name you choose. Everything happens within Him. Time and space are measurable only on Earth. When the soul exits the body, time and space do not exist. Gross can only measure the time and scale, not the subtle. The soul is subtle. The Supreme Father is subtler. The soul is still an entity. When the soul completely merges with the Father, it cannot be identified, just like a river merging into an ocean.

---

[1] Means endless, limitless, eternal, infinity. Also, refers to Sheshanaga, the celestial snake, on which Lord Vishnu reclines.

A merged soul extracts itself when there is a need for a *dharmic* existence. That birth is not due to *karma*. It is not like our birth. It is a birth purely out of *dharma* or duty. Like the Sun is doing its duty everyday. This birth is pure, uncontaminated and without any emotions or *karmas*. Emotions contaminate our birth. It becomes a lower level of existence. Lower level means more dense or more gross. More gross means it is prone to re-birth.

❧ **Question:** Why are we of higher existence?

Mohanji: This is because we chose intellect over might for our existence. This is because we have the ability to real-ise the highest. An animal lives a pre-planned existence. It goes through birth, life, and then dies. It is not the same with a hu-man, who has different levels of existence. We have the pow-er to realise the Highest. The Highest is our Creator. As we go through the process of realising the higher, we become more and more subtle. Subtle means lighter. The body is the grossest which you can feel. The senses are subtler than the body. The breath is even subtler. The soul is perhaps the subtlest which you can experience. After death, even our soul remains more gross than the Father.

The Father is the subtlest and invisible. We go through the various levels of filtering until we become one with the uni-verse. We travel from the limited body to the unlimited ex-panse of the universe. Each location has its subtlety. Each *loka* or world is different in subtlety. Earth, Moon, Mars, and Ve-nus have different levels of subtlety or grossness. This trans-formation of 'limitedness to unlimitedness' cannot be achieved through doing. Doing only helps you to be with you. When you do *hatha yoga* etc., you may feel better. But, doing *yoga* with a mind wandering somewhere else is of no use. It may help as a physical exercise, but it will not tune your mind.

Most people are doing *yoga* at a physical level because no teacher tells them, "This is for you to bring yourself to you!" A scattered mind which goes out of your system with the senses should be brought back to the system. Then it becomes very powerful. Then, you become powerful because less energy is wasted. Energy is money. Energy is power. Let anything happen outside; it will not affect you. When you are more and more with your soul, you become subtler. Your words become commands to the universe. This is how Masters operate. Command the rain to stop, and the rain stops! The subtler you are, the more powerful you become!

Society – Duality's Role Play

Society consists of all sorts of beings. Variety in looks and variety in flavours makes life worth it. Monotony and stagnation always create boredom and stress and deliver a depressed existence. Motivation to excel helps maintain energy levels. Society works through systems. Various players make it complete. The job of a policeman, doctor, and engineer are distinct, and each of them adds value to the overall collective existence. A doctor is expected to cure illness, while a policeman is expected to maintain law and order. Each one has his chosen path and expressions. One cannot be replaced by the other, though there could be possible combinations.

There are expressions in beings which bring forth happiness, sorrow, or both. Various expressions from various flavours of love – the highest being unconditional love – to lesser emotions such as greed, hatred, jealousy, anger, and so on. These are all flavours that the scriptwriter wrote in his personal drama of life, out of choice or out of ignorance. What has God, the audience or spectators got to do with it?

If someone ever states that God or *Guru* should prevent evil from spoiling the broth of life, it is indeed a sign of perfection in non-understanding. Just as the soul, (the energy and electricity), does not interfere in our thought process, words, or action and just assists fulfilment, so too God shall not remove duality at any cost unless It chooses to remove relativity and dissolve everything back into Itself. Until the huge universal drama ends, the smaller, many micro dramas will continue. God shall not pull the plug.

Coming back to our realm, if everyone plays his part well, society will be a better place. If a policeman handles law and order honestly and purposefully, people will live in peace. If the ruler is objective, selfless and benevolent, people will live fearlessly. If laws ensure justice on time, crime will be less. When greed and selfishness dominate a society, calamities will happen. When purposelessness dampens the morale of society, wars will happen. These are some of the basic ground rules of existence.

Thus, as individuals are creating their script of life, society is built up on collective scripts. No God or *Guru* is responsible for that. Duality or relativity made life possible in its existing variety. Minus relativity, there is no creativity. Minus creativity, there is no experience or fulfilment. Minus fulfilment, there is no reason for existence. So, how can God interfere? He is the facilitator and not the creator of the micro dramas. If your rulers and policemen cannot prevent crime, if the education systems cannot develop higher awareness in society, what has God got to do with it?

It is a problem with the operating levels of society which consists of people. It is not the job of a Saint to maintain law and order. His job is to guide those who choose to come to him, follow him and stay with him, to higher levels of awareness. In that effort, miracles can take place. No true *Guru* will perform miracles of higher or lower impact, just for the sake of creating thrills in people, because *siddhis* bind and often enslave the performer. It is indeed the faith of the disciple that facilitates it. Those who come to test get nothing. Those who develop faith can spontaneously experience higher realities. As Jesus said, "May your faith heal you".

No true *Guru* will interfere in the free will of the people or society. The star villains of our epics, such as *Hiranyakashipu, Kamsa, Ravana,* or *Mahishasura* had their own free existence before being deleted from the system by *Avatars* that came specifically for this extermination job. There were Saints and higher Masters living in those periods too. Why was duality maintained? This is how the universe operates. Societies that crave for peace should create awareness. They should shed greed and jealousy. When greed for profits achieves insensitive proportions, the soul of Earth suffers. The environment decays. The *Guru* or God has nothing to do with it.

One last question on the same subject – Even if a *Guru* or God comes forward, volunteers to cleanse the society, and prescribes ways to do it, will the subjects follow it unconditionally? If the answer is yes, then we would have already done that. We would not have assassinated Jesus and Socrates – those who only spoke the Truth. We would have lived according to the teachings of the Bhagavad Gita, the *Ashtavakra Gita*, the *Avadhoota Gita*, or the great eternal teachings of the Saints who followed *Sanatana Dharma*. We would definitely have lived by the teachings of the Gita and *Satcharitas*. There should be a clear understanding before we complain about our state. Who is creating them, maintaining them, and enjoying them? This is important to realise.

Life's Varied Dimensions

Is Life Precious?

Indeed. Life is precious. Every moment is precious. We have already missed many diamonds while we were busy collecting stones.

Is Life about Liberation?

Indeed. But it is not about escapism. It is not about discontentment with what we have, and lust after what we do not have. It is not about comparisons. It is not about sadness over inequalities. It is not about resistance and turmoil inside. Liberation is about liberation – an existence in which you have everything but need absolutely nothing. Whether a material is available or not, there is no agony or ecstasy. Nothing is essential. True liberation is a lack of dependency on anything and being grateful for everything.

Is Life about Achievements?

Indeed. But it is not about the cups and trophies in the cupboard. It is about the blessings that we render to the helpless. It is about our ability to make a positive difference to another being. True achievements cannot be counted on the fingers, but can only be measured through one's spiritual progress, one's level of liberation. True achievements are the tangible moments that we lived selflessly. This is the only place where everyone wins. Otherwise, all achievements are a material gain for some and a loss for some.

Is Life about Thoughts?

Indeed. What you think, so you become. Thought is the first level of creation, where energy is released. Thoughts arise out of an inherent desire existing in the subconscious in the seed form, blooming in the right environment. Thoughts, if powerful enough, lead to further expressions such as words or images. If the words are powerful enough, they lead to action. Action combined with emotions becomes *karma*. *Karma* leads to further births. Thus goes the life of a man.

Hence, every thought is important. Nothing goes wasted in our system. The collective thoughts of a generation create events. Oppression or suppression brings forth an *Avatar* who will destroy evil and reinstall *dharma*. A lifestyle based on procrastination and lethargy will provoke wars and change. Thus, at every point in time, all are participating in creating a collective destiny, which in turn becomes the individual destiny, to whichever degree it should.

Is Life about Food?

Indeed. The body is a sheath made out of elements. The elements nurture that sheath until death and disintegration. The body is linked to the mind as much as the mind is linked to the body. The mind keeps emotions, including emotions related to food. The mind's need for satisfaction supersedes the needs of the body. The mind rules, and the body obeys. Obesity happens. The body does not need as much food as the mind needs. The mind nurtures craving. The body has its intelligence. Our food habits reflect our character and destiny. Unconscious eating, emotional eating and craving lead to overeating, obesity and sudden deaths.

Food that is cooked and stored, food containing dead organisms (which lacks *prana* – life force) and food that is contaminated gradually decrease the consumer's vital energy and make him vulnerable to many diseases. One who is in control of his consumption can be considered an emperor of his life. Moderate eating fills one-third of the stomach, while one-third remains filled with water and one-third with air, which is supposed to be the ideal quantity for healthy living. Moderate eating, moderate sleeping, and moderate exercise, along with personal hygiene, make a superb human.

Wastage of food is a crime and should never be entertained. Take only what you can effortlessly consume. Never take food for granted. Our body has consumed tons of food and gallons of water to date. Much more is also wasted. We live in a world where some starve and steal food, while some fight obesity. Feeding the hungry is the noblest of all charities. The hungry can be a bird, animal or human being. Irrespective of the body type or species, we must educate our children to feed the hungry. This will arrest their stress and make them higher beings in flesh and blood.

Is Life about Success?

Indeed. True success in life depends on our growth in awareness. Success is in our spiritual evolution. Success is in our kindness expressed. Success is in liberating ourselves from all kinds of dependency. Success is in gaining simplicity. Success is in knowing oneself. Success is in success itself. All material successes are temporary and transitory. They come and go and involve either happiness or sorrow, but not equanimity. Yet, equanimity in happiness and sorrow is true success.

Is Life about Faith?

Indeed. Faith happens, sooner or later. When the ego subsides and gets nullified through consistent downfalls, faith happens. Faith leads. Faith soothes. Faith reinforces. Faith nurtures life. Faith elevates life. Faith stabilises life. Faith liberates man.

Faith increases with experiences. Faith decreases when we disown our experiences, swapping them with others' opinions or book knowledge. Faith increases when surrender becomes absolute. Faith decreases when the ego becomes predominant. Faith is real if it is spontaneous. Faith is transitory if it is induced or inherited. If a man's herd instinct leads to certain faith, it ends when he turns a new corner. Such is the passing faith that has no longevity. Faith based on conviction is more real if the conviction is based on Truth.

Is Life about Giving?

Indeed, but only when giving becomes unconditional and devoid of any expectations. Giving is not about wealth or money. Giving time, energy, knowledge, guidance, information, space, food, water, medicine, clothes, books, healing, and everything else, with pure intentions and without expectations, indeed transform a man into a 'human.'

One who gives, glows. One who selflessly moves in society radiates positivity and hope. Even if his life is short, there will be life in each moment. His purposefulness itself will radiate life. Life is not worth it if lived without any benefit to the world around us; it is not superior to an animal's existence. Life is in giving. Giving is essential in life. Giving strengthens and raises man to the level of God. It liberates him. Unconditional existence always liberates man.

Is Life about Gratitude?

Indeed. Gratitude liberates and positions the mind in the present. Being in the present itself is liberating. Gratitude makes the heart rich. A rich heart is more precious than a rich wallet. Gratitude invokes child-like wonder in the mind. It makes life worth living. When gratitude becomes the essence of our character, excesses vanish, the ego vanishes, and anxieties vanish.

Gratitude supports faith. Gratitude provides equanimity. Gratitude reinforces unconditional love. If you have to choose one quality in life, choose gratitude. It is worth it. Everything else will fall in place by itself.

Is Life about Power?

Indeed. The real power lies in the control of intellect over the mind. When a man becomes emotional, intellect shuts down. The uncontrolled senses and mind amount to human weakness. The mind in control of the senses and the intellect in control of the mind make a man powerful. The real wire puller is the soul, which is all-powerful. But it does not express its power. It never overrules any decision of the mind or intellect. Having power but not expressing it or having to express it, is real power. Power, if used to create harmony and love in the world, is truly noble. Power, if used for conquests and suppression of other beings, is demonic. How we wield our power depends on our basic character.

Power makes a man naked, as it exposes his true nature. Some use power benevolently and for the benefit of all. They are a true expression of the Almighty. They never entertain any barriers within, such as caste, creed, culture, countries, colours, communities, etc. They are universal beings. Their nature of expression is unconditional love. Some use power to control other beings through fear. They are insecure. Those leaders who create fear and control, indeed lack character and quality. An individual or organisation is the same in this context. An organisation is a body consisting of many individuals.

Power should be used for wiping the tears of many. It should be used for protecting rather than destroying. Power should be used with awareness and not emotion. Power is a double-edged sword. It could hurt the one that wields it. History is full of examples. One who has absolute power needs to be absolutely careful. Power should create harmony, love, and peace. That is real power. One who has one's mind in control is powerful too. Nobody can shake them ever. They will never be insecure. They will live a life of equanimity. Thus, the real conquest is the conquest of the mind.

Is Life about Choosing Aloneness?

Indeed. Choosing to be alone with full integrity and strength for the sake of subtlety (which means pulling away from the senses and gross body, to the level of the soul) where you are all-powerful; then you are very powerful. This is a time when people get attracted to you, whether you want it or not – because your strength is much higher than that of an average person. The dissipation of energy is much less in you.

How is energy dissipated? It is through the senses and the mind. It gets dissipated through the oscillation of thoughts between your past and future, i.e., guilt about the past and anxiety about the future. These two things suck your energy away. That annihilates you. This is not the annihilation of Shiva or annihilation for the sake of dissolving; it is of the *karmic* push. It is painful, and then you crave. When you crave, emotions happen. When emotions happen, another life happens! That is why situations are repeated over lifetimes.

We have the choice of what to do with the situations of this life. You have only the present to work on—nothing else. The future does not exist if the present does not exist. That is why all the Masters always point their fingers to the present and say, "Do this now." If you are in the present all the time, then no need for meditation, no need for *Gurus*, Just Be.

I like to walk alone. As a child, a teacher once asked me what I would like to do. I said that I'd like to be alone. He got annoyed since he thought I was making fun of him. He could not understand a situation where one would love to be alone and that it is possible. It is fine. I am alone. It should not be escapism, though – "I cannot get friends, so I want to be alone".

This is theoretically easy to understand but practically very difficult because there will always be someone who gives you anxiety about the future, saying, "What will you do after ten years?" That is all! This is what we are. That's our nature. Let us accept it. Only through acceptance can we correct it.

Is Life about Purity?

Indeed. Purity of thought, word, and action liberates man from everything. It strengthens his existence. Purity is power. Purity is Truth. Truth is pure. All elements resonate with Truth. Our whole being resonates with Truth and purity. The whole universe resonates with Truth and purity. When we live the Truth, purity happens. When we live a life of purity through consistently expressing purity through every thought, word and action, we elevate ourselves to an existence of supreme consciousness. There are no barriers in the realm of purity. There is supreme strength in purity.

The power of purity is tangible. The power of purity unburdens on various levels. The power of purity liberates. The power of purity immunises from the rocks and shocks of daily existence. The power of purity radiates. Purity empowers. Purity strengthens. Purity liberates. It brings gratitude to existence. It quells the wandering mind to a thought-less state. It quenches all questions. It brings contentment. It brings stability. It makes our very existence a great experience. It fills our existence with life. It brings purpose. It fills life with faith and hope. It connects us to the highest Consciousness. The power of Purity is unfathomable. It is the nature of the Supreme.

CHAPTER 2:

...Fuelled by Dharma and Karma...

The Power of the Subtle

🌿 **Question:** How is *karma* created?

Mohanji: Thoughts are the first level of creation and energy is required for that. Words are the second level of creation. Energy is required for each word uttered. The last level is action. Major *karmas* are created through emotions attached to each thought, word, and action. Emotion is the glue that attaches every thought, word, and action to your subconscious. This makes you take birth again. Being detached from your action, observing yourself and being fully present with every thought, word, and action liberates you. You will not be bound or emotional. You must feel for other people, but not be emotional about it. Feeling is a part of the system.

This also means that you should do a hundred per cent of what you can do. Then offer gratitude and remain detached. Do not get affected by what you have done. This detachment is your liberation. You will always do your best when you operate in the detachment mode. You will not compare yourself with another person. You are unique; the other person is also unique. You are a *karmic* being; the other person is also a *karmic* being. Different *karma*, different constitution! How can you compare different constitutions? When comparison stops, the heart becomes lighter. You will not be worried and then no anger, no jealousy, no hatred! You are then operating in the plane of absolute Consciousness.

All scriptures are teaching us the same. We get stuck with words and forget the essence. Hence, we do not progress. All Masters who came to Earth till today have said the same thing! Times were different, situations were different, and people listening to them were different. The collective consciousness was different in the past and is different in the present too. The past Masters had to use certain words and ideas to address their subjects, but the essence is the same.

What is cleansed through the Power of Purity meditation is your inner space. This also cleanses your activities. The roots must be clean so that the sprouts will also be clean. We dress up well and show ourselves to society, but usually, the inside is terribly contaminated! We are still keeping a lot of baggage, trash, and heavy burdens, while we smile externally and deceive others and ourselves! Pretensions! Grave pretensions! That is why people cannot trust anybody. They do not even trust themselves. When they start trusting themselves, they will also trust others.

> ❧ **Question:** There are people who are going through similar experiences to learn the same lesson. When I am learning a particular thing, some other person from a different continent also is learning the same lesson. Why is this required?

Mohanji: This is because the awareness is different, the agenda is different, and also *karma* is different. There could be similarities in desires, or even a pattern of existence between two individuals. But they are not exactly the same. The syllabus is the same for all the students of a classroom, but the purpose and consciousness are different. Even if they learn the same subject, their understanding and assimilation would be different. Two bodies are taken by two different souls because the aim is different experiences.

If you take it a step further, this can be a completely different topic, just like life. Your understanding of a matter will depend on where you stand. It depends on where you can see, what you can see, or how far you can see. This is why a judgment based on partial understanding could become quite catastrophic for many. Take for e.g., those dictators who ravaged nations and life; selfish politicians elected by the people, for the people, yet working only for themselves.

Creation is *dharma*-bound. What you are saying is *karma*-bound. Human experiences are related to *karma*. You do not know what makes your reality. You are creating *karma* through thought, word, and action. Thus, you get parallel experiences. But creation is something else. The macro creation is about consciousness and *dharma* or duty. You are supposed to create. An architect is supposed to design a building and it is his *dharma*. *Karma* provokes life. You know how *karma* is produced through thoughts, words, and actions, plus emotions. The collective consciousness of society also contributes to it.

If people or society feel that you are someone great and behave that way with you, that could build your ego and *karma*. You may also think that a particular person is good, but others may not think so – this is individual perception! Some people are humble and well balanced, while some behave in a humble way because of low self-esteem. A two-dimensional society. However, society can see only their expressions, not their dimension. A rich man may think that people love him because of the attention he gets from society, but most likely, people love his money and not the man. You can see this kind of disproportionate life everywhere.

In the highest Consciousness, there is no lack of proportions. There is no inequality. There is one existence. Expressions of one existence. I am you and you are me. Gender, time, and space cannot matter. You express what I want to express. This is why all Masters are at one level. All Masters operate from one Consciousness. There is Krishna, Jesus, Buddha et al. You choose who you like. No problem. But the Consciousness remains the same; the operating level also remains the same – completely unconditional, completely selfless, and the operation is *dharmic*, not *karmic*. Krishna, Jesus, and Datta have no *karma*. They came to safeguard *dharma*. Do not confuse our *karmic* operating levels and higher consciousness creation levels.

Talking Thoughts

One may ask if a man is accountable for all his thoughts, especially the violent or reactionary ones, or is he only accountable for the thoughts that he puts into action? It is true that it is difficult to control our thoughts. Because thoughts are produced by inclination, inclination is produced by *karma*. If there is no *karma* to smoke cigarettes, one will not have an inclination for cigarettes. If one does not have an inclination for cigarettes, one will not even have a thought to smoke. If one does not have a thought, then one will not have a word about it. One will not even say to somebody, "I want to have a cigarette."

If one does not have a word, there is no further action. 'Word' in the sense of a particular activity or transaction and not just speaking. It leads to actual activity, to actual smoking. So, what is *karma* in the beginning, is fulfilment in the end. *Karma* takes a course and it gets fulfilled. If it is not fulfilled, it becomes another desire. For e.g., "I smoked this particular brand and I want to smoke another brand." That is a desire which is pending; the next movement is towards that one. In this way, we are going in circles continuously.

Thoughts which invade our mind come uninvited. The reason is that thoughts are created by *vasanas* or inclinations. They happen only as per linear time. Our life goes from the first birthday till the last birthday. We travel in a linear fashion through time and all our experiences are according to time. So, a particular thought can happen only at a particular time. Like an experience, for e.g., of what it is like to be a mother, one cannot experience this at the age of five. One has to attain a particular age to be a mother. So, each thought will happen or each activity will happen, only as per the right timing.

Thoughts are happening without our knowledge because that is the right thought at that time. If a 90-year-old man decides, "I want to go to college and get educated, or play football," all the things which a twenty-year-old would do, it is impossible for him to do those things. Because the time has already passed. Likewise, everything is linear to time. A particular thought is happening at a particular time because the time induces the thought, and the *vasana* will become a thought only at that time. It cannot happen before or after. But these thoughts are uninvited because this is coming as per one's destiny, the path of destiny called *prarabdha karma*.

Thought is the first level of creation. Energy is released with thoughts. So, the more positive thoughts one has, the more positive results and realities one will have. Man's *karma* is accountable for the thoughts. The base of thoughts is *karma*, which then becomes an inclination, *vasana*, which next becomes a thought. Definitely the base is *karma*. *Karma* is accountable and the thoughts are the first level of creation. Thought has potential. When we bless people, it reaches them. It has potential. It is a positive thing. Thought plus emotion is equal to *karma*. Thought minus emotion has no value. Thought has a particular value if there is emotion attached to it.

The question is then, if the thought stays as a thought, is the person accountable? It depends on whether there is emotion attached to it. If there is an emotion, it can become a reality, sooner or later. Even if one is watching television and becomes very angry or upset, that can recur later in one's life. One may attract that emotion; it need not be what one is doing in life, but what one sees, hears, and gathers from other people. These are all inputs into one's system. All the things people talk about, one may think it is innocent gossip, but it is not so. One is gathering the essence of it, and one is keeping it inside. Some day it will become a reality, and one will probably suffer because of that.

So it is very important before one goes to the good company, to shed the bad company. Bad means somebody who pulls one down, only talks gossip or says, "This will not work, that will not work," thus only adding oil to the fire of insecurity. There are many people like that. It is important to segregate into the positive and if one can help them and bring them around, it is ok, good. But one should not be rescuing somebody who is drowning in the water, in that one should not jump to the rescue and be drowned themself. This should not happen in life.

To those who have worked with me, I always say, "Do not tell me things which you cannot do. Tell me things which you can do. Let us start working from there." People always come back and say, "I cannot do this, I cannot do that..." When one observes society, there is more 'No' than 'Yes'. Where is this coming from? Insecurity. Inertia. Lack of energy. Lack of fire. So, this becomes their destiny. Who can help them? Nobody can. Because if one chooses to bring the fire back, definitely a lot of people will help. But if one chooses to be in that inertia mode, it is very difficult for anybody to help. How many deep, dense, and negative people does one handle everyday? However, one can stay uncontaminated. One can stay pure. This is one's choice. The right choice helps.

If there are violent and reactionary thoughts, is the person responsible for them? Yes. Because violent and reactionary thoughts are expressions of emotion. If the person is peaceful, there will be no violence inside. They will never hurt anybody. They will only love. All the violence inside is the expression of emotions of the past. One has kept the violence inside. At some point in time it is coming as anger, coming as insecurity, coming as hatred; all these things are happening because there is a seed already in the system.

Free Will is a Myth

ꙮ **Question:** I would like to ask about free will and decisions in everyday life. To be spontaneous and be like a river is an imperative of our spiritual life, but we cannot be totally passive in that. We sometimes have to do something with all respect for God's will. Even if we have faith in existence, we are in a position to act, but we often have the dilemma, whether to go right or left. So, how to cover this gap? Could you tell us about free will in everyday life?

Mohanji: Free will in everyday life is more or less like a myth. When we were in our last life, we gathered a lot of emotions, desires, understandings, and misunderstandings. All these things put together created *karma* in this life. Before we started this journey, before we took this birth, we clearly decided, 'these are desires, these are emotions, these are materials that we want to experience in this new life'. When we thus decided, we almost completely gave up free will. Because we chose from our first heartbeat to our last heartbeat, where we will be born, to which kind of parents, what sort of experiences, the place, the education, relationships, all these things we actually decided before we came here.

This is why we are born in a particular place, to a particular set of parents, and we have certain tastes, education. Some people like to do yoga, some people like to do sports, play tennis... All these qualities, all these characteristics, we chose before we came. That is why our children have distinct characteristics. They are very clear about what they want, more or less; they have a clear character. This is because they had chosen it before. So, to live now, the understanding we need to have is that whatever we are experiencing today, is what we have chosen, and whatever we will experience tomorrow, is what we have chosen. At the same time, we can choose one thing: we can choose not to accumulate more desires, more emotions while we are living. This is our advantage, this is free will.

If you want to stop accumulating more desires and more emotions, you should have complete understanding about your daily life, your Now. That means acceptance of everyday as it is and no resistance, no storage of emotions, whatever comes to us, just let it come and go. We remain always clean and pure. If we can operate on that level, there will be no accumulation of new desires and new emotions. That is exactly our free will. Our free will today is not to have further emotions, further desires. When we are enjoying and experiencing everyday activities, our mind is completely here, in the present, enjoying that activity fully and experiencing an event fully, completely, so that we are satisfied, fulfilled each moment, that is exactly the free will that we have.

There is also one more thing. When you lose interest in something and you say, "Ok, I've had enough of this experience, I'm fine, I'm happy," including a relationship, that desire and that emotion also get dropped. That is also free will while living. This is the only free will we can operate on because we have chosen our lifespan, how long we will live, we have chosen our activity and all the qualities of our activity, our character, our shape, country, culture, even the food we consume, and the tastes we enjoy. All these things were decided before. So, your free will is: first, do not accumulate any more, and second, you can always grow out of an emotion, grow out of a taste and say, "I had a sufficient amount of it, I don't need any more". Then that drops off, so that you are more and more liberated. Each moment you can liberate yourself.

🌀 **Question:** You said we should accept everything that comes our way and that we should totally accept it, then you said something about enjoying it, but what if the experience is very bad or very painful? Should we also totally accept that?

Mohanji: If an experience is painful, understand where the pain exists. The pain exists only in the waking-state mind. It cannot be translated into your dream state, nor can it be moved to your deep sleep state. The mind, which is conditioned with so much of our education, our culture, our upbringing basically, that is the mind which gives the suffering. Emotional suffering is always related to the mind. But we can understand, "Ok, this is coming and going, but we are not bound by people, personalities, time, space, situations, country, culture, anything."

Because we just experience that. We are experiencing and we are moving on. As an effect, nothing can bind us. Nothing can conquer us, because we are free, right from birth to death. But the mind does not allow us to be free most of the time. The mind will say, "This is an injustice; this should not happen. This should be different," and we always manipulate based on the mind's opinions. That is the time when suffering happens. Otherwise, we could say, "Ok, I had a relationship which was not to my taste, it did not suit me. Let me go away." In this way, we can step aside and watch the whole show. At that point in time, we are very powerful. We cannot be defeated. The mind actually pulls us down but if we use our intellect, we understand that all these things are passing and they cannot bind us, if you move with the clear understanding that everything is just experience. Everything is just experience; there is no pepper or salt in it.

꙲ **Question:** I was in a conflict with someone and I'm aware of our different opinions, different attitudes towards life, and I tried to detach, but that person is attached to me. Do I have to be born again just because that person is emotionally involved with me?

Mohanji: Yes, actually this is the complication of life. Maybe you got out of it, but that other person may not have got out of it. It is important to nurture it in such a way that you slowly have to take his hand and put it somewhere else. You have to divert that person's attention to something else. Because what happens is, one person is completely relieved or detached, but the other person still holds on. It means the hook is still on your flesh, so it is important to detach slowly. Slowly with understanding, awareness, make them feel just like the mother slowly, slowly detaches the child from having milk. Similarly, you have to slowly, slowly detach that person. People are like children, in this example.

꙲ **Question:** The more I try, the more angry or the more frustrated he gets.

Mohanji: You have to handle it carefully because this is life and emotion. Make that person realise that this is over, as if somebody had died and gone. What would you do? You cannot do anything, right? That stops there. Similarly, we have to handle the relationship in such a way that the other person is very clear that it cannot continue, or change the pattern of the relationship. For e.g., suddenly you become motherly or something else that does not suit the other person, and the person says, "Ok, now the relationship has changed." Like certain people after divorce continue to be good friends, so the old emotions do not exist anymore. I've seen many people like that. We have to turn the relationship in such a way that it relieves you, detaches you, liberates you.

How We Create Our Destiny

Question: If free will is a myth, what then is the purpose of life? Why are we here? If everything is predestined, what are we doing here on Earth?

Mohanji: Simple, what you are experiencing today, that experience is what you have chosen. That is why you are here. It is almost like an automatic mode. We have a clear understanding of all our thoughts, words, actions. If we do not keep emotions with them, we will not come back. But what happens is that we resist, we have anger, we have anxiety, we have fear, we have love, it is all a mixture of all these, and this comes out as desire. For e.g., a man tells a woman, "I love you so much! I would like to be your son in the next life" or "If only I was your son!" The desire becomes very strong and the relationship has to materialise in another life. This is how we create our destiny.

Likewise, two people are fighting, and one person says, "I will kill you! I will surely kill you!" and they become very angry with each other. However, if they cannot complete that anger with each other or sort it out, unconsciously, they will come back again in the next life as brothers, or brother and sister, or father and son, and there will be a big fight in the family, because the anger transferred across lifetimes. So, unconsciously we are creating our destiny. After our death from this life, we are preparing for the next life and we have this agenda of our desires, of what we would like to achieve within one lifetime.

This is clearly defined, and decided, and laid out in that plane between death and the new birth. That is the time when the whole format is made and while the format is being made, you have full free will, only free will. But once you say, "This is what I want to do, I've created my agenda," and then you close it, you cannot change it. So, unconsciously we create our lifetimes. But while living, we never understand that. People cannot meet if there is no *karma* behind it. You will not listen to me if there is no *karma* behind it.

✤ **Question:** Does the soul have to experience all that?

Mohanji: The soul does not experience; the soul is like the petrol in the car. It just helps the journey. It is not deciding the destination. Each soul has a different set of experiences because each soul operates a different body. The same food will be different for different people; some people say this is good, some people say this is not good. The food is the same, but the taste is different. That is why each soul operates as a different machine, a different body.

✤ **Question:** If someone has a health problem in this life, which is a problem from a past life, does this person have to suffer from this illness their whole life, or can he or she be somehow healed?

Mohanji: I would say both. Physical illness is a result of emotions. When you trap emotions, it becomes physical later. It is important to let go, relax and leave it, so that even the diseases may not materialise or manifest as much as they could. Many times, diseases are kept and captured by emotions, our mind.

If somebody does something good to you, try to compensate in some way. I normally pay people or do something for them if they do something for me, so that it gets equalized. Likewise, if it is hurt, I wouldn't recommend hurting the other person because that cycle continues. If somebody hurts you, you hurt them back, then they hurt you again... Because this is an ego issue.

My suggestion is that the best thing to counter any kind of hurt is through love. Or we can deal with the whole situation with a lot more maturity using the brain, so that it stops there. I was telling one person who was writing a letter saying a lot of bad things about the other person. I suggested a reply saying,

"Thank you very much for letting me know, but my love cannot change." That stopped the communication. There was no further argument, no further discussion. Thus, it is better to cut short something negative as early as possible.

The Nature of Karma

   Question: Everything has been decided about our birth and death. Destiny has been written. But we do not know what will happen in the next moment. The next moment also depends on you, if you do a good thing or a bad thing. But, on the other hand, everything has been written and pre-planned. I cannot correlate both together. I find it very confusing.

Mohanji: I have explained this point clearly before. But it does not matter. I will explain again. I like to explain again, and further.

The destiny that you talked about is the *prarabdha karma*, the *karma* that provoked our birth on Earth in a particular place, to a particular set of parents, in a particular environment, to fulfil a particular set of desires. This agenda is your shopping list. This was decided before you ventured out of the house, which means before you took this birth. Before you went to the supermarket, you prepared a list of essentials that you wanted to buy. You carried sufficient money to buy such things as well. Maybe a little extra cash as well, in terms of life, a few breaths extra! So, breath is your money to continue with the journey and complete the journey. You have the shopping list and you started the journey. This is the road map and this is the destiny. Are you clear about destiny now? This is from each birth till death.

Now the free will you are talking about is very limited in this bargain. On the way to the car showroom, you decided to buy a Rolls Royce, instead of the ordinary car that you had originally chosen. Do you have sufficient money? You may not have. If you had gone to buy a Rolls Royce in the first place, if you had sufficient money for that, you would have taken the money and accomplished the deed. But that was not your original agenda. It was not on the original list. This is the *karma* that you added today. This new addition or change in the original plan may need postponement; you may have to take it with you to another life, or another trip. Consider one trip as one life. You have to take another trip to buy such additional things. That is destiny.

Now, what is your free will at this point or period of time in this journey? In a second, in an environment like this place, this space, this time, this moment, you can only lift the left hand or the right hand. So if I lift the left hand, that moment is gone, the time has expired. It is over. I cannot lift my right hand at this time. I can only lift the right hand at another time. So is your free will limited amongst your pre-planned, predetermined destiny.

What is the nature of your journey? Simple. What made you come here for meditation today? You could have gone to the pub instead. Such events tell you the nature of your journey. Where you started travelling, which is the path you are taking, which would be your possible destination? Why you do not understand the whole journey is because your conscious mind – the limited mind – cannot understand the master plan. Because this mind – the brain which you are using to understand the world, is acquired in this life, just like the place you are living now. Of course, the *karmabhumi*, or platform for action, did exist before. Your body is new and the new body cannot understand in totality the whole agenda of your past lives.

But who can understand? Your higher self can understand. But your higher self usually has nothing to do with your local *karma*. This is something which you acquired now. Just like your soul, your higher Self sees all, detached. It has no interest in your agenda, but it helps you. You are not communicating with it enough so that you know why you are here, what your job is, what you are going through, and where you are going to. The moment you start mixing with the higher self, you become complete – in 360 degrees. Full! You will know your past, present and future at one time. This is what we call a complete merger, *moksha (liberation)* or *mukti (freedom)*. At that point in time, your desires are totally wiped out, the complete meaning of the whole of existence falls into place, and you are totally complete – *sat-chit-ananda, sachidananda*!

Until then, when you are operating in the micro level, you can never fully understand the macro level. A first-grade student cannot understand what a tenth-grade student is experiencing. He may only know that the tenth-grade student is also carrying books and attending classes. He might also imagine that he could sit in the tenth-grade as well! But he cannot, because his eligibility level is different. His intellect is not developed to the same level as the level of the tenth-grade student, so that he can understand the subject matter of that grade. Evolution of consciousness happens. Evolution must happen, evolution is required.

It has nothing to do with physical age. There could be an eighty-year-old man with no spiritual evolution, and a five-year-old boy completely evolved. So if you look at a man's physical age and decide that this man is indeed evolved, but without knowing the Truth of his level of existence, you will be terribly mistaken. Physical age has no meaning in spiritual terms. It only tells how much you have travelled in this *karmic* life. That's it. Some people have travelled for fifty years, some people have travelled for sixty years, and some people have travelled for eight years. It has no meaning on the spiritual level.

Understanding levels or awareness levels are always different. So you cannot underestimate a small child who is very evolved. Spiritually he could probably be much more mature than his grandfather. Do understand this and feel the differences, because this is the total perspective. Go through the book, 'The Power of Purity'. I do not give half-cooked food; I either give cooked food or no food at all.

So, is it clear? Do you get the idea? Do you get the idea of what free will is and the extent of free will that one has during his *karmic* life?

Now I will give you another dimension of it. You are very much active in the dream state. You know, you are also exhausting your *karmas* in the dream state because your space is different. In the dream state, you do not have the binding of the physical body. You are operating from a larger dimension, so you can move in different planes. You can change your character, you can change yourself. All that is binding in the physical state is absent in the dream state. You have realities happening there as well. These are also desires getting exhausted on another level. These are also present in your life. Do you understand the different dimensions of yourself? Each day is different. It is not a one-time affair.

The third level is the deep sleep state, where you visit your home, your hometown. Where is your hometown? It is the astral plane where you go after your death. That place is very familiar to you because you have been there after every death. This physical place, this city, is not familiar to you because only in this life have you come here, and even if you have visited this place before, the roads or at least road signs would have changed, if not the city itself. You may not even have come here in another life.

However, the astral plane is very familiar to you. Hence, you go there every night. This is what people call astral travel. It is no big deal. It is your nature to visit your hometown and make sure everything is ok there and meet familiar people there, shake hands with a few of them and come back to your current body, without any awareness attached to it. If I say I can actually take you to the astral plane, I will have to give you a course to travel to the astral plane, right? But, you already know the train to reach there anyway! It is very simple.

When the body activities are very quiet, when the mind is inactive and has no value, when you are in perfect deep sleep, where you have annihilated all your characteristics, all your qualities, even gender, space, time, plus all identities related to this existence, nothing matters because you do not exist. You do not know that you are sleeping, you do not know whether you are a man or a woman, you do not know about time or space, you have no idea about the quality of your possessions, you have no idea about your professional position, or about social situations, you become completely detached from everything.

At that time, you can get out of the body and go to the astral plane and come back – because the body is stationary, safe and inactive. This is what you do. Sometimes you come back and have some memories of some meeting with somebody or at least some information that you could use here. You may think it is a dream. But it is not. Many people tell me – "I met you, Mohanji and we discussed this matter and you told me what to do". It was real, because the answer was clear. You got a clear answer. It was given in another plane. If you are able to bring back one answer from the astral plane that is crystal clear in the mind, back to this physical plane, it is indeed great, as it is always relevant.

Somebody has actually given you that right answer. Was that your imagination? How did you know this relevant answer to a live situation, which you did not know of before in the physical plane? The answer is crystal clear. You met somebody, you discussed, and you brought it forward as you had to use it here.

36

This knowledge had to be used here. That is why you brought it here. Otherwise, you will not bring it. You need not bring the astral road map here because you cannot use it on these roads. You can only use it there, like the roadmap of your Indian hometown, where you belong. You cannot use it in Dubai or Muscat, right?

Information that you may need in the physical plane- here, right now, you may carry forward from the other planes, with the permission to go ahead and use it. If it helps you to have clarity, do it. You might forget other information which you cannot use. You may consider this information and those experiences as vague dreams as you never needed to remember them, and this is the beauty. We do not carry garbage in the astral plane. We discard what we do not need. There is no accumulation. It is only here on Earth that we tend to accumulate all things wanted and unwanted. All the garbage happens only here in the gross plane.

Death

❧ **Question:** I read a story of Ramana Maharishi. A family lost their only son in a waterfall. The family asked Ramana Maharishi the reason for the death of their very young son. Ramana Maharishi answered that his *karmas* were over in this life. He could not live more. Mohanji, what does this mean?

Mohanji: There is nothing further for him to do in this life. Whatever he came to experience is finished. If you are only going to the shop to buy éclairs, you bought éclairs and finished the desire, right? And perhaps you did not bring money for anything more. That is it. Some people go with a bigger shopping list and fill the cart. There is a special counter for people who buy one or two items. This is how our life is.

You see in the transit lounge of airports that so many people come together, going to various places, everybody sits for only a very limited time. This is the space between life and death, only so much time in that lounge. Some people may stay for one or two hours and some stay for half an hour, or one hour. Some people go to the smoking chamber, some go to eat something, or some may read the newspaper. Each person expresses his character and disappears. Fresh people keep coming. The whole world is just like the transit lounge of the airport. This is life. Very simple life, not complicated at all.

   ❧ **Question:** So when children die young, does it mean that they were a high soul?

Mohanji: Usually, if the child exits before the age of five years, it is usually a higher entity that came to fulfil a certain mission and left. It may not be a *karmic* birth.

   ❧ **Question:** Is it also related to the parent's *karma*?

Mohanji: Not entirely – Higher souls come for a higher purpose, for a higher reason. Of course, the parents also experience happiness and sorrow in the bargain. Usually, it is said that real *karma* takes root only after the age of five years. *Karmic* life starts after the age of five. If a child exits before five years of age, it is purely a *dharmic* existence. Existence before five is rarely a *karmic* existence.

You come to achieve a certain *dharma*, to establish a certain *dharma*, to create a certain awareness, not only for the parents but for higher things. It may be for a whole family, or a society – it could be anything. It depends on the size of its mission. Having said that, all that the child is supposed to experience within that brief period can indeed be considered as *karmic*, even though the *karmas* are not sufficient for a long life. I hope this is not too confusing. *Karma* is always complex. It is difficult to decipher because it has multiple dimensions. It is not an action-reaction theory, even though it appears to be so.

❧ **Question:** Can I ask you about abortion? When does the soul really enter the body of a baby? Some say it is after the fourth month, so if you have an abortion, it does not affect the soul's travel.

Mohanji: Abortion is violence. Prevention is better. Anyway, coming back to your question, it is not easily definable that way because I do not believe in such definitions. I believe that when the child starts growing in the womb, it is alive and has to be considered as a living baby. When the heart starts beating, it has to be considered as alive. Whether the soul enters or not is not the point. It is when the heart starts beating that life has taken place.

❧ **Question:** But is it important whether abortion happened before or after the soul enters the baby? Does it make a difference?

Mohanji: No, life has formed, life has happened, when the heart starts beating. As I said, I do not support violence of any kind. I consider abortion as violence. One could always prevent pregnancy. Why kill the baby?

❧ **Question:** I know someone who had four miscarriages. It was revealed to her, in past life regression, that those children came again in some other lives because they were affected by this. But these were miscarriages and not abortions.

Mohanji: It does not matter what the reasons were. That is why we were talking about the *Naga Devatas*. You have to be in harmony with nature. Then miscarriages and such things will not happen. If you are not in harmony with nature, when you are self-centred, such things will happen. That is why you can never be self-centred in life. You have to be in tune with nature. You have to work as one with nature, respect and love nature. Things will be fine. The moment you think, "I am doing something," you start falling. We are not the doers. Things are happening through us. Situations are happening. Of course, we chose situations, just as we decide to take birth quite before the actual birth.

After birth, the journey is taking you. You chose the destination before the birth happens. But what control do you have after birth? How does your heart beat? How is your circulation happening? How is your digestion happening? How do thought processes happen? Can you control your thought processes? Do you have any idea what you will be thinking in the next moment? We are so helpless. Absolutely. Then why this ego? Why do we believe we are the doers? Things are happening. The moment surrender happens, divinity takes over. Grace flows. Be grateful... Are you clear about this?

   Question: Replying to that young girl, who told the story of the child who died young because he finished his purpose. Now, a child has been born; he is one or two years old. He is bubbly, happy and makes everyone happy. Then he dies. What higher purpose could that child have had?

Mohanji: The higher purpose is that the child could have taken away a lot of negativity of a community or an individual family or a collective family with his death. It would have shifted certain dimensions within the family. There are certain roadblocks in the *karmic* life. The child sees that, through its unpolluted, unbiased absoluteness. The soul is full and omnipresent, even though it is within a child's body. It has come here for a purpose, due to the *karmic* eligibility of the family, to help them and protect them. At death, through intense sorrow, it shifts the consciousness of the family members.

Everybody has certain protecting angels or guides from above. They decide to give a helping hand, as they see that these persons may not know the course of life, or what the roadblocks, or the obstructions are, along the way in the path of life. So, this child could be one of the protecting angels as well. From a higher perspective, everything is clear. From birth till death, the whole thing is clear. We are just not aware of it. Then there is a collective level of obstructions which is acquired by the family over generations. If there were disagreements, if there were problems in the family, fights, all these things that are accumulated in the family, that also partially becomes the *karma* of individuals living in the family. Such things are clogging the whole family's movement or obstructing their free movement.

During such time, the higher beings will say, "Ok, we will come back and take birth here in this family, just to cleanse the whole thing, just to clear the stale air." Then they come and spread this warmth around, and they collect all the garbage, and they disappear, in a *dharmic* way. This could be a guiding angel, a protecting angel, or maybe a higher entity who chose to come there and then cleanse the generation from the accumulated *karma* or the accumulated roadblocks. Such things happen many times.

Take a look at an individual. A woman had a desire to have a child. How does *karma* play a role? For e.g., one lady had thirteen children in one life. She was living in a particular community where birth control was not accepted. She was not allowed to stop childbirth in any way, so she kept having children. After thirteen children, she was sick and tired of this whole thing. She was praying to God, "God, please do something; please stop this misery." It was too late to pray in that life, because she already had all those children. Even though it did not work in that life, it worked in her next life. Because what she asked for was not possible in that particular life, her prayer bore fruit in her next life.

Since that desire was carried forward to the next life, which is this life, she bore no children in this life. Now, she started praying to God to give her at least one child! It is natural for a woman to think of having a child. She does not know what her state was and what she was praying for in her last life. Then, with all this desire, she got a child, but the child survived only about a year or two because the intensity of the desire was just to have a child. It was not to have the experience of all the stages of motherhood through time and ages of the child. So, the desire to have the experience of motherhood was fulfilled in this life. But the child did not live on to give her the complete experience, because that was not supposed to be in this life. This is how *karma* works.

When the child came and left, it actually removed a lot of roadblocks and burdens, and it elevated people to a certain level of awareness. People who were going in a completely materialistic and emotional path were shaken by the death of the child. They started thinking – "What is the whole thing about life and death? What am I trying to do here?" Suddenly everybody became introspective – "Am I doing the right thing? Is it really worth it? What is this whole thing about? Is there a God?" Slowly they shifted to thoughts of spirituality. Till that time, it was impossible because a sudden shock was required in the family to tilt their level of awareness. To bring them to a certain track.

The child did that job. It does not matter how long it lived, but it lived sufficiently so you had those nice smiles and cries of that baby. These feelings are essential. If the child had died within ten days, you would not remember it that way. But, if the child stayed on for some time, and created its own impression, then you would remember. Then you cannot forget, and that changed the consciousness of the people. They started seeing things differently. We understand the larger purpose. So, every event has a larger meaning. Everything has a deeper purpose.

The Nature of Dharma

Dharma is the Basis of the Universe

🌾 **Question:** What is the purpose of being in *Dharmic* mode?

Mohanji: *Dharma* is not a purpose. It is a pure duty. Animals always operate in *dharmic* mode. The sun, moon and stars operate in *dharmic* mode. They have a specific system of operation. If there are lots of deer and a few tigers, a tiger will never kill a deer for the sake of fun or to control the population! A tiger will kill a deer only when he is hungry. We humans do not do that. We kill for pleasure. Thus, it becomes *karma*. The sun rises everyday. It does not say, "I am tired today; I will come tomorrow." *Dharma* is the base and basis of the universe. *Karma* is the basis for individual life and its corresponding happenings and experiences.

The Dharma of Existence

When the destination is clear, the journey is effortless. Sense objects do lure us. That's the *dharma* of sense objects. The *dharma* of the senses is to run after sense objects. The *dharma* of the mind is to experience the sense objects by aiding the senses. The *dharma* of the soul during terrestrial existence is to aid the mind, body and senses and facilitate the role play that we are currently enacting. Thus, different sets of *dharma* underline our existence.

An *Avatar* does not appear just to re-establish or re-invent *dharma*. *Dharma* is always well established. *Dharma* always exists and is enacted within us and outside of us. *Dharma* never goes out of circulation. *Dharma* has to exist for the world to exist. *Dharma* could decay with the flow of time, and repeated use and abuse. When we repeatedly use something, wear and tear happens to it. *Avatars* appear to mend this wear and tear, and bring the generation back to its natural track. *Avatars* are excellent mechanics. They make the huge vehicle, called *dharma*, prim and proper and maybe as good as brand new!

CHAPTER 3:

...To Create 'I' and 'You'

The Original Man

Time evolved man. Man evolved time. Man's very existence became related to time. He forgot his true state of timelessness. He forgot his true nature. Man became another species on Earth, detached from the 'Father'. A vulnerable species, his basic existence revolved around his emotions, feelings, impressions, and ego. He reduced his divine stature, to the stature of his own mind. He looked at the world through his own eyes.

He steadily lost his capacity to look at the world through the winding journey of explorations of himself and the deep quest to find himself. Man's search for himself continued through time and existence in various times. To find himself, man wandered through lands and oceans. Time after time, drop by drop, his consciousness evolved. Thus, we reach the study of the evolution of the consciousness of man. This is the story of Original Man.

Theory of Evolution

Charles Darwin said that man evolved into his current state from the ape. Let it be so. No arguments. Darwin contributed a lot in moulding the mind of the twentieth century man. Along with Karl Marx and Sigmund Freud, he sowed great imagination into the minds of twentieth century men and influenced the thought process of the entire generation, thus changing the course of history and thought pattern of modern man. Respecting the contributions of Charles Darwin, especially in making people think differently, let us look at the evolution theory objectively.

If liberation is the reason for existence, as we spiritual seekers believe, why do we reincarnate again and again? Why this tedious process of trial and error? Well, one cannot reach the highest grade without going through the lower grades: that is the answer. In that case, we have to agree that God has been experimenting with beings with lower consciousness, allowing them time and space to reach His consciousness by themselves. If this is true, then the old Vedic principle of 'Neti neti', or 'Not that, not that', becomes more relevant.

The *Guru* never taught the Truth to the disciple; instead, he just gave hints. The student meditated on those hints and came back to the Master, asking if his finding was the final knowledge. The Master would just say, 'Not that'. The student went back and contemplated further. Thus, with the aid of nature and sheer contemplation into himself and his own existence, he would eventually reach his own soul. When the student culminated his search at his own soul and from there to God Consciousness, he would never go back to his Master. Until then, he kept going back, asking the same question and receiving the same answer – 'Not that'. So, if we follow the theory of evolution of man from unicellular being to the super conscious being, our consciousness has taken ages to reach here. This is quite a possibility, right?

Theory of Devolution

Let us contemplate on the fall of man. God created man in his own image. This means Man was created with all the power and potential of God Himself. Let us call the first man Adam.

We must keep a few things in mind here. God is formless. God is omnipresent. God is not prone to emotions. God has unlimited intelligence. He exists in the Superconscious state. God can multiply Himself at will. God expresses Himself through all materials. God creates, maintains and dissolves all materials from Himself into Himself. So, Adam should have all those powers.

But the difference here is that Adam is made up of elements while God is consciousness. Adam is matter, even if the identification is temporary. God is pure energy. That difference became too expensive for Adam. God operates through His consciousness and Adam operates through his mind and intellect. This is a heavy limitation. But when God created Adam, He also gave him the potential to realise his true stature by installing three subtle energy meridians branching out throughout the etheric body and a three-and-a-half-turns coiled Serpent (*kundalini*) near the root *chakra* (energy centre at the bottom of the spine).

The serpent always sleeps and that allowed Adam to believe that he was the limited body. When the serpent awakened, and especially when it moved, he experienced strange sensations happening to him. He often became helpless, emotional, vulnerable, erratic... So, in order to feel control over himself and the space outside of him, he unconsciously allowed the serpent to sleep. Therefore, the theory of devolution amounts to the fall of Adam from his original stature of 'God Man' (man who had the potential and power of his Creator) to that of ordinary Man, who is close to animals in stature.

The Fall

The male Adam wanted a female body as his companion because he saw animals procreating, and his identifications naturally drifted to that of animals. He was indeed far superior to animals, but he had nothing to compare himself with. At least nothing higher than himself. So, he asked for Eve. He had the power to create Eve at will. Some species still possess that power. When all the beings of that species become one gender, some of them convert themselves into the other gender to help continue the species. This is usual with certain amphibians – frogs, etc. Since Adam was superior to amphibians and since he had the power of God, he created Eve. Actually, Adam did not realise that he had the power to create many selves at will, because that is the way God creates.

With creation, his *kundalini* also got awakened. When *kundalini* started moving through his *chakras*, strange emotions started to surge and spurt out. Sexual desire was the most powerful of them all. As the *kundalini* moved through the earth element (*muladhara- the* root chakra) and pierced the water element (*svadhisthana- the sacral chakra*), he could not control his sexual urge anymore. The call of the elements and the surging *kundalini*, (the serpent), tilted Adam. He ate the forbidden fruit: he procreated with Eve.

Adam began to feel 'naked'. He fell in consciousness, from the supreme Consciousness of God and the ability to create at will, to a lower consciousness of having to procreate to keep the species going. The fall was from unlimited Superconsciousness to limited consciousness associated with his body, mind, and intellect. Thus, he reduced himself to the nature of elements, or in other words, the nature of animals and inherited all the associated woes. The fall of consciousness happened there. The body, which is made out of elements, had to be re-created through procreation, not at will. Man lost the power to conglomerate raw energy into matter and thus create another human. His consciousness fell to the level of animals.

Nature and the environment intensified the fall. He slipped again and again. Ignorance shrouded the Truth. He lost his direction. He forgot his way back home. He lost his destination. Then, through generations, with the help of many Masters and evolved souls, man started climbing up, step by step, to the highest consciousness. It was a difficult process, an up-hill task, especially as he had to fight his basic, inherited, primal nature and grow in consciousness, while the primal nature always lurked behind. God patiently waited. He allowed the time for his son to find his way home because God has always been existing in timelessness. Man played with *Maya* (worldly illusion). *Maya* played with Man.

The Territorial Man

As the level of consciousness fell, man became territorial, like animals. He began to guard his territory, property and people. He became possessive and vengeful. He guarded his territory and, whenever he could, he tried to expand his territory. 'Dissatisfaction' got written in bold letters on his forehead. Man could never satisfy himself. He came back again and again; to further satisfy his ever-growing desires. Ignorance helped here. He lost his memories of his bizarre quests and thus repeated them, basking in his ignorance. He asked many questions of himself and of others. These were just expressions of his confusion, as he never lived the true answers. He kept avoiding the Truth for the available tangible delusion or *Maya*.

The Greedy Man

Man fell to greed and extreme possessiveness, associated with ignorance of his true nature. Along with defined territory, power happened. Power bred greed for more. Possessions were displayed in tangible formats, such as gold, precious stones, captive women for pleasure or many wives, many captive animals, many soldiers, etc. Man collected trophies to prove his superior status to others. The vacuum created by loss of stature was filled with greed for social status. He groomed himself to do anything to make money, attain power, and enhance his social status. His society also blindly supported material success, ignoring the crimes behind his unlimited wealth.

The Saintly Man

There have been detached beings in every society, who could have anything, but needed nothing. When money, power, wealth and women lured the average man, these people stayed afloat in the social existence, unaffected, like a lotus flower above the water. Even when they were standing knee-deep in the mud of existence, they expressed the beauty and radiance of the Divine on the surface. Early kings were advised by such Saints. They advised the kings to rule the country based on *dharma* or basic noble duty. Their advice kept kings grounded and pious, and their subjects at peace and harmony.

They sowed unconditional love on the path of the existence of the kings as well as their subjects. They said, "Wherever all people are not protected without discrimination, wherever mothers cannot feel safe, wherever children cannot play without fear, wherever power is not used to help and save the poor and hungry, wherever animals are not protected, wherever trees and plants are not respected, wherever life is not respected and nurtured, disease and decay will happen. Downfall and destruction will take place."

The Business Man

Man learned to wield power effectively. Power was the key, while control was the method. Fear was the tool. As time evolved, the duel between the positive and negative continued in every mind. The Saints were discarded and the glitter-bitten kings chose businessmen as their kin and advisors. They believed in profits. They believed that time equated to profits. Time would never be spent for free ever again. Time would be spent provided there were gains. Life became transactional.

Relationships became transactional. Love became conditional. Rule became profit-based.

Power was with the businessmen. They also started creating rulers. Wars happened to satisfy the greed of man. Weapon manufacturers became the ones who decided the future of societies and countries. People assassinated people. People tortured and killed people. People were exploited. Everything was camouflaged and done in the name of religion and *dharma*! Man fell further and further in consciousness. His consciousness became demonic. Some people who lost everything in the bargain, had nothing further to lose and started rising up in consciousness. Higher Masters held their hand and helped them to walk the winding path. Some struggled and fell, disillusioned. Some clung onto faith and survived. The business man thought he was having the last laugh. But that was an illusion too.

Time after time, the new replaced the old and the more cunning survived. They insensitively ravaged their very seat of power – Mother Earth. The Mother watched the whole show in tears, helpless. On her chest, man killed fellow man, destroyed property, and dug deep holes into the very existence of future generations. Greed for profits spilled the very guts of Mother Earth. It imbalanced her very existence. Greed continued and profits justified all the aberrations of mankind.

The Family Man

Man shrank. He became family-oriented and started shrinking to responsibilities related only to his immediate family. His territory became his family. He became selfish. His whole world became himself and his family. This narrow mindedness and insensitiveness about others, glued his consciousness to the limits of his family. Poor man. Every blow in the harmony of his family affected his heart deeply. His expectations killed him. He often died heartbroken.

The Social Man

The social man was a bit better. He also cared for his society and the poor and downtrodden. Karl Marx provided wind to his wings and the twentieth century saw the fertile imaginations of many social people taking flight and organising revolutions. Their intentions were good. They cared for people. Maybe just human beings. Still, it was better than gross insensitivity and inertia. Yet, every society consists of the good, the bad, and the ugly. Each carved his own dimension into the social structure. In all these times, those who slipped into higher consciousness or those who could see beyond the box and dared to talk about what they saw, were assassinated or eradicated.

As human beings, we have always despised those who chose to be different. We love to burn challengers to our beliefs. We hate to think differently. We choose continuity of thoughts and beliefs. We have always been afraid of changes. Thus, society killed Socrates, Jesus, and many others, who were different and had the ability to show the light of higher consciousness to the average man. Ironically, we can be proud of our tenacity to stick to the errant path!

Society created dos and don'ts. Society also created morality and an acceptable code of conduct. Some societies even created rigid morality and severe punishments for those who disobeyed. Men started to pretend. Pretensions became the acceptable mode of existence. Pretensions entangled men further into social bindings.

Some people live their whole life on pretensions and waste it completely. They pretend happiness, they pretend love, they pretend care, they pretend benevolence, they pretend spirituality, they pretend knowledge etc. Eventually, when they have to meet reality, they will have already lost their life. This sad story gets repeated in every society, for many people. Yet, people refuse to get real and resort to their pretensions to gain social acceptance. Those few who dare to walk alone, stay liberated, despite social persecutions. Pretension is one thing that is definitely anti-spiritual.

Society created morality for the middle class. The rich and the poor have nothing to do with it. The middle class contains the most pretenders too. They are neither rich, nor poor. Since by nature, due to his erect spine, man likes to look above his eye level, he tries to be what he is not. (If you ask a child to write on the wall, he will write above his eye level. This is the nature of man.) The more the morality, the more the violations too. Along with violations, gross suppressions also happen. Suppressions lead to restlessness. Social restlessness leads to calamities and revolution. Thus, the ignorance of man, combined with a lack of effort to maintain hygiene in the inner world, makes our society a filthy alley.

The Cunning Man

The cunning man has always survived. He is street smart. He is intelligent. He is manipulative and well-spoken. He has beautiful presentation skills. He is selfish, but conceals that skilfully. He is handsome and effective. He is considered a good businessman.

With the fall of consciousness, those who displayed their intellect in any manner possible, and those who successfully attracted money or power, were worshipped. Cunning became a symbol of success. It was often re-named a 'strategy for success'. We saw many cunning men who effectively eradicated good but passive people and climbed up the ladder of material success. Society made statues of them and honoured them wherever possible.

The Political Man

The cunning man often left his business and opted for power instead, or played a dual game. They played the game of politics and business simultaneously. Everything is fair in politics and war. They re-defined the territories and walking spaces of the common man. Passive social men were led, misled, and at convenience, manipulated to gain their ends. Political man blamed all sufferings as inevitable in the path of ultimate freedom and independence. Generation after generation saw the same dish served on different ornamental plates. Passive men were happy to see the changes in the plate and ignored the dish. As long as there is food, life goes on. Thus, suffering never ended. The promised freedom never happened.

Political man changed his costume time and again and appeared to appease bonded minds with promises which they never meant to keep. All manipulations were called 'strategic decisions', which confused the social man. They knew that the best way to rule is to confuse. Faces changed but confusion remained. Life went on. Dictators came and went. Wars came and went. Many got killed. Many survived. Life went on. Never was any politician punished by the law. The long hands of the law managed to reach only the gates of the politician's abode, but never dared to touch him.

When the law got too close, he sacrificed someone else to satisfy the hunger of the law, and escaped from that situation. The law was applicable only to ordinary people. The rich politicians had nothing to do with it. They were lawmakers. They have always been immune to the law. Even when Saints, who guided generations to liberation were burnt at the stake, politicians were never touched for even grosser crimes they had committed. History has seen this phenomenon consistently, repeated time and again with every generation.

The God Man

There were a few God men, who stayed away from the eyes of society, maintaining a higher consciousness and avoiding the contamination of social life. Whoever came into society out of compassion was scandalised, ridiculed, imprisoned or even assassinated. Those who escaped society searched for the princes among the frogs. They had to kiss many frogs to get a few princes. They guided those true seekers and elevated them to the highest possible level of consciousness within the possible time. They left the rest to fight out their survival in the quagmire of lower consciousness. God men were very few; however, they helped balance the gross negativity. They often burnt themselves like candles. They served without expecting anything in return.

Negativity never needed any nurturing. It came uninvited, like a weed, and overtook the garden by force. It feasted on trees, plants and sometimes, even the gardener. Many fell; some survived. Those who survived showed the rest the light of true existence and evolution. Some followed the light. Those who missed the glow and procrastinated got dissolved in time.

Man, who fell from super consciousness to animal consciousness, is slowly climbing back up, step by step. The path is difficult. It is filled with thorns and danger. The uncontrollable mind that lures man is the biggest danger, together with the ego and all identifications. This journey of liberation is only possible through determination and awareness of the present. Those who get there will rejoice. Those who fall back, will come back to try again.

The Types of Men

An ancient classification states:

Mineral Man – Selfish, not interested in anyone else but himself. Usually greedy and self-centred.

Plant Man – Selfish to the extent of his family. He is not interested in anything beyond his close family.

Animal Man – Selfish to the extent of his family and his community. He is not interested in anything beyond his community.

Human Man – Selfish to the extent of his family, his community and his country. He is not interested in the welfare of any beyond his country.

God Man – Selfless. He loves beyond all man-made barriers. He does not care for caste, creed, communities, countries, colours, or classifications. He loves everyone, just as the sun spreads its rays equally around, without discrimination. Man's consciousness reaches its human zenith when he spontaneously becomes a 'God Man' – a man beyond barriers.

Where do we stand? Contemplate! It is worth knowing...

Four Types of People

🌼 **Question:** There is always a thought that I need to do something about injustice.

Mohanji: This is our usual response level. But use your intellect: respond, do not react. That itself is a big war won. If emotion is coming forward, it will suck all your energy away and you will be exhausted. If you respond using your intellect: you will be much better, as energy will not drain away, even if you feel that somebody is using you or abusing you for some reason. Do you know what you are doing? Do you have control over your actions?

Awareness is the best way to overcome all sorts of things, but awareness must happen to all people for perfect peace to occur. If a person is not evolved to that level of awareness, he will never understand and he will continue with his reactions. However, you could certainly get back to your own inner peace and let the world happen as it will. Do not try to change others. Change yourself and lead by example. That is much more powerful than a million words. This is why Gandhiji is honoured and respected even today: he lived his teachings.

That is why I have explained the predominant characteristics of people in 4 ways: Aggressive good, aggressive bad, passive good and passive bad.

Aggressive Good is a very intelligent man and is also selfless. He uses all his intellect and all his power, for the general well-being of society. Examples are Krishna, Jesus and Buddha. They did have feelings, but never operated from the realm of emotions.

Aggressive Bad is a person who is extremely intelligent in the same way as Krishna, Buddha or Jesus, but is using everything for selfish means. They are also very, very powerful and you can see such people in our own society. They are often politicians. They are very powerful people, yet mostly cunning and are primarily only looking out for themselves. They even harm society for selfish ends. Society sometimes stands by helplessly, because the Aggressive Bad are intelligent and they play their cards very well. They also get away with their treachery. How many politicians get punished by law?

The third level is Passive Good. By nature, they are good. They like to go home, be with their wife and children and take them to the shops, but they are passive. They cannot respond. They use emotion more than intellect. They are controlled by the Aggressive Good or the Aggressive Bad. If the Aggressive Good are controlling them, they will be highly beneficial for society. If the Aggressive Bad are controlling them, these people's goodness is used against them. You can see such people in society.

The last is Passive Bad. They are bad and negative by nature. What do they do? They abuse people. Sometimes they are a part of the mafia too. If their boss, the Aggressive Bad man, tells them, "Go and kill that man!", they will just follow the order without feeling anything. They do not think. They do not even ask, "Why should I kill that man?" By nature, they are negative. Such people are plenty, but these people can also be influenced by the Aggressive Good and the Aggressive Bad. Most of the time the Aggressive Bad influence them and they get used as tools to achieve the Aggressive Bad's selfish ends. If the Aggressive Good influences them, they will slowly turn towards goodness and selflessness.

If you look at society, you can see this classification working. These are broad classifications. There are mixtures of these too. It is like a pyramid. Just draw a pyramid and then start putting the lines on. Aggressive Good people are scarce, but they are powerful enough to change the course of history. Aggressive Bad is a slightly bigger group. Since they are heavily selfish, they could also sow negativities and create wars, agony, and hatred in society. Then there are slightly more Passive Good than Aggressive Bad. That is why we have armies. They are passive, but they are good. They take care of the country, but they obey rules. They are good-natured.

Yudhisthira from the Mahabharata is a great example of Passive Good. He is a very good man, but if you follow a Passive Good leader, you could even be led to the jungle! It is because his nature of goodness was not useful for himself. Yudhisthira was manipulated by the Aggressive Bad Shakuni, the maternal uncle of Duryodhana. Yudhisthira was good by nature, honest and truthful, but that was not used in an intelligent way. He should have known that if he played dice, he would not beat his opponent. Yet, playing at dice was his weakness. That intellect was missing. Instead, he upheld the Truth, "I am a *kshatriya* (warrior); if someone challenges me, I should accept the challenge and fight."

In such situations, one should use the George Bernard Shaw principle: 'I will not stand in front of the gun. If you want to do that, you may stand. I know that if they shoot, I will die. It is foolish to show bravery by standing in front of the gun!' It would be more sensible to be alive and tackle matters, rather than die and become a statue on the wall for the birds to decorate with their offerings.

So, this is the intellect's capacity for discrimination. Consider Passive Bad Dushasana of the Mahabharata. Duryodhana would tell him to go and kill a man and he would do it and come back and drink his tea. He would not even think twice. Dushasana would never ask the question why he should kill somebody at all. He liked to break people's bones because that was his nature, his hobby. He went around and did that. All contract killers are of this kind. They do not care. They like to inflict pain and misery and rejoice at their handiwork.

> **Question:** The Creator or Existence is benevolent. But if you look at the entire world, it seems that it is ruled by the Aggressive Bad. So much so that one tends to conclude that bad prevails. How does creation let this happen?

Mohanji: You see, creation happens at various levels. The first level of creation, when *Parabrahma* (The Supreme Father) decided to experience himself – the first form, the form of an egg happened. There was only purity. There was no division. Then relativity made room for hundreds and thousands and trillions of creations or possibilities. Thus there are creators from the level of the Almighty to creators at our level. That is, we create our destiny in our own way with our available materials. If creators are of varying levels, their creations will also have difference and variety. That is why the universe is full of variety.

The Almighty just energises the creation. It is just like the petrol of the car that never tells you where to go. The soul never tells you what to do, what to create. You use your clay – your intellect, *buddhi*, *ahankara*, and *chitta*. You create within your understanding levels, with your education, with your knowledge and available materials.

The Almighty certainly has a much higher awareness, or complete awareness and he may not even get involved in the creation. Just as an investor would create the first company, appoint people to run it and develop it, and then his staff set up further companies out of the profits from the first company. Creation happened through many hands and continues to happen so. Each staff member may not possess the total view or macro view that the owner has; hence, his creation will also be at his level of consciousness. The owner will allow you to create. I will give you an example. Look at the consciousness level of animals. It is almost like a one, two, or three-year-old human child. They feel and they respond to love, just like a small human child. So, the highest IQ or intelligence level in an animal is the same as that of a human child.

So, where do we stand in consciousness? There are 'animals' and 'God' in men too; that is why we create many realities such as hatred, anger, jealousy, and fear, as well as love. So, who put the clay together for animals? Who created those? There are entities that designed such things. Some entities were extremely artistic. They created those beautiful birds, colourful fish and wonderful flowers.

There are so many creation levels in the universe. It is not created by one person. We can refer to it as *Brahma*. *Brahma* has various dimensions. *Brahma* has four faces, four dimensions of creation, isn't it? Four represents all angles, all sides or the total dimension. All the dimensions of creation are expressed in the universe and projected into space, and it is not only on Earth, but also in very different and diverse locations or positions, unimaginable to the human mind. Thus, when the creator created the creators, or when the creator – that is *Parabrahma*, the Supreme Almighty, created the original creators, there was some kind of uniformity, or same IQ level, because they were original expressions of the original creator.

Further creations were at different levels of consciousness. Still further creations were of various levels of consciousness. It also depended on the location, time, space and available material. In this way, the world has hundreds of different levels of consciousness. They have no uniformity, but they have one destination – eventually to merge with the supreme father – *Parabrahma*. The clay is of different colours and flavours. At the end of the day, behind every creation, is the one Supreme Entity who created it all. Definitely!

There is no doubt about the Supreme Entity, but that entity is just watching the show. Perfect witness-hood! He likes to see the show. They are all His projections. One day he could withdraw everything and say, "Ok, the show is over, get back home." Finished! This is certainly possible. Since time has no existence in the supreme, because time needs relativity to exist, we cannot predict on which date the Almighty will wind up the show. It could be in the next trillion years, from the angle of time and relativity. Why bother? We have only today to play with. So, play on...

You are Not Alone

Every moment, all we do is just echo the glory of existence in its absoluteness. When the conscious mind blocks our vision, we fail to see its grandeur and completeness. This is the design of existence. Since the conscious mind is filled with conditionings and related expectations, we fail to see the obvious when we are at it. We cover our weakness with reasoning and arguments that are nothing but expressions of our ego. Yet our heart knows the Truth. The spiritual heart that guides you as to which way to go, puts people and thoughts together, and explains the meaning of life the way it is.

There is no coincidence. We met for a reason and we will travel together for the same reason. When we look back, we will see the reason for the journey. Neither before, nor while at it, can we see the purpose in its completeness. This is the nature of existence that runs parallel to time. When our existence shifts to timelessness or being-ness, everything becomes one, just expressions of one large being. Nothing matters then. We will meet soon. There is much to do. Do not worry. You are not alone.

We are Relationship-Oriented

If you look at your whole life, it is just like the cinema. No situations are repeated. We go along with time. I can only lift the right hand or the left hand at this second. By the time I lift the right hand, my choice is finished. Then it is another second, to lift the left hand or the right hand. So just like a movie, things are moving forward. If we understand that clearly, we will have less sorrow. We feel we control our life. However, something else controls us, because time is given, space is given; intelligence and choices are very limited. So, why do we complain? Whatever happens outside of us, if we are peaceful inside, we can survive. If we place the remote control of our life in somebody's hands, they will keep changing the channels. Who suffers? We do.

So, if our life and our happiness and sorrows depend too much on other people, we will suffer. I'm not saying that we should not talk to other people, but we should take other people as other people. If they are happy, or they do good, or they smile at you, it does not change much within you. However, we are usually relationship-oriented. When we are relationship-oriented, a lot of people have an influence on us everyday. So how do we handle this? Through increasing awareness. Whether there is sunshine or rain, life goes on. Whether I'm happy or not today, life goes on. Whether I'm fat or thin, it does not matter. Life goes on. Another thing is that we always think that if we were somebody else, it would be better. Because we think we have defects, and other people do not have defects. For e.g., say I imagine, "If I were Arnold Schwarzenegger, everything would be better." It is impossible, and he will have these problems as well, that we do not know. Furthermore, what we think about other people also influences us. One way other people control our lives is because we give the remote control to a lot of people. Likewise, we think other people are better off, whether better looking, or have better finances or position... Something better than us.

But one thing I can guarantee you. I have met many supremely rich people, and what I have found is that they have much more insecurity than a normal person. Most of them cannot sleep well. Most of them are terribly worried, as they have created a prison around themselves to protect themselves. At the end of the day, they fail to enjoy what they have. To top it all, while getting money takes a lot of effort, sweat and blood, maintaining that is even more difficult.

I'm not commenting on whether money is bad or money is good. It is energy. If we have enough money in our hands, we control it. If we have money above the neck, it controls us. Many people who are rich and famous are prisoners of their own fame and fortune. So don't think, "I'll be happy tomorrow", or "I'll be happy when I have a lot of money." Can you be happy now? This is the only reality. If tomorrow happens, thank you. But I cannot guarantee.

Most of Our Relationships are Binding

❧ **Question:** How do you control your mind – anger and restlessness?

Mohanji: You cannot tackle the mind directly. You have to watch it. That's the only way.

What makes the mind strong? Your participation in the thought process! If you get emotionally involved, you will have agony. However, when you are rooted in the spine, you will automatically observe your mind. Our conscious mind that generally drives us crazy, is a product of this life. The subconscious mind, which has the full data, is a product of many lifetimes. So, over all the lifetimes, you have had the same agonies, same emotions, and frustrations. Then you took this body, a fresh body, with a fresh mind, which does not know the past. Only your soul knows your past.

Where is anger coming from? Mostly from expectations! We say we know something, but what do we know? We say we know many people, but we don't know anybody. A husband does not know his wife fully. Children don't know their parents and so on.

We are all living in a blinded world, and we do expect, "He should behave in certain ways; she should behave in a certain way etc.", because we like to put people into frames. We have certain ideas about people, but will they always behave in that way? The point is to watch your thoughts. Where is the hook of your anger buried? It has to be in something from the past and the related expectations, and it is usually related to relationships. Relationships cause us a lot of problems in life, usually because we have expectations. However, at the same time, if a relationship is based on a larger purpose – sometimes people come together to elevate each other to higher dimensions – then there won't be any conflicts. Then it will be a beautiful relationship. On that level, nobody will bind the other person.

Most of our relationships are binding and conditional: "If you behave in a certain way, I love you, and if you won't, then I don't know you." This is how most relationships work these days. Worse is a relationship of convenience. To be with someone because you are bored or have nothing else to do – and you form a relationship just to fill the vacuum. It will crack because of varied expectations.

If this is the case, rather than forming a relationship of convenience, it is better to be alone and concentrate on your personal evolution. Otherwise, it only amounts to nuisance value and further agony. I always say, "Please use this life to understand life and stay liberated." Liberation is a state of mind – when the mind is not controlling the body and when the senses are not controlling the mind. If intellect runs our system, we are safe. Remember, we can only control our actions, not the results.

The Naked Truth

Our relationship is not accidental. We have been connected through many lifetimes and will continue through time as well. So, the familiarity that some of you are experiencing today has deeper roots than your limited mind can perceive. Please do not mind if what is given below is a bit too informal and straight. I know this will provoke some thoughts in you.

ᰰ **Question:** Relationship with (husband, wife, son, daughter, neighbour, boss) is not working.

Mohanji: Is your relationship with yourself working? Sort that out and all the external relationships will work. Connect to yourself first. This 'yourself' is not what you see in the mirror. It is the formless that keeps what you see in the mirror alive. Connect to that formless within you and everything else will work.

  ❦ **Question:** Who is our real friend, our true friend?

Mohanji: Your Self; Your own soul. Nobody is closer to you than your soul.

  ❦ **Question:** Who is our worst enemy?

Mohanji: Yourself. Nobody can destroy you as much as you yourself can do. You can be 'defeated' and 'killed' only if you choose to. You can be liberated from everything if you choose to. It depends on what you choose. Your worst enemy and your best friend is yourself. All others are secondary. So, how can we blame others for our weakness or our fall?

  ❦ **Question:** Why do friends part?

Mohanji: When the joint *karmic* agenda ends, people part. When it begins, people meet or come together. The same applies to marriage, partnerships, love affairs, etc. People need a common *karmic* agenda to be together. It can never happen otherwise.

  ❦ **Question:** How do we live with people who pretend to care yet do not, who praise you in front of you and talk bad about you elsewhere?

Mohanji: Ignore them. Behave with them as you would with a person who is ill. Be kind and compassionate, yet detached. Do not carry their baggage on your shoulders.

  ❦ **Question:** What do you mean by binding or bondage?

Mohanji: I would say everything is binding. All relationships are binding. Dependency on elements like water and food is also binding. But we need this binding too. We cannot say that we will exist without all that. We have to slowly grow beyond all that. Evolve stage by stage and step by step. Masters will come and guide you. When you are ready to walk the path, guidance is for sure. But when you sit in the drawing-room and think, or if you are procrastinating, nothing will happen. It is an individual path. No one can carry you on his/her shoulder and walk. You must walk the path yourself.

ॐ **Question:** What about successful relationships?

Mohanji: Do not try to prune the tree. If you allow a person to be natural, the person will be reasonably peaceful. Accept the other with their pluses and minuses, like you yourself have. Most people who go wild have been suppressed. In a relationship, you cannot bind anybody to you. Allow each other the freedom to be. You cannot control anybody. We don't even have control over our children; if you try, they will abandon you.

You see, everybody comes with a particular shopping list for their life, which is not necessarily yours, which we have to accept. Everybody comes with enough potential to finish the shopping list in this life.

Often, we are very dictatorial in our relationships. A *Guru* or Master can be dictatorial because sometimes you need a kick to leave your comfort zone. But a relationship is a mutual journey and if the purpose is clear, it is more enjoyable. However, don't take a destination like enlightenment as the purpose of your relationship. That does not work.

Standing Alone or Escapism?

ॐ **Question:** Is it possible that, even though there are friends, you know that you can be without them. You are not dependent on them. You are there for them rather than needing them. What do you do in this case? Can you stand alone?

Mohanji: Yes. Be yourself and be benevolent. Express love and compassion. Standing alone should not be escapism. "I stand alone because I do not have friends", is escapism. You have friends, you love them, but you are not dependent on them. Dependency leads to emotions and expectations. Expectations always bring agony. We were supposed to go for lunch together, but he did not come! Expectations are difficult to handle in life. We all have them. Great Masters put an axe at the root of the expectations. Hundreds of people are waiting to see a Master, and he never turns up. You shout, "I waited for you! I wasted my time!" Those eligible will wait. Even if you do not see me, you will still get me.

Deserving Levels

✤ **Question:** Is it possible that you may not find someone that you can look up to?

Mohanji: It is possible because it depends on what you need or deserve. What if you increase your deserving level? How can you increase your deserving level? If you have the experience and qualification of a CEO, you enter a CEO position. Can a tenth-grade student become a CEO? Increase in eligibility is always based on detachment. Why, after some time, do your friends change? It is because your position changes, as well as your communication level. Only corresponding friends will happen. Some previous friends may not understand what you are doing! They may not understand your evolution. You may measure your progress by the number of friends dropping away!

Measure the depth of expectation of yourself. Write down all expectations and then ask yourself, "Do I deserve all this?" Don't underestimate or judge. See where you stand. We always analyse others and never ourselves. However, be aware that we can never understand the third dimension of another person. We see what we can see, and see how they operate in the external world. The tragedy is that most of us operate in the external world on pretensions of what we are not! We are dependent on society to call us good!

Faith is important. "I have faith": this statement is not important. Faith should be practised at every point in life, with surrender. For e.g., this is a situation, this is me and my intelligence, and I have done a hundred per cent from my side. As for the rest, leave it to the Masters, whichever Master(s) you believe in.

Surrender at His feet and never look back. It will work. Or it will be like planting a seed and digging it out all the time to check whether it has sprouted.

The Best Medicine to Counter all Negativity is Love

❧ **Question:** When there is some injustice happening, for e.g., to your colleague in the office, should you do something about it or should one keep quiet?

Mohanji: The best medicine to counter all negativity is love. It is not easy. But it is the best medicine. Eventually, people become helpless in front of love, unconditional love. When you start expressing love unconditionally, and express benevolence all the time, not only to the person who is trying to harm you, but to everyone, all will shower you with love. If you are steadfast in love, and your path is that of love towards all beings, birds, animals, trees, people, it disarms and diffuses all negativities and elevates your consciousness to great heights. It also removes and destroys all kinds of psycho-somatic blockages too.

This is the best. Usually, when somebody does an injustice to us, our ego is hurt, and we feel hurt. This discriminating factor makes us react. Reaction always harms. But the moment you shift it to the intellect: "What is he doing? What is this person doing? Why is he doing this? Ok, he is doing this for me." There is some kind of education happening in this whole thing. You start understanding the wholesomeness of an event, and you start responding instead of reacting.

Response is with the intellect. Reaction is with the emotions. Try to discard emotions and start responding with the intellect. It disarms the other person or opponent because it is not what he expected from you. The moment you react, the other person will be happy: "This is what I am expecting", an emotional outburst, crying or whatever. This is why the non-violent movement of Mahatma Gandhi became so effective. It disarmed the opponent.

 ⚡ **Question:** But, when the opponent is your own colleague?

Mohanji: In such situations, what you would do is let there be peace or those kinds of chanting or *mantras*. You can dilute the situation that way. But one thing you must understand – everybody gets what they deserve. Thus there is a certain deserving level playing inside all events. Everybody does not get what they desire, but they do get what they deserve. There is the inevitable deserving factor. You cannot really contradict that. However, with awareness, you can overcome it.

Each person is playing only his or her role. Nothing more or nothing less he or she can do. They come together to get a thing done, and then they disappear, go in separate ways. You cannot do much about that. Yet, you could keep responding with kindness. The most disarming weapon in the whole universe is love. The other person will become helpless eventually and come to terms with himself. 'Life' starts to blossom within him too. Real life is a life totally based on selflessness and unconditional love, not in-sensitiveness, competition, accumulation and greed.

Reaction vs Response

❧ **Question:** If *jnana* (knowledge) creates ego and blocks one's progress, how do we stop it?

Mohanji: First through understanding, then observation. Observe your thought, word, and action. You have two choices to deal with society – one is to react, and the second is to respond.

Reaction is always a consort of emotions. It always originates from emotions. When you are agitated or someone abuses you, you react. *Buddhi* or intellect is out of focus at that time. *Buddhi* becomes blurred and does not exist at the time of the reaction. This is why whenever you get angry, since the intellect is not there to control it, you will regret it later.

When you respond, *buddhi* is working. Emotions are not circulating. The response will have longevity. Reactions have a short life. Reaction also leads to catastrophes of life.

Life gets deeply affected when a person is in a reactionary mode all the time. It creates a lot of guilt and calamities. All this needs to be observed. When you express something, observe. For example, when you get angry you have to express anger, so that the other person understands. Express anger, but do not get emotionally involved with it. A child is sick and is not taking medicine. The mother gets angry and says, "I will not give you sweets if you do not take medicine!" Here, the mother is not angry with the child; she is doing it out of love. At the same time, if you are emotional about it, or you behave in an authoritative way, the mother-child relationship gets strained.

Anger, ego, hatred – everything can be tackled only through observation, clarity, awareness. The mind also can be tackled through observation. The nature of the mind is to be restless. You cannot do anything about it. That is the way you are born. When the nature of mind is restless, allow it to be restless. At the same time, observe and be detached from it. Watch how the mind functions. When you watch how your mind functions for a period of time, it itself will stop functioning. The gap between thoughts becomes longer. The empty space gets extended.

That is the place of peacefulness and silence. That becomes you and your character. Your expressions will change. You will operate with peace in society. That attracts people to you. When we need something, it annihilates peace to a certain extent. When you need nothing, peace happens within, and expressions of peace within happen outside. You will operate with unconditional love. You will love for the sake of love, and not out of any desire. You do not need anything from anybody. Once that happens, you are liberated. All thoughts, words, and actions based on unconditional love are liberation. You will not take more births!

Otherwise, we keep coming back. There is so much pending activity. If you are tired of today's work in the office, you have to come back tomorrow and finish it! Is it not? Nobody else will help you. It is the same here!

The Glorious Dead

A friend of mine died last evening. He was ill, hospitalized, and had been in a helpless condition for a long time. None of his relatives displayed significant compassion. He was a schoolteacher and none of his ex-students provided substantial help.

His own children were not too happy at the 'loss of money' on behalf of their father. Only his wife was at his side till the end. She did her best to keep him comfortable. This being the state, after death, many people came to pay respects. Society called for a meeting to mourn his death. Many wept, looking at the dead body. Many grieved in public. I sat and watched the show with a smile. It all looked like a comedy show to me.

I am always surprised at the emotions people display when people die. I always think, "Where were these overflowing emotions when the now-deceased were alive in their respective bodies?" Most people cannot handle personalities and see only differences between one another. Yet, they display profound emotions when these same people die. An amazing world of pretensions indeed!

One thing must be remembered. Human relationships are grossly conditional. Any close associate or friend can turn around and scandalise you at the drop of a hat, for a paltry reason. Relationships are based on relevance. A sick old man often becomes irrelevant in the gross world of time, money, and profits. Their past contributions to the family and society become irrelevant with time.

Words of gratitude dry up with time, too. Utility value is calculated in detail even by their own children. It is important to shed expectations as we grow older and consider whatever comes our way as Grace and blessing. In the modern age of mad rush for profits, this is the best attitude for survival in peace. Keeping sufficient money for a decent burial at hand's reach is also a good idea. There are no emotions here. Just hardcore acceptance of reality and Truth as it is.

It is also important, as we grow older, to catch God, slowly detaching from terrestrial entanglements. Merge into God consciousness more and more consciously. This will take away the suffering from our pains. This will help us detach from ourselves and our silly emotions, too. This will dilute expectations and increase our level of satisfaction. It is important to be real. It is important to understand and differentiate between the real and the unreal.

A practice, which just occupies the mind temporarily and leaves us back in misery as soon as it is over, is certainly not the right path. Perpetual bliss, objectivity, and equanimity must be achieved. This needs shedding of our old patterns, habits, fears, expectations... so on and so forth. As we grow older, if we move more and more into realms of equanimity, rather than differences, life will become complete. Liberation will happen sooner or later.

We must be aware that we are bound by concepts, especially pertaining to *kundalini*, *chakras*, aura, so on and so forth. In the absolute sense, they all are distractions, the mind's playground. Concepts delay our spiritual evolution. They alienate us from the Truth. Sensations are experienced by the mind. It craves more. It craves repetitive sensations. Repetitive sensations create habits. Habits bind us and lead to stagnation in the spiritual journey. Spontaneity and fluidity are essential for growth in spirituality. This clarity is a minimum requirement for any seeker.

I meant this note just as a statement, an eye-opener, about our own spontaneous pomposity, a mirror to our shallow existence of gross pretensions. If we are able to gather ourselves away from our pretensions, we are redeemed. If not, there is no other choice than repeated births and deaths until total nullification.

Remember – *Shivoham*. We are truly the seed of God. Choose God-hood.

Section 2:

...CREATES THE WORLD OF NOISE...

"Know silence – NO sounds.
NO silence – Just Noises.
Silence has permanence.
Sounds are temporary.

You have to enjoy noises to dive into silence."

CHAPTER 1:

You are not your...

Possessions

*A*nything that provokes pride and ego can be considered your possession. Anything customary or of social necessity could be regarded as *dharma* (duty). I am explaining it in this way, just for clarity's sake. There are only thin lines of difference. A *Guru* will exist in your life, as long as he needs to. Once he leaves, only gratitude for him should remain. All the teachers who came to your classes always empowered you to move on and move further. They needed nothing from you. All you could have meaningfully expressed is sincere gratitude.

We have to examine our emotions, one after the other, to determine the ones we can live without. What are we clinging to? Possessions generate multiple fears. Even if the possessions are qualifications, experience, or just degrees, we fear. Our fears are of various types. An educated person's fear would be more about correct positioning in society than those who are not so educated. He is constantly afraid of losing his status.

Even a job loss creates a big ripple in his inner space because he has imposed that kind of expectation on himself. A rich man fears the loss of his wealth. One who loves another, fears the loss of the other. Thus, fears are aplenty. Liberation from all these fears through higher awareness and understanding of the impermanence of our situations will liberate the mind and man. Those who are thus liberated, dare to walk alone. They become self-sufficient.

Remember – one who does not possess anything owns or commands 'everything'. Possession is a limitation. Society is possession-oriented. The more we amass, the more we are feared or respected in society. Most of us live our whole lives in fear of society, and do everything to maintain our image. Some choose to be different and are not afraid to walk alone. They evolve higher. Possessions granted by *prarabhda karma* should be handled with sincere gratitude and not pride and ego. Attachment and greed bind people to people, materials and Earth. Higher awareness and understanding of our true nature liberate people from it. Use all possessions with utmost gratitude. That makes this life useful and, in that context, successful.

Mind

Small innocent things that attract the mind could become a trap in the path of liberation. Small things may also include music, food etc. This attraction of the mind and senses could be very detrimental in the path of liberation. It is not easy to avoid all these traps, but what helps is being aware of the trap. You should enjoy everything but enjoy with detachment. This means whether that particular material is available or not, life goes on.

The mind should be fully present with every thought, word and action. This is very important to avoid repetition. For e.g., while eating ice cream, your whole concentration should be on the ice cream. You must be fully present. Each bite should be completely enjoyed. Then, a second ice cream could be avoided. Temptations could be avoided. If you are fully present in the activity, the second time around the mind may say, "Umm, not again!"

An activity with emotion becomes memory. When the emotion is missing, an activity does not stay in your subconscious as deeply as it would with emotion – which glues it there. If you are doing an activity unconsciously, the mind will say, "Yeah, no problem, do it again!" This is because our wandering mind prefers a repetitive action rather than a conscious action.

Anything in moderation is fine. Any food that binds us and makes us dependent on it is anti-liberation. Coffee pumps up our system and is unnatural. In that sense, coffee gives a temporary sense of rejuvenation. Tea is more subtle. Herbal tea is even better. In short, any addiction is bad. If you can stay liberated from all of it while using it without attachment, everything is fine. All kinds of dependency are anti-liberation.

Gains and Losses

Do not worry about gains. Gains and losses are part of your conscious mind's conditioning. Life is beyond gains and losses. Life is only about a stream of experiences from birth till death. Concentrate on feelings. What expands your heart? What makes you and others happy? Do that. I do not mean that you should do things that you do not want to do or compromise beyond limits for others' sake. Subtlety is caring. Be caring. Be love, without expectations. Express love sincerely. That is better than any words. Feeling is better than words. It makes a difference in lives.

Expectations

Question: Can liberation be a reality?

Mohanji: Indeed, but that depends on the seeker's attitude. You get what you deserve. The *Guru* appears at the right moment when the disciple is ripe and ready for him. You detach from a true *Guru* when expectations creep in. True *Gurus* consistently destroy the tendency towards expectation in their disciples. Unripe disciples fall. They get disillusioned and walk away to more predictable Masters. True *Gurus* are unpredictable. They do not conform to the regular, expected norms of society.

Expectation is the biggest treason. All are prone to its lure. Expectations alienate minds. They build boundaries, create traffic jams and roadblocks. Expectations create calamities. They shrink the heart *chakras* and the ability to express your true nature, which is to love without expectations. Expectations make love conditional. Expectations take away the real flavour of life. Expectations even destroy, at times.

Thus, liberation depends on the seeker's attitude and ability to move from moment to moment without expectations, like a gliding fluid, completely present in the present moment, operating through the vehicle of unconditional love, selflessly and with commitment to the Truth, until they realise that there is no distance between the seeker and the sought. The seeker then merges with the sought.

Lust

☙ **Question:** Can sex deter from the path of liberation?

Mohanji: No. The need to have sex is a deep-rooted *samskara* (impression). Avoiding it is escapism. Overindulgence is attachment. Attachment is bondage. Equanimity in sex will never deter liberation. Even *amrit* (celestial nectar) in excess can work as a poison for the one who consumes it. Escapism only postpones an inevitable action to a later date. It never eradicates the seed of that action. Whatever the action, it is more appropriate to go through the action, if you have to, rather than keeping it suppressed. Every thought, word, and action has the potential to create your destiny. Hence, everything that you experience today has been voluntarily created by yourself at some point in your multiple existences.

There is no point in comparing, complaining or postponing. Acceptance and ownership, in that respect, will reduce your agony. Postponement will only harbour heaviness due to non-action. This is not only about sex, but everything related to life. A society-bound man often lives in pretension, fearing a tarnished reputation. This only brings him back, again and again, to this terrestrial existence. At least one day of unpretentious living is much more important than a lifetime of pretentious existence.

Attachments

What are we doing here? Have we ever thought about it in-depth? What is our purpose? What is our mission? Why are we here? Where else can we be? Every man harbours these questions. These questions haunt us more, if our path is that of liberation.

Liberation! That is so beautiful. Liberation is not escapism. Escapism is running away from *dharma* (duty). Liberation is natural detachment, without any effort, while performing *dharma* with detachment – like the sun or a flowing river. No object on Earth can make us happy or sad. Liberation makes us perpetually self-sufficient.

The nature of our soul is liberation. It takes the subtle body through many births and deaths, but never gets contaminated. It is as pure as ever. Let us look at ourselves closely. We have never considered the soul. Every thought brings an attachment. Every word invokes an attachment. Every action is with an attachment too. Every meeting is with expectation. Every decision has an expectation. A result is expected. Results are bound to happen. That's the nature of action. Attachment to results causes bondage. Expectations cause bondage. We suffer. The moment we shift from these expectations to pure action, we become liberated.

Bondage is of various types. All attachments are bondage. All expectations are bondage. All relationships are bondage. The *Guru* can be bondage. Disciples can be bondage. Body, mind, and intellect are bondage. Knowledge is bondage. All habits are bondage. Dependency of all kinds is bondage. All *samskaras* are bondage. Thus, life is full of seen and unseen bondages. This makes liberation even more difficult.

The best way to transcend bondage is through higher awareness. It is like growing up through many classes, just as we experienced in our school days. The awareness level keeps changing and we realise at each stage that we were not aware of many things earlier. Clarity improves and dependency reduces or at least shifts, as from a toy to a bicycle, a bicycle to a motorcycle and so on. Habits change. When a habit is replaced with the deep, pregnant silence of spirituality, we are liberated. The need for action is formed out of *samskaras*. When *samskaras* reduce, actions reduce too. But usually, we fill the space with more *samskaras*. We are afraid to die. The birth-death cycle has become our habit because of repetition over lifetimes.

Anything can bind us and keep us away from liberation. Our identifications make death painful. Identifications such as name, shape, nationality, religion and everything else. Even a mirror can prevent a smooth exit. A mirror re-establishes our physical image in our psyche so much so that, when the soul departs from the body, it feels lost. It stays on. It refuses to transcend. So, if you look deeply, you can see that many things hinder our progress. In that situation, if you are still able to translate knowledge into wisdom and experience wisdom, that nullifies the push of your *samskaras*. Then life becomes easier and transit becomes effortless.

Nothing is either good or bad. There are no dos and don'ts. These are all created by our mind. What is right for us is the exhaustion of our *karmas*, whatever it takes. What is right for the soul is to stay as the soul – without the baggage of *karmas* and the push for many re-births. Right and wrong are relative and it also shifts modes time after time. Nothing is permanent in terrestrial existence. If we can fully understand this fundamental Truth and live it to the brim, we are relatively better off.

Staying in the path of liberation is not easy. Every person sends messages. Every message comes with an attachment. Every attachment is like a virus. It makes your system dull and sometimes even sick. When we are constantly in the web of life, we stay trapped and bound. Liberation needs serious practice. We cannot suppress *karmas* and attain liberation. We have to exhaust *karmas* and get there. We have to grow with awareness and detach because we do not need it. It is far different from the state where we reject it because we cannot reach it.

When the world was speaking about 'haves' and 'have nots', India always had a third segment: the true liberated Masters who had everything but wanted nothing. They lived in plenty with no need for any terrestrial objects. Terrestrial love, like relationships, is temporary and often conditional. The soul is liberated and unconditional. That is the shift that we are talking about here. The shift from our limited mind to the unlimited soul. That guarantees liberation.

Success or Failure

ᴡ **Question:** How can I bounce back from failure without harming myself?

Mohanji: Remember that ego brings you to an artificial world. For e.g., you fought hard, you did so many things, and it all was successful. You became successful. Thus you naturally developed an ego. Yes, you are reasonably successful; you are a successful person, you have made money, you have riches. These were all events or situations that rapidly enhanced your ego. Ego then led to expectations. It led to firm conditioning. You started telling yourself that you have to be continuously successful, that you cannot be anything but continuously successful, and that you cannot afford even one drop of failure.

Failure refers here to the social state, according to social criteria. You cannot afford failure; you do not allow it. If that should happen, then your self-esteem goes down. You will start calling yourself a loser. A small loss can mean a lot in that situation. It sometimes even leads to suicide. This is the fall. When your self-esteem goes down, fears and anxieties creep in. Again, you fall back and then you have to climb up. You may need assistance to climb up too. This pulls you down. Sometimes people really fall hard, and sometimes they fall out of the game of life too. Success and failure should be handled with equanimity. Both are part of the same existence.

Do you see how the chronology of existence works? Success leads to ego, ego leads to expectations, and expectations narrow the 'walking space' of your path. This means, first of all, the 'failure' side is not acceptable, so you only have the 'success' possibility. Life, however, is not like that. Life has both sides. You cut off all the failure sides, and walk the narrow path of success. If you happen to switch to failure, you have not found permission for that, and you fall out. Sometimes you pull yourself down completely with that. Sometimes, you will even pull your relatives down with this.

Hence, please accept failure gracefully and be grateful that it leads you to a new awareness. Tell yourself that this is fine and that this is part of our very existence. No problem. That way, you can move on. Otherwise, your self-esteem will fall so much, and you get very hurt inside. That situation is totally unnecessary. You can counter your failures with the awareness that 'this too shall pass'.

Realise that success and failure are determined by ourselves! Society has nothing to do with it. We judge, criticise and censor ourselves much more than what society does. We do not accept failure at all. We think, "What will they say? What will the 'four people' say?" (four people being society, of course) We are worried about the 'four people'! We then try to modify ourselves to fit inside such limitations; we become bound by the 'four people'. Oh! What will society think if I am like this? I cut my hair because they will think I'm crazy if I have long hair.

In this way, we are bound and controlled by society. This is our fundamental cage. We created this cage with our fears of what others think! Do we have the guts to live our life? Do we have the guts to be ourselves? If yes, that is the fundamental shift that will lead you to subsequent liberation. Indeed, we create several cages, or walls, around us.

One is the 'four people' (fear related to social standing), another is our own expectations about ourselves and others. The third is our non-acceptance of our own reality as it is: we want to accept our reality as we'd like it to be, which is not possible, as primarily we have to accept ourselves as we are and before that, we should know who and what we are and why we came here. The fourth wall is resistance to changes. These essentially make up the walls of our cage.

Then, of course, there are others, such as desires, education, all the conditionings, etc. They are also part of our cage. Everything adds to that 'reality', and finally we end up with no walking space. Sometimes, we pretend we know. This is silly. We do not know and it is better if we accept that. The easiest way is to pretend. Most of us are living a pretentious life. We fake happiness, we fake love and we fake everything. Finally, we forget the difference between reality and make-believe, because we are so used to faking! Look at your own daily life. You will know what I mean. Do not kill me for telling the truth...

We become a victim of the cages that we ourselves created, with the help of our society that believes in cages, so that everyone becomes predictable. We love predictions and predictability. We are used to killing those who were unpredictable, e.g.: Jesus, Socrates. Our society is rule-oriented. Rules that ensure predictability, which in turn restricts our walking space. This is not a joke. Look around. Our society is not creating men. We are only creating bricks that are identical!

Addictions

᭼ **Question:** The problem of addiction seems out of control everywhere in the world. How can we tackle it?

Mohanji: Addictions start with a thought. For e.g., before you start drinking, you think you would like to have a beer. Before the thought comes up there is an inclination, which provokes the thought. Thought is born out of that inclination. Look, I never think I should have a drink because I don't have the inclination to drink alcohol. What comes before the inclination? Karma!

The root, which you carried forward from another life, because you wanted to experience alcohol. The seed for drinking alcohol is already in your causal layer. When the environment is right, this seed will sprout. This seed is the *vasana* (tendency) and when there is the *vasana*, then you get the thought. You might suppress the thought, but that does not mean it has disappeared. In specific situations, the thought becomes a word and you might say, "I want a beer." Then, someone gets you a beer and it becomes an action.

Unfortunately for society, people are unique, even if they look alike. That is why you sometimes see people behaving in a strange way. They may consume alcohol, drugs or seek strange sexual experiences. They think that this will help liberate them. This is actually escapism. They are feeling so suffocated here, in their current reality. They want to do something else. That is why, unconsciously, people are doing it and you can't blame them for it. You have to blame the cages they have made for themselves. Otherwise, if you are going to have a drink because you love to have that drink – that's a different thing. But is that the way people are resorting to alcohol these days?

For many, an innocent habit has become an addiction. They are helpless victims of addictions. Addictions created by ennui and boredom. Addictions created by vacuum. So, are people happy? Mostly not. They are drinking because they want to escape from something else. But it does not happen. Reality always re-surfaces, in an uglier way than before. People waste a lot of money on dancing girls and such things. What is the benefit? It is a momentary pleasure. You give money to the dancing girl, she smiles at you and you feel very good. What is the big deal? Some kind of ego satisfaction! What are they trying to do here?

We are jumping from one cage to another. One habit to another, trying to fill the emptiness within us. The new habit fascinates us for some time, just like some people marry many times. The new wife fascinates them for some time and then they become bored. The quest continues. They never reach anywhere, let alone liberation. Simple logic. How can you be liberated if you are too bound by hundreds of materials that you continue to fancy? When we try to skip from one habit to another, temporarily we feel fine. This is especially so, when we start on hyperventilation (*pranayama*) or *yoga*. Then, it becomes a habit. It is like buying a new car from the showroom. For a few days, it will be thrilling to drive it. Then it becomes monotonous.

Too much dependency on external objects for our internal fulfilment! Food, films, wine, women... Life has got to be more liberating. Right? We are just trying to fill the vacuum due to the absence of a sense object with another. We are afraid of the vacuum within. When we start falling in love with the vacuum, emptiness becomes a deep, pregnant silence; the silence of the Divine, which leads to detachment and eventual bliss within; and most importantly, we will not be pressured for pleasure anymore. We will not be afraid to be alone. Being alone will be in being-ness: being-ness in bliss. The pressure for doing-ness will change. Doing-ness will become purpose bound: action for the sake of necessity, not for the quest of external pleasure.

Escaping from their routines, their own cages, people are trying to do something else, and they do not understand that this other thing is merely another trap. All they are doing is jumping from one trap to the other. They are just flying from trap to trap. Liberation is very difficult. Liberation is conscious awareness. There is no conscious awareness here. There are only traps, traps and more traps. You jump from this trap to another, from this habit to another. Even if it is a spiritual habit, it is still a trap. For e.g., "I cannot live without my meditation." This is a trap. You should be perpetually fine. This is the liberation that we are talking about. Whether you meditate today or not, you feel good. Whether you do yoga today or not, this is fine. Can you be in that mood? That is where you attain your liberation.

Escapism

✤ **Question:** I don't feel like doing anything except searching for wisdom. I want to move or run away from society, away from my professional work and relations. Any remedy, or should I face the consequences?

Mohanji: This is called escapism. Sheer escapism. You cannot run away from anything. It is your mind that is saying so. What faculty in you is pushing you like this? Your mind. When the mind says, "I don't like this, I need to go elsewhere," what is the guarantee that you will be fine there? The same mind will start provoking questions, and thoughts, and problems in any place you go. Now you don't like this because it is routine, it is creating boredom, fine. But even if you go elsewhere, the same thing will start again. Don't think that spirituality can be enhanced through running away from realities. Instead, being in reality, being one with reality and operating in reality will enhance your spirituality. It does not matter whether you are sitting in the *Himalayas* or in busy places in Mumbai. You can still be spiritual. It is actually the thing inside. You can be completely spiritual.

I'll give you a small example. One person decided to leave everything and join an *ashram*, a *Guru*. He went there and he saw that most people were sitting down and meditating, so he also started meditating. Then every second day, they had to clean everything. The *Guru* came and said, "Now, this group cleans the garden, this group cleans the temples, this group cleans the dormitories." A few groups were formed and they went around cleaning. Then this man said, "I did not come here to clean! I can do that at home!" Then the *Guru* said, "No, this is the *seva* we do for this *ashram*." With a lot of difficulty, he cleaned, but most of the time, he was cheating on it. He was just pretending to be cleaning and he was not doing it.

Then the *Guru* said, "Today we are fasting." This man became very upset. He said, "No, no, no, I don't need to fast. I'm not interested in fasting. I only like to meditate, that is why I joined this *ashram*." Then the *Guru* said, "This day we need to detox. Fasting is just to detox. It is not for anything else." At 10 o'clock in the morning, he started having headaches and fell unconscious. The *Guru* allowed him to have some food and he was fine. In a week, by doing all this, he came to the *Guru* and said, "Guruji, I thought that *ashram* life is much easier. There is a lot of peace here; we sit and meditate; we have food at the right time; we get up at the right time."

The *Guru* replied, "This is all fine, but what about your duty, your *dharma*, your *seva*? That should also happen simultaneously. The *ashram* is not for escapists. The *ashram* is really for those who want to evolve spiritually, and be focused. There is a single-point focus on one activity or one purpose. That purpose will take you further. That is why this *ashram* life is prescribed for some people. *Ashram* life cannot be for you." He went back because he could not stay in the *ashram*. He did not want to indulge in any of these *seva* activities like cleaning, cooking and so on. He just wanted to eat, sleep, read some books, and meditate. But that is escapism.

No true *ashrams* allow you to be an escapist. No true *ashrams* will give you room for escapism. It is a wrong understanding, "Oh, I don't like this, is there an escape?" Where is the escape? You cannot escape from life! Then what are we talking about? What are you escaping from? Wherever you go, whichever place you are in, you have to do what you have to do. We are not escaping from food, are we? We don't escape from going to the toilet. We mostly escape from taking a bath, but this is also essential because we are in society. All these things are part of us, so what are we talking about? Where are we going?

"I want to leave this job". Then what? You must create sufficient sustenance even if you leave the job. Who will give you sustenance? You have to create your sustenance, right? Everybody is expected to work. Don't think that *Gurus* don't do any job. *Gurus* work. They empower people, and they usually work more than normal people. They create various ways where people can understand some tough material in simple terms. They create a lot of baby food. This is work! Many *Gurus* are deeply involved in *seva*. This is work. It is not that they are sitting idle and sitting quiet.

If they are getting funds, those funds are also used to serve people. Even if you give me ten meals, I can only eat one meal at a time. The more money you have, the more visibility you have. Do not think that you can consume more. Greed can happen in every path, but it does not take you anywhere. It is complete ignorance. Greed is equal to ignorance. So, that is not a solution. Thus, leaving one place thinking that another is better is also ignorance. It is a wrong understanding. It cannot take you anywhere. This is the answer.

Pseudo Spirituality

❦ **Question:** Why are many still groping in darkness as far as spirituality is concerned?

Mohanji: Good question. This is because people are going after 'feel good' stuff, cults and organised patterns. While each one of us are unique creations, every capsule cannot suit everyone. Comfort zone spirituality cannot ensure any growth. Stillness is the nature of the supreme God. If the aim is to achieve that, shedding is important. Everything should dissolve and there can be no duality. Only oneness with God. Until we achieve that, we need to practise witness-hood, objectivity, and stillness. Many people who are on the path are just entertaining themselves with activities, believing that more activity will get them more results. This is perfect non-understanding. Being-ness evolves the man, not doing-ness.

Pretensions

🌺 **Question:** Sometimes we just listen, and neglect what we have heard.

Mohanji: Not only that, but most people live based on pretensions. We pretend to be what we are not, or we pretend to be what society needs us to be. This is why we are not progressing spiritually. The moment you accept your weaknesses, the moment you accept exactly who you are, without adding pepper and salt, then you will start progressing. But we don't allow that. We pretend to be what we are not over a period of time, maybe till the end of our life as well.

Sometimes we even enter into certain 'cults', or we happen to be in some spiritual sects – we make ourselves believe that we are on the right track and then we adjust to it. It is almost similar to the boiling frog syndrome – you adjust so much to the rising temperature that you cannot get out of it. We adjust and we move on with the same process until we are not able to get out. A lot of insecurity is created, such as, "If we get out, what will happen?" The comfort related to the sect, or comfort related to the situation, bogs us down, and in a way, destabilises or immobilises us. The energy to get out of the situation never happens.

This is not spirituality. This is anti-spirituality. Actually, if you want to be spiritual, you have to be kind of fluid. Keep flowing. It is a journey in which you get a lot of road signs. The choice of looking at the road sign is yours. If you know the way, you can go further. *Gurus* are only road signs, just directing you to your Self. *Gurus* have no further role. Of course, the Grace element will be there provided there is an attitude of surrender and deep faith. Divinity then takes over. Otherwise, when we are progressing on the path of spirituality, we just go through the path, follow the road signs correctly and then there will be no problem eighty per cent of the time.

But what happens is that somebody else, who is also a seeker, guides us saying – "Oh, I had a wonderful experience – why don't you come along ?" This could be that person's experience and have nothing to do with you. We still go for it, or make ourselves believe that it is the right path, and get stuck there. In this way, we get stuck at various points. Our journey is delayed. Eventually, you will reach the destination. However, it may be a lengthy journey, over many lives!

To measure how far you have progressed in this life, revert to how much you have travelled in your past life. We have done some spiritual activities in our past life. We can't prove this scientifically, though now we can prove it to some extent through regression therapy, etc. We do not remember the activities because we are operating from a new intelligence, and not from the old subconscious when we did the activities. This data has been carried in the form of 'impressions' to this life.

But the faculty we are using is the new fresh body, fresh mind and fresh intellect. This fresh material, which is the conscious mind, body, and intellect, cannot understand a thing that happened in past life, as it did not exist in that life. It is a new tool. A bulb does not know where the electricity originated from. That is why we always have to shut off the conscious mind to revert back to the original self. That is why we practise meditation.

Everything is important, everything is good. The most important thing is this – Where do we want to stand? And where do we want to go?

Doubts

The conscious mind creates doubts. It also creates fear of the unknown. It is the inherent characteristic of the conscious mind to create doubts and subsequent insecurity. Doubts are based on the level of consciousness. On a sunny morning, when basking in the warm rays of the sun, the conscious mind is sure that it is morning and there is sunshine. However, a person who sleeps under a blanket with curtains blocking the rays from entering the room, can never be sure of the situation outside their window. Their mind speculates. So, the available data and the level of consciousness create doubt.

Doubts block progress. Doubt about anything is a hindrance. Those who dare have always found some result. Sometimes it is just a mediocre experience. Sometimes it is blinding truths. It is certainly good to be brave. The roots of doubts rest in inertia, or *tamas*. The more *tamasic* a person is, the more doubts he will have.

Reasonable risks always help progress and self-esteem. Foolish risks often ruin a man. Reasonable risks stem from the intellect. Foolish risks are the offspring of emotions. Whatever is born out of intellect has longevity, while every action born out of emotion usually carries the seeds of catastrophes.

All doubts will vanish with higher awareness. When you have doubts about the weather outside, just open the curtains and look outside. Likewise, whenever doubts arise, do the action and do not resort to speculation. The best way to beat doubts and even inertia is by resorting to action.

Gunas (Flavours)

🌿 **Question:** What is inertia?

Mohanji: *Tamas* or inertia is part of us. That part of us that gently guides us or suggests that we go to sleep, plus our innate lethargy, postponement and escapism, anger and defensiveness, are all aspects of *tamas*. Everything that handicaps us is *tamas*. Everything that binds us is *tamas*. Postponement and lazy inaction is *tamas*. Purposelessness is *tamas*. Intellectual churning, constant analysis which leads to subsequent inaction, is *tamas*. *Tamas* is our inherent enemy, one that stays with us, within us always, and only manifests during our waking hours.

It induces procrastination and brings forth a series of failures; life can even get totally wasted due to its influence. Craving for *tamasic* food such as old food, the flesh of living beings (meat), alcohol, etc., are all signs of inherent *tamas*. Some proudly boast that they hate vegetarian food! They have no idea how much they are exposing their own weak constitution in this way. *Tamas* is our constant companion and mostly responsible for all our seeming failures in life. Beware of *tamas*. Be aware of *tamas*.

❧ Question: What or who is the enemy of *tamas*?

Mohanji: *Rajas*. Action. The best medicine to counter *tamas* is compulsive action. Action for the sake of it. Work hard. Only entertain adequate sleep. Organise yourself. Do not postpone things. Believe, decide that there will be no tomorrow, and today is the only space in time that you have for yourself to fulfil and complete all that you have to do. Do everything today. Do not look or strive for too much satisfaction and absolute perfection. There should be adequate perfection, and more than that, there should be adequate attention, consistency and application. If *rajas* is expressed on the platform of selflessness, spiritual glory is accessible to you.

❧ Question: What is the role of *sattva*?

Mohanji: *Sattva* is the ideal state of equanimity. Absolute objectivity is its sign. Unconditional Love, selflessness and compassion are its spontaneous expressions. It is difficult to stay in that plane. Just like a day has only three hours of *sattvic* time, from 3 a.m. to 6 a.m. approximately, in order to exist in that level of consciousness is a tall order for the average man: one who lives in the routine world that we see around us. The average man is predominantly *tamasic*, then *rajasic* and seldom *sattvic*.

Even one who visits temples, churches or mosques, and one who is always immersed in chanting and worship may not be in the realms of *sattva*. You need keen observation to understand its subtlety. When *rajasic* mode shifts to selflessness, man touches the realms of *sattva*. Still, he could fall back into *rajas* or inertia at any time. We can see even Saints wasting their lives in relative luxury and pomposity, falling prey to *tamas*. *Tamas* is indulgence, compulsive indulgence and its associated slavery.

❧ **Question:** What creates anger?

Mohanji: Unfulfilled expectations. *Tamas*.

❧ **Question:** What creates hatred and jealousy?

Mohanji: Ignorance. *Tamas*. The common factor in all negative emotions is *tamas* or inertia.

The Frog Syndrome

The frog is an amphibian. A cold-blooded creature. It can respond to temperature much better than us. If you put a frog into already boiling water, it will jump out of it immediately. It will not be affected by the temperature. At the same time, if you put a frog in water of normal temperature, it will stay floating in it. If you start heating the vessel from below, as the temperature of the water changes, the frog will keep adjusting. Finally, by the time the water starts to boil, the frog will have lost its capacity to jump out. It will die in the boiling water.

Many people display this kind of syndrome. They 'hang on' in one company or place of work, and sometimes in the same position for a long time. When a catastrophe like the company closing down or merging with another happens, they will display total inability to change or move out. They have been adjusting so much for so long, that their whole initiative for change will have evaporated completely. This is *tamas* – inertia. Beware of *tamas*.

Procrastination

🌺 **Question:** Someone wants more clarity on procrastination. He is asking if designed postponement is procrastination. For e.g., "I know I have to do this job, and I will do it in the evening because I have some work now..." Is this procrastination?

Mohanji: This is not procrastination. Postponement with a purpose cannot be called procrastination. Procrastination is *tamas*. Expression of *tamas* is procrastination. *Tamas* is inertia or laziness. It is also escapism. *Tamas* induces these qualities of inertia, laziness, escapism – for nothing! The person just does not want to do it. Postponement, not because he has some other work, but because he does not want to do the work. That is procrastination.

🌺 **Question:** How do we overcome procrastination?

Mohanji: There are three *gunas* – *Rajas*, *Sattwa* and *Tamas*. *Tamas* is the densest of all. In order to get out of *tamas*, one must enter *rajas*. You cannot move to *sattva*. *Rajas* is action. *Tamas* must be diluted, or conquered with action. Deliberate actions are a must to beat *tamas*. I would say, just go jogging, do aerobics, play tennis – whatever. Just get into good physical exercise or physical action. That beats inertia. When you have extreme action, you shed *tamas,* and that leads you to *sattva* automatically.

Sattwa means a very subtle state in which awareness will be very high. In *sattva,* action will be for the sake of action, and not for the result of the same. Actions will not be out of expectation. You will perform an action objectively. You will perform actions without any conditions. Operating in the *sattva* plane will always give you tremendous equilibrium. It will give peace of mind because you are not expecting anything. I am not talking about expecting results in the evening. In the office, we have plans, generate revenues and achieve targets.

What I mean is in our attitude, that we will only do a task if we get something in return. This is a *rajasic* transaction! Transaction in *sattva* will be completely from the heart and with equanimity. Please do not misunderstand. I am not talking about the emotional heart. I am talking about the higher spiritual heart! These transactions will be completely purpose-bound, like those of Jesus or Krishna. Their every moment was purpose-bound. However, to slip from *sattva* is very easy. Expectations bring you back to *rajas.* Lack of objectivity slips you back into the *rajasic* mode.

Avatars always knew, with absolute clarity, exactly what to do and why something was happening. As you move higher, you have more vision and much better clarity. *Tamas* is the lowest state, and is a zone where you are sufficiently lazy to be inclined not to do anything. To beat that, you have to go into *Rajas* mode. Get into action to beat inertia. Take my word for it. It will help you tremendously. *Tamas,* like a weed, will pull people into depression. This is happening more and more in our society. Inertia is dangerous. Without your knowledge, it will suck you in. A week later, you will realise that you have been lazy all week long. So many things pass you by during times of inertia.

Expectations

The great Hindu epic, the Mahabharata, is about the war between cousins, the sons of two brothers. They fight a war for the kingdom. The war is orchestrated by an *Avatar*, Krishna. During that period, war was based on Truth. So, they would not fight after sunset. It was like a 9 a.m. to 5 p.m. job! As the war was finishing, Krishna and the most senior member of the opponent group, met to see the battlefield. They were checking what happened, how many people had died that day. Suddenly, a beggar came by. He said to the man who was with Krishna, "I'm hungry, can you give me some money?" The man, however, did not have his wallet, so he said, "Come back tomorrow, I'll give it to you." The beggar went away because he got nothing.

Krishna started laughing, and he laughed and laughed. The man was surprised, "I did not crack a joke, so why are you laughing?" "No, no, I'm laughing because you are so sure that you will be alive tomorrow to give money to the beggar, and I'm not." Krishna was an *Avatar*, and He said, "I do not know my future". The other person, who was ignorant, was quite sure about his future. This is human existence. We postpone things thinking we have a very long future and sleep on it. What Krishna says is, "If you can do something now, do it. Do not promise for something in the future. If you cannot deliver, you will have to come back again to deliver."

Life is as simple as that. We make it complicated because of our expectations. We keep increasing our shopping list, so we are not able to fulfil it. God has nothing to do with it. God blesses you all the time. I always tell people, "I fail to understand why you complicate your life. Eighty per cent of the complications are related to expectation." One small example: we are born thanks to two people, our parents. They brought us up until we were able to be on our own, and make our own living. But at the age of forty, if one says, "Where are my parents? They are not helping me", it does not make sense. So as life goes, relationships also change.

Parents remain the same, of course, we don't change them. However, the intensity, the connectivity, and relevance also differ. After some time, you may even look after your parents. While you were a child, they looked after you. This is how life goes. Life goes from today, to tomorrow, to the day after tomorrow, but take your mind with you when you go. The body is definitely going, because we are getting old. Take the mind with you. For e.g., if you leave your clothes in different houses you have to collect them again, right? So better to take clothes when you go.

Then when you do not have the choice of stopping time and staying young, take the mind with you. The mind goes from event to event. Body goes from time to time. If these go together, you are a peaceful person. Your presence will make others peaceful as well. They will want to meet you and discuss something with you, at the least lay their burden on you. If the mind can travel along with the body, then you are in control of your mind. You will never feel like a victim, "Oh, I'm suffering because of this or that person."

Sometimes we think we have certain blockages. What we think is the most important one may not be the most important. What is removed (through Grace and certain practices) is the most important one which prevents your progress. Then miracles happen. Miracles do happen, if we allow them to. Once Jesus said, "I refuse to show miracles," because people were getting stuck on the miracles, not him or his consciousness. Jesus had his whole consciousness to offer, and people were coming to see the magic. What can we do? So, what did he say? "Connect to Me and you will reach the highest, the Father."

Yet how many people went to Him to reach the Father? Nobody went to him to reach the Father. They went to him asking, "Can you remove my cough?" or some equally mundane thing.

People pray to me, "Please, can you get me parking, so that I can come for your meditation?" Our requirements are sometimes very low. Because I did not have onions, I couldn't cook a particular dish. However, though there are many other vegetables available to cook a dish, because our mind was focused on the onion, which was unavailable, we forgot to eat, or we could not eat.

So what is worth investing in, in this life? One thing worth investing in is awareness. Awareness is the larger vision of life. Seeing, not from these eyes, but from the third eye. When you start seeing from the third eye, the past, present and future stay at one point. Then we are deathless. Because in the absolute sense, just like a film, we have been projected to the world, to Earth. Just like a film has a three-hour duration, we have about eighty years of duration. In between, we see many situations, many people, many events, and we act in it all. Then the film ends. Another film comes along. It is never-ending.

So, continue acting. If you do not want to act anymore, stop desiring. Do not enter into the next contract. If you do not want to enter into another contract, it would be better not to have too many relationships, which means friends, or enemies. It would be better to be kind rather than venomous. So people will say, "Okay, bless you." It helps. The vibrations help. The more you are kind and able to express it, the more liberated you become.

It is not about spending money for poor people. It can simply be if somebody is not feeling good; just support them. This is good. Kindness. Charity is not only about spending money. It is being kind in every situation. Everybody responds to love. Not only human beings, but all the animals, birds, plants, every being responds to love. When you express love consistently, you operate in a very liberated plane. Your image will be reflected in everybody's eyes. You and the universe become one. That is how you become deathless, because you merge with the universe.

Guilt

✤ **Question:** Is it wrong to think only of my own spiritual journey?

Mohanji: All of you have come to this mega-mall called the 'world' with your own shopping list. This is fine. There cannot be any other way. So please go ahead and exhaust the shopping list before the money (your breath) completely leaves your wallet (your body). This journey or shopping list is your own. Even your close relatives have nothing to do with it, because they have their own shopping list.

There are common things to buy, such as household items – tables, chairs, refrigerator, fruits and vegetables etc. Your shopping list will agree with that of your relatives as long as this match exists. There are individual items as well, like your toothbrush. You will not want to share it with anyone. Hence, allow time, space and privacy for everyone.

Do not judge the purchases of others. There is nothing right and nothing wrong, in the absolute sense. You are carving your own destiny. Kill guilt. Kill anger, anxiety, jealousy, revenge, enmity, distrust, hatred, comparison and desires. They will all make you spend your money faster. They all make you spend emotionally. When you are spent and sick, you will suffer a painful death. Have nothing to do with it. Just love and serve. In this way, when you die, you will die in peace.

Guilt is very powerful. It glues us to Earth. Have nothing to do with it. Do what is right, according to your conscience. It may not be right for others. Never harm anyone through thoughts, words, or action. Otherwise, your right is your own right. It will suit you. Trash guilt, whatever it may cost. Be relaxed. One thing is guaranteed – you have brought sufficient breaths to complete the original shopping list of this life. Do not add more. You do not have sufficient funds for that. You did not bring them. Time borrowed is pains borrowed. You have to repay it with interest. Be aware of that.

Age

You look at the mirror many times in a day and re-establish your own image of yourself! If the image remains intact, and you like what is in the mirror, good enough! But if there is a change, such as old age, then what happens? It is the annihilation of some image. When that annihilation happens some people just go haywire. They cannot accept old age gracefully. This is human nature. Whatever we are getting over-attached to is not good. Of course, as a person, you need to be presentable, I can understand that. But how dependent are you on your own image? This is one aspect of how attached you are to your own life.

The changes happening may not be graceful. They may be forced changes. "I cannot help it. I cannot get it. I am getting old." Then, we start getting frustrated about all the age-related problems.

This is because we are not deciding the changes. Society decides and we obey. Society decides that a twenty-year-old must have a boyfriend or a girlfriend or should get married, and we inherit that. It is our responsibility to practise it! At no point do we think – "why can I not be different?"

Anxiety

🌿 **Question:** How to get rid of an anxious state?

Mohanji: I already explained that. Connect to your spine, feel your spine, stay away from your mind, start watching your mind, detach from your mind, and slowly, slowly, slowly the mind will become still. It is like, if you do not energise one hand for one year, you won't be able to use that hand because the muscles become weak. So if you do not energise your mind, especially your fears, your anxieties, your insecurities, they will start dropping off. They will not be there. Detaching from the mind is very important. When I say the mind, it also contains ego and it also contains intellect. The discriminating factor, the emotional factor, the ego factor.

Fears

❧ **Question:** How does fear happen? Fear of money, fear of society?

Mohanji: Just watch: when does fear happen? What time does fear happen? How does it happen? Fear happens when you are awake, at certain times, and only when you are awake. There are no fears when you are in the dream state or in deep sleep. Of course, there could be some fearsome dreams, however they vanish when you wake up. Some do linger on, nurtured by the conscious mind. There are no fears at all during the deep sleep state. Thus, all fears are temporary. They have a nature of passing through. Understand that fears are also the opposite of love. When love is predominant, no fear happens.

It is just like darkness and light – when light is predominant, there is no darkness. Darkness means absence of light. Fear means absence of love. Love is the antidote for fear. Hence, if you increase love, fear disappears. If you bring light, darkness disappears. Every fear has a weak root. It is temporary and fleeting in nature. Ignorance leads to fear. Non-understanding of something leads to fear. For e.g., if there is sufficient light, you have no fear about the room since everything is visible in the right light. Then you switch off all the lights and there is darkness, lack of visibility and fear happens.

Uncertainty and non-understanding lead to fear. Non-understanding leads to insecurity, as well as fear. Fear is an off-spring of non-understanding. So, if you understand something very clearly, there is no fear, misunderstanding or related insecurity. However, if you do not understand something, all the fears come and anxieties happen. If you just look at the events of your own life, nothing stays, right? Everything is passing with time. Everything is temporary. A very healthy man becomes very sick! A sick man recovers dramatically! Rich people become poor and poor people become rich overnight! There is nothing permanent.

However, we expect things to be permanent and we try to bind time with events. Time has value only as a milestone, which you see while travelling from one place to the other. Time is travelling. Each point of time is also just like a milestone. You cannot stop anywhere. You are pushed forward in time. Something (an event) happens at this particular time, a particular place or at a particular kilometre. An event happens at a particular time. It can only happen at that particular time; not an hour earlier or an hour later. Thus, you look at time just like an odometer. When this happens in a simultaneous way, each event has value only at that time.

You have value for lunch only at the time of lunch. You have value for a certain thing at that moment only. When you were growing up, your parents bought you a motorcycle. You had value for that motorcycle at that point in time. Now you have grown beyond it, and you have probably bought a car. Then you look back at the model of the motorcycle; its value is much less. Maybe you use it because it is there, or maybe you have sold it. Time and value have a certain correlation, and it changes. They cannot be together forever.

Similarly, fears are transitory in nature. There are certain fears that are formed out of experiences of the past, for e.g., traumas related to accidents etc. You carry forward the trauma until you realise that it was wastage. Sometimes as a child, you have a fear of ghosts. Ghosts could be something unknown. You do not know them. Then, when you grow up, you feel, "What was I worrying about? What was I afraid of? What was I not understanding? Why is this happening? What is this changeover?"

"Oh! Ghosts- it is not a problem. So far in my life, none of the ghosts have been a problem." Then, through understanding, you overcome your fear of ghosts. Likewise with fear of altitude, fear of water. Such fears are a part of your *karmic* baggage which you carried when you took birth. Human existence is always transitory; one point to the other point, from birth till death. That is it. Beyond that there is no meaning. Then it is another life. We take things too seriously. We believe that certain things are very important for us. Actually, they are not. They are also part of the baggage or transit.

You are driving a car and there are passengers with you. They may get off at some point in time. They may say, "I do not want to travel with you any further." It is as simple as that. Even if you force them, they may not continue the journey. However, you may have to go further, because this is your interest, not their interest, and likewise people keep travelling together as long as they have to, and then they drop off. Likewise fears travel with you and they do not exist when you are in a different mode, such as sleeping. When you wake up, you may wake up with fear and anxieties. Sometimes you may wake up in a different environment and you do not feel any fears, because all the fears are gone. So, look at it from this angle and you could understand fears better.

❧ **Question:** What about fear related to a job?

Mohanji: Whether fear of job or life, every fear is the same!

❧ **Question:** How about materialistic things? Like, "Will I get something or not"?

Mohanji: Such thoughts will happen. These are anxieties. Whether I will be able to have the deal or not? Sometimes no, sometimes yes! Many times, people judge you on 'not achieving something'! That is also part of this anxiety, as people are hiring you because they have expectations to be fulfilled through you. "I am hiring you provided you deliver me this!" I will not take you in if you do not perform to this level of my expectation! If you are not living up to that, because of whatever reason, no problem! That is not the end of life. That is only a juncture, or a transition point. You tried and it did not work well, or as expected. No problem! That does not mean that you are a failure.

It means that at a particular time, in a particular space, in a particular environment, something did not happen. It had happened in another environment, at a different time. You may not have been able to implant the same thing in another environment. This is not a failure because there are so many factors associated with that. Thus, people consider a person to be a failure, judging him based on certain situations, activity and corresponding result. It is like asking a fish to climb a tree. The fish cannot climb. Then I call the fish a failure. However, if I ask the fish to swim, it will swim very well. Can I ask the fish to climb the tree so that I can call the fish a failure? Can I tell the fish it is a loser, because it is unable to climb a tree?

❧ **Question:** Is the identification of resources for a particular assignment also our responsibility?

Mohanji: To make a curry, you need certain ingredients. If those ingredients are not available, you cannot create that curry. It is as simple as that. You need to assemble many things to create certain things. If those things are not present, it will not work. You will have to make something else with the available material. That does not tell one if you are a success or a failure! It should not. If we start assessing a person based on such events, then the deficiency is with us. We do not know how to assess a person, because our understanding is always limited. It has nothing to do with the other person. Nobody is a failure that way.

However, we are too judgmental. Most of the time we only look at people two-dimensionally. Our vision is so limited and we cannot help it. We miss the third dimension, which is the real You. When we miss that, we miss the whole thing. That is the point. This is very much applicable to an HR Manager. What is a wholesome personality? A personality, which not only directly reflects on the effect of the job, but also on the background. What leads a person to a particular place – what is the complete man?

Ego

Consciousness is existence. Love is spontaneity. Love is the basis. It needs no creation. Creation itself is love. As consciousness grows, love establishes. As subtlety grows, strength happens, detachment from the gross happens. Thus, the process itself will give the result. We need not do anything. Just be. Just love. Just control expectations through conscious living and acceptance. Man becomes God. Man minus ego = God; i.e., God with ego = Man. Ego is body consciousness, mind consciousness, intellect consciousness, and also ego consciousness. When ego evaporates, god-hood awakens. Man realises God.

Obstacles

🌿 **Question:** If one wants to achieve a goal, and encounters a lot of obstacles or even one obstacle which is tough and seems too difficult to overcome, should we consider it as a sign that we should turn to another direction, or should one persist and endure, slowly waiting to achieve that goal?

Mohanji: The speed is not the point, whatever it is. Your movement is important. Are you moving ahead or are you stagnating? To keep moving is important, not the speed of your movement. Time is like this. Actually, time itself is not slow, however there are many obstacles so that we become slow. You should ensure that even if movement is slow, you keep moving so that you will eventually reach your destination. So please keep moving, I'm holding you.

🌿 **Question:** A lot of negative things have happened in my life recently. How do I get rid of negative emotions? I can't control my space to be clean and peaceful. I'd like to escape somewhere deep within, but how to do that?

Mohanji: This is common for everybody when there are some kinds of emotions which are residues from the past . Not only you but all people are also storing it and suffering because of it. Look at your life now. Is it fifty per cent positive and fifty per cent negative, or are your thoughts more positive or more negative? This is the first level of analysis. Positive is that we are in good health, we are eating all right, we are sleeping all right, etc. First, start with what is there. Thus, start with what you have, what is in good condition in your life. Start from there. This will help you to increase your positivity.

Then, the second thing is when you look at the past and things that happened in the past, if you store those details, then it is likely that they will happen again or get repeated in the future. Whatever happened in the past, understand that it was a different time in the past, a different space, and a different mind. Thus, start looking at it like, "Ok, that is the past, that is dead, and that is gone." Today you are a new person. This is your reality, today, now. You are not the past, you are not the future, and you are perfectly new. At this point in time, you are very powerful.

You do not know about the past because it is already finished. You do not know about the future because it is yet to be. Now you are very powerful. If you focus yourself on now, with all the pluses and minuses, the past or future does not matter. If you focus yourself on the right now, you will be perfectly fine. You will always do good. When the mind goes to the past, especially guilt, you must tell the mind, "That is history. I am different now. I have gained more strength for today from the past, despite my past. Today I am more powerful."

This is the way to tackle the current mind. The mind will definitely go to the past; however, bring the mind back to the present. You should always be conscious. You should always think, "This is the only reality I have. I am living today. I am working today. I am talking today. This is my only reality." From here, you start working. All the people who are with you are your current reality. Be with them, harmonise them. Give love, share love, so that everyone is happy when you are around. That way you can make your future much better.

CHAPTER 2:

Our conflict with nature

Velocity of Violence

Unity in Diversity

We live in a relative world. Though we are striving for unity in this diversity of people and perceptions, thoughts clash, words aggravate, and actions violate. This saga has been going on since mankind began. Disagreements are rooted in non-understanding. Non-understanding is based on the level of perceivable frequencies, and this is individualistic. Numerous frequencies are accessible in the universe. Numerous waves of vibrations. Numerous flavours. Our human constitution is also varied and individualistic, just like the numerous gadgets we have made.

Each one has their own capacity and compatibility with respect to frequencies. Lack of compatibility of frequencies creates divisions. It creates affinity at the level of 'birds of the same feather' types. However, all frequencies are always available for all kinds of species. All species, except humans, almost always conform to a certain specific frequency of existence, and they continue that way. They do not aspire for the higher, unless it becomes inevitable, or someone brings them to it, or they come into contact with those frequencies and get attached to them.

Human beings all have the capacity to raise themselves up to the higher frequencies, which elevates their vision, perception and understanding levels. This is especially possible when the energy and frequency around one are conducive or reasonably uncontaminated. The subtler the external energy, the easier it is for internal subtlety to grow. This is why people retreat to the mountains and quiet places to pursue their spirituality. A powerful Master's presence can give a similar effect.

When the mind goes silent in the presence of an awakened Master, the students can effortlessly raise their capacity for higher frequency. Their constitution, inner emptiness and *karma* will determine how high they can go. The key detrimental factor to a disciple's capacity for elevation is the stored negativity in his or her inner space. Usually, the Master allows this freedom of choice to the disciple because 'the eyes to see' is a personal choice. Even if a Master bestows it to a disciple to accent his progress, maintaining it against all odds is the disciple's responsibility. A lower frequency is very easy to achieve because it does not need skill, and the basic faculties provided with each existence can certainly and effortlessly connect to lower frequencies.

The higher and subtler you go however, the more you will need tenacity, determination, as well as constant and vigilant observation to maintain those frequencies. All the differences that one experiences in the terrestrial plane are of the lower frequency. If one experiences unity in diversity at all times and does not ever ask the question "Why?" at all, one is always experiencing the higher frequency. Between the lowest and the highest, there are numerous frequencies. It is also very difficult to make it finite – such as, "This is the absolute lowest and this is the absolute highest".

Crossing Frequency Barriers

As we attain higher frequencies, our operating levels also change. Our perception, outlook, and requirements are no longer the same. This clearly shows us where we stand at a particular point in time. Some people experience spontaneous shedding of meat, alcohol, certain relationships, unconsciously or not, because of the change in their operating vibratory level. We can see this all around us. The moment someone unconsciously upgrades their vibratory level, they shift gears in life.

Unconsciously, we disclose our frequency in everyday life. If we observe keenly, we can see this. A person who does not care about the pain and agony of others, is essentially operating at a lower frequency. When a person or society becomes insensitive, we can understand that the frequency of the whole area is lower. Then again, some souls may choose such a location for their incarnation to help show a light, to some at least, amidst the total darkness. These are elevated souls. They are used to higher frequencies and not too bound by personal agendas.

Emotions are usually rooted in lower frequencies. The ego is the same. The intellect is rooted in or equipped with a slightly higher frequency than mind or ego. This is why we usually have no regrets when we use the intellect. When the intellect is used to manipulate other minds, the frequency is lower in essence. This means you are using a good tool with a capacity for the higher, for a lower, personal agenda. When a person displays selflessness at all times, he or she is connected to the higher.

Selfishness is lower. Consuming intoxicants is lower. An animal product, which has a history of violence, is necessarily lower and it keeps the consumer in a lower frequency too. *Tamas* or inertia has a very low frequency, *rajas* is slightly better, and *sattva* is the best to have in the human periphery.

Terrestrial beings have frequency barriers. The key barriers are their own senses and mind. These are followed by the ego and intellect. Frequency barriers can be crossed when one moves more and more towards the soul. The Soul has no frequency barrier. Frequency barriers are also almost always related to elements such as body, senses, mind, intellect, or space and time. Upgrading from the ordinary squarely depends on your ability to establish connectivity with your own essence, yourself.

There are mechanics and guides available, as you know. However, the connectivity and capacity are individualistic. A Master can deliver the 'eyes to see', but a disciple cannot use them unless he raises his awareness to that higher level to adapt to the new software. The new software is useless unless it is placed in a compatible gadget!

The more violence there is in thoughts, words, and actions, the less the atmosphere is compatible for elevation. All negative emotions have systematically contaminated the atmosphere. A thought, word, or action never dies, because with every thought, word, and action, energy is released. Energy carries these vibrations to the world outside.

A negative thought might seem very innocent. However, it can determine the destiny of a man. Violence in thought could eventually trigger violence in words and actions. This could also get transferred from one mind to many minds. This could create events. This could launch wars, anarchy, and deaths. Hence, violence in thoughts is equally or more important than in words and actions. This should be closely observed, as this is individualistic.

Increasing the frequency is the remedy. Increased frequency leads to higher awareness. You will be able to see from above and help a situation objectively.

Existence in unconsciousness is also related to *tamas* and lower frequency. This means routine habits, unconscious behaviour, mind not in the present, compulsive behaviour patterns, eating habits, so on and so forth.

We eat flesh or other animals, unconscious about the torture and trauma they went through before they became meat. No animal wants to die. Nobody dies with pleasure so that we can eat them. Are we aware of this at all? Again, the profits and associated greed of an industry keep consumers unaware of the realities. Nobody visits a dairy farm or an abattoir. Even if they did visit, they would only be shown what is good for the eyes.

I was deeply shaken by the following three stories from the recent past.

Delivering on the Way to the Slaughterhouse

A pregnant dairy cow was being transported to the slaughterhouse. She delivered her child on the way. The truck driver discarded the calf, leaving it on the road, and drove off with the cow. The picture showed the mother cow yearning for the calf, looking out through the bars of the truck for her child and the child lying on the road. The mother cow was taken to the slaughterhouse and slaughtered. The police, fortunately, found the calf and it survived. In human terms, can we call this sanity? Every mother and child enjoy the same frequency of unconditionality.

The mother-child relationship is one of the most subtle and most powerful of all relationships. Subtlety is power. The dairy farm had promised so many 'heads of beef' to the meat producer and they never cared about the emotions of the cow or the calf. The truck driver was bound by duty and hence he could not care either. A new mother was slaughtered because the meat industry had committed supplies. Thus, the whole circle of profits and unconscious insensitivity destroys the fabric of subtlety. This is one of the tragedies of human existence.

A Mother's Love

Some CCTV footage in a British abattoir: A large group of sheep was herded into the abattoir where workers were stunning these beings. As they were brought in, I saw a sheep and her baby. The baby was glued to the udder of its mother, drinking her milk. The man at the abattoir started stunning these beings. First, he stunned the mother while the child was still drinking the mother's milk. As the mother fell down unconscious, the child was running around in fear and confusion. Then, the worker caught the child, stunned her as well and slit both their throats. What else can we say?

The killer at the abattoir is insensitive. He is doing his job. He does not care if it is a baby and her mother he is killing. He has been paid to do a job and he has been given timelines for completion because consumers are waiting for their product. The product need not have feelings. The consumer never understands that their product was alive and had aspirations for life. It is just meat on their plate. They eat a bit and throw away the rest. Life is totally wasted! The consumers are not aware of the tragedy that happened to a mother and her child. Unknowingly, they eat their flesh and thus participate in this *karma* of cruelty. Unconsciously, their demand or their need for flesh ultimately created this cruelty.

Calves are Trash for the Dairy Industry

A video shows a cow delivering a calf. The cow is tied to a wooden enclosure so that it cannot turn its head much. The calf hits the floor and struggles to get up. Finally, it gets up. The mother cranes her neck to see her baby. The calf inches towards the udder of the cow. The mother is eager to give the baby her milk. Before the calf's mouth touches the breast of the cow, a tall, heavy man in boots comes in, picks up the calf, and throws it aside. The calf falls down. The cow, in obvious distress, cries helplessly. The calf was not allowed even a drop of milk. It could not even taste its mother's milk. Then, the man lifts the calf and puts it in a wheeled carriage and takes it away.

Tears flow from its mother's eyes as she cries and cries for her baby, whom she will never see. The next scene shows many such calves in another enclosure. They all look bewildered and frightened. They are all looking at the camera. Then, a man stuns one of the calves using a machine and lifts it up with a string. He hangs it upside down while he slits its throat. He cuts one of its hooves while it is still alive using a sharp knife, to keep count of the babies he slaughtered that day. One by one, he thus kills all the babies!

These videos and pictures wrenched my heart. I felt deep pain and agony. I felt suffocated and helpless. I have posted them on Facebook. I keep wondering if this planet is worth living on. We make hue and cry of some celebrity sex scandal. Millions of letters in print fly for that. However, ultimately, who really cares if one makes love to another? They are not harming or killing anyone. The atrocities and insensitivity over beings of other species are totally un-ignorable. The letters and posts should fly for that. With their beautiful presentation of smiling cows, the meat and dairy industries effectively mask the agony behind it.

People who buy the products cannot understand the pain of death. This is like a beautiful advertisement inviting people to hell. Only when we take time to explore will we understand that what is shown outside is not the reality at all.

We are what We Eat

The same goes for game hunting. Many of the species on Earth are almost extinct. Many have disappeared forever, thanks to the brilliance of humans! I saw supporters of game hunting posting comments that they are actually animal lovers and are committing this crime to prevent overpopulation of the animals they kill! This is absolute nonsense. Humans just cannot understand the laws of nature. If you take a look at the Earth that we live on, you will understand. Earth is filled with waste that humans have created. If we had awareness, we would never do that.

Coming back to game hunting, since well before human existence, Earth has maintained a balance of its own. Earth has perfect symmetry and balance. Animals never kill for pleasure or fun. Animals only do things for a purpose. It is man who has destroyed the ecological balance. When we kill tigers and lions, the deer population grows. When we kill deer, lions and tigers starve, and so on. The deer and the lion are aware of their interdependence. A deer is never afraid of a well-fed lion. A satisfied lion never bothers a deer, even if it sleeps next to him. Furthermore, the law of nature is symmetrical. No animal mates for pleasure.

Their life is always purpose-bound. They eat to sustain their body and they procreate to sustain the species. Simple. How then can we say that we kill so as to preserve the ecological balance? Do we have the kind of macro vision that Mother Nature has? These kinds of claims should actually be immediately discarded and the hunters should be taken to task. Superstition also kills many animals. Aphrodisiacs made from the horns of rhinos have made them extinct. If animal organs were a good substitute for human organs, today, no animal would exist on Earth.

Our animal farming is the root cause of poverty on Earth. We are conditioned for meat, so we breed animals. Eighteen pounds of grain consumed by a cow produce only one pound of meat. Eighteen pounds of grain could sustain one family for at least two weeks. One pound of meat can appease hunger for only a single meal. We use one-third of the world's agricultural land for animal feed. Furthermore, this imbalance of production has now accented global warming.

Catastrophes are, to a great extent, instigated by the insensitivity of man. Our food supply chain is immoral, unethical and insensitive. We are what we eat. We must pay the price too. Our diseases, our calamities, our agonies are all derived from the agony we have inflicted on other sentient beings. We are violating the purity, the space, Earth, and the whole constitution of existence. We are being violent within and outside. We are.

There simply cannot be humane killing. Any killing is violence. It destroys life, the will for existence, and any captive killing amounts to murder.

The Species Conflict

Species collision is the biggest, highest and most devastating disaster Earth has ever seen since the ice ages. It is irreversible too. This is totally man-made. No other species on Earth trusts humankind. This lack of trust between our species and others is alarming and crippling our existence on Earth. With our insensitive life patterns, we have created such vast fields of distrust between ourselves and all other species on Earth. Every human walking on Earth is responsible for the species collision. It is an inherited curse. This breach of trust started about the same time domestication and farming of animals beyond the boundaries of ethics began.

Because of our lack of sensitivity, we have lowered the vibratory levels of the surface of Earth. We have violated the harmony of the vibratory plane between other species and men. This is the same equation for both land and sea. We have put our hands everywhere. The segregation of harmony in vibratory levels, which can be understood only through senses beyond the usual five, is irreparable in the immediate future. It may take a few lifetimes to achieve this, if at all. The other option is re-construction after demolition. This is Earth's choice, based on its state. Earth uses natural disasters to equalise the imbalance and make way for re-creation. We asked for it.

Passivity in moderation is good, if the passivity is based in awareness. Passivity with awareness can also be called patience.

Do not be deluded. All humans are not on the same vibratory plane. There are high and low planes of operation amongst people. We can see the subsequent devastation on the world as well. Political philosophies which resulted in human massacres are a clear sign of variety in operational level. Every being living on Earth has its own frequency. However, apart from humans, all other species use their own inherent skills rather than external objects to manoeuvre on Earth. Only humans mutilate, manipulate and destroy beings of other species indiscriminately. Since we do not 'feel' enough, we fall through greed for pleasures.

Man is eternally searching for happiness. Man is searching for inner silence and peace. He works hard for it. Many times, the weight of lineage and the weight of social *karma* delays his movement. He strives for perfection. Still, there is delay. In between, mind wreaks havoc. Mind compares, criticises, judges and alienates man from himself and his guides, banking on a broken concept – often inherited, and stored in the mind since eternity. The barriers are many for man to evolve and see the light of Truth. Many barriers are created by oneself and many are acquired from the world.

That which Creates, can also Destroy

Whatever the conscious mind gathers, the subconscious mind will not necessarily store. What is repeated though, is definitely stored in the form in which it is entered. This is just like a computer. We type a message and if we do not save it, it will be lost from the memory of the computer. We are storing in our subconscious only that which we have consciously energised and emotionalised. Likewise, a matter that is stored can manifest again in time, anytime. This can also become your destiny.

The world is turning fast. It is a good time for man to evolve spiritually. What are the factors that are hindering his progress and not allowing him to take advantage of this god-given chance?

1. Mind – When I say mind, I would like to include the intellect and ego. It is the collective mind. Mind is the trash can that contains all the stuff that man has acquired over generations, and that he has stored using emotions as the glue. The concepts, phobias, fears, apprehensions, anger, hatred, jealousy, craving, love, kindness, compassion, so on and so forth. This mind-conglomerate rules our life. It never allows us freedom from it. At any given point of time during our waking state, the mind produces some character trait that is stored in its storehouse, manifests it and thus distorts our reality. We judge, criticise and condemn other people or situations based on that. Usually, when we become negative, we connect with other people of the same vibratory level. When we experience positivity, we tend to isolate ourselves. This also means being objective at all times. Beyond the influence of the mind lies real spirituality. It leads to liberation. Nothing constructive happens in an agitated mind. Nothing can be built on shaky ground.

2. Species – I would call it the burden or curse of our species. We carry the responsibility and burden of being born into the human species. We are superior in intellect. We can manage choices. We can think and act. We can modify materials and we can create new things. So, we are better creators than any other species on Earth. Creation comes with responsibility. Destruction amounts to irresponsibility. Destruction of ma-

terials and life alike are clear signs of misuse of power at hand. Man has failed miserably to act responsibly.

His emotional nature and his greed have damaged his very abode –Earth. The biggest damage of all is the lost trust between species. Man has become totally isolated. There is no trust between the animal kingdom and the human kingdom. There is already a split on Earth. This has happened because generation after generation, we have captured, tortured, and killed beings of other species, as if they were war criminals. We have wiped out many species as well. We are still doing the same as I write this.

The breach of trust which came along with the permission or choice of existence on Earth has become a lack of mental equilibrium for mankind. No peace. No real peace is possible because the atmosphere is filled with victimhood, torture, and bloodshed. When we began treating animals as food materials, breeding, raising and killing them for the sake of human taste buds, we lost grip on our own conscience. We lost our grip on ourselves. When we kill any being, when we deny the right of existence or shared space towards any being, we are committing a breach of trust.

Every being has its character, its consciousness. Every being is equal to a human being, including other species. They have the same rights on Earth. When we breed, raise and kill them, the trust they develop for us is also assassinated. They feel that we are benevolent when we feed them on time. They start loving us unconditionally. Then, when they realise that this love was selfish, just for the sake of their meat, they release many negative vibrations into the atmosphere. They feel cheated, betrayed and they die broken-hearted.

I shall not re-iterate the agony that beings of other species experience in our collective farming, which I have narrated many times before. Ultimately, as man restricts the movements of other beings for his benefit, and as he insensitively wipes out beings of other species for his own trigger pleasure, we are already actively involved in the species war. We may also experience a false feeling that we are winning this war when we kill them indiscriminately, but these atrocities are constantly being registered in the consciousness of this platform called Earth. The final judge is Earth. Earth could choose to annihilate the oppressor completely from its face. Every cry of pain stays as a vibration on Earth. Everything is registered.

As Above so Below, As Within so Without

Species conflict is destroying Earth's vibratory level. Millions of animals and acres of environment are destroyed each moment. This has alienated man and will also bring forth doom to the species. Unconscious food habits, unconscious habit patterns, and living unconsciously or emotionally have isolated man from himself. So much is already destroyed in the internal and external world. The wounds of the internal world are reflected in the external world, and the wounds of the external world are reflected as human ailments.

The species war has a lot to do with our current state of restlessness, anarchy and lack of equilibrium. This is increasing day by day. Natural disasters have everything to do with the change in the vibratory plane. The victim-hood of species is affecting the masses. The restlessness that exists in the air is making mankind suffer more hurdles in the pursuit of Truth. One of the key reasons for our agonies, sorrows and depressions is the change in vibratory level caused by the species war. This is a silent war. Many people may not even realise there is such a war.

When we visit the stores and see or buy meat products in attractive packaging, we hardly realise that consumers of such products are actually sponsoring the species war. The more the demand, the more the casualties. All the beings that are killed for the benefit of humans are not faceless. They had a character, a constitution and a will to live just like humans. They also had the right to share Earth with humans. They feel the same way humans felt during the holocaust or Pol Pot's regime. The feeling is the same. Inevitable death! Helplessness! Resigned to their fate! Tears! Pain! Helpless surrender! Every being of every species that dies everyday feels this way. Trust me on this.

If Earth has to be a better place for humans and other species to live peacefully, then co-existence must become a Truth. This should be based on respect. There is harmony between all other species except man. A deer understands and appreciates the hunger of a lion. One deer from the clan may even sacrifice its life to save the rest and honour the species harmony. A lion does not kill for pleasure. Hence, there is predictability which the other species understands. On the other hand, in the case of humans, we kill, capture, torture and mutilate animals for the sake of our sadistic pleasures.

Canned hunting and human-controlled species protection using advanced machinery to reduce animal populations are all signs of our lack of conscience. Nature has its own effective control systems in place. The lions and deer have different breeding patterns, patterns of growth and styles of life, including appetites. Grass grows faster and the animals who survive on it, keep it trimmed. When the deer populations grow, lions control them, so on and so forth. When humans breed, there is no sensitivity. They overpopulate and take over the world of other species after destroying them. Thus, lack of effort with regards to co-existence has separated the human species from all other species. The concrete jungles that we have created for ourselves are then further alienating us from our own kind.

The species conflict has a major role to play in the psychosomatic illnesses that we experience each day. The agonies and pains that mankind bears is the weight of our crimes towards other species. We must be aware of it. Species war is the largest disaster that mankind has unleashed on Earth, with the technological era. All of man's conquests are external and worthless. No inner conquest has been made. Man has epically failed to realise that the only worthwhile conquest in his lifetime, is his inner conquest.

We must do whatever we can to bring back the trust between species. We need to re-unite and re-bond. We need to bring back peaceful co-existence based on respect and harmony.

We MUST TALK because They CANNOT

Man is quite famous for his selfishness. When our selfishness stretches to torturing other beings for our momentary pleasures – I feel this is exactly what we are famous for! We are famous for our insensitiveness, sadism, and cruelty. We torture and kill our fellow beings. We bind them and imprison them for our pleasure. We teach our children that it is fine to see a monkey in a zoo. It is fine to keep animals in cages for our pleasure. We do scientific experiments on them without regrets or concern for their pain and inconvenience. We skin them alive because we love to wear their skin.

We are so insensitive that we never feel the other's pain or agony. However, we certainly complain if we have a small injury. Understand that the same soul operates in all. We should feel. We definitely should feel. There is no point in being emotional about it. There is no point in reading and forgetting about it. If you cannot help it, at least spread the awareness of this matter. Remind people of our true nature – We are love incarnate. Why do we nurture everything that is opposite to love?

We talk and preach about God. How can we reach God when we cannot even see God in every being? The soul element of every being is God. When the soul element leaves, we call it a dead body. We have to see God in all creatures and respect that. When we start looking at all beings as expressions of the Almighty, can we hurt any being at all? All beings collectively become the true expression of the Universe. Who gave us the authority to live the way we want and hurt every other being in one way or another? We have no authority to kill or torture any beings, as they also are true expressions of the Almighty.

Maybe your voice is singular and may get dissolved in the ocean of voices of this world. However, the energy that travelled with your voice can never die or decay. It will come together with similar voices and make a change in the system, sooner or later. Hence, voice the expression. Animals are not made to feed us or entertain us. They have similar emotions just like us. They feel pain and sorrow. They weep and cry. They feel deeply for their fellow beings.

How can we treat them so insanely and so insensitively? Remember, all the beings that Mother Earth nurtures are equally important to her. None are better liked than the other. We must live sensibly, sensitively, and with love as our primary, secondary, and final expression. That is what we essentially are. We are incarnates of kindness and compassion. The capability to express love and kindness, in all adversities, is our actual strength. Let us remember that.

God-Given Energy Resources

ꙮ **Question:** The current development all over the world is actually leading to destruction. How to go back to ancient systems, for e.g., free electrical energy, not using and depleting fresh water, coal, and oil, etc.?

Mohanji: There has been an evolution in the thought process over a period of time. It is mostly based on greed. The mighty always control. The mighty, whether in terms of wealth, political connection or power, control the weak. This is how the system has operated. I'm not saying this is the ideal system, but this is the system we are experiencing. For example, a person with power runs over the not-so-powerful. This is happening continuously. So, to bring forth changes for the better, the awareness of the people should be increased. This has to start from top to bottom, and from bottom to top. This is a process.

What happens is, in the past, people who were more *sattvic* and wiser, created many things. However, by the time of the technological uprising, greed-based economies had happened. For example, ammunition is made to protect the country. Yet it has a duration, an expiry date. So, what happens is that before the expiry date, it needs to be used. War has to happen. Destruction has to happen. So, this kind of wrong understanding, these wrong calculations, wrong moves and most importantly, this war creates pain. It creates agony.

If people decided that peace was more important, and not war, then that itself would cut down the military expense. Furthermore, every country should cooperate towards this. Politicians should feel for the people, for mothers, and children. However, they only look at their wealth. None of the politicians have been brought down in today's political world, whether in terms of economy, finance, or stature. Some scandals happened and they were affected, but ultimately, they all started somewhere and made much more money over the months and years.

Nobody has been serving the people. Politicians are supposed to serve the people. Rather than serving, they have instead earned quite a lot. In this kind of situation, what sells is what they are capturing. They do not consider what is good for the people. What they consider is what makes profits, and what is more beneficial for them. When rulers are like that, society is already contaminated. Society is also forced to feed them. Moreover, manufacturers control politicians through bribery and such things. When such a vicious circle continues over a period of time, destruction has to happen in the civilisation.

If free building through awareness cannot happen, then awareness has to rise and rebuild the whole system. God-given energy resources are the sun, wind, and water. None of these God-given energy sources contaminate Earth. We chose to take the oil. We chose to break the mountains. We chose to dig and the digging has affected Earth, because it is puncturing Earth too much. What will happen in this case? Destruction. Only destruction can happen. Only then can things be rebuilt. If we cannot change, time changes us. If we do not change ourselves, time will change us. This is happening. This is to be expected, especially during the shift.

CHAPTER 3:

We shoot the messenger

The Cycle of Rise and Fall

For the last few days, I have been bombarded with calls and emails asking for my comments on the incident related to 'N'[2]. I have answered all your questions personally and in our *satsang*. I would like to write my thoughts here, so that raging minds may find some relief. I am objective. I am not involved with his institution. However, I like his style of teaching, his clarity and the pearls of wisdom that he has given forth profusely over all these years. We cannot ignore what he gave to the hungry world of sundry seekers. We cannot shatter his image because of a scandal and ignore his teachings.

I am not justifying him not practising his teachings or our notion of dishonouring the sanctity of saffron. Time will tell the Truth. Let us exercise patience. Please wait and watch, and refrain from being judgmental.

I am watching human nature or the nature of the mob with amusement, where hundreds of good messages and teachings were ignored and disowned because our mental image about 'N' was shattered. Why do we have to disown the *Guru Tattva* that travelled through the medium called 'N' to the out-

---

[2] Refers to a Master who was in the news at that time due to a scandalous incident.

side world? Why do we have to disown our experiences as well as knowledge? Mental images are bound to get shattered sooner or later. Let us realise this fact, as this body will also perish one day.

The Tragic Flaw

In the Aristotelian teachings, there is a heavy accent on a principle called 'the tragic flaw'. This means that one flaw or deficiency in one's character triggers his downfall. Othello had jealousy. Hamlet's flaw was delay. Every human being possesses one or a few tragic flaws in him, which eventually cause his downfall. Suppressed sex is such a flaw. Does this change with enlightenment? We shall see that in the following lines.

Guru Tattva

The *Guru* principle is like the ever-flowing Ganges. It keeps flowing, through various cities, nourishing various regions and beings. The *Guru* principle began when life began. The *Guru Tattva* operates through any being, any mouth and any words that matter to us, time after time. Just as different teachers have guided you in different classes, aiding you to reach the higher levels, the *Guru* Principle works through various beings and helps us climb steps to higher awareness. The *Guru Tattva* flows eternally. Nobody can deny this.

All external teachers are only representing this principle. Our soul also represents this principle. God represents this principle. That is why we say the *Guru* is God. The *Guru* is transitory. The *Guru* changes from grade to grade, or from time cycle to time cycle. The principle though, never changes. The *Guru* principle travels through eternity and takes any mouth to convey wisdom. The mouth is not important, as it is transitory. The message it conveys is important for you. Trust the message. Cherish the message. Experience the message. They are the eternal truths. This will help liberation. Marry the wisdom, not the *Guru*.

Equanimity

Our Tradition teaches us the path of equanimity as the best path. Perfect balance through happiness and sorrows. If a seeker approaches spirituality with extreme equanimity, he will be well balanced in *Guru Tattva*, with supreme gratitude to existence and all the mouths that expound the *Tattva*. If emotion is driving the seeker, and especially if 'doer-ship' is predominant in him, he will tend to get attached to the image of the *Guru*. They miss the *Tattva* and fall for the *Guru*. They build expectations and mental images. When the images fail to hold, they fall flat too. Many get disillusioned. Many get out of disillusionment, and finally leave their need for the supporting stick and start walking on their own thereafter.

The Path of Liberation

Our Tradition has always accented liberation from the birth and death cycle. Our Tradition has never bound anyone to any system, and has allowed free choice for all. This is the true path. In this path, The *Guru*, our Soul, and God are One and the same. Our soul is our primary *Guru*. The external *Guru* is only an exponent of the eternal principle called *Guru Tattva*. In the path of liberation, sooner or later, the image, name and form must get nullified and the *Tattva* should shine bright. So, whatever image we hold on to for our immediate progress will vanish, and will be replaced by another and another, until the completion of our journey. The path of liberation is always a path of annihilation. Everything, including our body, mind, and intellect must perish and dissolve, sooner or later.

The Body

Hunger sustains the body. Sex sustains the species. When one takes the body, one also inherits the relevant urges. Hunger and sex are essential for sustenance in different levels, all amounting to existence. When the accent on the body reduces, and man establishes his consciousness in the Omnipresent, all the requirements of the body will take a back seat. It does not mean that it has vanished from the system. It exists in a dormant state, in most cases. When that person has to operate continuously through the senses and body, such as teaching or nurturing establishments or people, these urges can come back and bother him. It is possible. This, the primal urge, may also cause the fall.

Enlightenment

Enlightenment establishes one in unity with his own soul. It leaves aside all caution and allows nature to take its course, like a tree, even if it means cutting it off from its roots. Enlightenment aligns all the *chakras* of the vital system in perfect order and converts the man into a mirror. He will start reflecting what comes in front of him and will usually maintain a fluid state. He will be like the water that attains the flavour and form of its container. This level of being-ness often brings forth personal chaos. Especially when the person consistently operates on the terrestrial plane, his larger awareness takes a back seat. If lust takes over, it gives room for degeneracy. Lust could also be acquired. Like a sponge, he could acquire any feelings from another person.

The Image

Our body, mind, and intellect are temporary. When over-dependency on any image happens, it gets shattered. This is the law of nature. The public image that we consciously or unconsciously create is transitory or temporary. Sooner or later, it will fall. It will definitely fall if we do not conform to the image that we create and do something contrary to it. The image that others build about us is also transitory or temporary. The difference here is that, even if we allow changes in ourselves, others will not want to change their image of us at all. Then, if we are casual about the image, others could crucify us, because we do not conform to their mental image anymore. Society likes to keep images of its people. The larger the image, the tougher it is to maintain, let alone change it. When such images break, society becomes cruel.

Expectation

Expectation is the biggest treason. Expectations are inevitable, as long as we operate from our conscious mind during the waking state. Expectation is part of our mind mechanism. The more expectations there are, the more our sufferings will be. Expectations create walls much stronger than the ego. Expectations always alienate us from the Truth. Expectations thus should be nullified before we realise God. When we build expectations about individuals, they are bound to perish, because almost all people are *karmic* beings and unless we see the third dimension of individuals, we cannot understand their operating levels.

Enlightened beings operate in the *dharmic* mode. In order to understand the operating levels, we need to have unity in consciousness. Since each person operates in his own consciousness, and cannot migrate into another, this is very difficult. So, expectations are bound to perish sooner or later. The shock that follows wakes us up and relieves us from our dependency on our expectations to their nullification.

Gratitude

Gratitude is essential for growth. Every *Guru* has given us something. Everyone has aided our growth. What we are today has come with the support of many *Gurus*. We should be grateful. If a *Guru* behaves in a way which is contrary to our expectations, we should understand that the problem is with our expectation. We may have failed to understand the third dimension of the *Guru*, which was not fully obvious. All we need to do is accept and appreciate the teachings.

The Power of Sex

Sex is very powerful. It is powerful because it is inherent in all beings. It is inherent because it is essential for the continuation of a species. Sex is used only to maintain the species – by all beings except man. For man, the sexual act also amounts to pleasure and recreation. Celibacy is a test. Being a celibate is not easy, because the needs of the body sometimes play havoc, just like hunger can take a person even to the level of murdering another. Being a celibate in a forest is much easier than existing in the marketplace amongst all kinds of lures. Thus, all these matters can acquire the power of tornadoes at times, unless overcome.

To win over the elements, which are essentially the basis of our body, we need stillness and being-ness. In the extreme doing-ness of social life, even if a person exists in the being-ness of his realised state, the needs of the body could always play an important role. The shift from the all-pervasive omnipresence to the limited body consciousness can be considered as inevitable, when the interaction at micro level is continuous and consistent. This is at the discretion of the Saint. He could very well transfer himself into a *grihastha* (householder), get married, have sexual gratification and even help continue the species, if need be. He could also renounce fully and pursue his spiritu-

133

ality in anonymity, like *avadhootas*. If he chooses to serve the world and also maintain perfect celibacy, he needs to exercise great restraint. It is not easy.

Sex has lured Masters since time began. Sex is the temptation that tilts humans because we are used to suppressing it. Society condemns it. The middle class preserves it. Upper and lower classes have nothing to do with morality, usually. Morality is the property of the usually deprived middle class. We pretend to be immune to it and fall flat at times, unable to handle its immensity and weight. This is the way we are, whether we like it or not. Like the Great Master Lahiri Mahasaya, who also led a family life, said, "When sexual desire takes place, it takes place." It is as simple as that.

Adi Shankara migrated his soul into another body to experience sexuality. Vishwamitra fell for the charms of Menaka. Osho has remarked that without addressing our inherent sexuality, there is no progress in spirituality. Now, the question is about the image that we have created and the reality that we experience. If there is a big disparity, the fall is inevitable. The equation is in coming to terms with ourselves. Nobody is immune to sexuality. Everyone has fantasies. If someone pretends otherwise, beware. Sex is natural. Accept your sexuality. There is nothing to be ashamed of. Use your discretion while going about it, that's all. By suppressing something, we cannot solve it. Period.

My Request

My request to all Mohanji family members is, please respect the teachings of 'N'. Please respect the *Guru Tattva* that he translated into many lives. Please respect the teachings as well as the experiences. Do not despise anyone, let alone 'N'. If you criticise and hate any *Guru*, the *Guru* principle within you will be affected. Just be grateful for what 'N' gave you and the world. Only our expectations were shattered. Our mental images were shattered. A big bubble burst. They are bound to be shattered today or tomorrow. Nothing stays permanent in life. Be respectful.

Never use any violence in thoughts, words, or action. Do not judge anyone's actions. There is no need to justify, as it is none of our business. Remember one thing – the Truth will remain the Truth, despite the Master's image. Also, be careful about who is benefited by desecrating and burning the ashram? Why do we become emotional? Why do we become violent? Are we all such pure beings to throw stones at another? Are we not all a mixture of everything? Look within first. Then look outside. True spiritualists should maintain calmness and serenity. Marry the teachings. Do not marry the *Guru*. However, always have gratitude for the teachings or *Guru Tattva*.

One person has insisted on my answering his question about whether I approve of it or not. My friend, the world does not operate on my approvals. Your mental processes happen beyond my approval. I have seen a shift in flavours without any concrete reason in life. People change in moments. Their thought processes change. We never know who will do what tomorrow. Who will be alive tomorrow? What will happen to us tomorrow? We are so fragile and momentary. You and I can rise or fall anytime. Tides can turn anytime. So, let us not be over-enthusiastic in cherishing somebody's fall. We do not have to approve the sexual preferences of anyone. They will go ahead with it, well without our approvals, if they have to. When we cannot even control our own thoughts, how will we control others? Do we have to, at all?

I appreciate your stressing on morality and Sainthood. History has seen much suppression and subsequent liberation. Let us not argue this fact. I do understand that mental images have been seriously shattered. That is bound to happen, because our path is that of liberation from everything. Just understand one thing. With or without us walking this planet, life will go on.

Nothing changes with our protest or concern. Violence within will only affect us. Hence, express gratitude for everything and allow people to walk their path. Let us not be judgmental. We have no right. Let us take everything as part of our learning process. Hence, marry good teachings which help your spiritual evolution. Never marry any physical *Guru*.

Love all. Forgive all. Be kind within. Do not judge another.

Who is Afraid of the TRUTH?

We believe that practices take us to perfection. Not always. We have practised life and living many times over, yet we still remain imperfect! We believe that performing *sadhana* (spiritual practices) helps us reach God. Doing-ness is bound by time. We believe that reading and acquiring knowledge takes us to perfection. Intellect is bound by time too. Retention has a duration. Memory has its limitations. All that we learn from outside may not even become our reality, as we chew much more than we can digest. Anything in us which is bound by time cannot take us to the timeless.

Only the timeless within us can merge our consciousness to the timeless. That timeless is the true you. That is your true nature. So, as we start our journey on the path of spirituality, such questions will keep cropping up: "Am I on the right path? Am I that, or is this the Truth?" Whatever limits you, including food, clothing, sex, shelter, space, time, relationships, concepts, fears, phobias, terrestrial love, hatred, possessiveness etc., does not represent your true nature. Causeless love is definitely an expression of your true nature. Causeless is the real you. Causes are just expressions. Causes are bound by time. Measurable time is expression-bound. Measurable expressions are time-bound. Thus interconnected they are!

We live in a world of extreme variety. There is a constant tug-of-war between Truth and untruth, the real and unreal, illusion and reality, the good and the bad, between good and evil. We watch it being played out everyday on television channels and in our own minds, when we try to digest scandalising 'truths' vomited out by the media, which are mostly modified to suit their audience, or whoever pays their bills. The common man is always confused. He is always kept confused. This state in society is needed for the media to stay in business.

What has led me to write all this, are the hours of discussions about a recently released book on 'MA'[3], which has created quite a storm. I have not read the book, nor have I touched a copy of it. However, since many people have asked me whether I agree or disagree, I have decided to make my position on this very clear. I look at life objectively, without any emotions. Whenever there is emptiness outside of us, it is just a reflection of the emptiness within us. Inner void and outer void are inter-connected. Yet, to change the outer void, we need to change the inner void. Inner strength is always reflected in our outward expressions. This being the case, I look at the history of mankind with amusement. There has always been a struggle between the binding, controlling, law-making side of humans and the liberated, unbound and selfless 'Truth-sayers'.

Time and again, whenever someone spoke the Truth, they were scandalised, even crucified, but later philosophies and religions were formed based on their teachings after they had been shamelessly assassinated. In short, a true Saint was not recognised during his time. It always took the future generations to honour a Saint. I can quote many examples. John the Baptist, Jesus, Socrates, even our own Shirdi Sai Baba, Bhagavan Nityananda, to name a few. During their time, none of them were truly honoured or respected.

---

[3] A contemporary spiritual Master

John the Baptist was beheaded. Jesus was crucified. Socrates was given poison and killed. Shirdi Sai Baba was taken to court for a paltry matter. When Radhakrishnamayi became pregnant, people accused Baba of being the child's father. Bhagavan Nityananda was asked by local officials to reveal the source of his income based on complaints made by the very people who had tremendously benefited from him!

When the officials threatened to arrest him, Bhagavan Nityananda took them to a pond and told them it was there that he got his money from. When the officials decided they were being fooled, Bhagavan jumped into the pool and came out with a pot of gold coins, saying his finances came from here. When the officials recognised the stature of Bhagavan, they left.

The point is that contemporaries never recognised the stature of any living Saint and it always took the next few generations to honour a past Saint. Generation after generation, the same habits continue. We scandalise, arrest or kill a Saint, or anyone who lives and speaks the real Truth. There is only one absolute Truth – that we are indeed one with God. In other words – *Aham Brahmasmi* (I am *Brahma or God*). Those who cannot see beyond relative Truth, who identify themselves with limited identities such as their body, mind or intellect and who are proud of their terrestrial stature, have never agreed with any liberated person living beyond man-made rules.

No generation has ever appreciated a living *Guru*. They have only idolised the dead. When we scandalise anyone, someone who does good to society, the world, to people, birds or animals, be aware that we are just following the same old repeated history of intolerance. We are no different from those who crucified Jesus, poisoned Socrates or Osho. We are no different from those who burnt people at the stake in Europe. The same people who orchestrated the inquisition, ethnic cleansing, and all the wars and worries of the world. We are the same.

We have been seriously concerned more about the private life, and specifically the sex life, of a public figure, than his message/contribution to the world. We never appreciated the contributions of great people while they were alive, however we did glorify and idolise politicians, who cheated, stole, and danced with borrowed feathers (money and talent). The names of our streets carry the name of politicians who perhaps even swindled money and manipulated people. No Saints are honoured even in their own home town.

Adi Shankara got no support from the local people of his community to cremate his mother. Today, we respect him as the Master of the era. The great *Sant* Jnaneshwar and his brothers and sister were made to starve by society. His parents were asked to commit suicide by the people of their time, as repentance for shedding renunciation. All the great Masters have endured deep humiliation by their own society. Look into history, you will know. We have nothing to be proud of. If we can correct ourselves now, well and good. Otherwise, history will repeat itself. It is repeating itself over and over again.

Character assassination is usually a byproduct of jealousy. There is also jealousy in spiritual circles. The phenomenon of one-upmanship and its associated power struggles are happening in all aspects of society. The spiritual world, despite the isolation and self-oriented lifestyle, is not immune to the egos of existence. Instead of unification, many so-called spiritual *Gurus* are keener on building walls and dividing people between groups. All spiritual teachers are relevant because they cater to someone in society. We cannot under-estimate any, nor can we question their relevance.

However, what example should they set to the sundry seekers of the world if it is not peace, harmony and oneness beyond even the species barrier? The key aspect of any spiritual path is self-actualisation. There are many paths one can choose to achieve that, as per his or her inherent constitution. Who can question that? One is free to choose his or her *Guru*, even though the scriptures declare that the one who appears to you is the right One for you, just like our school grades where the teacher that appeared in one grade helped us cross over to the next.

The power wars within the spiritual circle, the silly egos and disagreements among spiritual *Gurus*, the extended disagreements of their disciples; in short, a lack of unity is destroying the very fabric of the age old, time-tested principles of *Sanatana Dharma* or the basic ground rules of our very existence. Name, fame, money and power are going to people's heads. Under the masks of spirituality, crimes are committed. Religions are waging wars even at the cost of destruction of lives. Unless the purpose becomes solely the elevation of the awareness of the masses, unless efforts become unified, unless unity consciousness happens among spiritual *Gurus*, there is no protection, hope or continuity.

If all the spiritual teachers stay separated, the whole path of *Sanatana Dharma* will decay. Unity for the preservation of the age-old Tradition of tolerance is important, more than ever, at this juncture of time. Character assassination always has a strategy and profit motive behind it. There is a definite vested interest behind character assassination. If you looked into the minds of the so-called moral police, you would see dark desires lurking behind their seemingly benevolent expressions. There is an agenda being played out. It never affects a real Saint.

Jesus made his point through the cross that he is beyond the cross and because his conviction shook the conscience and consciousness of generations, Christianity was born. People are waking up to Osho more than ever before, many years after his death. Even people of the time never spared Shirdi ai Baba when they blamed Baba for Radhakrishnamayi's pregnancy! Today, Shirdi Baba temples are in every corner of the world.

Character assassination has been attempted towards almost every contemporary Saint by their contemporary generation and there is someone's vested interest in it. Who is afraid here – other Saints, other religions, businessmen, regular followers who come with expectations, or the politicians of the country? Someone is affected for sure by the overwhelming presence of the Saint. Someone is benefited by their character assassination.

Truth always wins eventually, even though the history that the world gets to see is not always the absolute Truth. It is usually choreographed, or the opinion of someone who witnessed it or assessed it. This may not be the absolute Truth. It is usually a version of the absolute Truth. People usually never get to know the absolute Truth. Everyone is fed versions or opinions, under the pretext of Truth, by the manipulators of the world, or by those who run the world – the politicians, media moguls, other religious heads, etc.

Truth is given on a platter in the form of an enlightened Master and society chooses to crucify him just because the Truth sounded like blasphemy to conditioned ears accustomed only to relative truths! With the body thus destroyed, the consciousness that survived starts to perform without hindrance and this becomes an eye opener to many! "Oh My God! We missed a chance! The good man has died. Let us make a religion out of him!" This is how Masters are missed, and religions are made.

Commerce rules the world today. Everything sells. Even spirituality is sold in packets as courses. This is not what we want to discuss here. This is not our cup of tea. This commercial network also is a marriage between businessmen, spiritual persons and politicians. This is a completely different story. I do not even want to comment about it because there is nothing spiritual in it except the name or flavor. Control, power, money, and possessions are the norm here. This is totally a terrestrial matter. We can talk about it some other time, if it is worth the breath.

Remember, once again, no Saints or *Avatars* were accepted during their time. Almost all are posthumous celebrities. Jesus was a man of flesh and blood at one time. He ate food and slept. Krishna and Radha were two human beings who existed five thousand years ago. They also ate food, drank water, used the toilet and slept. Shirdi Sai Baba, Akkalakoṭ Maharaj, Ramana Maharishi, Swami Vivekananda, Buddha were all Saints who lived in flesh and blood at some point in time. We remember them and revere them with respect today. This is because they added value to our life. We value their time when they add value to our life.

We do not consider the time they spent on themselves, even for meditation. It does not matter to us. Value for us is when value is delivered to the world by any Saint or philosopher. However, a word of caution here – all that glitters is not gold. There are many fakes in the world. Usually, the ones who possess only acquired knowledge but resemble past Masters in form, name or title. We can ignore them. They are not connected to the source. True Saints are only those who have crossed over and are connected to the source. We are only talking about these here.

Those who are connected to the source lead a completely different lifestyle. Many will be unpredictable to the core. This is because *dharma* is their guiding factor, not *karma*. Vyasa impregnated Amba and Ambalika because the reigning dynasty was coming to an end. He also impregnated the maid to bring forth an unconditional, wise man called Vidura into the court of selfish royals. If it happened today, there would be hours of debates on our channels supporting and criticising Vyasa. Vyasa, Vasistha, Krishna, Buddha, Jesus, Ramana Maharishi, Sai Baba and all other Masters knew exactly what they were supposed to do on Earth. They never wasted even a moment of their existence on paltry, self entertaining matters. They did everything for a higher purpose.

Relative Truth vs Absolute Truth

The war is between relative Truth and absolute Truth. Relative Truth is based on faculties of perception and faculties of action that come within a frame called the body. Absolute Truth is related to the energy that runs the machine called the body and its associated infrastructure. Relative truths are based on approved methods and patterns. Approved realities and perceptions are those that can also be categorized as morality.

Morality is a word that people use when they need to shield themselves. Morality is relative in our society. It changes with generations, time and space. It changes with religions and interpretations too. So, morality is a flexible piece of equipment. Usually, it is used by one person or a group of people for taking advantage of another. Morality is a sensitive tool. It can wreak havoc.

Avadhootas such as John the Baptist, Bhagavan Nityananda or Shirdi Sai Baba never cared about this pretentious morality and always revelled in the absolute Truth. They went on with their work irrespective of what others thought about them or not. This is a clear sign of a liberated Saint. They have no opinion about others, nor do they care about others' opinions. All are *karmic* beings. There have to be ups and downs in all. This is the variety of existence.

Let us look at the relative Truth that propels our life forward. (Well, forward, backwards, or status quo is debatable). Look at the flip side of the relative Truth that we enjoy each day. A politician, a rock star, a film star, or a rich man womanises or abuses drugs, hoards money or accumulates wealth; the whole system comes to their rescue. Even if they are arrested and imprisoned for crimes like stealing public money, they get special preferences in the prisons of the world. Their wealth will buy them prestige. They get re-elected to power and positions.

There are even terrorists and dictators who have massacred people and yet are honoured. For e.g.: Pol Pot of Cambodia who killed more than 2 million children, women and men, died of old age. Even in his last interview with the media, he said, "I did it for the country," and the world pardoned him! Men who make ammunition and weapons that destroy lives are well accepted in society and even considered as protectors or harmless, while someone who tries to do good without consideration for profits or benefits is crucified! Drugs are experimented with on humans, prisoners, and victims from every species in the name of science and progress.

Human greed has destroyed more than half the forests of the world. Most of the spaces thus made are used for factory farming and human housing. When natural habitats were removed, many species perished. Many species are on the verge of extinction. Seven billion people are consuming twenty-one billion birds and animals each year. One-third of the grain cultivation of the world is used to feed animals for slaughter. The same acre of land that produces animal feed for 250 pounds of meat, can produce 40 000 pounds of potatoes, 50 000 pounds of tomatoes. What a gross wastage of our resources and environment!

Genetically modified food is destroying the human species. Naturality is lost. Holocaust is happening every minute. Millions of living beings are slaughtered for food each day across the world. An average factory in a developed nation kills more than one hundred cows in an hour! Remember, almost all living beings have an awareness level of a two-year-old human child. They feel love and fear. They feel the pain of separation. They have the ability to love unconditionally. They care for their offspring. Man imprisons them, tortures them, and kills them for selfish pleasures.

Superiority of race, if there is anything of that sort at all, should be expressed in our ability to express unconditional love and compassion beyond time barriers. It is our ability to express kindness that makes us human. It is our refinement in thoughts, words and action, not greed and selfishness, that truly qualifies us as human! If we can protect and care for other lives, we are worthy of being considered as humans. Otherwise, we are worse than animals, with intelligence but no sensitivity, compassion, kindness or wisdom, let alone awakening.

History said, "Never again," when millions of Jews were slaughtered by Hitler's militia. Yet, history has seen the same type of crime and gross injustice repeated in Cambodia under Pol Pot when he systematically assassinated men, women and children; during the Nanking Massacre by the Japanese military where they made campfires and burnt children alive in front of their mothers; and with the killing of countless men and women in Iraq, Egypt, Syria, Afghanistan, Yugoslavia and so many other countries.

We still kill thousands of beings each moment. Why is killing a being of another species considered natural, while killing humans is called murder? Pregnant cows are slaughtered and the calves in their wombs are put inside incinerators. This is not punishable by the laws of any country in the world. Where is our sense of justice? Where is justice? When we accept such blatant acts of cruelty, what can we cry for? Crime breeds crime. Insensitivity creates revolution in society. Sexual suppression leads to sexual anarchy. Suppression of anything leads to eventual anarchy. The human mind craves for whatever is denied. This is the nature of the human mind.

Every human being walking on Earth must focus their attention on things that matter to themselves and the generations to come. They should be concerned about the state of the world today. They should be aware of the destruction that has taken place already and the decay happening each moment. They should know that the world is dying each moment; it is becoming more and more uninhabitable. We are cutting the very branches of the trees that are housing us.

In the last hundred years, mankind has destroyed and devastated Earth more than ever before since mankind began. Especially during our very time in the past fifty years. We are on a destruction spree. Totally indiscriminate. Unfortunately, the development in technology is increasing the potential for destruction. Earth has deteriorated to the maximum in the last hundred years. We must be aware of this. We must do something about it.

Money

Money is a big deal. This is one of the key issues in the book, as I understand it, against 'MA'. How does money happen? What attracts money? The answer is simple. Stature attracts wealth. When a person moves from the basic gross existence to the subtler aspects of himself, the grosser becomes attracted to him or her. The symbol of *Ananta Shayana* in the Hindu system is a clear sign of this point. Ananta is infinity, the snake which coils as a bed for Mahavishnu, the preserver of everything to rest upon. Mahavishnu lies in *Yoga Nidra*, which is a state of *samadhi*, when your consciousness is spread all over the universe and has merged with the universal consciousness, in other words, when you have become the Source.

In this state, there is no individuality; there is only universality and hence everything that is part of the universe is also part of you. You are the universe. There is no individual *karma*. There is only *dharma*, truthful and unselfish duty in the performance aspect. Lakshmi , the wife of Mahavishnu, sits at His feet. Lakshmi represents wealth and prosperity. In a nutshell, when a person embraces the subtle, wealth is at his feet, or at his disposal. There is purity and legitimacy in this wealth.

When a gross person chases gross wealth, it eludes him and often, he gets it contaminated. People even sell their souls to earn wealth and suffer through lifetimes. Subtlety of existence is the key to wealth. Subtlety attracts material benefits spontaneously, and by that time, the person who has already embraced the subtle may even have nothing to do with physical wealth. (I believe '*MA*' is in this state. She has nothing to do with wealth. Wealth happens to her spontaneously).

They are already in the absolute bliss state of *sat* (the essence of creation or the essence of the supreme), coming into contact with *chit* (the unit or our substratum which feels and experiences the alienation from the *sat*). The '*ananda*' or bliss takes place when *chit* merges with *sat*, and there is absolute bliss of unity in consciousness. In this state, money or wealth have no value. They come to you spontaneously, because of the simple fact that subtlety always attracts the gross or even wealth.

So, when people talk about '*MA*' hoarding wealth, my opinion is that '*MA*' does not need wealth. She has sufficient wealth inside of her. Real wealth is that which is not visible to human eyes. The wealth of spiritual bliss! This wealth cannot be conquered. It has got to be earned through the constant shedding of all the identifications that keep blocking the spiritual progress of an individual. Whether '*MA*' has hoarded physical wealth or not, she is obviously truly rich inside. This energy, this wealth, is visible to all, all of the time. She is never tired, and this inner richness was visible in her calm and composed reply to the scandal to the public. No remorse, no complaints, only love!

Emotions and Sex

Spurious food leads to contamination of the body and deterioration of health. Spurious emotions will lead to contamination of the mind. The more we acquire such information, store it and energise it, the more it seriously affects our consciousness. Ignorant people lead a contaminated existence without any knowledge of the levels of contamination they are carrying. Most of what we carry in our minds today is unwanted and insignificant material or the trash of the world.

The organs of perception can only see the superficial. They cannot see the third dimension of the individual, and simplicity happens with subtlety. Subtlety brings simplicity. Nothing that the world can ever offer matters to a liberated Saint. Then life becomes simple, without the conflicts produced by the mind.

Several political party members and religious leaders have been speaking on television about this matter. Listening to their verbal diarrhoea, my thought has been: "Those who have not 'sinned', may throw stones at her". Who has the right to point a finger at *'MA'*? Honestly, I feel that if a rape has happened in the *ashram*, it is important that the victim should immediately bring this to the attention of lawmakers, police or at least *'MA'*. Forced sex is not acceptable. We have no right though, to condemn consensual sex between two adults who indulge in it with full awareness and desire.

There is a thick line between the two. One is exploitation, molestation etc., while the other is gratification. Every being walking, crawling or flying on Earth is bound by food and sex. Nobody can deny that. Food to sustain the body because the body is made from elements, and food being a supplement that nourishes the body. Likewise, sexuality sustains the species. No beings on Earth other than human beings use food and sex as recreation. Hence, all the rules and regulations pertaining to these two integral aspects of human existence apply only to human beings.

If someone who operates in society came to me and said, "I have overcome my need for food and I have no sexuality," I would immediately think, "Either he is sick or he is lying." In spirituality, when *chit* merges with *sat* and the person attains states of *samadhi*, sexuality and the need for food dissolve. This is a state of bliss. We should not compare that with the mundane existence of an average human being, an ordinary sexual being. Hence, lack of sexuality is something I never buy, when people boast about their detachment. Often, these are the very people who scandalise other people, because what they could not achieve is sour for them in every way and jealousy haunts them.

I do not believe that '*MA*' is bound by any of the above two. Hours of sitting at one place without food definitely signifies an altered state of consciousness. Who can achieve such a feat without a no-mind state? I cannot buy the idea that '*MA*' is a sexual being. She has a human body. In case she is, then it is none of our business. She has the right to privacy just like any of us. She has the freedom and eligibility as an Indian citizen to lead her life, within the boundaries of the laws of India.

Again, I insist that forced sex, rape and molestation should be reported to authorities as and when it happens, and not fifteen years later through a book. This is a big disfavour to fellow Saints or sadhus, because if it is true, within fifteen years, so many more could have been affected. In this context, please also remember that sexual frustration leads to aggression. Many people who embrace the life of renunciation have arrived there out of tragedies or insecurities, and not because of a genuine desire to merge with God. God-consciousness is not a choice. It is a state. It has to happen through nullification. It cannot be forced. God realisation is a happening.

Suppression, oppression, or masking of inherent traits never help actualisation; on the contrary, it takes one away from the track completely. Even if we are in a marketplace, or if we are a non-renunciate as per the regular norms, God consciousness can happen at any time for sure. It does not matter whether you are a family person, whether you are having sex or not. So, when sexuality is suppressed due to the pressure of the robe or renunciation, aggression can happen. Whatever is suppressed will erupt sooner or later. Hence, either obtain gratification at

the right time, in the right way, or increase awareness to sur-
pass bodily needs by withdrawing the senses from objects of
sensuality. This is easier when a person chooses no contact with
any being of its kind.

Perfect renunciation! When a Saint is constantly interacting
with the sundry people of society who carry various emotions,
fears, desires, and perceptions as well as sexuality, it is very likely that control of the senses can become a big problem. Hence I
suggest that consensual sex should be fine because it is a choice
that the person makes. Non-consensual is definitely unacceptable and should be condemned. Once again, I fail to see why
an event is not conveyed as and when it happens. Why does
one have to wait all these years, as is the case for the author of
the book, to come out with such revelations, fifteen years after abandoning *her ashram*? There could be a conspiracy. There
could be vested interests. This is my reading.

I personally feel that each being that walks on Earth deserves to have privacy. It does not matter whether he is a bird,
animal or a human being. It does not matter whether he or
she is a Saint, businessman, celebrity, public figure, or a person among thousands of others. Everyone has a personal constitution, character, needs and desires, apart from the generic
ones such as food, sleep, toilet, and sex. I believe that we should
allow this privacy to all individuals. Why are we haunting celebrities? Why can't we accept their teachings instead of their
bedroom stories? Bedroom stories never elevate anyone's consciousness. They only tickle or rather contaminate one's inner
space.

The teachings though could be quite elevating and purgator-
ial. Please have a conscious thought about this. Do not get carried away with scandals or others' opinions. Just ensure you remain objective at all times and keep asking the question – "Do
we have the right to criticise another at all?" Certainly, raise
your voice against injustice and violence, but only do so with

first-hand confirmation, not because of others' words or opinions. We may have tremendous regrets about it in the future.

Recently, some people who came to see me asked my opinion about the life of Jesus. Questions asked included: "Did he
survive the cross? Did he live the rest of his life in India? Did he
have a child with Mary Magdalene?" My answer was straight
and simple. "I do not know and I do not care." Jesus' public life
ended with the cross. As far as the world is concerned, there
ended his physical relevance. If he lived beyond the crucifixion,
it has no value for us, as his public life ended with the cross. His
teachings survived through his followers. This is the relevance
that he left behind.

We need to be concerned only about that. Seekers should
concentrate only on the teachings of the *Guru* for their personal growth. We have got Jesus' teachings through the mouth
or interpretation of his disciples, those who walked with him.
Nobody told any further stories of his life after his crucifixion
or about his further life. We should stick to the relevance of a
Saint. I look at life in terms of effective years and non-effective
years. Effective years are those when the Saint was contributing
to the world with what he had, the non-effective years (as far as
the world is concerned) are the ones which the Saint spent for
himself. So, if we stick to this method, we shall remain reasonably clear and also pure inside always.

Furthermore, why would I care if Jesus had sex with Mary?
How does that help our spiritual growth? I would like to think
of it in this way. First of all, it is no big deal as it would have
been consensual sex. Secondly, if it happened, it would have
been for the sake of fulfilment as unfulfilled desires become fuel
for another life. Hence, it would be better to complete and exit
from this life. So, before we judge another, we should look within. Thirdly, does this information help us today in any way? Is
it elevating our consciousness at all? Or are we just trying to
find excuses for our own fickle desires or character deficien-

cies? Hence, I would urge the reader to marry the teachings and not the *Guru*. Use the teachings for one's own higher evolution and not to choose for intellectual comparisons and eventual judgment.

If Lord Krishna was living today, he would be talked about more because of scandals rather than his Bhagavad Gita. His relationship with Radha alone is enough. Apparently, Radha was already married when Krishna used to visit Barsana, which was a few kilometres away from Vrindavan, under the pretext of grazing cows, to see her. Barsana was her husband's house. Today, we worship Radha and Krishna. We celebrate their romance. His legitimate wives such as Rukmini and Satyabhama are not worshipped as much as Radha is. When we can accept this, why then are we so fascinated about a holy mother's private life?

I am confident that a Saint of *her* stature is well beyond all the needs of the body. It is obvious. However, society loves scandals, especially sex scandals. Why are sex scandals so important and how do they sell so much? Because of generations of sex starvation and pseudo morality. In a sex-starved world controlled by pseudo morality, the best tool for character assassination is a sex scandal. The media loves it because sleaze gets maximum viewership. The very rich and the very poor are immune to it. They do what they like and let the winds of morality blow wherever with their money or lack of it.

Lack of money gives freedom as there is nothing to lose, just as having money also gives freedom because you can buy almost anything with it, including respect in the society. Actually speaking, it is a waste of time. As I said earlier, aggression which becomes oppression for some, should be controlled by the law. Otherwise, we should definitely respect the privacy of every person. The more suppressed we are, the more aggressive we become within. This will take us further away from a peaceful existence.

Stature of a Saint

We create our realities. Whatever we fear will appear in our lives. Whatever we love can also be ours, if the intensity is right. Yet, what we fear has a better chance of manifesting in our lives because the mind nurtures the negative more than the positive. This only pertains to human beings because our acceptance level of reality and life is much less than the beings of other species. If we have experienced certain realities in our life which did not lead us to a happy state, it is because of such trapped fears and insecurities or stored negative emotions. We should not blame others for our predicament, if we understand how the law of *karma* works. Moreover, most people cannot change, or evolve into the higher in one lifetime. Metamorphosis is a process. It takes lifetimes of trials and errors to finally catch the ultimate Truth from a quagmire of relative truths.

Look at the total population of the world. Let us take seven billion people and try to classify them for understanding's sake. Please understand that this classification is generic and there could be exceptions and mixtures. We look at people in terms of their orientation, such as physical, emotional, intellectual, spiritual, and beyond everything. There could be physical, physical-emotional, emotional-intellectual etc. Hence, please consider this generic dissection only as a guideline to understand a point.

At least thirty-five per cent of the people of the world are 'physical' oriented. They indulge in physical, sensory gratification and lead a life of momentary pleasures. Another thirty per cent live in the emotional plane. They are more inclined to emotional gratification, gossip, sleaze, anxieties, fears so on and so forth. They live with their mind, totally controlled by the mind. These are the people who are hooked on to soap operas which churn out nothing but emotions and related suffering. These people always make room for gossip and emotional negativity.

They always react to life and call themselves victims of circumstances. They are more prone to psychological disorders.

About twenty per cent of the total population lives in the intellectual plane. Their gratification is through their intellect. They do not have much to do with physical or emotional gratification. The so-called intellectuals such as thinkers, planners, strategists, scientists and all other intellectuals fit into this category. They consume knowledge, as well as many other intellectual methods of self-gratification. They usually feel much more superior to the other categories, ignorant of the fact that the concepts they are consuming are binding them eternally.

Many of them are self-centred and even cut off from society. Many of them do not care for other beings' pain or suffering. Many churn out theories using their brain, which pushes development, but not always real progress. Most creations add material comforts at the cost of alienation from nature, which directly affects every aspect of immunity that protects physical and psychological existence on Earth. Many of the medicines and gadgets that man has made have harmed mankind. Many creations of man have destroyed the Earth. Many of them are non-productive too. They just live in their own cloisters.

About ten per cent of the population can be considered as spiritual. They are exploring spirituality and this interests them a lot. But, they are still only exploring. Many become escapists in the name of spirituality. Many fall into depression mode and either withdraw, or repeat the same thing over and over again, without much benefit to themselves or others. Many do not know what they are looking for and, of course, where to find it. Many fall into the traps of rituals, predatory religions and cults.

The remaining five per cent actually attain the highest, beyond the duality of existence. The rest fall either backwards or forwards. All the physical, emotional, as well as intellectual members, are also exploring the unknown through spirituality. However, they have limitations. In the case of the physical, it would be transactional worship for the sake of some bene-fit from God, with complete non-understanding. Most of the 'physical' people queue up in front of temples and at the door-steps of astrologers to pacify their insecurities.

Emotionally oriented people will either have blind faith rooted in devotion or follow others blindly. Emotion clarified is devotion, which can take one to the ultimate merger. Very few attain the capacity for total surrender and acceptance of everything that happens in their life with total willingness, en-durance and non-resistance as the gift of God. This level is achieved through higher awareness, which is achieved by con-stant contemplation on the energy that runs our system, which is also called God. The power of all the great Saints has been this surrender and acceptance with no doubts about them-selves, their path, their *Guru* and their destination. This is not easy to come to.

The intellectual path is even more difficult because those on that path need reasoning for everything, which slows them down tremendously. They face duality much more than any-body. Doubts and analysis plague them often. Acceptance is less in them. They try to understand the workings of the sub-tle through their gross intellect. This is as tedious as making a camel cross through the eye of a needle. The spiritual types have actually crossed over many barriers, such as the physical, emotional, and intellectual walls, and they are determined to cross over to the realms of the subtle. However, they could also be controlled by their egos and sense of achievement, just like their cousins of other categories.

Ego lurks in every state. It appears and disappears with-out calling. Ego is a permanent ingredient of human existence. Thus, out of the ten per cent spiritually inclined, five per cent actually attain the highest. Thus is the case of the spiritual jour-ney. It is not easy. All paths are good. All paths run parallel to the same destination. So, there is no need to worry whether a path is right or wrong or whether a *Guru* is good or bad. All that liberates you time and again is good for you. All that liberates you from each level and leaves you liberated is good for you. Anything that binds you is bad for you, irrespective of whether it is a person, a place, a situation, or an action. You are born free and should die free.

Terrestrial existence is temporary. You cannot be bound here. The body is borrowed from the earth for the sake of experiencing Earth, just like you hire a rent-a-car when you go to a new city to travel through the city and do your errands. In our case, the soul has borrowed this body for this journey on Earth. *Karma* is the agenda for the journey. Senses, mind, ego, and intellect are the operating tools or navigation guides. The body must be given back when the job is over. So, living a liberated existence here and now is very important.

Wasting time on the bed-time stories of other people has no value in our journey. All have such stories. There is darkness in every corridor. There is good and bad in everyone. Only those who have never sinned have the eligibility to throw stones, and those who have never sinned will never throw stones either, because they know very well that throwing stones at anything or anybody will pull them down for sure, and one *karmic* being has no right to judge another.

I read that '*MA*' herself responded to the criticisms against herself and her organisation. She said three things in very polite and matter-of-fact language:

"Many children come to me with many expectations, large expectations. When these are not fulfilled, they turn around and criticise or scandalise. Children should not become angry like this. Anger is definitely a weakness. It is negative and can pull a person to the depths of negativity. Patience is strength. Children should exercise patience and not negative emotions.

'*MA*' is an open book. Our ashram is also an open book. Any financial transaction happening here is recorded and filed with the government. Anyone who has a doubt can verify it anytime. I never call people or ask people for favours. I have never asked anyone to come to me and serve me. All have come voluntarily. In the same way, all have the freedom to leave too. Why do you complain?"

This shows the stature of '*MA*'. Absolutely calm amidst a storm! This shows the stature of the individual. Totally unaffected and unperturbed! This also means that she is innocent. If there was any speck of pollution, anxiety or fear, it would have been visible. She is not a politician to mask all crimes with expertise, and still go to the people asking to be elected to power again, as if nothing had ever happened. The calm declares her purity.

Again, it would be a grave mistake to assess the stature of a Saint by the yardsticks of his or her disciples. Usually, very few disciples could rise up to the stature of their Master to receive the mantle from him or her. They will all be operating in different levels of consciousness. So, never measure the stature of a *Guru* by looking at his disciples. The *Guru* has accomplished the highest.

Disciples are with the *Guru* because they are aspiring to reach the status of their *Guru*, if not the stature. So, they cannot be considered the same. Status can be bought with money. Stature has to be earned. Stature is a state that cannot be bought. It takes a lot of effort to become totally detached. When a person is totally detached, whether he drinks alcohol or smokes (like Shankar Maharaj, Shirdi Sai Baba), sleeps with women, or visits brothels, it does not make any difference in their still state of mind.

Stillness can never be disturbed by an activity once the Saint attains it. The common man cannot understand the freedom that stillness of the mind or the mind-less state provides. They judge based on expressions and they fail to touch the real because of their mental blocks. Not being able to touch the real while existing is one of the real tragedies of a terrestrial existence.

Sometimes the Saint observes silence amidst the storm of scandals. This is not because of his inability to speak out. This is because he is not pressured to speak. He is objective. He speaks only when he has to. He will not counter anyone's emotions because he has nothing to do with it. Mind is still. Often, it so happens that the Saints foresee the calamity and also use it to shake the tree of their own setup.

This could help them shed many dry leaves which do not help the tree. This will also help shed the *tamas* (inertia) among their disciples and swing them into positive action. So, silence could be because of foresight and have a positive purpose. A scandal always works as a positive filter. It filters away the feeble, unsure, or fickle and retains those who are truly connected. Hence a scandal is a good idea as a filter.

True Saints are soft targets in the gross world. They are usually defenceless. Many of those who have money, power, position, and contacts get away with anything. However, there are those to whom money flows because of their sheer stature and subtlety. They will never use their position, power, money, or connections to save themselves. They will never manipulate minds. They are selfless. They are immortal while in the body and keep the body only out of compassion towards their followers.

The gross world which cannot see the subtlety of a Saint always pumps bullets of scandals into their defenceless lives. The Saint loses nothing. He was never bothered about his body anyway. He would just leave the body behind and expand into the ever present super expanded consciousness well beyond the body. The loss is for the world. Every generation has had many soft targets like this through the history of mankind.

Established religions, priests and preachers with acquired knowledge always become terribly insecure about a true Saint who is connected to the Source. They manipulate minds against the true Saint. The Saint does nothing to protect himself. He has completely surrendered to the will of the universe, a *dharmic* existence, almost like a being in the wild. From birth until death, they are surrendered to the will of nature. They cannot manipulate, accumulate, store, or be greedy. They consume only what is essential for them. Even if there is excess or abundance of anything, it is distributed evenly for the needy. They only know how to give. They give all that they have.

It increases insecurity in the minds of the established priests and religious heads who sow fear to harvest people. Fear conquers minds much more easily than love. It is a very effective tool. They use the people to secure their own future, ensure power and maintain supremacy. A true Saint has nothing to do with these. They are crucified, as they are innocent, soft targets, and since sex scandals get maximum media attention as well as audience, they are the best ammunition against an unarmed Saint. If you study the history of most of the scandals, you will see the thread of this phenomenon deeply embedded in every incident.

If expectations are not fulfilled, it leads to anger. Anger leads to the need for justification. Justification demands the need for companionship or isolation. In order to avoid guilt, people make themselves believe or convince themselves that what they thought, spoke and did was the right thing and they deserve attention from others. They become heavily insecure with their own proposition. Some people (usually of the same feather) will buy their story, sympathise with them and give them company. Some will avoid them. These are all aspects of the play or *Maya* or relative Truth.

Truth will always shine forth even if the clouds of doubts obscure the Truth temporarily. Be aware of it and stay clear. No true *Guru* who is connected to the Source needs anyone or any kind of support. They are in the marketplace out of compassion for humankind as well as other beings. They are walking reminders for you as to who you really are. They represent the state which is your destination. You need them to be a road sign or a reminder to reach their stature. Be reasonable with yourself.

By scandalising a *Guru*, you are destroying your own chance for the highest. This is because you are destroying the *Guru* principle (*Guru Tattva*) which you carry within yourself. You are free to be with any *Guru* and you are also free to be away from them too. However, let your detachment from the *Guru* arise because of your accomplishment in terms of a higher state, not because you have differences in opinions, which is essentially a mind factor. If you want to know the stature of your *Guru*, you need to go beyond your mind.

From Separation to Oneness

It is important to respect every individual at every time, even if the person is harmful to society. If a person is harmful, use the law of the land to deal with it and save society. We should never judge or condemn another. This will affect us more than the other. When poison for the arrow is manufactured in your house, remember, your house will have more poison than what the tip of the arrow carries to others. Your inner space should remain pure. Using that state of purity, observe the contributions delivered by the Saint to the world.

In the case of '*MA*', how many people has she touched in this lifetime! How many have been given hope and solace by '*MA*'! How many have been healed! How many people attained fulfilment! How many charity activities! How many acts of kindness! How many beautiful instances of guidance and teachings! This is what we should cherish. This is what we should nurture. We should look at the value of a Saint who lives with people in society primarily from two aspects – A. The clarity in her teachings. B. The charity that she does. In short – The relevance! The physical and spiritual relevance. Let us never ignore that.

A request to all those who talk ill of '*MA*' or to all the people who talk badly about Saints in general: please check how their life has added value to the world! How many people have been benefited! It is easy to live and die in one's own cubicle of personal agendas, selfish pleasures, ownership, possessiveness, concepts, fears, personal family-ship, happiness and sorrows. When you decide to live your freedom, there is bound to be opposition. Those who cannot walk the path or those who cannot understand the path will certainly create roadblocks. Do we have to budge? Do we have to change tracks?

Live your own Truth and discard the borrowed relative truths. Your experience and your Truth have much more value in your life than others' opinions. If you clearly understand that, it would be a great favour that you would be doing to yourself. In the path of dissolution, in the very end, when the disciple merges with the consciousness of the *Guru*, every relationship ends. There is no duality to maintain a relationship. There will be no *Guru* or disciple. However, cutting the relationship before total dissolution, would be a terrible mistake as well as a tragedy for the seeker, even though it never affects any *Guru*.

In the beginning of the journey, a disciple will only see the superficial differences. It takes a lot of time and effort to see the unity of consciousness. There should be patience, perseverance, conviction, and commitment. Otherwise, disciples will get stuck with the superficial. The problem with the superficial is that it only provides comparisons, infatuations and eventual disassociation, if not depression. The agony of separation is usually terrible in the beginning. But, as the disciple comes closer and closer to the *Guru's* consciousness, beyond the facade of superficial expressions and image, the pain slowly gets converted into bliss.

Finally, when the merger of consciousness happens, there is only bliss, oneness. There is no separation, nor the related confusion. So, in the end, even the image, words, and expressions will dissolve when you become the *Guru*'s consciousness. This is what we call totality or complete liberation. Here, by the word '*Guru*', I mean One who is connected to the source, not one who is imparting acquired knowledge. Be aware of that.

In the beginning of the journey, there are only differences. The mind only recognises the differences, the comparisons, and the superficial. When the disciple gradually approaches the unity of consciousness, the mind is forced to dissolve. The mind must dissolve to experience unity of consciousness. A struggle happens – often a bitter struggle, a war. The mind brings forth everything that could create alienation. This is a very confusing time. The mind asks you to run away and save yourself. The mind objects to the idea of the merger of consciousness and counters it with deep-rooted fears such as death, destruction, wrong paths, wrong *Gurus*, fears of the unknown, etc.

The real war is between the Truth and illusion, or between the soul and the mind. The mind likes to keep its comfort zones. The mind likes to keep its identities. The soul wants liberation from the illusory existence. Illusions capture us more than the soul. The soul exists in a liberated state always, which we will only know when we touch or feel the soul. Illusions keep us blinded from the Truth. The *Guru* represents the Truth. The fears, doubts and illusions that the mind carries immerse the consciousness of the *Guru* in delusion, by projecting the superficial aspects such as the form and habits of the *Guru*.

This is why we discuss the superficial aspects of a *Guru* rather than his or her teachings and guidance. We are looking at the disparities or differences much more than the unity in consciousness. We are more connected to the terrestrial aspects of a living *Guru*, including his wealth, sexuality, attire, mannerisms etc., rather than the projection of the supreme consciousness or his connection to the source that actually made him *Guru* material. Masters, who are connected to the source, will shine. No cloud can permanently take away the glory of the sun!

Why are we so bound by time and differences? It is because we are identifying and operating in time zones and not absolute-ness. The body has a duration and that duration is measured in time. Having a body keeps us hooked to time. Hence it is essential to search for and understand the timeless in us. The timeless is our real state. That which is absolute in us is what we are, and not the body which is bound by time. The search begins in the mind and ends in the mind-less state.

The very material that we use our mind to explore can only be understood when the mind is absent. This is something which every seeker should understand. Mind is the barrier between man and the absolute. Mind includes ego and intellect too. When we merge with the absolute, there is no need for the mind because there is nothing apart from you. You have nothing more to 'know' or 'understand'. You are that! *Tat tvam asi.* So, who is afraid of the singular Truth? Who is afraid of the Truth at all? Your mind. You are not your mind. Be aware of that.

Appreciate their Love and Care

Why do we need the proximity of great Saints at all? Why do we crave it? The reason is that they represent the peace that has been eluding our lives since lifetimes. They represent our original state. They represent what we could be or what we are already, which our mind has hidden from us for so long. If the mind gets connected to a *Guru* either due to infatuation or helplessness, the relationship cannot mature into unity of consciousness. When you are unable to cross the first mile of your road home, how will you ever reach your bed to rest upon?

The proximity of the *Guru* should be reflected in you as your inner stillness, peace, strength, resolution, so on and so forth. Usually, a true *Guru* will reflect your own state. Their reflection of anger mirrors your pent-up anger; their overflowing love reflects your bottled up or unfulfilled love. They could even reflect your sexuality, hunger, and all other personality traits. When the *Guru* operates in unity consciousness, he or she becomes what appears before them, because they have already dissolved their mind and just honestly reflect what you are to yourself!

This understanding would help a seeker when they approach a *Guru*, provided they stop measuring their *Guru* using their mind, including ego and intellect. The proximity of great Saints is a constant warning, a constant reflection, constant removal of personality traits, and also constant burning and churning of blocking negativities that distract one in the path of God. Many people prefer a *Guru* who is not in his/her body because they cannot handle the personality of the living *Guru* or they get terribly disillusioned by the living *Guru*'s personality traits.

The dead Master is easier because what is in your mind about him is your reality. What he was or what he could have possibly done if alive does not matter anymore. The teachings, often expressed through others and not directly by the Master himself, and their personal interpretation can easily provide a comfort zone for the confused seeker. They cannot think of changes within themselves. They would rather change the *Guru*! A living *Guru* eats, drinks, sleeps like any other man. A living *Guru* may wake you up, even rudely, from your pretensions and fears. If this is a problem, I would suggest staying away from a living *Guru*.

True *Gurus* are honesty incarnate. They only want the best for their disciples. Often, the disciples are not ready for the best. What you already are, you do not know. The mind has kept you disillusioned. When the mask of the mind is removed, you will know what you already are, and the difference between what you 'thought' about yourself and what you actually are! Huge difference! Huge awakening! Here, the Master is a road sign. He or she just guides as per your path. He never intrudes, yet will slap your hand when you are indulging in anything that prevents your progress in the path, whether your mind likes it or not. Comparing a true Master, who has dissolved his mind, to a seeker operating a hundred per cent from his mind, is an absolutely wasted exercise.

Hence, spirituality needs acceptance and spontaneity. It needs understanding. In summary, live and let live. If crimes are committed by someone, or by a group, inform the legal authorities. Always exercise restraint and approach everything with caution and not reaction. Respond spontaneously and do not react violently.

All that any Saint or Master who is connected to the Source does is accept support (including monetary) from those who can afford it, and then pass it on to cater for those who cannot afford it. They are creating a balance in society. They are diluting the imbalance between the rich and the poor. They lead by example. When such a Saint's living time becomes more valuable and they are provided with comforts to maintain them, this is only natural. When their horizon increases and more are benefited by their presence, they will have to do more to make themselves available to the world, irrespective of whether it is a fast car or a private jet.

Everything depends on the value they add to society. It applies to every human being and not only a Saint. A CEO of a conglomerate will have to use sophisticated gadgets to run his empire. If a person who runs a small unit envies him and suggests that he should be simpler, it is absolute ignorance. Likewise, money and wealth come to a Saint as per the relevance of the Saint to the world. However, they use it to give back more to the world. They hardly use anything for themselves because their terrestrial needs are minimal. This enhances their compassion and makes it more effective. We must appreciate their love and care and not be jealous of their facilities.

As per requirements, facilities will happen. It is absolutely right to be contemporary and use all the contemporary gadgets, especially if the mission involves the public or the world. If the Saint is sitting in the quiet of a cave or mountain, none of these matter anyway. The contemporary Saint may not even be demanding it from anyone. It comes to them, as I stated earlier: they are the people who could have anything, but need nothing. They will never be understood in two-dimensional class divides such as haves and have nots. This is the simple Truth of existence.

'MA', from what I have understood, single handedly supported almost 30,000 students after the tsunami in Japan. She is said to have contributed more than what the UN or anyone did post-tsunami in Indonesia. She built one billion rupees worth of houses for tsunami victims in India, which no organisation, politician, spiritual leader, political party, or government did. She is definitely using her wealth for good causes. Which politician who is hoarding public funds have we heard of doing anything close to what 'MA' has done for the world? Do they even share a cup of tea with a poor person? What are you complaining about? What right does anyone have to complain about 'MA'? What are you worried about? What are you afraid of? Her sheer stature is attracting people to her. No amount of envy can change that.

Finally, "The evil that men do lives after them; The good is oft interred with their bones." (William Shakespeare; Julius Caesar, Act 3, Scene 2) All the good things a man does are easily forgotten. Only the wrongs are spoken about! This is true through time since the history of mankind. We are eternal gossip mongers, one way or the other. This is why we are more interested in Jesus' sex life than his glorious teachings. This is why we are more interested in the private lives of all the public figures. This is why sleaze sells. We have always been like this. We bury a thousand good things that a man did for the world along with his body, and talk about a few follies or acts of frailty through time.

I was told that one channel alone used three hundred and eighty four hours to telecast the news when the Shankaracharya of Kanchi was arrested. The same channel aired the news of his acquittal for three minutes! This is just an example of how negativity sells. Sleaze has its evergreen market. Buying into gossip, and ignoring our experience, is an absolutely useless exercise. Cherish the acts of glory and discard the acts of negativity.

If a person is harmful to society, pass him or her on to the hands of the law with evidence. There need be no emotions about it. Those who ate salt must drink water. There should not be any compromise. Character assassination is the sign of the weak and is a cowardly act. If there is disagreement, it should be discussed face to face and dissolved in good time, because our inner space should always remain clean and uncontaminated as we walk towards the path of total liberation. It is easy to contaminate the inner space, and difficult to clean it. Beware.

Stay with the Truth

An old Saint conveyed a message to me through a friend who visited him. The message is, "M, you know the Truth and you are not afraid to tell it. This will make some people uncomfortable. Some egos will be hurt. Some may leave you. This is fine. This is their loss. However, tell the Truth anyway because your path is that of purity. There cannot be any pretensions here." This sums up my existence in a way. Many times, I have experienced alienation because I chose to stay with the Truth and articulate it without dilution.

In the path of liberation, one has to stay with the Truth, or else decay will happen. Decay of character leads to decay of conscience. There is no harm in performing a difficult task (difficult for the mind and ego) for the general good of the people or the world. If the intentions are pure, even if alienation happens, one should go ahead. If intentions are of a selfish nature, decay must happen. Truth is often bitter. In today's world, we prefer to hide our head like ostriches in the sand called the internet, and pretend that we are fine in the virtual world.

We post quotes of others and post pictures of ourselves and our families and indirectly tell the world, "I do not care about the world. Only I and my family exist," or "I am also as knowledgeable as you will accept one to be. I am not a lesser being." Clear signs of insecurity, self-centredness, ignorance, *tamas*!

We choose to hide our own personal experiences, personal truths and conform ourselves to the socially accepted relative truths and make ourselves and others believe in our pretensions. This hinders our progress. We hate to accept bitter Truth and we tend to remove true friends who articulate Truth from our friends' list. When we cannot see reality, we blame others for our incapacity! We deny the miracles of our existence because of our incapacity to accept them. We even deny God at times, because we cannot comprehend God.

When man becomes so secluded, the world, which is like a mirror, ignores him and leaves him alone. When calamities happen in his household due to stagnation and isolation, or being in the self-created comfort zone of the artificial world for too long, or because of losing touch with reality or even because of acquired decay and *tamas*, one witnesses himself in the depth of despair and depression. A professional psychologist whom I met in an airport lounge told me, "Business is good. Thanks to the internet. Disillusionment is very high. The youth have lost touch with reality and pretend that nothing exists beyond the virtual world, and when reality strikes hard and they cannot handle the Truth, they come to me." This sums up today's life and lifestyle.

There is no hope for salvation here. No salvation because that is the reality that they chose to experience. They never listened to the cry of the world outside themselves. They never even listened to the cry of their own kin, because they were so overwhelmingly engrossed in virtual realities and pretended lifestyles. If you tell them the Truth, they will destroy you, they will spit venom.

They never do anything to expand their consciousness, to evolve, to touch the Truth. They never do anything to embrace the world with selflessness, unconditional love. Even if they do something in the outside world, it is because of their inherent insecurity and as an attempt to safeguard themselves from rainy days. They never realise that they lost their sunshine long ago. They hate the Truth. Instead, they choose a shrunken world of expectations and pretensions. Life becomes perpetual agony. They become useless to the world.

I urge you to use this blessed life of yours to elevate yourself to the highest. Take care of your family; you must. However, also take care of the world the way you can. I wish you fulfilment. May your life be truly complete.

CHAPTER 4:

It's time to change

In the Name of the Lord?

How many children became orphans in the last seven days! How many children died? How many people lost everything? Who will answer? In whose name is this happening? Land? Power? Politics? Supremacy? When will man understand? Gaza is burning. The world's conscience is burning, even if we try our best to ignore it. Whether it is Gaza or any other country, conscience must get burnt where beings are bound or murdered.

Awareness is the key. An eye for an eye will leave the whole world blind. These are not my words. This is a famous Truth. There is no way we can buy justice through wars. One man's gain is always another man's loss. When will we understand that? Our soul cannot be owned by anybody. Likewise, Earth cannot be owned by any being. It can only be used for a certain period of time. What is expected during this time is peaceful co-existence.

Earth cannot be owned by anyone. Earth is just a platform. Temporary possessions give the illusion of ownership. Transactions on paper make us feel proud and money's worth. However, when we die, we leave the paper and the property behind. Who owns Earth?

Who will answer for the death and destruction that takes place in the name of land, religion, and politics? All people are the same. All countries are the same. None is higher or lower. None have the right to oppress or suppress another. Life must continue. When we walk on the blood-paved paths of existence, our feet must hurt. Tons of accumulated atrocities and murders have weakened the natural vibration of Earth and made the planet less and less habitable.

When emotions are ruling, wars are inevitable. Expect the backlash. A hit on the conscience causes guilt. Guilt travels through time and lives. When collective guilt takes over, destruction takes place. We may feel lucky to have shed the body earlier, before the backlash expressed itself fully. However, we may either come back, or our generations to come will curse the past generations for having taken the soul out of Earth, for killing the 'life' of Earth. None can escape the fruits of their action. This is an eternal Truth. To turn a blind eye towards a crime is equal to committing it.

We are too selfish. We only like to sit back in the virtual world, looking at the images of dead women and children on Facebook, and hitting 'like' in support of the cause, irrespective of whether it is towards or against. We live in an artificial world of make-believe and deceive ourselves into believing that everything is good outside and within our own household. The children who are brought up completely in this virtual world are total misfits in the world outside. Everything happens for them in the virtual world and they could not care less about other people's suffering. We never consider even once that inertia has indeed left us totally bound and helpless. The only parts of the body that actually move are the fingers which click 'like' on Facebook.

Now, I know that even these words here are useless. I know because it is not possible for individual consciousness to fight against the gross and ugly collective consciousness, hell-bound for destruction and death. It is useless, because the comfort zone-oriented man will just consider any positive words as too tall an order, and discard any potential for collective action. I know very well that even if a thousand of us join hands against human atrocities, we will all be crushed mercilessly. The only permanent solution is increased awareness and a different system of education.

Motherhood should happen in a more profound way. No mother would order the killing of any children. It has always been man. Love should prevail through motherliness.

Now, this is meant as food for thought. I am with the suffering and helpless. I love those who help heal even a small wound of the body or mind. I always hope that peace will prevail. Again, the collective consciousness is too strong to grow any seeds of sensitiveness. Yet, let us not give up hope. Let us grow seeds in our own garden and distribute selflessly to others' gardens too.

Children of Vipers

Mankind has expressed cruelty towards its own kind and all other species for generations. Hence the Bible said, "You children of vipers, repent".

"You brood of vipers, how can you who are evil say anything good? For out of the overflow of the heart, the mouth speaks." Mathew. "John said to the crowds coming out to be baptized by him, You brood of vipers! Who warned you to flee from the coming wrath?"

"You serpents, you offspring of vipers, how will you escape the judgment of Gehenna?"

This question still stands today. Mankind continues to create its own hell. How can meditations, *Shaktipat* and proximity of Masters help if you keep your inner world contaminated? Forgiving is important and repentance is even more important.

A few weeks ago, a man called me and apologised for spreading rumours, stories created in bad taste about me, which he knew very well were not true. He did it out of spite. I told him, "I do not feel anything because of your words and action. But, how do you feel? If you truly repent your action, if you really mean to apologise, call up all the people whose minds you have contaminated, tell them you were wrong and remove their wrong understanding. If you can do that, repentance is complete. If not, handle the wrath of your own words and action. Nobody can help you. I may pardon you. However, you will not pardon yourself."

Helping the helpless in any way possible is a sign of repentance, feeding the poor and the hungry beings of Earth etc., are always good actions. Selfless actions help purification. It is time to unhook from an unholy lifestyle. It is time to clean up our closet and keep our insides tidy and clean. This is a wake-up call.

Section 3:

...UNTIL THE GURU...

~~~~~~~~~~

Being in one path, being with one guide, one systematic practice with concentration, conviction and discipline is very important for any seeker of Truth. Those who put their legs in different boats eventually fall into the water.

CHAPTER 1:

The path and the tradition

The Right Path

The Essence of Yoga

We know that yoga means to unite. Hence, whatever unites man to the Supreme Consciousness can be called yoga. In other words, yoga has no boundaries or barriers. Yoga essentially subscribes to the very nature of man. Yoga unites, or whatever is uniting, is yoga, irrespective of the nature of every being.

There are various paths – service to humanity, devotion towards an object of power or God, paths of contemplation and meditation, the path of conscious renunciation, the path of shedding the aspects of the mind, the path of the breath, path of silence, the path of nurturing awareness, the yoga of action, the yoga of inaction, the yoga of restraint, and so on. All these paths are aspects of yoga and aim to dissolve the limited mind into the Supreme Consciousness.

Each path has potential. Each path is relevant to someone. How to choose the path? Simple – It is the path that chooses you, based on your nature. What makes you connect easily is the right path for you. What feels comfortable to practice will work for you. What adds stress is not your path. This is the problem that man faces when he follows others' opinions. Others cannot understand your nature completely. Only you can experience your nature based on what suits you.

The nature of a being is not always clearly understood by one, and it depends on likes and dislikes to determine one's nature, orientation, and so on. Nature is formed out of character traits. Nature represents the true constitution of the individual. One can be aggressive, passive, silent, loud, creative, destructive, optimistic, pessimistic, kind, cruel, sadistic, cynical, compassionate, loving, etc. Nature is always a mixture of many aspects as well. Nature can also be situational.

Having understood that, it must be clearly understood that a path suitable for one may not appeal to another. Hence, it is important to walk one's path towards liberation based on instinct, comfort, do-ability, inclination, and most importantly, nature. Therefore, apart from the royal path (Raja Yoga), the path of knowledge, path of devotion and path of liberating action, are clearly defined in our ancient scriptures. Everything suits somebody.

The very reason for all the paths and all the religions which represent the different paths, is man's quest for liberation. Liberation is what the soul craves. Liberation from birth and death! Liberation from all the lower frequencies of existence such as anger, hatred, jealousy, revenge, and the inclination to hurt others for the sake of positions, possessions, and possessiveness. Every aspect of lower frequency binds man to Earth and repeats his existence through many bodies, as well as time and space.

When man awakened to this fact, he chose to seek liberation. Liberation does not come easily. Every desire must dissolve, and the mind should become still or thought-free, before a man can raise his awareness to that of universal awareness.

The craving of the trapped soul, which repeatedly took birth on Earth for the sake of gratification, pushes the mind towards liberation. Expressions in the form of spirituality – spiritual seekers, Masters, *Gurus* and religions – are all the visible expressions of this craving of the soul for liberation. In this craving, whatever unites man to the path of liberation is called yoga. Thus, yoga unites oneself to one's self as well as uniting one's self to the Universal Self. One's nature is the gateway to one's self, while one's self itself, is the gateway to the Supreme Self.

Follow the Path That Suits You

Many people are image-oriented. They will only accept messages that they hear from the person or mouth that they are used to. They shut their minds off any new person or image. This is human nature. Let us not blame them or force them. They can only accept the path that suits them. We should never force anyone into any spiritual practice. We should not force ourselves, either. Just follow the path, teachings or *Guru* that suits you. Whatever we force eventually becomes a burden to us. Be spontaneous and flexible. The supple tree can survive any storm of life. Thus, images do not matter, including my image. Only consciousness is real. That is permanent.

Images will come and go. All live images have a prescribed longevity. Even this body will go sooner or later. Please do not be attached to images or be affected by them. Just stay with your Truth, your soul – which is your personal *Guru*, and your path towards liberation. All true Masters rendered the same Truth – *Tat Twam Asi* (you are That). You are the universe. You are the creator too. There is nobody higher or lower. All are children of the One Consciousness. All are One. Plants, animals, birds and humans. All are expressions of One entity, the Supreme Father – *Parabrahma*. All are His children.

Brahma, Vishnu, and Shiva are all aspects of the same God Supreme. They represent three different aspects of existence. Jesus and Buddha are One. Krishna and Rama are One. Zoroaster and Mahavir are One. *Parabrahma*, Father and *Allah* are

One. You and I are One. Beyond every form is the One God. Just like you can only wear a dress that suits you, so too your chosen path should be suitable for you. Then the destination is reachable. Otherwise, detours are inevitable.

✤ **Question:** Many paths, which one to choose?

Mohanji: Simple. The path that is in front of you. You cannot choose anything else (any other path).

The right path is a relative term. It is individualistic. Every *karmic* being must accomplish all that they came for, before they can liberate themselves from the cycle of birth and death. Thus, their right path is the exhaustion of *karmas*. Even though the soul aids the execution of *karmas*, liberation from repeated births is its aim, and hence it is the right path. We cannot escape experiences that we came here to enjoy, irrespective of whether the experiences are good or bad. Thus, the right path is being present with full consciousness when it is happening, moment by moment. That will help liberation.

There are hundreds of paths leading us to the same ocean. The path you choose should depend on the path that suits you. All paths are fine. There is no need for any conversion. All *Gurus* are the same too. Your personal choice is the best choice for you. Never regret it. Essentially it is through being-ness that we achieve the Ultimate. Doing-ness has tremendous limitations. It also leads to the creation of habits and attachments.

The Nath Path

✤ **Question:** Can you tell us about your path?

Mohanji: Numerous paths are leading to the same ocean. In the Tradition that I follow (the path of Shiva), most of the activity is done by the Master. In our path, the biggest requirement for any disciple is an empty space. It is not based on activity. It is based on being-ness. We say that being on our path is like being a monkey's child. A monkey's child clings to the mother. It does not have the power to climb the tree. The mother climbs the tree. All the monkey's child does is cling to the mother. Similarly, in our path, a disciple must have a complete connection with the *Guru* or the Path or the Tradition and everything is delivered.

Have you heard of Sai Baba of Shirdi? He is a great Master from India who is no longer in the body. He left his body in the 1900s. Somebody asked him, "Tell us about your *Guru*." He said, "My *Guru* was very powerful. But he taught me nothing. From morning till evening, I kept looking at him. I sat down and looked at him. He gave me everything." Here, the practice is being empty and surrendering. Just by connecting to the *Guru*, one achieves the highest.

I'll share another example of Sai Baba. Sai Baba had a disciple called Upasni Maharaj, who used to do extreme practices – more or less playing with his life. He would sit in a cave in the forest and meditate for days without food and water. He would go to various places which other people could not even access. He would just sit and meditate, just to attain the highest possible level a man could reach. He was not connected to Sai Baba. Whenever Sai Baba saw him, Sai Baba would catch him, bring him to Shirdi and make him stay there. But he was used to the forest and isolated places and hence, couldn't stay there. When Sai Baba was not looking, he would run away. Sai Baba would then catch him again, bring him to Shirdi and keep him there.

This happened a few times, and he became as powerful as Sai Baba. After attaining the highest level, he lived in a burial ground, about four to six km from Shirdi. Sitting there, he would know whatever happened in Shirdi. A man went to meet Sai Baba in Shirdi but was disturbed when he saw Sai Baba smoking. He said, "He smokes? Is this a *Guru*? I don't want to bow to him," and went away. He then went to Upasni Maharaj and tried to bow down to him. Upasni Maharaj refused and said, "Go away. If you cannot bow down there (in Shirdi), don't come here." This was in the 1900s when there were no telephones for instant communication.

A lot of people come to see. Very few go higher. This is not a problem at all. It depends on the receptivity of the seeker. Many flowers bloom on the tree, yet very few become fruit. In our path, there is only one criterion – empty space. It does not matter if you are black or white, rich or poor, from this country or that. The only criterion is, "Are you able to receive?" However, the *Guru* will test your eligibility.

I was talking to a divine mother in the Himalayas. She said, "People climb the mountain to reach the *Guru*. After a lot of effort, they reach the top and meet the *Guru*. However, the first thing the *Guru* does is kick them. Some may get disappointed, Oh, I climbed all these mountains for the Guru, and he kicked me." But some may kiss the feet of the *Guru*, and then the *Guru* hugs them. If you survive the test, then you are taken in. Then, there's nothing to worry about. It is an anecdote, but it gives an idea of the path, where the only eligibility is emptiness. No ego, no mind, and then God fills in the empty space.

Our Tradition originates from Lord Shiva, who is called *Adi Nath* (the primordial Lord). The Tradition is like merging two rivers as one – the coming together of Kriya yoga with Babaji and all the associated *Gurus*, and the Dattatreya Tradition with all the Siddhas (perfected ones). On both sides, there are powerful Masters. Each caters to a different set of people. Some people need activity and to do certain things to reach the highest. In contrast for a Siddha, it is about emptying – nullification. The Tradition is called the Nath Tradition.

Numerous Gurus have walked the path of the Nath Tradition. Nisargadatta Maharaj, Bhagavan Nityananda from Ganeshpuri (who left his body in 1961), Shirdi Sai Baba and Sathya

Sai Baba are all Nath *Gurus*. Sitting in one place, they can work in many places. They are only using their bodies to be on Earth. However, their consciousness is vast. If you connect to their consciousness, you will automatically be elevated. The only criterion is to keep emptying. "This is not me; this is not me, ..." Once you nullify yourself, they completely take over.

When someone enquired about him and his *Guru*, Lord Dattatreya, just said, "I am merely a lover of nature." That level of humility and nullification is the sign of our Tradition. In the path of Shiva, it is all about dissolution. Each and every aspect is dissolved. The ego is dissolved, the mind is dissolved, the intellect is dissolved, and you become completely one with perfection. When all limitations are removed, you become extremely powerful. You become one with the universe.

One person asked a Nath *Guru*, "How can I get initiated into the Nath Tradition?" He said, "That's very simple. Jump into the river, and the river takes you. All you need is simplicity, love, compassion and just be empty. Remove all the concepts. Be naked." When ego, hatred, division and all the things we have stored in the mind go away, the mind itself will go away.

It is like we don't need a trash can if we don't have any trash at home. The trash can is our mind. We are producing trash and keeping it in our mind. If we do not remove our trash from our household for a month, we can't enter the house. Our mind is like that. We have kept the trash for lifetimes. We can't enter now. That's it. Throw the trash can away. I always tell people if they want to leave something here with me, leave their mind and go. Be free.

Thus Spake the Masters

❧ **Question:** Mohanji, why do you attribute everything to past Masters? You have spoken about ownership. Isn't this against it?

Mohanji: This is our Tradition. Even the great Lord Krishna says, "Thus spake the Masters". Traditionally, we respect and revere our *Gurus*, the stream of Masters who transferred wisdom to people over generations. They have said everything. If we look deeper, we know that everything started from Lord Shiva – "*Sada Shiva Samaarambha*". The *Guru* principle flows eternally. So, how can I take ownership? I am only one of the mouths of Eternity. Since I follow the Tradition of great Masters, I attribute everything to the past great Masters who delivered everything.

None of the past Masters took ownership of the eternal Truth or knowledge. Shirdi Sai Baba always said, "*Allah Malik*" (God is King). Hence, none of the existing *Gurus* can own anything that they are teaching. They are all part of the Tradition of Masters. Please understand this clearly. If a *Guru* says, "I invented this", understand that they lack depth and clarity. Humility and gratitude are automatic when enlightenment happens. Spiritual evolution makes people humble because it is a path of nullification, of dissolution. The context where I said, "own your experiences" is different. This means, when you have profound spiritual experiences, during meditation or in the company of Masters, do own them, nourish them, cherish them. They are your own. That is the point from where you will grow.

The mind may have some borrowed ideas, to ignore your experience and believe in someone else's, that might hinder your progress. That is a fundamental mistake. We are not the other person. Their experience is unique to them. You are yourself. Your experience is unique to you. Own that. Be proud of that. Start your journey from that point. You will evolve higher and higher. Information is in the air. When your antenna develops the capacity to decode the information you are eligible for, you will automatically receive it. The *Guru* principle will ensure that. Thus, there is no need to worry. Own your experience and be proud to talk about it. Do not worry about others who might ridicule you. They are doing so because your consciousness is unique to yourself, and others cannot see what you see. Believe in yourself – Your Self.

A Heart That Touches Truth, Overflows

The eyes see the Truth. The heart feels the Truth. When we come face to face with the eternal Truth, every cell of our body exclaims, "It is true." Truth has that power. It touches the soul. This is the quality of Truth. All the while, our heart knew that Truth exists but could not touch it. When it finally finds it, our whole constitution moves into a trance state. Whether it be what you read, words, or a song you hear, or a dance you see, the Truth always touches our soul. Tears of bliss are spontaneous expressions.

Just keep your heart steady on the Truth Eternal. There is no other *sadhana* more appropriate for complete liberation. Never allow your mind to sway with inevitable external storms or calamities. You will exist in the realm of the true Masters. Understand that expectation is the root cause of all personal calamities.

Be Free. Live Free.

Freedom is a state when the mind is free and unruffled, without control or expectations. The bridge to this state is a clear awareness that we control nothing in life. "Shed your weight and run." The weight sits in your mind as concepts and sundry conditioning. When you consciously shed them one by one, you will become lighter and lighter and reach ecstatic states of joy and wonder! This is freedom!

Let your detachment from a person, place or situation be due to your liberation or freedom from it, not because you hate it. Whatever you hate will persist. Hatred and liberation are bitter enemies. They cannot live together at the same time in the same mind that creates it. It is usually either one or the other. So, beware...

Freedom begins in the mind and shines in society. Freedom is primarily individualistic. When one is free from the clutches and conditioning of one's mind, the expressions of freedom echo in society. Being free is important, but allowing freedom to all the beings around us is vital. Freedom liberates oneself, and others. Be free. Live free. Bless all beings with the freedom that they deserve.

Simplicity is Godliness

The reason for worry is expectation. If expectations are not realised, it leads to frustrations. The remedy is: acceptance of every moment as it is, without resistance. Allow life to flow. Acceptance of yourself as you are is also equally important. You are already with all *Gurus* and God. If you reach closer to your soul, you will realise, feel and experience the proximity. Nothing can separate you from them because you are one with them.

Remember – Simplicity is Godliness. Man minus ego is God. Lack of expectation means absolute liberation. Equanimity at all times is supreme strength. An objective display of anger is our strength, while subjective, spontaneous, and uncontrollable anger is our weakness. The former leads to liberation as there are no emotions attached to it, while the latter leads to *karmic* bondage and diseases.

The foremost point is Liberation – to liberate oneself from the birth and death cycle. Sai Baba and all true Masters, true representations of the Supreme Father *Parabrahma*, have always guided us towards liberation through their words and their lifestyle. Use this life to get out of the traps of your mind, emotions and ego and to overcome desires. Never suppress them. Just swap them for the higher until everything gets nullified. Senses and mind always wreak havoc. Let them do so. We should be completely focused on liberating ourselves. Serve all, and if possible, guide others towards the light of wisdom.

❧ **Question:** Can you recommend some books for this purpose?

Mohanji: Books cannot take you to liberation. Reading also amounts to doing. Through doing, none can get enlightened. Only through being-ness can one get enlightened. Being-ness is a perpetual state. Being-ness is existence in awareness. This cannot be achieved through books. Books can explain to you what being-ness could be, as an intellectual understanding. It can also limit you because you will start expecting similar results in your spiritual practice. Expectation binds and takes away the beauty of experience, especially if your perception or expectation of a result does not match reality. There should be a deliberate attempt to limit doing-ness and shift to being-ness.

It can be achieved effortlessly by just deciding to operate in the present always, deliberately bringing your mind to every thought, word and action, having the presence of mind and the sincere practice of expressing unconditional love and gratitude against all odds. This will lead to being-ness. Perpetual being-ness will necessarily lead to liberation. There are some books that help your clarity and awareness, such as the Bhagavad Gita, Autobiography of a Yogi, Sai Satcharita, Chidakasha Gita, and so on.

Knowledge (*jnana*) is not a burden, provided it is useful for your further journey. If knowledge is a key to open a door, it is good. Knowledge is a burden if it becomes intellectual weight. If you are using knowledge to "show off" in front of others, or are using it to express your ego, it is a burden for you. "In the feast of the ego, everyone goes home hungry". No one is satisfied when ego is at play. We all live this way!

Too much knowledge causes heaviness. It also deepens your ego emotion. When knowledge becomes a burden, it slows down your spiritual progress. Less luggage, more comfort. This is the fundamental Truth of existence.

❧ **Question:** What helps liberation?

Mohanji: Spontaneous and effortless shedding of habits that you could not otherwise have lived without. The wisdom behind the shedding itself is a confirmation of personal spiritual evolution. *Gurus* will happen in life automatically and guide you further. *Guru* is a principle. It could take a mouth and talk, or it could come as a message from nature. The bottom line is, the *Guru* happens in life when you need them the most.

❧ **Question:** Is enlightenment the aim of life on Earth, or does each of us have a unique purpose and does this purpose change through time?

Mohanji: Enlightenment is the purpose of the soul. This is mainly because the soul is trapped in the body. The soul wants liberation. The soul will appreciate it if you reduce the baggage. If there is no baggage, it is enlightenment. But the purpose of the substratum (our constitution, body, mind, intellect) which the soul carries, which we call character, is to experience Earth and express our constitution on Earth.

Every person is a bundle of *karma*. Firstly, what provoked this birth, what provoked you to take this body, from your first heartbeat till your last heartbeat. Secondly, you have a collection of *karma* which is inherited from your family, from your lineage. Thirdly, we have collected *karma* as we live this life. All this is a part of inherited, individual, and collective *karma*. We are a combination of all three *karmas*. We cannot segregate them.

When you are looking at me, you see a physical image and the words I speak. These are only two dimensions of my existence. If you want to see my consciousness, you have to merge into my consciousness. That is when the exact understanding happens, and that needs awareness. You have to increase your awareness and connect to my consciousness.

If you look at my cards[4], there are always eyes on them; the eyes are a gateway to consciousness. The eyes can never lie. They always carry the Truth. It transcends through lifetimes. If you connect to Consciousness, you will understand that you and I are one. There is no difference. Physically we are different. You look at the physical form; we have so many differences. But the moment you connect to Consciousness, it is a hundred per cent peace. It is a beautiful feeling.

We can read and understand lots of stuff. There is plenty of information in the world. Even the internet can give you many things. But if you do not digest the information, they are just theories. They never help you to evolve. If you look at the whole of spirituality, there is only one message: "You Are That." Just one message. Whatever you are searching for in the world out-

---

4   Business card size picture cards printed with Mohanji's eyes that were distributed in the past.

side, that is you. If you understand that, you have understood the whole of spirituality.

How do you know 'you are That'? When you finish all the searching outside, you become tired. Then, you start thinking: "I'm not finding what I am looking for. Where is it?" Then you slowly withdraw. Once your whole search ends, you find yourself. This is the whole of spirituality. Whatever you do, whatever you say, or whatever you practice, one day everything will stop, and you become still. Then you know who you are.

Until then, you only have a relative idea. You have not experienced yourself. The moment you experience yourself, you are totally at peace. There is nothing more to experience. These are fundamentals in spirituality. On the path, you sometimes get frustrated, sometimes you become angry, sometimes you feel you are not reaching anywhere, sometimes overwhelming love, sometimes overwhelming hatred, all such emotions will manifest. This is all sitting in you. At that time, people usually change the *Guru* as they themselves cannot change. But that is not a solution.

When you are going after God, nothing should stop you. You do not need a priest or anybody else, because you and God are already One. This is all you need to understand. Experience it. God can never be understood; God has to be experienced. First, before you experience God, you have to experience yourself. When you go more and more into silence, what will come out initially are all the things you have collected and stored in you. They will come, and they will bother you. At that time, you have to cling on further to the purpose. Whatever happens, do not deviate.

Remember, God is One. God has no form; it is pure energy. It does not matter what name you give God; God is One. Until you catch God, do not stop. This is my advice to you because it is worth it. I cannot explain the kind of things which you experience once you achieve that energy. It is very difficult to explain. On travelling the spiritual path, more and more calamities can happen. But that is the time when you have to hold onto faith. Nothing should stop you until you achieve the highest. Whatever happens in the middle; let it be. Use this lifetime to reach the highest.

Secondly, the Law of Attraction is equal to subtlety. You can attract wealth. You can attract anything, provided you are operating in the subtlest possible. The body is gross. The mind is still gross; you can feel it. You have to go beyond the body, beyond the mind, beyond the intellect, and beyond the ego, and you reach a state of stillness. When you operate from that state, everything will come to you. You will not have a shortage of anything. What you want will happen. But if the mind is operating, you cannot get everything because the mind keeps changing. The mind is never stable. If the earth is shaking, you cannot build anything on it. Similarly, you cannot attract anything operating from the level of the mind.

One suggestion I always give around the world: Never miss the opportunity to be with a person of higher energy, a higher vibration, or a higher frequency, because you will automatically be elevated just by being in the company of people who have touched the higher frequency. Just by being. As I mentioned earlier about Shirdi Sai Baba's response when people asked him about his Master, "My Master was great, but he taught me nothing. All-day, I sat down and looked at him, and he gave me everything." This is very important to understand. Being in the company of people who have attained higher frequency, automatically raises your frequency.

Firstly, do not judge. If you judge, you never understand. If we start judging another person even in our life, we stop understanding the person. We stop appreciating. We create walls. Secondly, you will get many sensations in the spiritual path. As you evolve, you will have many experiences, many feelings. I would always say they are good, enjoy them, but never lose your focus. Catch God. Do not lose your focus. You are not just here to experience a sensation; you are here to experience God. Until you touch God, reach God, connect to God, don't stop.

Keep evolving. Nobody can stop you. You have the power; you have the resources; you are already that. Nothing can prevent you. So, be yourself. Be as powerful as yourself. If you feel weak at all, understand, that is the mind at play. The mind is keeping you weak. You are not the mind. The mind is part of you. You can never be bound. You are born free; you will die free. In between, do not allow your mind to conquer you, subdue you, and make you feel weak. This is my message for you.

❧ **Question:** How do we know that we are awake?

Mohanji: In spiritual terms? Simple. When we become aware that we do not exist. When no gross exists, and we cannot experience duality anymore. Then we will know that we are awake.

Love All as God

True Love is Unconditional Love. Love as your inherent nature, without any reason, is sacred. Conditional love is not love at all. Love all as God, as all are part of God. This is right.

This Earth is very old. Our soul is very old. We have walked this Earth many times before this birth. We have entertained the same emotions at all times. The proof is our distinct character in this life. The proof is our wisdom or elevation. The proof is our level of understanding and awareness.

Everything has relevance. All of God's creations have relevance. All emotions have relevance. All decisions have relevance. Sometimes, we may not understand the relevance when we are at it. We may have to go past a particular time and look back to see why a particular thought or word happened at a particular point in time.

Nothing is wasted. There is no wastage in God's creation. No thoughts or words are wasted. Wastage happens only in our creation. So, it is important to accept. It is important to understand. It is important to respect. It is important to have faith in a higher justice. Every event has a reason, and the reason is sometimes intangible to the limited conscious mind. Never mind.

The need of the hour is love, nothing but love. Unconditional love has just become a theory. We witness it in the words of orators, but not in reality. Just as we watch stuffed animals and birds of extinct species in the museum, so we hear about unconditional love from the mouths of politicians and Saints. It never gets converted into action. We need true expressions of unconditional love, not articulation of theories such as love and care beyond man-made barriers. We have had many theories, which have caused us indigestion for generations. Let us now experience love, spread love and live love.

When I think of all the Great Masters who walked this Earth in the past and those who are still contributing to the welfare of this planet and also the universe, in their own way, I feel humbled and so insignificant. Just as an ant is so small and often hardly visible in our daily existence, I am less than an ant and insignificant in cosmic existence. Think about some of the spiritual giants who walked this Earth – Lord Dattatreya, Agastya, all the Siddhas, Akkalkot Maharaj, Bhagavan Nityananda, Ramana Maharishi, Shirdi Sai Baba, Mahavatar Babaji, Narasimha Saraswati, Adi Shankaracharya, Kabir Das, Jesus, Buddha, the Avatars of Lord Vishnu, Socrates, and many Masters who spoke all that we know to date. There is nothing new to say. They have said it all.

What you hear today, through many mouths, are the same words that the past Masters uttered. Thoughts and words are ancient. Truth is ancient. What is my significance? What is my contribution? My beloveds, I am no *Guru*. I am an ordinary man, perhaps more ordinary than you who are reading this. As long as I exist in this body, I am just like any other man. What is different in me? Nothing. I am just another instrument of the Almighty. I have nothing to give you which is my own. As long as I exist in this body, I articulate. As long as I stay in connection with you, you will witness me. Otherwise, depending on your faith, you will feel me. There too, you are feeling the Lord Almighty, not me.

This body is a temporary entity. It can perish or vanish at any time. The Lord remains, through time to infinity. I am just another expression of the Lord, just like you are. What can I call myself? He exists. I do not. So, do not be confused. Do not be disillusioned. My existence in this capacity depends on your need, faith and understanding. When your need evaporates, I cease to exist in this capacity. All I try to do is deliver what I can, with the purest of intentions and without any expectation. This is all I can do.

ᴥ **Question:** I love You!

Mohanji: Do you? You should love yourself first. Love your family. Love your neighbours, friends, and colleagues. I am total. When you love totality, when you become unconditional love, you do love me. If you think I am this form, this is non-understanding. When you hate someone, you do not love me. Loving me means loving the universe. Loving me means loving unconditionally. When you see me in every being, you do love me. You will feel my love too. I love you through all beings.

ᴥ **Question:** When does true love blossom in the heart of a seeker?

Mohanji: When detachment happens love will be for the sake of love. Love will become truly unconditional. The true beauty of existence can be witnessed only through divine sight or through the third eye. The more you operate through your third eye, the more you can only witness the grandeur and beauty of creation and the Creator. You cannot see imperfection. The eyes that witness imperfection are regular eyes, combined with the regular mind. A being of higher awareness can only see perfection in the whole universe. That, which is beyond, is perfect. This, seemingly limited, is also perfect. When the illusion of limitedness gets dissolved, only the grand perfection remains, in its unlimited form.

The Art of Elegance

Everybody has potential. Everyone craves it. Everyone gets it at some point in their lives. Everyone cannot maintain it. Everyone suffers from a lack of it. Everyone misses it. This is the story of elegance.

The intellect is integrally attached to elegance. It gets reflected in one's thoughts, words and actions. Being elegant is an art. This cannot be pretentious. Pretentious elegance cannot be maintained. It becomes situational. Many celebrities are victims of it. They often become disillusioned when they cannot bridge the gap between the fake and the real. They fall to self-destructive abuse and even death. All the tantrums they display are usually expressions of their deep insecurities. These are clear signs of not coming to terms with themselves and their acquired status. Status can be acquired, but not stature. Stature has to happen. It needs eligibility. It needs grounding.

Stature happens with an increase in awareness. It needs a deeper awareness of the thread that runs between status and activities performed each day, which runs between the man and the mission. The thread that unites everything to the place of action and the thread that keeps the beads of events and life together. Being with the thread, being aware, will reflect as maturity, groundedness or even elegance.

Elegance can be nurtured, and for that, the intellect should be in command at all times. When the intellect is in command, there will be no excesses. Everything will be in moderation. Elegance cannot be acquired from outside. It has to happen inside, with the right attitude of flexibility. Situational elegance can be termed pretension, or even a facade. Elegance through time and space needs equanimity and a clear understanding of the role-play of life. It can even be called spiritual and social maturity.

Elegance never permits complaints of any kind. It is a clear understanding as to what happens, why it happens and for whom it happens. The purpose is clear. Even if the purpose is not clear, there is no resistance to the events of life. There is only management of everyday matters as they appear while keeping the boat of equanimity steady. Elegant acceptance of reality as it is, makes a man irresistible.

Elegance has nothing to do with habits. It is not dependent on whether a man is a gambler, an alcoholic or a womaniser. These traits, if left uncontrolled, could lead to his downfall, but they do not affect his elegance, per se. If weaknesses bind him, they pull him down. If he is socially compatible, it usually shows his nature of flexibility. Elegance does not mean compromising or conforming to every whim of society. Elegance is in accepting realities and living them in style. A non-conformist could also be elegant. Elegance has nothing to do with social morality either, though social acceptance does help in life. If someone compromises too much to be socially acceptable, he cannot be considered elegant.

Any activity that provokes and maintains weaknesses of any kind should never be entertained. Every habit can be termed a weakness. Every emotion can be termed a weakness. Notions, knowledge, and understanding can also lead to weakness. The operating tools such as the mind and intellect can lead to weakness of character. Elegance is in independence. Elegance is in existing in freedom within. Elegance is in flowing with life. Elegance is in not stagnating, physically, mentally and intellectually.

The factors that pull a man down are primarily his constitution, such as the state of mind, thought processes, fears and phobias, dependency on other people and dependency on a time, space or activity. Any dependency can bring forth weakness.

Truth is something that stirs your being. It gets reflected in the mind. Elegance is basing oneself on the real Truth beyond dualities. This makes man fearless. Elegance is fearlessness. Man exists on Earth based on relative truths. This destabilises his mind and confuses his existence. When he shifts to the absolute Truth, he attains equanimity to the very thread that gets reflected as beads. He attains elegance.

Once this is attained, nobody can pull him down. Nothing can affect him anymore. He will start seeing through the ups and downs of life in perfect equanimity. Stature that is based on the absoluteness of existence creates spontaneous equanimity. To achieve that, witness-hood is necessary. Witnessing one's thoughts, words, and actions without emotions will lead to power over them. This is not situational power. This is perpetual power. That power can take one above mundane existence to absolute being-ness.

Elegance exists through happiness and sorrow, time, space, and situations. It is a perpetual state. It is a state of no excesses. It is perfection in existence. It never sways the mind. It never gets affected by people, places, or events. Elegance is a perpetual state. It is being-ness.

When good or bad events do not affect a personality, when nothing can adversely affect them, when the operating level is based on equanimity, that person has transcended mundane existence. That one has liberated himself.

Elegance can be consciously nurtured when daily life is handled only by the intellect and never by emotions. When the intellect rules, man has no regrets. A lack of guilt and regrets help maintain elegance. When emotions rule, it gives room for all negative emotions. That leads to downfalls. Emotion only creates regrets and dissatisfaction. It can never give perpetual fulfilment.

Emotions lead to temporary pleasures which cannot be termed as absolute fulfilment. The fulfilment that a person experiences out of emotions is usually temporary. It leads from emotion to emotion with decreasing levels of satisfaction, and eventually, it tires the person into disillusionment.

Elegance happens as wisdom increases. When awareness enhances wisdom, equanimity takes place. That leads to elegance in lifestyle. All true Masters have consistently displayed extraordinary elegance, even if some of them led a life of a *fakir* (a Muslim religious ascetic living on alms) or a beggar on the street. Their elegance was unmistakable. If you digest the lives of Saints well, you will see the underlying elegance displayed beyond time and space, and even through death. A lack of dependency allows absolute elegance.

Where does elegance come from? Equanimity. Equanimity happens out of awareness. When you are aware of the temporariness of your thoughts, words, actions, and even your existence on Earth, the mind becomes silent. The mind stops jumping from tree to tree (of desires). The mind keeps quiet.

Less desire leads to better equanimity and balance in existence. This never takes away the pleasures of life. Instead, you will enjoy the fruits of existence better, without the mental barriers and expectations. This will help better enjoyment of life because the pressure for pleasure is less. When the mind stops pushing man for pleasure, whatever is available is more enjoyable. Otherwise, comparisons and corresponding dissatisfaction prevent all pleasures of existence.

Elegance is attractive. It transcends beauty, power, money, position or status. The inner stability reflected through the life of purpose brings forth irresistibility. An elegant man becomes irresistible to society. He becomes an icon. He need not prove anything. His lifestyle itself becomes his message. It attracts people to him. An elegant personality is highly irresistible.

Elegance springs out of a life managed by intellect instead of emotions.

Elegance needs absolute selflessness. Selflessness in thoughts, words, and actions keeps a man elegant.

Elegance needs equanimity through time and space.

Elegance cannot be affected by persons, personalities, situations, time or space.

Elegance is beyond the mannerisms or immature states of other people. Nothing can affect an elegant personality or his perpetual elegance.

Elegance is not in dressing up or showing off. It is in handling life elegantly at all times.

An elegant lifestyle is an art and a perpetual expression of how life can be.

Elegance is in inner stability beyond changes of time, space, situations and people.

Elegance is in the ability to see through situations into the thread that runs through time, people, place, and personality, and remain unaffected.

Elegance is in being happy irrespective of whether a person, a situation, a dish or a place is available or not.

Elegance is in the discipline of life, not influenced by emotions, time, people, or space.

Elegance is absolute objectivity.

Elegance is the ability to keep one's position steady against all odds and storms of emotions in life.

Elegance is in conviction, and the ability to act accordingly against all odds.

Elegance is in being you through time and space.

Elegance is in being kind, compassionate, and non-violent irrespective of time and space.

Elegance is in being elegant. What do people like in a man or a woman? It is not their beauty. It is their elegance. Beauty is transitory. It changes with time. Elegance is permanent. It stays through time. Elegance maintains the beauty of character. Elegance maintains a life of equanimity. Elegance maintains relationships beyond emotions.

Elegance enhances you and makes your life complete and satisfied. There are no dos and don'ts in elegance. It is not in what you do but how you do it that determines elegance. It is your attitude associated with every activity.

Wish you elegance.

CHAPTER 2:

Pillars of the tradition

Have Faith and the Rest Will Follow

Duality is part of the very existence of the universe, let alone us, human beings. There is always dark and light, white and black. Both have power. The difference is that the black captures or binds beings to itself and the white liberates them. Black and white are symbolic, not actual colours per se. They signify the negative and positive. When you hold on to positivity and liberation with all your might, the potential threat of dark forces will drop off. Unfailing faith will lead to salvation or perfect merger with the Supreme Lord. With your surrender and faith, you will always be protected. There is nothing to worry about.

> ❧ **Question:** I was thinking today that we always say that the Master's Grace is there, but it depends on our receptivity to receive it. I feel receptivity is not just listening but listening, understanding, assimilating, and implementing. Do the four combined together become receptivity?

Mohanji: Yes and the core is faith. The spine of all is faith.

> ❧ **Question:** So if we have faith, then all four will follow?

Mohanji: Yes. Faith and purity are pillars in the path of liberation, just like patience and devotion.

❧ **Question:** I have faith.

Mohanji: Do you? Is it conditional or unconditional? Think again. Do you really have faith? How much faith? The word faith has become a cliché. Faith is not just a word. It is a state, a perpetual state. Most of those who say, "I have faith," doubt themselves and certainly even their faith. Their faith is often conditional and sways with others' interference, opinions and words. They need to work harder to achieve a total state of absolute faith.

True *Gurus* Never Bind

❧ **Question:** What message can we give to people with different belief systems. For e.g., people believing in different religions, who think that their way is the only way of salvation and are fixed about it. I feel they are in delusion. What message can we give to those people?

Mohanji: This could be your understanding. They might be quite evolved. We should not judge or criticise another. Anyway, have you thought about why they think so? It is because of their level of understanding or consciousness. That consciousness could be of the first-grade[5], second-grade, or third-grade. They can only understand things in that way. Allow them to be. In the absolute sense, there is no Hindu, Muslim, or Christian; nothing. There are only human beings. Just another species. And God? There is only One Entity. All are expressions of that Entity.

It is only in the waking state that you think, "Oh, you are a Christian, you are a Hindu, or you are a Muslim." But when you are sleeping, where is the Christian, Hindu, or Muslim? All gone! There is no deep meaning in any of the religions except

---

[5]   As in the grade in a school

that they are just another path leading to God. Whichever path you follow is fine because it is up to you. Whichever religion you may want to follow, be good and do good. Be kind, generous and compassionate. At the end of the day, that is the only thing that matters. Finally, only your inner peace and the cleanliness of your inner space matter. Inner peace matters a lot, because it becomes outer peace.

If people feel that there is a difference between religions or that one is better than the other, it only reflects their level of understanding or consciousness. Allow them to be. If they are open and receptive, you can say, "Okay, have a look at this," or "Why don't you look at it this way?" What happens to your religion at night when you are sleeping? Then, why do we have to worry about religion? If you like to worship in a Muslim way, please do. There is no problem. If you like to worship in the Christian way, please do. If you want to follow the Buddhist principles, please do. These are all fine. This is your journey. Walk with faith and conviction.

No true *Guru* will ever say that this is the right way or the right path. Everything is relative. If the path is of liberation, nobody can bind you. If I bind your leg with my leg, I too cannot walk, right? A *Guru* who is steadfast on the path of liberation can never bind you. He will never do that. When binding happens, understand that there is a lack of awareness, or the level of consciousness is really low. Those seeming *Gurus*, who are insecure themselves, may put the fear in you that you will have a big problem if you don't come to them every week. Thus, they put the seed of fear in you. It will grow by itself.

When you are not going for their meditation and fall down by chance, then you will think, "Oh! I did not go for the meditation. My *Guru* had said that I will fall down, so I fell down!' Automatically, the fear will create more fear. The *Guru* need not worry. The seed of fear that they sowed in the disciple will automatically grow. This is totally against the path of liberation. I would say, "Whether you come here or not, no problem – I am with you. This is your home. This is the path of liberation, and this is the Truth. I like to remain fearless and keep you fearless. There are no insecurities and fears in our path. We need not even meet. We are connected with the strong rope of faith."

If you look at all the great Masters or Saints over time, they were always steadfast on the path of liberation, not binding. Binding never happened. In today's world, why does binding happen? Political interest or money, just money and power! If you do not come here, how can I take money from your pocket? Thus, I make sure you come here. The best method is fear. I create fear in you, so that becomes a chain and I bind you. If I liberate you, you may go and spend the money elsewhere. Then what will I do?

Do you understand the problem? Do you see this clearly? Be aware of how the world operates. There are so many traps in the path of spirituality. All that glitters is not gold! Insecurity of certain people and certain religions are visible all around! People who handle religions often have serious insecurities. That is why fears are created in their subjects; otherwise, when a man is on the path of liberation, fears cannot exist. In the path of liberation, fears have no value. If fears exist, there is a total lack of awareness and understanding.

But we need not preach. We should not preach. We should not argue or fight. We need not deliberately educate people or tell people. If they come to us, we answer, we guide with love, affection and objectivity. We should not try to convert either. No one can convert another, but can convert only themselves from the accumulated filth of the mind to purity. No other conversions have any permanent value. Hence, lead by example. Live the Truth and peace that you have experienced. Do not sell your mind to other people and allow it to be influenced and utilised. Live your Truth and live your understanding. Do not allow others to manipulate you and later complain.

You express happiness, contentment, desirelessness, higher awareness, love, selflessness. Then, others will think, "Look at this fellow! How can he be so liberated living with the same terrestrial standards as me?" They will ask you, "What is the trick? What is the secret?" At that time you can say, "Try this path. This path has no binding". We never say that you will be ok if you meditate or you will not be ok if you don't meditate. This is unacceptable. It is a path of liberation, a path of pathlessness, where anything becoming a habit is not accepted. We have to eventually shed everything to move on towards liberation, including our body, mind and intellect.

You can follow the path of meditation and if it does not take you higher, drop it. Even if this *Guru* is looking good, if he does not take you any higher, drop him. Be on the path of liberation just like you travel through the various classes in school. Different teachers may come and guide you. Have faith in that side of existence where all the *Gurus* say the same thing. Different mouths are giving you the same information. Mohanji may die tomorrow and somebody else will come and guide you. This is fine, because it does not matter, as long as you are guided, you are protected, and you have faith. It is your faith that matters. Remember this clearly.

If you cannot hold on to your experience and grow from there, if you are completely suffocated by the image of the *Guru* which you have created, and if you expect that *Guru* to fit into that image and discard him if he changes, where does the problem lie? In the *Guru* or in you? If the message is good for you, you should take it, if the message is not good for you, why do you bother? Drop it. Just drop it. This is my sincere advice. Do not come to see me for my sake. Come to see me for your sake.

Think about what your experience has been, and hold on to it. Others can have their opinions, but you need not necessarily buy them. Why do you buy things you do not need or will never use? Buy only things that you need. That will leave more walking space in your home, which also means peace of mind. In the path of liberation, no one imposes anything on anyone and no one ever binds anyone to anything.

I tell you to meditate; that if you meditate, you will reach certain levels. Why are a lot of people still coming together and having experiences with the Power of Purity meditation? This is because of their openness and faith. This meditation is a communion where you are actually communing with your consciousness and soul. Results have to happen. How can results not happen?

If somebody speaks against the *Guru* and you change, how deep is your faith and how shallow is your experience? Think about it. If you discard your experience for another's words, you could be terribly insecure. Strengthen your *muladhara* (the root *chakra*). Gain more stability.

We have to start walking from where we stand. I can start walking only from this point. I cannot walk from where you are sitting. I can start from there only if I go to that place – correct? We have to start walking from where we stand, and that is our experience. Start from your experience and keep progressing. Do not keep shifting your faith based on others' words. If you want to leave Mohanji, it is fine, but this message stays true wherever you are and whichever path or *Guru* you are following.

From experience to experience, until finally all experiences become one and you become one with the universal experience – this is how it should grow. Others' words have no value. You know, it does not really matter; my love towards you is eternal.

Consistency

I would request one thing from all those who are following me in various countries: Be consistent. Don't be too analytical about your experience, about your progress, about where you stand today, whether meditation is helping, or whether you are connected to Mohanji or not. It does not matter. Have faith. The pillar of our Tradition is faith. You should have faith in yourself, which is your self, which means your soul. This is the permanent entity in you; it can never change, it will never divert from its purpose. That is you. Thus, if you are purpose-bound; your objective is clearly purpose-bound; nothing can thwart you from the destination. Nothing can prevent your journey. You will be completely guided; you will be protected, and you will always attain your final destination. This is for sure.

Thus, your purpose should be very clear, and should not be ordinary: not just a few sensations. You can easily attain sensations. In meditation, there are various experiences happening. Even if you are not meditating, if you are connecting to my consciousness, you may feel an elevation. If you are connecting to the *Guru* consciousness and if you are connecting to your spine, you may experience so many changes within you. Even if you do hyperventilation, you could be touching the altered states of consciousness, but this is not the end. These experiences are only steps to the ultimate trip, the ultimate journey. The destination is not these experiences. You need to cross over all these experiences and be one with God.

To be one with God, you should be one with yourself. Thus, my request to all of you is to take time off and experience yourself. Experiencing yourself means first of all, acceptance. You need to accept yourself. You may have all sorts of thoughts about yourself, criticism about yourself, and judgment about yourself. Forget about all that. Be yourself. What you are today is what you have created yourself to be. This is exactly what you wanted to be. You may not have done that with conscious choice, based on the consciousness of the available state of mind which you have now. This is not the whole you. This is just an expression of you.

The available consciousness that you are operating in, or let us say, the available awareness level which was chosen by you for a particular reason. Because of that reason, you wanted to experience a set of desires laid out over a period of time, using this awareness. This is why you chose it. So accept it. This is what you are. But understand yourself. Take your time, feel yourself. Feel life. Feel life more and more. When you feel yourself and feel life, you will stop judging people. You will stop criticising people. You will be completely focused on purpose. Once you are completely focused on purpose, these emotions will take a back seat.

Emotions will not worry you or bother you so much. It will be more on the plane of the intellect. The intellect is the subtler aspect of your mind. The subtler the aspect, the more powerful it becomes and the more consistent it becomes. Once you stop criticising, analysing, judging, or comparing yourself with other people, automatically, the intellect takes over. Once the intellect takes over, life is smoother. There will be a purpose-bound existence. Once existence becomes purpose-bound, then you will be stronger and stronger, clearer and clearer. You will have absolute clarity. Also, you will be peaceful. *Shanti* (peace). This is exactly what we are looking for.

In order to become peaceful, you need to have consistency; you should not enter into any kind of violence in thoughts, words, and actions. Even if they arise, consider them as flowers and put them at the feet of the Master, of your *Guru*. Whenever there are negativities happening, collect them, take them in your hand, and put them at the Master's feet and say, "This is not mine." Likewise, praise happens, the ego develops, ego happens, or aspects of the ego that you experience, take them all as flowers, and put them at the Master's feet. There is no comparison, there is no jealousy, there is no criticism. You will automatically raise your awareness, and your awareness will grow until you reach complete liberation.

207

Complete liberation is a continuous task. Liberation has to happen from every aspect of your existence: even your name, your fame, your habits, your vices, your good aspects. All these things are a part of your binding. You have to liberate yourself, you have to liberate yourself from every aspect. Detach yourself from all that you think you are and start working or walking towards liberation. Liberation is worth it because we have been bound even without our knowledge all throughout our lifetimes. This is why we are here today. We are here today because we have been bound by *karma*. We have been bound by destiny. Today, right now, we are bound by our destiny. This is exactly the blockage we are planning to remove. If you have to remove this, if you have to be free from all these aspects, you have to be consistent.

You should have one purpose, a clear purpose, and walk towards that purpose. The *Guru Tattva*, the principle, will guide you. It will help you, when you need the *Guru* principle most. Just like your shadow, it is with you full-time. Always. So never underestimate the *Guru* principle. Never feel that you are alienated. The *Guru* is with you one-hundred per cent, twenty-four hours, 365 days. Full-time. Just have faith. Trust and do not be bogged down or do not worry about the mannerisms or the superficial aspects of any *Guru* who is in the human form. Because then you will never understand the Consciousness.

You will be stuck with the superficial. It is easy because the senses always connect to the superficial. The senses are oriented towards the superficial. When you are using your senses and mind to recognise or understand or feel the principle called *Guru*, you will never get there. You need to go beyond the senses, beyond the mind. To connect to the consciousness which operates through the principle called *Guru*, who could also be in human form. Never make the mistake of judging a *Guru* using your available understanding, or available awareness. You will never get to the real core of the principle.

Let the glow, the energy, the brightness of the principle called *Guru* brighten you, burn inside you and let this plane always remain inside your heart and let it shine forth. Lead by example. If you would like to convey something to the world, do it, live it. If you do not live it, if you just preach, it is just noise. It will have no effect. It will not matter to the world. But if you live it, you are actually making a statement to the world. This is more appropriate, and much more important in today's times.

I wish all of you across the world, who are connected to me, to know that I love you, I love you deeply, and I am constantly with you and concerned about you. I care for you and I will remain so. You are connected to me just like one family. So, please live harmony, please live love, unconditional love. These are the expressions of higher awareness. If there are differences, take a step towards solving them, sorting them out, making people understand that life is short, there is no time for differences. We have great things to do for the world. Help all without thinking, without discriminating, especially those who are helpless. This is our commitment and our responsibility, to help the helpless. Always be available to help the helpless. When you help the helpless, you are actually supporting, or you are explicitly performing the *tattva*, the principle called *Guru* in you. Always do that.

I am one with you. I am not separate from you. I am always with you and you are always with me. We are eternally connected. We are soul-mates; that is why we came together. That is why we recognised each other. Remember this clearly. Let us be one family. Let us remain so. Let us be connected and let us evolve into the highest possible: liberation in one lifetime.

Purity Matters

Time is racing past. At the same time, it is empowering people to experience higher dimensions too. Those who are willing to take at least one step towards liberation from the various bindings of Earth are being abundantly assisted by time and Masters. Hence, do use this time wisely, shed doubts, suspicion, jealousy, guilt, greed, silly ego and anxiety, and move on to the next level. There is nothing worth holding onto which is of permanent value on Earth.

🌼 **Question:** What is more important – purity or *sadhana*?

Mohanji: The most important matter in the path of spirituality is unconditional love and purity. Purity in thought, word, and action is much more powerful than any *sadhana* that we could get addicted to. *Sadhana* without leading a life of purity and selflessness is of no use. We often get deluded that those who get closer to higher Masters are those who perform rigorous *sadhana*. This is not true. *Sadhana* can only help us organise ourselves into a discipline. It is our inner purity that finally takes us there. I am sure you have recognised this Truth too.

🌼 **Question:** How do we define an act as good or bad, in the context of a spiritual being?

Mohanji: My answer is purity. Purity in thoughts, words, and actions while living life on Earth. If your act is for the well-being of the receiver, if your intentions are pure and unselfish, it is a good act. If you do anything to satisfy your own desire or ego, it is a bad act. A spiritual person should maintain his objectivity. Many people attain spiritual powers quite rapidly. These are baits of spirituality. If you use the acquired spiritual powers for your own benefit, you will fall. If you use the acquired powers for the general well-being of society, you will always stay liberated from them. The utility of a knife depends on its user. A knife can harm you and help you. It depends on how you use it.

Remember the old story. Two monks were walking on the bank of a river. One was quite young, in his twenties, and the other monk was older, in his sixties. While walking they saw a pretty young woman taking a bath, half-naked. They ignored the sight since they were not allowed to have such distractions and moved on. Suddenly the woman slipped and fell into the river and started to drown. The young monk dropped his shoulder sack, jumped into the river and rescued her. He lifted her and brought her to shore. She had become unconscious. He brought her back to consciousness and when he knew that she was fine and could manage on her own, he took his shoulder sack and left the place. He did not look back or expect even a glance of gratitude from her.

The older monk was watching all this. After walking for a while in silence, when they sat down for lunch which they had carried, the older monk told the younger one, "I do not think what you have done is right. We are monks, celibates. We are not supposed to touch a woman, let alone a naked one. In that regard I feel that you did the wrong thing". The young monk smiled and said, "Nowhere in the scriptures have I read that an act of compassion is wrong. The situation demanded appropriate action. I acted. I left the girl at the shore. She is far away from my body and my mind. Why are you still carrying her?" This silenced the older monk.

The young monk acted objectively based on the need and purpose. He had no fears. The older man represents our current society. He never considered that the woman needed to be rescued or that saving her life was the most important thing at the moment when the incident happened, or that it was the appropriate action at that point in time. Instead, he was totally pre-occupied by the man-made dos and don'ts for monks. This is an example of how society, which consists of people of various evolutionary levels, will think and act, and how it thinks you should think and act as a spiritual being. Again, the bottom line is purity. Action without selfishness.

In the spiritual path, when *siddhis* or spiritual powers happen to you, I suggest, "behave like a doctor". A patient is in front of you. Emotions have no value. Objectivity is important. The right diagnosis is the key to the cure. Look at the patient objectively, diagnose and do whatever is the right treatment at that time, using all available knowledge, technology, and understanding without worrying about the consequences. There are many occasions in the history of medicine that show the confidence and purity of the doctor working miracles on the patient. If we are pure within we need not worry. If the intention was pure, never worry. Society may not understand the 'eccentric' spiritual being. You need not worry about it.

When you have spiritual powers (*siddhis*), if you consistently behave in selfish ways, they will erode away from you. Objectivity is important. Who is in front of you is not important. What you need to do is important, and that you are doing whatever is needed is all the more important. Once you have completed what you have to do, objectively, move on without any expectations. In today's world, misunderstandings are quite common. Each person entertains his own view of how a spiritual person should be. They have no consideration or idea about his operating level of consciousness. So do not expect all people to understand you. It is also not worth being scared of society and not doing what you have to do because of fear, or not doing what you meant to do with your available life and powers.

The best way is to be objective and perform to the best of your ability. Your conscience should be clean. Your inner space should never be contaminated. Only if you entertain purity, can you deliver purity. There should not be an inch of selfishness within you. Having no fear is the sign of a true spiritualist.

When you are performing from the level of purity, even if people do not understand you and your actions, it does not matter.

Remember, many people did not understand the actions of Jesus in his time, and they criticised and condemned him. Many people criticised and condemned Krishna. For e.g., the whole Kaurava clan. Many people considered Sai Baba as a madman. Many people hated Osho. Take any spiritual Master and you will see that some loved them, some hated them. Some moved with them with their own personal agendas and expectations. Some left them because of unfulfilled personal agendas and expectations. When this is the way the world works what are we afraid of? Just ensure that you stay liberated and pure at all times. Only then can you help others to see the light of liberation.

❧ **Question:** What is the Crystal Lotus?

Mohanji: The symbol of purity. The lotus remains pure and unattached even while existing in the mud. Water cannot drench it. Gods rest on the eternally pure lotus and display their presence at times. It is the symbol of subtlety and detachment. Nothing affects a lotus. It lives and dies in purity. A crystal lotus has no birth or death. It symbolises purity and faith.

Strip Before You Enter

About 200 years ago, in the current Pakistan region lived a Saint who observed silence most of his life. He lived in a small hut, along with his wife. They had no children. He had a long beard and was partially blind. His house had only three rooms. The land in front of his house was open, and the floor was paved with cow dung, a natural disinfectant. A line of planted shrubs served as the fence, and there was a small gate, which always remained open. The shrubs grew so tall that from the gate, one could not see the inside of the compound. The ground was nine steps high from the gate. At the gate, instead of 'remove your footwear here', which is common in front of all ashrams and temples, there was a distinct signboard: 'Strip before you enter'.

The Saint always sat at the front of his house, stark naked, looking at the gate. He never spoke a word. All the visitors would come in silently, sit on the floor in the open yard of the house, clothed, looking at the Saint and never spoke a word. The only message that the Saint ever conveyed was that of nakedness and silence. The difference between the visitors and the Saint was not just physical nakedness. The Saint was naked inside and outside. The visitors wore various degrees of clothing, inside and outside.

Even though there was no word uttered, everyone left for home happy and fulfilled. None felt hungry or thirsty. None felt cold. Even though there was no discourse, everyone's questions were answered. The only offering or *dakshina* the Saint asked for was 'nakedness', or the state of emptiness and non-pretension. By stripping, he meant that all those who enter should strip their ego, anger, hatred, jealousy, pretensions, fears, insecurities, etc. outside his gate and enter naked. His only teaching was silence. Since his aura spread all over the premises, people automatically got healed in his presence. He never travelled outside his compound. Mostly he remained still and silent.

It so happened that many people who read the board were quite distracted and did not enter the premises. They were quite afraid to be naked! There was one rich woman in the neighbouring city. She had lost her son and was under tremendous sorrow. One of her friends heard about this silent Saint and suggested she visit him. She decided to travel. It took a day for her to reach the abode of the Saint. However, when she read the signboard: 'Strip before you enter', she was so distracted that she left without entering.

This is the case with most of us. We are not ready to 'strip'. We are not ready to leave anything. Yet, we expect the Saint or God to give us everything. When the inner vessel is filled and overflowing with insecurities, ego, and similar negativities, how can the Saint, or the silent God deliver anything at all? We support ourselves and justify our insecurities! We miss the Saints of our time!

We all are essentially naked. However, we have learned to clothe ourselves layer by layer and the clothes have started to control and restrict our movements. We have started to become immobile and stagnant. In many cases, we are proud of our immobility and stagnancy, which we even call stability! Real stability is flexibility. Real stability is fluidity, motion. The most rigid tree is the most ready for the axe!

"I Do Not Know" Keeps the Ego in Check

ᴪ **Question:** I do not know anything... Each day this feeling is increasing. Please help.

Mohanji: You are on the right track. The moment you feel: "I know", you stop growing. Your spiritual evolution stops there. The more you feel: "I do not know", the more your ego is in check. Your ego is not overpowering your spirituality. The tallest of all egos is the spiritual ego. It traps a seeker in illusion. Knowledge is an illusion, *Maya*. The more we feel we know, the more the ego will grow. The more we feel insignificant, which of course is the Truth, the more we grow. Sooner or later, we have to shed everything. This includes all our identities, such as name, fame, position, Tradition, path – everything. Nullification has to happen and that means liberation. If we live liberated from everything, including ego, our transit to the higher will become effortless. We will live a life of unconditionality.

Surrender Means Egolessness

✤ **Question:** Why is surrender so difficult for people?

Mohanji: Ego. Surrender means egolessness. When you prostrate, your heart and head are in one line. Why do we touch somebody's feet? We consider that this man, whose feet we are touching, exists in absolute consciousness. This is our assumption.

When we touch elderly people's feet that does not mean that they exist in absolute consciousness. We respect their age, experience and evolution. Actually, the soul's age should be considered and not the physical age. Physical age has no value because everyone will become old one day. The consciousness level in which he operates is the most important thing.

Enlightened Masters like Shirdi Sai Baba and Bhagavan Nityananda behaved like ordinary people, or even like beggars. It confused people. How can he be an enlightened Master? Again, mental images block our vision. Our mind does not allow us to touch their feet. Mind pushes us to touch the feet of the glamorous, articulate, and pompous, rather than the true and the real! Thus, we miss great opportunities. He is available! He is standing there with his feet for you!

✤ **Question:** I surrender.

Mohanji: Do not deceive yourself. Surrender means leaving out whatever you surrender completely from your system. Do you do that? Total surrender needs absolute faith. Complete surrender is a complete state of annihilation of a certain aspect of you. It is a state of dissolution. You are removing something you do not need from your constitution. Your *karma* gets trashed. Think again when you use such words. Do not deceive yourself.

Surrender Matters

'Surrender', is one of the words in human languages that is most misunderstood in usage. Surrendering to someone is a big hit on one's ego. It diminishes one's self-esteem. Having to surrender is considered a weakness or a deficiency, in terrestrial terms, where ego decides actions.

However, in spiritual terms, this is a good thing. Man minus ego equals God. So, surrender nullifies our ego and then the God-hood within us starts to shine. This is why we prostrate in temples and monasteries. When our head and heart come in one line, horizontally, the ego is under control. When we bow down in reverence, we nullify our ego, at least temporarily. *Bhakti* or devotion has a lot of value because it brings the ego under control. Ignorance expands our ego, while surrender brings it under control.

Traditionally, our ancestors used to practise some simple methods to maintain health and keep the ego under control. Here are a few chants and their explanations.

When we wake up in the morning, after lying horizontally the whole night, the energy pattern in the body would have changed. Its frequency would have altered. While sleeping, the energies of our body have attained a tranquil, passive state. It is more latent energy. When we wake up, we must give time for the energies to start moving, preparing the body for action. In order to provide this time, they suggest lying down and looking at the palm of the hand instead of jumping out of bed and being vertical all of a sudden, which can affect the heart's rhythm and adversely affect the meridians of our system.

There is a *mantra* to ease our getting up. Look into the palms of your hands and chant: "*Karagre Vasate Lakshmi, Kara Moole Saraswati, Kara Madhya Sthitha Gauri, Prabhate Kara Darsanam*". This means, at the tip of our hands or fingers stays Lakshmi, the Goddess of wealth. Lakshmi never stays constantly in any place. Money changes hands. Fortunes change too. So, it always stays at the tip of our fingers. Saraswati, the goddess of knowledge stays at the opposite side, that is, the root of our palm near the wrist. Acquired knowledge stays with us till we die. It is more stable in terrestrial terms.

In the middle stays Goddess Parvati, kindness incarnate, the Mother. She balances knowledge and action. She enhances wisdom. With this knowledge, if you see your hands and remember the pattern of our existence, it will give sufficient time for the latent energy to move in an even fashion within, as well as giving us a balanced outlook. It also enhances our commitment to selfless work. It activates kindness and reverence within us. This is also a reminder that it is the God energy in us that makes things happen in our life. This is also meant to nullify our ego and we surrender to the supreme.

There is also one version of the same hymn where it says that Lord Krishna stays in the middle of the palm (*Kara Madhye tu Govinda*). Well, He is the *Guru* of the universe. If He stays in the middle of the palm, we can only function with total equanimity and detachment. He has blessed us with the great Bhagavad Gita and if we follow His teachings and function with detachment, we attain liberation.

Then we sit up for a few seconds in our bed before we stand on our feet. This is good as it helps the body's rhythm and the flow of prana through our meridians. Our body has become semi-vertical from horizontal. Energy has started moving differently. Then, we need to earth it, as we were lying horizontally before. In order to achieve that, when the feet touch the ground, we chant: "Samudra Vasane Devi, Parvata Sthana Mandale,

Vishnu Patni Namastubhyam, Paadasparsham Kshamaswame"
and we bend down and touch the ground with our right palm,
which is the opposite side to where our heart is. Through our
right hand, we earth the excess energy that we accumulated or
conglomerated during our sleep, which protects our heart as
well.

This prayer is to the Goddess whom we call Earth, even
though we address it to the wife of Lord Vishnu, Goddess
Lakshmi: 'One who pervades the water and mountains,' or,
'One whose body is the oceans and mountains, I prostrate to
the Goddess and please forgive me, as I step on you or tread on
you. This is reverence to Mother Earth. If we have such reverence for Mother Earth, we will never be insensitive towards her
and destroy her. We thus seek her permission to walk on her for
our purpose. We remain in gratitude.'

This time also gives our body an easy pace for the transition
between horizontal, semi-vertical and totally vertical. It helps
to keep our energies even and well circulated. It maintains our
meridians. We are mentioning earth and water, the two basic
elements in our body. *Samudra* (ocean) represents the water
element in us, which is regulated by our *svadhishthana chakra*.
Parvata (mountain) represents the earth element, as well as the
potential for the highest elevation in us – the *kundalini* energy. Hence, this is also an invocation for the elements, mother
kundalini and also the other elements in us, to assist us as we
move through the day. If *kundalini* energy inspires us, wisdom
will flow. It also reminds us to be conscious right from when we
wake up until we sleep and always live on prayers and surrender. Then we are ready for the day.

Then we stand up, looking towards the rising sun in the
east, remembering Lord Vishnu or His *Avatar*, Lord Krishna,
the maintainer of the universe, and chant: "*Kaayena Vaacha,
Manasendriyaiva, Buddhyatmanaavat, Prakrite Swabhavaat,
Karomi Yadyat Sakalam Parasmai, Shri Naarayanaayeti Sa-*

marpayaami". This means, 'Whatever I perform today, with my body, mind, intellect, senses, speech, my nature and character, I surrender everything at the Lotus Feet of the Lord Narayana.' Narayana means the destination of man or the Supreme Father. Everything came out of Him and will merge back into Him. So, this prayer is to the Supreme Lord.

When we start our day with this prayer, and this understanding as well as surrender, we will accept all that happens that day with equanimity and poise and our desires or expectations will be totally under control. Even if things do not happen as we expect, we will not be perturbed and will start to accept it as the will of Lord Narayana. Then, we conclude our day with the surrender *mantra*, requesting complete forgiveness for all our actions, thoughts, and words.

This is the final prayer before we go to bed: "*Kara charana kritam va, kayajam karmajam vaa, shravana nayanajam vaa, maanasam vaparadham, vihitam avihitam vaa, sarvam etat kshamasva, jaya jaya karunaabdhe, shri Mahadeva Shambho, Shri Sainath Shambho*" which says, 'Whatever I performed today, with my organs of action such as hands and legs, organs of perception including senses, mind and intellect, all that I performed as per your wishes or against it, due to my ignorance and non-understanding, Oh Lord, please forgive everything, please forgive me, my supreme Lord Shiva, my Lord Sai Baba' (They are One).

As we surrender all that happened in the day at the feet of the Supreme Lord, whence everything originated and into which everything perpetually dissolves, we become free from all bondage. We become detached from all our thoughts, words, and actions. Thus, surrender purifies us completely. Also, we are surrendering all our activities of the day at the feet of Lord Vishnu who maintains and supports existence. He is the One who maintains creation. Preservation is His job. At night, we are laying ourselves at the feet of Lord Shiva, the dissolver. He dissolves existence. He merges us with our Creator.

Each morning, we are re-born, as we dissolve our identity during deep sleep and regain it as we wake up. We are requesting the lord of dissolution to forgive everything and help us dissolve smoothly into emptiness and provide us with blissful sleep. Readers may kindly note that in the morning, we are requesting for continuity in thoughts, words, and actions, so that all that we perform on that day may bear positive results and, in the night, we are requesting forgiveness which helps smooth dissolution into the lap of the Almighty, without terrestrial entanglements. Those who carry hatred and heaviness of heart may kindly be aware of this. One prayer goes to Lord Vishnu and the other to Lord Shiva. Both are essentially One. Both are expressions of One *Parabrahma*.

Surrender in the spiritual sense is a great thing. It helps liberation from the birth-death cycle. The same method can be followed by people who follow any faith of their choice. The main thing is the attitude of surrender, to your chosen deity or Master, or Prophet, and leaving all ownerships at His feet. He does everything. The whole existence belongs to Him. 'He' does not mean a male. Gender has no value here. It can be the Supreme Energy which is formless, genderless.

Thus Spake the Rishis

Remember the pieces of advice of our rich Tradition. Guidelines for successful living...

- Even if it is for fun, do not gamble. That will become your obsession and binding. Even if it is for fun, do not develop vices. They will eventually disable you.

- Do not go to bed without cleaning your feet. (Feet have links to every organ of the body. Dirt prevents energy flow and rejuvenation.)

- Avoid dependency as much as you can. Avoid activities that require assistance from others. Dependency essentially breeds expectations, leading eventually to sorrow, pain, and binding.

- Tradition says that a *Guru* can scold or punish his own children and disciples, even beat them, to correct them and lead them on the right path. He should not punish anybody else.

- Those who earn wealth or possessions by lying or stealing, those who live in the path of '*adharma*' (bad thoughts, words and actions or selfish existence) , as well as those who harm anybody will never lead a peaceful existence.

- The ill-effects of *adharma* may not be immediate. But, eventually, *adharma* will decay the whole family just like cancer destroys an able body. It will bring down their children, grandchildren, and further generations.

- Those who perform '*adharma*' such as stealing others' wealth, hurting or torturing others etc., may see immediate gains such as wealth, gain or prosperity, but, eventually, everything will decay and perish and the entire family will suffer the ill effects of one's selfishness and greed.

- When you have acquired legitimate wealth, do not feel guilty about it. Enjoy it and share it with others. Sharing will increase your enjoyment. When you have been given wealth, do not wear torn or dirty clothes. Respect and honour wealth. Use it well and share a portion of it with others, too.

- Do not eat emotionally. Eat intelligently. This is the secret of good health.

- Do not stop any creature who is drinking water and eating food. Wait till it has finished. It is bad *karma* to stop an animal from drinking water and a calf from drinking its mother's milk.

- Early morning and late night are not good for eating food. Dawn and dusk are the same. You can eat and drink at any other time.

- The one who leads a pious life, who does not hurt anyone through thoughts, words, or actions enjoys a peaceful life. He himself and his further generations will enjoy unlimited Grace.

- Those who do not consume animal flesh attain the Grace of a hundred fire ceremonies of the highest order.

- Do not take a bath after food or after 10 p.m.

- Those who scandalise their *Guru* have no place in any *lokas* (worlds). No *Gurus* will accept them. They will take birth in the lowliest of wombs, such as a caterpillar or centipede, and it will take ages and many lifetimes to attain another human form.

- Never consider yourself unlucky or talk so to others, even if you are suffering from the ill effects of your worst *karmas*. Surrender and acceptance of every situation lead one from bad *karma* to ultimate liberation from everything.

- Plucking one's own hair due to frustration or beating one's own head is completely inauspicious.

- Having equanimity leads to good health. Overeating, oversleeping, and over emotion lead one to illness.

- Never ridicule, despise or condemn the old, the ugly, the sick, the poor, the handicapped, a prostitute, the illiterate, other castes or religions, animals, or birds. Respect every creation. Respect every expression of life. Those who ridicule others are only expressing their inherent ignorance.

- Never use or utilise the property, vehicle, utensils, chair, bed, slippers, house or food of another without their permission. Scriptures say that a part of the sin (bad *karma*) of the owner of these comes to the user, if used without permission.

- Those who can calm the angry and help the helpless spontaneously are loved by all Gods. Grace flows to them constantly.

- If a truth leads to sorrow, better to avoid telling that truth.

- Avoid eating food with the plate on your lap.

- A *Guru* who is One with the eternal Truth may/need not follow any terrestrial norms. A disciple who is aspiring for the stature of his *Guru* must follow all the norms until he attains that stature.

- Anything in excess is bad; including excess sleep or no sleep, food, play, exercise, sitting, standing, lying down, etc. Everything in the right measure maintains good health.

- Food should be respected. Avoid talking while eating. Concentrate on the food.

- Do not make any sound while eating food or drinking water.

- The food kept for others should not be consumed. What is kept for others should go to the designated.

- Do not ridicule those who beg. We should provide within our capacity to anyone who comes to us as a beggar. Those who come to us as beggars might be entities who could save us from all kinds of ignorance and hellish lives.

- Fighting, hatred, and enmity should be avoided at all costs. Respecting and honouring the old, the sick, guests, as well as worshipping ancestors, family deities and invited guests, ensures prosperity through generations.

CHAPTER 3:

The guru principle

God, *Guru* and Soul are One

uru is a principle and not a form. *Guru* can take any form to convey the necessary message. The *Guru* principle works according to *Dharma* (Duty) of existence. The God element within us is our soul. The soul is not separate from God and we will feel God separate only when the soul is in a body.

> ❧ **Question:** I see her touching the feet of every possible *Guru*. Will it take her anywhere?

Mohanji: I have no interest in commenting on such matters. Isn't it at the individual's discretion? Who are we to decide what is right or what is wrong? It depends on various factors. Still, I am answering this question in a different way, only because I thought it is very important to clarify certain matters in general terms. Getting the Grace of all Masters is good, especially of those who are enlightened. Wandering unconsciously, not knowing what we are seeking is an absolute waste of time. This is the difference. Masters exist at a different level of consciousness than the seekers. Most people go to them seeking something tangible. This is the tragedy. Hardly any people actually go to a Master seeking salvation – *mukti* or *moksha*.

I have seen many wanderers. They are so insecure; they cannot anchor anywhere. They are so feeble that they shift their loyalty at the drop of a hat. They have heavy expectations and, if they do not get exactly what they expect, they not only leave the *Guru*, but also scandalise him. Stability and consistency are essential for spiritual growth. One who keeps wandering from camp to camp will never gather Grace. However, having no divisions within and accepting all as divine incarnations and being one with all the Masters is a great thing. There is no comparison there. There is only love. Unconditional love. Love without expectations. Such people evolve a lot in one life.

ᴫ **Question:** Many *Gurus*. Which one is my *Guru*?

Mohanji: None of them. Your *Guru* is your own soul. All else are reminders. Nothing that lies outside of you really belongs to you.

ᴫ **Question:** How to choose a *Guru*? Which spiritual courses to take?

Mohanji: All *Gurus* are One. The *Guru* that appeared to you is usually the right one for you. But, do not be confused as to whether you are on the right track or not. Just accept the *Guru* in front of you, or the one guiding you, even if you have never met him physically. Start walking the path with faith and confidence. Maybe you will meet more *Gurus* (road signs) on the path. Wandering in search of a *Guru* is absolutely unnecessary. This is because you will be searching for someone whom you think is the right one for you. The reality is your eligibility. Thus, learn to accept the *Guru* who helps you now. Whoever he is! Take this as your starting point and start walking from there with faith and devotion. The *Guru* will choose you. You need not choose any *Guru*.

If you want to choose a *Guru*, it is your choice. When you decide to leave this *Guru*, it is also your choice. If you shift to another *Guru*, it is also your choice. However, do not make your decision based on the words of others. You decide for yourself. Do not decide anything, just let things flow. If you decide to be with me, or leave me, it is also your decision. I do not invite anyone, nor do I ask anyone to go. I am all-inclusive.

The same is applicable to many spiritual cou   s. It is an intellectual requirement, not a spiritual requirement. You may like all the foods served at the buffet table and you may want to taste them all. However, you have your own stomach capacity. If you try to cram more, either obesity or indigestion, or both, will result. Take only as much as your stomach is comfortable with. There are hundreds of meditation techniques. Try a few and choose the one you like or what suits you. Do not follow others. You are unique. You carve your own path with the available materials. The same vegetables can be used to make different curries. Make your own curry with the available vegetables. Use your inner guidance. Just keep walking with faith in yourself and your *Guru*, whoever it is. Never procrastinate.

᭞ **Question:** Why do Masters distract students or disillusion them?

Mohanji: A true Master knows exactly what the student needs. He will distract the student to test his eligibility to receive the supposed knowledge. Also, he will check the maturity of every disciple to receive that knowledge. Many students come with their cups full of sundry knowledge. The Master shakes them so much that the cups will become somewhat empty. Some cannot handle this shaking and they leave. Some stay on and evolve higher. Masters have also displayed strange behaviours which often distract disciples. Some act like madmen. Some express seeming vices such as intoxicants, and the disciple's expectation gets affected. These are done to eliminate conditionings.

We are born and brought up with a lot of conditioning. These are affecting our thought processes and alienating us from our own true nature. Shirdi Sai was initially considered as mad, until many people started getting benefitted from his Grace. Our conditioned mind often cannot understand a true Master. Others also influence our thoughts. Negative thoughts breed fast, while positive thoughts take time. If one of your friends, or even your own husband or wife does not like a particular *Guru*, they may distract you, and you will eventually give up. This is almost always the case. We compromise our own Truth for others' words and suffer eventually. A will of steel is essential here.

First of all, the path should be clear. The track should be defined, such as path of devotion, knowledge, or action. Then, once you find your Master, once your internal churning about his stature is completed, stick on. Do not always be doubting Thomases. This is anti-evolution. It is true that along the path, you may reach higher Masters. This is like: after graduation, you step into post-graduation. A new Master welcomes you there. This is quite fine. This is evolution. There is absolute clarity here. This is to travel with gratitude for the path, the knowledge, and the evolution so far. This is how it should be.

As I mentioned earlier, true Masters are road signs. They never bind the traveller to themselves. True Masters always liberate you. Guaranteed.

The Master Framed on the Wall

There is a saying: "There are no two buffaloes alike." Each being is unique and different. Each being is complete in itself, even though we do not really acknowledge this fact. While we enjoy terrestrial life, we entertain our ego to a certain degree. Some high and some low. Our own personal ego will never accept another as possibly 'up there'.

With the dead, we have no such problem. They are no more. They are not in competition with our personal ego. We always feel superior to the next man. This is why no Master was revered when he trod the earth. Krishna was considered as just a friend by Arjuna for most of his life. He failed to recognise Krishna's divinity. This is more so because, for an evolved being, as his consciousness becomes more and more subtle, his interest in terrestrial standing decreases. He will feel that there is nothing to prove. Take it or leave it. So, those who are still caught up in a terrestrial quagmire will fail to see the real depth of the man. That's why we do not even recognise enlightenment in our own kin. It happens silently and it remains silent.

The Master within the frame on the wall (a photograph) is innocent. He does not interfere. We can interpret his teachings the way we want, according to our convenience. We can use him or abuse him. He is not going to come back with a stick and beat everyone. So, we stick to the picture in the frame. A walking and talking Master may not be too palatable all the time. He may scold you and even abuse you, as he needs nothing from you.

We prefer those half-baked, smooth-tongued Masters who only say what we like to hear. They pamper you and keep you in a comfort zone so that you will be happy even though unevolved. The mind likes to swap stagnation with comfort, which is the nature of the human mind. Spiritual evolution is a path of thorns and hazards. There are snakes and crocodiles on the way. A true Master will never stop you from that adventure. For those with endurance, a great result is certain. For those who cannot leave their comfort zones, there is always a next time and a next life.

✤ **Question:** Why do people worship *Gurus* – the ones who are in their physical form? Do we need to? I find it inappropriate and meaningless.

Mohanji: This question usually comes from a person who is on the knowledge path –a jnana yogi. There are many paths to reach God. The *Guru* is the guiding light. There are many types of people too. Everyone has his or her own style and approach towards any situation. Actually speaking, no true *Guru* or God needs anything from you, let alone worship.

Now, a person of an emotional nature, who chants the praise of God – usually the form that his mind gets connected to easily, melts himself or herself into that being or object of worship. These people need an object to worship. The human mind needs forms to associate with. This is fundamental. It recognises forms and connects to forms. The human constitution uses all its faculties such as the body, mind and intellect to connect to the chosen form. As the connection through faith increases, the individual personality takes a back seat.

The individual starts to merge with the object of worship. Non-duality happens. When oneness takes root, often the need for any of the individual faculties that the individual used for the primary connection also becomes redundant. Everything dissolves into oneness. This is the advantage of bhakti yoga. Usually, bhakti yogis merge with Supreme Consciousness much faster than the other paths such as knowledge, *sadhana*, and service. The tranquility and strength that they achieve through surrender cannot be fathomed by practitioners of other types of paths.

Likewise, the elevation that knowledge gives, based on non-duality, is not understandable to a bhakti yogi too. Experiencing God using the path of knowledge is like the pole of the pole vault. The pole is only used to lift one beyond the bar. Then, the pole of knowledge is shed when the bar is crossed. Then it is just a fall into the lap of Infinity or God. But, if the yogi holds on to the pole and refuses to let go, he faces a handicap in the game. He stays with his pole and cannot win God.

There is a saying: "If God and *Guru* come together, whom to greet first?" The answer automatically happens, "*Guru*, because he is the one who brought and guided me to God." This is one aspect and answer to your question.

Another aspect: in Shirdi Sai Baba's words, "My *Guru* was indeed powerful. But he taught me nothing. Day and night I served him and watched him. He gave me everything". This is another aspect. There are paths where there are no explicit teachings or courses. By just a mere glance or wave of a hand, Baba used to elevate people. By just being in the energy field of the powerful *Guru*, the disciple achieves everything. But, in those cases, the *Guru* would often display mediocrity and shallowness, to test the tenacity and conviction of the disciple.

In the path of courses and examination, the skill displayed is the criterion for elevation. In the case of the Path of Pathlessness, the ability to cling on against all odds, and the depth of faith and surrender are the criteria for higher elevation. Total surrender and perfect obedience was the path. This is often very difficult for a *jnana yogi*, one who is on the knowledge path and who needs answers for every simple thing. The *Gurus* of the Datta Tradition, the Nath Tradition or simply those who follow the path of dissolution will not deliver such answers. They even shake the faith of their disciples through abnormal and even unacceptable behaviour to test the mettle of the student. The jnana yogi often scandalises the *Guru* and escapes, but falls deeper into the birth-death cycle and disillusionment. The *bhakti yogi* stays.

True *Gurus* are Rare

✤ **Question:** Now, once again, how do you know a *Sadguru* – the true One?

Mohanji: There are some primary yardsticks. The most important one is your destiny. It is destiny that brings you to him. It is your destiny that makes you recognise the real One.

Second are certain signs of the *Guru*. Does he bind you with fear or does he maintain you unbound and free? If you are always kept unbound, you are at the right place. In this path, serving the *Guru* is your choice, yet it is also your elevation.

The third is, he needs nothing from you, or he gives you back much more than he takes – if at all. He changes your basic constitution, often based on conditionings and fears, to that of stillness and fearlessness.

Fourth is, when you are with him, you will know and recognise a definite change in your vibratory level, a shift in consciousness. The more you are with him, the more the shifted consciousness becomes yours. These are subtle aspects one must feel and experience within.

Fifth is non-conformity to any habits and mannerisms. He may behave in strange ways, often unacceptable to social norms. This is because a *Guru* who is established in supreme consciousness operates only at the level of cosmic necessity or purpose and not of individual karma. He is only guided by purpose.

He has nothing to do with social dos and don'ts. His operating level is spontaneity, uncontaminated by thoughts. For example, Sai Baba often scolded and beat people to drive away evil lying embedded in the constitution of devotees. People, who got offended, never understood the real meaning behind the action. They left him and went away. The loss was essentially theirs. Akkalkot Maharaj used to urinate in front of people, which distracted many. There are many such examples.

If the *Guru* is powerful, he will usually be very ordinary or will often act in strange ways. They scold people for their well-being. They need nothing from anyone. True Masters would not care about their mannerisms and will make no efforts to be socially acceptable. Those who are totally conditioned and bound by social norms and fears will run away from them. Those who stay get all that they can carry.

So, worshipping the *Guru*, considering him as representing the Lord Almighty or personification of the Lord, is definitely the path of those who are inclined to bhakti or the devotional path of spirituality. Understand that all the paths are suitable for someone. All the paths are not suitable for everyone. Do not judge from your level. If you do, you will only get more disillusioned. You may not understand the pleasure that a bhakti yogi derives from any acts of devotional nature. They often do not have duality. They become one with the object of their worship faster than the other paths.

The knowledge path keeps duality longer than other paths because intellect is the faculty used to digest knowledge, and the intellect is associated with our limited system. This constitution of ours which is tangible and that we call with a name is associated with a form. The intellect alienates and analyses. The intellect creates walls. When knowledge becomes wisdom, that means each unit of knowledge intake was digested well, and has merged into our constitution, duality slowly starts to dissolve. Oneness takes root.

Understand one thing clearly. No true *Gurus* or God need anything from people including worshipping their perishable physical form. However, for disciples, it is a reconfirmation, a confidence, and it helps in maintaining their faith. This is why they do it. Every practice has its value only if it is done from the heart. If mechanically, ritualistically done, no activity will have any value.

❧ **Question:** At which point is a person ready to become a *Guru*?

Mohanji: A *Guru* should happen. You cannot become a *Guru* through doing. You can become an *Acharya* (teacher) through doing. If you learn from a lot of books, you can become an *Acharya*. You can be trained to become a teacher! To become a *Guru*, it should happen by itself. That means that you becoming a *Guru* should happen to you. *Guru*-ship or *Guru*-dom should fall in place. At that time you may not want to talk to anybody. A true *Guru* is deeply connected to the source and operates in perfect equanimity with no desires. *Acharyas* are plenty. True *Gurus* are very rare.

☙ **Question:** Is it similar to *Tatwamasi*?

Mohanji: No. What is *Tatwamasi*? 'Thou art That'! That means: You are God. If it is just an intellectual understanding, it means nothing. When you repeat this understanding in the mind, it means nothing. You become God by expressing God. What is God? Unconditional love, a being full of love – you have no desires, your existence is for the sake of love. You exist in a bliss state, beyond all duality. That is God-hood.

The *Guru* is absolutely detached. Look at Bhagavan Nityananda or Shirdi Sai Baba. They wanted nothing. In the twentieth century, people were speaking of haves and have nots! However, in India, we have always had a third class, who could have everything if they wanted to; instead, they wanted nothing. 'Tat Twam Asi' is a great principle. The understanding of 'Tat Twam Asi' should be experiential and not intellectual. People most of the time talk about 'Tat Twam Asi', 'Aham Brahmasmi,' probably out of intellectual understanding.

The real core meaning of 'Tat Twam Asi' is becoming *Parabrahma*, Father, or *Allah*, whatever name you want to call it by. Become That, be That. It is a formless imperishable entity. The representation of that entity in you is your own soul. Be the soul. The soul needs nothing from you. It never interferes with your journey. When the soul leaves the body, we call it a dead body. You will call it 'X person's body'. When the soul exits the body, the body has no meaning anymore. The soul takes away the name of the body.

We are such fragile creatures, and still, we have a lot of ego. Eighty per cent of our vital functions are not controlled by us:

heartbeat, circulation, digestion, respiration. We make some silly decisions and then become egoistic about it. I am saying this for the sake of awareness. If our awareness level is high, we will accept our daily life as it is, and we will be peaceful. Suppose, someone tells you that at such-and-such a date and time you will die: some people will panic, as we are so attached to the body. They will feel, "Oh! My body is going, what will I do now?" But, some people will be okay with it. They will accept it as a true possibility, an inevitability and will be comfortable with it.

We are worried about small, small things. "Will I get parking today?" We operate only in such a level of consciousness. Baba can give us enlightenment, but we ask Baba for a vehicle parking space! He can take us to the highest level of awareness. Every day we ask about car parking, and we do get the parking. Faith is working and we do not realise that faith is working. We do not use the available rope to climb to the highest point in this life; instead, we stay stuck in our mundane troubles associated with our daily existence.

ﾐ **Question:** If faith is working, then why do we shift to so many *Gurus*?

Mohanji: There are two things. The first thing is that the restless mind takes you to too many Masters. The mind says, "This is not good enough, look at him! Let us go for somebody higher." The usual result is disillusionment.

The second thing is, you elevate yourself to a higher level and then the old *Guru* may not be able to teach you anymore. When you go from the second to fourth-grade, the same teacher cannot teach you. In the tenth-grade, another teacher must be available. This is elevation. This way you will change your *Gurus* or rather, the *Guru* may change. But this has to happen. Here, you are not changing anything. The new *Guru* is happening in your grade. When the mind says, "I do not want this

Guru, he smokes!" You disown that Master who would have elevated your consciousness, because of your prejudice – you discredit your requirements from that particular *Guru*. He does not vibe with your prejudice. Naturally, he will not. The problem is not with the available *Guru*, but with the mental image that you created for yourself. Your husband, son, daughter will also not obey you exactly the way you want. This is similar to that. Take another person who is a *Guru*, and you say he should not wear jeans and a T-shirt! This is the mind's job. The mind is telling you these things. Mental images are blocking you.

Then you change the *Guru*. You keep changing the *Guru*, especially if the true *Guru* dishes out bitter pills, and finally, you do not know where we are going. Then you surrender. You say, "I have had enough of this". Sometimes it goes to suicidal tendencies because you think you have wasted your life. Most people spend their entire life searching, without finding the *Guru*. When the actual *Guru* comes, you cannot identify him because your mental images block recognition! What a tragedy!

You already created mental pictures of the *Guru*. You already bought the frame. If the *Guru* fits into the frame, it is fine. What if the *Guru* is bigger than the frame? We discard the *Guru* and not the frame. This is how we function. Let us take a closer look at ourselves. We are indeed like that.

- ❧ **Question:** What are the qualities of a *Guru*? If we are looking for *moksha*, then how do we know whether this *Guru* will help us?

Mohanji: The qualities of a *Guru* depend on which grade you are studying in and the level you are operating from. Do you know the grade you are studying in? The *Guru* which comes in front of you is the right one for you. A student in the second-grade cannot decide what kind of teacher he needs because he does not know. This is a basic Truth. The teacher who comes into the class is the right one for you. If your quest is true, the right *Guru* will happen in your life. For that, we have to accept and be non-resistant. This is a fundamental principle of spirituality. "The food that comes to the table for you today is the medicine for you". So say the Vedas.

We may not like the food or maybe we never chose that food. We wanted *biryani* but got *dosa*! If you accept that food as medicine, then there is no friction within. When there is no friction within, peace descends upon you. When peace descends, you operate at the level of equanimity. This continuously brings you good things.

In our path of Shiva, the quality of the *Guru* will lie in being the one who helps annihilate or destroy all baggage, desires, *vasanas*, habits and all that is binding one to Earth. More things will be shed from you. Look at all the Masters of the Dattatreya Tradition. They never wanted anything. They were detached from everything and helped people to stay detached or unattached.

Why does Shiva wear ash on the body? What does ash mean? Ash means complete nullification of everything. Fire burns everything indiscriminately and forms ash. This is exactly what we hope to become. Liberation happens out of the ash. Shiva wears nullification on his body. It means "I belong there", i.e., in the perfect nullified state. The principle of Shiva is dissolution. This is even bigger than enlightenment. Do not confuse enlightenment and dissolution. Enlightenment is a shift in consciousness when you develop much larger awareness. Nullification or dissolution is a further process.

You have to observe each process and detach completely. Perfect *shanti* then falls upon you. If you are on a path of leaving the house to go wandering, the *Guru* for this path will happen to you. That *Guru* may not wear clothes or may not look crisp, clean, or attractive in the terrestrial sense. But in a city like this, if someone does not wear clothes, you discard the *Guru*! This is our level of operation. I do not like to mince my words.

The Grace of the *Guru*

❦ **Question:** These Masters also never said, "I will give you enlightenment." Is it that disciples are glorifying the Masters?

Mohanji: Disciples do not want to call themselves fools. Otherwise, society will ask, "Why are you going after this Master?" They hate to call themselves fools! Even if that Master is not carrying any weight on him, you add weight on him! When you glorify, two things can happen. Firstly, the person cannot take the weight and he falls. Secondly, he can develop 'hyper-ego' and will fall anyway. Ego makes you so heavy that you fall!

Not only today's Masters, but also look at the modern doctors and engineers. They are not serving the people; they are just trying to make money. Your competence is judged on how much money you make. There is no *satya* (truth) or *dharma*. So sad!

Let us look at how things evolved. During Lord Rama's time, great Sages were guiding kings, sitting in their court but they never wanted anything from them. They had a simple existence. Now businessmen are controlling empires. They count only profits. How much have we travelled- from Sages guiding the empire, to businessmen guiding the country! The makers of arms and ammunition are controlling empires. The result is war. Human life is traded in the street. Deterioration has happened everywhere. The same deterioration has also affected spirituality.

There is competition in spirituality now. How many disciples you have and how many I have! If I have one more, I am better off. People need to declare that their *Guru* is an enlightened Master! Look at various spiritual websites of our time; spirituality is being so heavily marketed. Nowadays people say,

"I am enlightened". They create a website to proclaim, "I am enlightened and I will make you enlightened." There are courses for "intense enlightenment" where you pay a lot of money. Sometime in the past, I attended a session in Dubai, where a woman told the group: 'I think I am slightly enlightened'. Everybody was clapping their hands. How can you be slightly enlightened? You are either enlightened or you're not.

First of all, why do you need enlightenment? Is it another trophy on the wall? Is it a thing to be collected? Secondly, who can guarantee enlightenment in this world? No one can guarantee enlightenment. Enlightenment is something that happens to you when the ground is ready. Enlightenment can only happen, based on the eligibility of the seeker. Even in the *Kriya* yoga path – I'm sure you have read Autobiography of a Yogi – you just raise the *Kundalini* up to the third eye level during *sadhana*, the rest happens automatically. You cannot decide whether you get enlightenment within a few days. It cannot be promised. Nobody can sell it or buy it from any shop. This is the reality.

Look at the old Sages and Maharishis. None of the sages ever proclaimed that they were enlightened. Satya Sai Baba never told anyone that he was enlightened or that he needed money–and nor did Bhagavan Nityananda and Shirdi Sai Baba. If a person is complete, self-sufficient, and enlightened, he will not come back to tell you, "I am enlightened!" He will never criticise anybody. He will do his job and say goodbye! Look at our Tradition. No Master, whether Ramana Maharishi or Bhagavan Nityananda, or Sai Baba, ever said that he was enlightened. They never invited you to their camp and promised more *ladoos* to eat!

They said, "I am available. You can come here if you like, but you are free to go wherever you like!" Nobody can bind anybody. Because, the very path is that of liberation, not binding.

The Eligibility Factor

Many saffron-clad people that we see today are just *Acharyas*, pretending to be *Gurus*. They have theoretical book knowledge. However, they pretend to be enlightened Masters. There is nothing original in them. They have to create ideas to attract. They collect material from many terrestrial sources, make different modules, and present it all to the world. As I always say, keep in mind that we get the *Guru* according to our eligibility. A post-graduate professor is of no use to a first-grade student. He will not get him either.

The government will only be according to the type of people who created it and the type of people who voted it to power! Ministers are voted in by people. They reflect society. Corruption happens because society's consciousness is such. A similar thing happens in spirituality. You will get a *Guru* according to your eligibility and calibre.

I met a person in the Himalayas. She had come from Brazil to learn Haṭha Yoga, and then go back to teach it in Brazil. She ended up in a camp on the beautiful banks of the Ganga. The camp taught all types of yoga. The first posture they taught her was to keep her leg around the neck! She became like a question mark! Nobody told her that one should be doing this posture only after the body becomes very flexible. Camps are advertising and damaging people. This is a reality in the Himalayas nowadays! That posture was advertised because it looked very interesting. It is eye-catching! A picture of touching the feet appears too simple. However, in the end, you may get injured. Who cares? You cannot measure teaching. When you do not do well, it is easy for a teacher to say, "I taught you perfectly. But Oh! You did not learn properly!"

Theoretical knowledge does not take you anywhere. Sometimes practice makes you perfect. There is no mission or vision about what a person needs. This happens only when a person with higher awareness looks at you. Only he comes to know what you require.

A disciple comes to a *Guru* and tells him, "I have heard about you and know you are somebody great." The *Guru* said, "I do not think so! This kind of thinking is your problem and not mine." This is their way of teaching. So strong! Only then, if the disciple clings on, does the *Guru* accept him. The situation here is different. You expect disciples to come from other camps! If one *Guru* falls, the other *Guru* is happy. He rejoices as it is more 'meat' for him! What kind of canvassing is this? When the teacher looks at the pockets of disciples, then degeneration is guaranteed!

The Grace of the *Guru* cannot be bought from the market! Grace has to happen. Sadashiv Brahmendra or Bhagavan Nityananda — you cannot imitate these powerful Masters. Can you just wear a loincloth and become Bhagavan Nityananda? The world however is operating by imitating somebody. You may become physically similar to him, but not in stature. As Adi Shankaracharya said, most of these things are 'gimmicks' just to fill the stomach and make a living. *Shaktipat* is a big task and a big responsibility. Those who give *Shaktipat* are aware of it. It is not easy to give and take *Shaktipat*. Some may say, "Oh, I have been giving experiences, let me start my own *Shaktipat* camp!" Be aware! God will pull the plug. It will be like a refrigerator without electricity.

Let me tell you a real story. My friend was fortunate enough to interact with Mahavatar Babaji. Babaji came in the physical form and was guiding him. Babaji made him grow from the level of individual interaction to the level of conducting seminars. So many people benefited from him because he spoke truthfully and his talks held high value. He also started TV programmes. He took lectures and seminars in the USA as well. His ego got bloated. He thought, "I am somebody great and I can do these things." One day the show was on; a live program was on and... Babaji disappeared!

This fellow was standing on the stage with no knowledge. He knew nothing and went completely blank. He did not know why he was standing there. His ego got completely deflated. Then he prayed to Babaji. "Babaji please help me." Babaji did not come! He realised the Grace element. Then he finally surrendered to Babaji and said, "I have understood the point. I am no one without your Grace." Grace cannot be taken for granted. If you take Grace for granted, you will be deflated sooner or later. Once he understood that, he left everything and disappeared.

We think everything is easy. "I can also give *Shaktipat*." Please go ahead and do it. It is not my discretion. I will not pull anyone's plug because I am not the One who is doing it. There is a higher Grace. That Grace is much higher than me. That Grace must flow. The criteria for Grace are faith, surrender, and purity.

Grace does not care about your money. No Masters ever equated any disciples with money. But these days, it is happening. Let me tell you clearly, those who are equating disciples based on money are *Acharyas* as they need the money for their living. They conduct seminars about the 'secrets' of making money, while they themselves struggle for money. Their disciples struggle for money. True *Gurus* never cared about money. They cared only for purity of the heart. Irrespective of whether you were rich or poor, you were not allowed in if you were not pure at heart.

Some also portray their pictures with movie stars to attract a crowd. This is because they need glamour. They need to say, "These big people are coming to me so you should also come!" The common man falls prey to this. My intention is clear. Please differentiate between *Acharyas* and *Gurus*. *Acharyas* are aplenty and many times pretend to be enlightened. They operate at your level to please you. They tune things for you to make you feel comfortable. True *Gurus* like Shirdi Baba may scold you, or even physically hit you. However, they are real Masters, and you will be immensely benefited by their Grace. You will be cleansed of lifetimes of *karmas*.

A king came to meet Akkalakoṭ Maharaj. As soon as the king entered, Maharaj slapped him! Everybody was shocked. His crown flew to the far corner of the room. Maharaj said, "I am the king here. Nobody comes here with ego." The king immediately realised that he is a true *Guru* and prostrated. Maharaj blessed him and everything was fine once again.

People do not like this kind of treatment. They want to be respected. People do not want their egos to be bashed. Those who want their ego to be massaged and maintained will go to *Acharyas*. *Acharyas* will give you all sorts of comfort. When this comfort zone is created around you, disciples do not progress. True *Gurus* do not let their disciples fall. Even if they fall, *Gurus* will bring them up. A true *Guru* does not need propaganda. They do not need a Public Relations Officer. Whatever they say is original. *Acharyas* usually copy-paste from others' teachings and pretend it is their own.

In Service of the *Guru* Principle

ﷺ **Question:** I have heard that Shankaracharya Chandrashekhar Saraswati would discuss nuclear physics?

Mohanji: Oh, Chandrashekhar Saraswati was an amazing Master. He was an ocean of knowledge. A great Master indeed. In those days, there were no means of communication like the internet or computers. Similar to Kabir Das, and Shirdi Sai Baba. How would people recognise them? Now visibility and communication are more due to technology. But the true Masters have gone to the Himalayas. The world is contaminated. They do not want to stay here. There are at least twenty thousand people meditating at great heights on the ice! Those who want to reach them will reach them. These Masters do not care about the rat race. They do not care about their photos – whether they are taken with lights so that their face glows, or not! They are glowing naturally.

There are hundreds of different ways of attaining God. There are people living in deep jungles or in burial grounds like the *Aghoris*. I am not only talking of them. Of course, they are sincere seekers. They want to conquer fear and attain Shiva. They want to transcend the fear of death and ghosts, which are major fears in our life. They have chosen their path. I do not want to talk about them. It would take hours to discuss that. Each one has their path. Please, identify your path.

We must differentiate between a *Guru* and an *Acharya*. I have said so many times already that Mohan does not exist. Mohan was never born and will never die. But the principle called *Guru* will always flow. This body will die. But the principle called *Guru* will keep flowing through different bodies. We have to catch hold of the *Guru* principle. The principle of *Guru* has operated over many, many mouths over the ages.

I repeat, do not equate a *Guru* with an *Acharya*. You may find others' expressions in *Acharyas*. They collect materials from various sources and present them to you. The expression of a true *Guru* is always original.

Acharyas also tend to ask their disciples not to go here and there to other Masters. They create fear and guilt in you to bind you. It is very easy to put trash in your inner space. But it is difficult to purify you. In the garden, it is difficult to cultivate a rose, but weeds grow and spread very easily, without your nurturing it. Your minds are the same. Contaminating someone's mind is very easy.

Acharyas may create fear by saying that if you leave them, you may fall out of Grace. Something wrong will happen to you.

However, if your pockets are empty, they do not need you. A true *Guru* will never bind you. If you want to leave him, he will simply say, "*Atithi Devo Bhava* (the guest is God). I am always available. It is up to you".

ᴥ **Question:** I feel the critical thing is we cannot measure the effect of meditation. Many techniques and packages are projected to make the mind feel that it is great. We cannot measure Grace.

Mohanji: Let me tell you a story that I heard today. I am equating that to spirituality.

In a village in India, a raging bull attacked a boy and tore one of his eyes out. He was taken to hospital. After the usual first aid, he was immediately shifted to the neighbouring city. A good ophthalmologist gave a sincere and truthful opinion, "I am sorry. Nothing can be done to save the eye." However, unconvinced and relying on hope, his relatives went to another eye doctor. The second doctor said, "Oh, this is very critical. Let me try. I will operate immediately." He knew quite well that it was useless to do any surgery. He took the patient to the operation theatre, stitched the wound again, charged forty thousand rupees and then said, "Sorry! I tried my level best, but his eye could not be saved."

Both doctors said the same thing. One doctor was straightforward and told the Truth upfront and the other cheated the boy's parents. People want those who would say, "I will help you," with an undercurrent of cheating! When someone talks straight, people do not like it. I hope that answers your query. May God guide you all.

ᴥ **Question:** Please talk about the dependency on the *Guru*?

Mohanji: Shirdi Sai Baba has enlightened many. Adi Shankaracharya, Buddha, Ramana Maharishi, and Bhagavan Nityananda have also enlightened many. By just following the *Guru*'s instruction, by just surrendering to the will and instruction of the *Guru*, by just serving the *Guru* without expectations, people have attained enlightenment. Faith is the key here. Faith can take us to the highest. Through complete and perfect surrender to the *Sadguru*, by making Him the main object of worship and obeying His words to the fullest, disciples can cut out the weeds of uncertainty and attain supreme bliss. All *Sadgurus* test their disciples to make sure that they have attained the right eligibility for receiving the highest. Faith, surrender, and patience mature a disciple and help his elevation. The *Guru* takes care of his well-being.

    ❧ **Question:** What attracts people to a spiritual *Guru*?

Mohanji: Their need for spiritual evolution.

    ❧ **Question:** What ensures spiritual evolution?

Mohanji: Faith, concentration, devotion, and patience.

How to Tap into the *Guru* Principle

We are not apart from the *Guru* Tattva, the principle called *Guru*. The principle called *Guru* exists inside us, within us, and this is driving us towards the ultimate realisation that we are one with the Guru principle. The *Guru* principle is you. You are the *Guru* principle. The *Guru* principle that rests in all beings is the soul element. Once we connect to the soul element, we are one with the *Guru* principle. While we walk this path, the path of spirituality, it does not matter which religion, which *Guru*, which concept or which practice you follow in life, to attain the highest possible in human existence. It does not matter who you are, where you are, or what you are, as the *Guru* principle is always with you.

To tap into the *Guru* principle, you must have a few things which are extremely important, such as discipline. Discipline is simple. If you are not disciplined, it takes you further and further away from the principle called *Guru* and it always makes you feel alienated. Alienation is a state of mind. It does not exist. We are always one with the *Guru* principle. You are always one with the *Guru*. You are always one with eternity, or the principle that guides us or maintains us. But sometimes the mind comes forward, the mind becomes overactive, and we feel that we are separate from everything, separate from the *Guru*, separate from the path, from the Tradition, from what you want to be, from what you want to achieve.

Whenever you feel separated, understand that there is no discipline in your journey or your effort in reaching the Ultimate, using the principle called *Guru*. The *Guru* principle could also come in human form. But the human form is given only because you need someone to relate to, someone to talk to. The *Guru* principle is everywhere. It is in the sun, it is in the moon, in the air, in water. In every being around us, we experience the principle called *Guru*, the *Guru Tattva*. Once you have discipline, once you are fully disciplined and fully focused on the principle, in your effort to reach the principle, then next comes consistency.

Whatever you do, do it with consistency. There should be consistency. You can remove all your consistency when you become one with the *Guru* principle, as then you will be fully integrated into the *Guru Tattva*, the principle itself. Until then, you need to have consistency. If you are not consistent in your practice, if you are not consistent in your *Guru*, if you are not consistent in your message, or the message which guides you, or the path you follow, then it always leads to alienation. You will be separate from the Tradition or the path, or the *Guru*. The more you wander, the more you alienate and get disillusioned. Eventually, you will feel that you have earned nothing. This was all a wasted exercise. So be consistent.

And whenever you are walking this path of the *Guru*, or the *Guru* principle, always have firm conviction. Always take your time to understand the Tradition. Take your time to understand the path. Take your time to check if this is good for you, or whether it suits you. If it does not, you have every reason to discard it. However, while you are walking the path, have firm conviction. If you do not have firm conviction, it will not take you to the desired destination. The *Guru* principle is available to you, it is within you. At the same time, if you don't connect yourself to the *Guru* principle, it cannot take you to the desired destination, or desired result.

Now, what does the *Guru* need from you? Actually, the *Guru* needs nothing from you. The *Guru* is just like a road sign, or the electricity which is sitting in your wall, waiting to express itself. But you have to switch it on. You have to press the button. Then it displays its brilliance. The *Guru* principle is similar, it is the principle that is available through time, always available to you, but you need to press the button. The button is first of all your willingness, your conviction, your consistency, and your application. You need to apply yourself. Otherwise, you are expecting the *Guru* to deliver everything to you, or serve it all to you on a plate. It will not happen.

Why will it not happen? Because, according to the *Guru* principle you cannot interfere with anyone's free will. Free will has been given the ultimate or utmost importance in the whole of creation. You created your destiny, you created your life, and you created your path. You chose everything, including your parents, your body, your character, your constitution; all these things are chosen by you. Now, the *Guru* is coming just to guide you as a road sign to your ultimate destination. So, while you are walking this path, the *Guru* can never interfere or change things that you have already chosen. But at the same time, when you surrender, when you are convinced that, for example, liberation is your ultimate aim, the principle called *Guru* will bring you everything which helps you to attain liberation – ultimate, complete liberation. But you must definitely take the step. If you do not take the step, no *Guru* can help you.

You can follow any *Guru* you like, you can follow any path you like, but it is all about being here, now. Being available. Availability is emptiness. Basically, if you are empty, you are available. You are being available just by being empty, being receptive. If you are filled with ideas, if you are filled with concepts, if you are filled with thoughts, and expectations, then the *Guru* can give you nothing. The *Guru* is a living, walking, talking example of what you should be. A true *Guru*, who is connected to the Source, is a real living example of who you actually are. Whatever you see in yourself is not your reality. These are relative realities. In relative realities, everything changes.

In the ultimate reality, however, there is only permanence. Stillness. Absolute stillness of the mind. Absolute oneness with the constitution, the Truth. We have a saying, *"Satyam, Shivam, Sundaram."* The Truth is Shiva, Shiva is Truth, and this is wonderful, this is beautiful. Whatever is true is permanent. Whatever is permanent is eternal, or it is Shiva. The principle called Shiva is exactly the principle called *Guru*. That *Guru*, the principle, stays inside us. This is our soul principle, the principle called soul. This is one with us. This is the only aspect within us which is permanent and this is exactly where every *Guru* leads you to.

The *Guru* is showing the way into yourself, connecting to your own soul. Once you connect to your own soul, you are connected to the whole world, the whole universe. Every being operates from the level of the soul. But because there are differences, because there are cosmetic differences, like different bodies, different minds, different equipment, such as intellect, ego, species differences, all these make us feel that we are separate from each other. This is the wrong identity, the wrong identification; this is exactly what the *Guru* principle points at or tells you to look at.

Once you are connected to the *Guru* principle, all these differences will evaporate. They will dissolve, and then you will see the soul element within every being. When you see the soul element in every being, you cannot find differences. If there is disturbance from outside, you will not see any external differences, but perceive it as an extension of yourself. This is because soul-wise, we are related. Another body is creating the sound, creating ripples on this canvas called existence, but you will feel that it is just like the grumbling of your stomach, that it is an internal thing. You tend to accept it.

When there is a problem inside our system, we will do something about it. We will tend to accept it, we will tend to overcome it, we will take some medicine, we will find some remedy, some cure. Likewise, external disturbances will not matter to us because our extended entity is inside them. This is all our extended identification. Everything is us. There is no difference between a plant, a flower, an animal, a human being, the stars or the sun or the moon, no differences. This is all extension of our constitution, our consciousness, the oneness, the Truth which is called the *Guru*, the principle, which is extended everywhere. In that mode, you can never alienate yourself. You will be one with the whole cosmos, and you will be merging beautifully into the whole thing.

Once you start experiencing that, you become the *Guru* principle. The principle starts working through you. The primary difference you will feel is that nothing affects you. The second difference you will feel is that you will be fearless. You will have no idea what fear is because there is nothing to be afraid of. Thirdly, you will feel that whether you exist or not, there is no difference because actually everything is you. You always exist. The soul always exists. You will be identifying only with the soul, you will always exist beyond time and space. You will be one with the whole universe. There will be no differences between the Gurus, or any beings. We will consider any beings of the universe as one, the same, all are One. Once we attain that state, we are the Guru principle. We can experience this.

Living with a Saint

Saints have always been ordinary men. External glitter never mattered to a true Saint. The halo in the picture is a reflection of the viewer's mind. In real life, we hardly see any halo. When Shirdi Sai Baba lived, some people considered him mentally unstable. He used to talk to entities invisible to human eyes. He used to behave in a strange manner. He was living the larger Truth. Who can understand that? Only those who dare to rise up to his stature.

Saints who chose to operate in the marketplace have always run the risk of ending up in mental asylums. Many never understood them. Many underestimated them. The extraordinary powers that we read about create mental images. People live within those images and then when they choose to live with a Saint, the whole glasshouse starts to crack and eventually fall apart. Truth is One. One who lives in Truth also is one with the Truth. Everything else is an illusion for him. He does not need to pretend. He cares not for ordinary glories, of which we are usually victims.

There is nothing to prove. There is nothing to see. Look through my eyes; you will see the Truth. Truth is as stark as the blazing sun. You chose dark glasses. That was your choice. Truth is always stark and non-dual. When you chose the company of a Saint, you chose uncertainties also. That's actually the essence of life. Saints live impermanence externally and experience permanence internally. This is the irony. They enjoy the growth and decay of cells, and do nothing about it, even if they have the power to change, reverse or recreate anything. When you are with the Truth, you also possess the power of the supreme Truth. That becomes part of your existence. Yet, you will do nothing for yourself. That's the way true Masters are.

They need nothing. Neither favours nor sacrifices. They live as moving monuments of selflessness. As signposts of liberation. If you read the life story of Shirdi Sai Baba carefully, you will understand what this text is all about. We need to see through his image to know the Master. A great Master has to be the most ordinary. Empty pots are noisy. Filled up pots maintain a deep, pregnant silence. When they die, we see them in pictures. Monks sitting naked with a big halo around their heads. We bow to them. We revere them. We meditate on them. This is all fine, because we do not have their physical proximity.

It is physical proximity that is the problem. They eat and drink. They use the toilet. They sweat. They display human emotions. They love, and they abuse too. Sometimes they even display seeming cruelty. This is bound to shatter all our concepts and mental images. It shatters expectations. Only through dissolution is re-creation possible. You have to empty first to fill in again. This is the bottom line. As the saying goes, do not get too close to a Saint. Accept and enjoy his teachings, if you can. This is important if you want to maintain your mental picture of the Saint. If that is what you choose. Getting closer to a fire will burn you. Getting close to a Saint will burn your expectations and even certain inherent traits. Beware!

Living the Teachings

  ❧ **Question:** What is the best gift you can give to your beloved *Guru*?

Mohanji: The best gift you can give to your beloved *Guru* is to live his teachings. When you live his teachings, you become one with your *Guru*, whoever your *Guru* is. It does not matter.

But, if you respect your *Guru*, if you appreciate his teaching, live it. That is the least and that is the best you can do for him.

The purpose of *Bhagavan* Sathya Sai Baba's living was to give us the full guidelines for life. What more can we give to Bhagavan? Because he knows very well how long he should stay in his body. Will you pray to keep him in the body? What can we pray for, for an Avatar?

The best gift you can give to any *Guru* is to live his teachings. The *Guru* does not want anything else. When you live your *Guru's* teachings, *Guru* is happy. His life and time on Earth become worthwhile. What else can you give to a *Guru*? You may give him medicines to sustain his body, but is Bhagavan interested in that? Living in the body itself is painful for *Gurus* and real Masters or Avatars. It is also a big restriction because you need to operate through the body. Perhaps, it would have been much better for Sathya Sai not to have been in the body at all!

But then, people would not understand him. People need to touch and feel. People need tangibility. We cannot understand the Omnipresent *Parabrahma*. Sai chose to take birth and live in a body so that he could communicate with you. You need a tangible format so that you see the *Guru*, you hear him, you see him talking and walking. Or you will not know him. The omnipresent *Parabrahma* is here, but we cannot see him. We do not feel him. We cannot see air. When air leaves this place, you understand that you are suffocated, you gasp for breath. We take the air around us for granted. We do the same with Grace.

What is Grace? What has it got to do with life? Simple answer! What has an umbrella got to do with rain! An umbrella does not stop the rain, but prevents you from getting drenched. Grace protects you; it does not stop an event. Grace flows. It is pitched against collective consciousness. The collective consciousness creates situations. For example, it elects the ruler or the king! Grace protects you from the sun, but cannot remove the sun. In the rain, some water will drop on you from the sides, but overall, with an umbrella, you are protected. You have to suffer, but you suffer less! You will get wet but not as much as if you were standing under the rain. This is the importance of Grace. Similarly, when *Guru* leaves the place, we feel he is gone. While *Guru* is in the body, we do not actually appreciate him. We take him for granted.

It is not a tragedy for *Bhagavan* or for the Universe when he leaves the body, because he has done his job. It is a tragedy for human beings who could not catch the message and need the physical form.

I sincerely want to convey that *Bhagavan* has done us a great favour to be here on Earth with us[6]; whether he continues to stay in his body or not. His teaching is basically love and Truth. If you love *Bhagavan*, live and love his teachings. That is the best gift you can give him. Then the purpose of his *Avatar* was worth it. Otherwise, however much we pray is of no use.

Do not just spread his teachings by writing messages or posting them by mail, live his teachings. We remember his teaching by living it or practising it. Because there should be the application of teachings in real life. Otherwise, we will just talk: "Oh, He was a great Master, He was an *Avatar*...." What is the use? The Master does not need any of this nonsense. He came here to raise consciousness on Earth. Whatever you do which is not in tune with that, is of no use.

Bhagavan once said, "After staying in this body for eighty years, people still have not understood me! Even if I live for another eighty years, it will be of no use." Once, on *Shivaratri*, he said, "Why are you sitting in front of me like a frog, looking at me?" This expressed his anger. It was very unlikely that he would use such words. *Bhagavan* is very compassionate. He talks in a very mild and soft manner. He then told the person, "Go home and serve selflessly at your place."

---

6   This discussion happened with Bhagavan Sathya Sai Baba was in the body

Many people have left their homes and are staying in Puttaparthi to be around him. Interestingly enough, Bhagavan often keeps extremely arrogant people around him all the time. They are rude and aggressive. Did I tell you this story? This is a story that I have heard. *Bhagavan* had a driver who served him for twenty years. This driver was a rude and angry man. When someone would come to Baba, he would shout and antagonise them. Some people got really affected by this behaviour of his. They thought, "We are coming to see *Bhagavan* from far and wide, and this fellow throws us out". "Can something be done?", they asked *Bhagavan*.

Bhagavan did not say anything. *Bhagavan* tolerated the intolerance of his driver. After twenty years, one day Baba told him: "You have completed your job. Go home in peace; I will take care of you." The driver left. Someone then asked Bhagavan: "Why did you keep such a rude man as a driver for so long? He does not reflect your stature at all." *Bhagavan* answered: "I stayed with him for two days while I was in Shirdi Sai Baba's body. I repaid that debt." Understand that *karma* works for an *Avatar* too. He did not erase it. He continued with the flow.

Have you been to Puttaparthi? You might experience rude behaviour from many people there. Of course, there is a dire need for good security. Everything is done on account of security. But, our ego may not enjoy us being suspected, treated like a terrorist! You may think, "Is this necessary? Is this what I have come here for? Did I come here to experience this kind of treatment? Why do we experience this at the abode of such an enlightened Master?" This is especially so with people from Western countries.

However, there are reasons for this. One is, these people have irritable characters. They are an irritation for society, and so *Bhagavan* collects such people, keeps them near him and thus saves society. Being in the vicinity of *Bhagavan*, these people benefit a lot. They undergo tremendous inner cleansing.

Another strong reason is that people visit *Bhagavan* with eagerness and inquisitiveness to see a *Guru*. All are coming from different walks of life, with ego. Through these irritable people, *Bhagavan* bashes the ego of people coming to visit him. The volunteers around *Bhagavan* never care about the social status of the visitors. They scold them and impose rules on them indiscriminately.

People may think, "What is this? What kind of people are these?" But if you are sincere, you will survive all that and reach *Bhagavan*. You may reach the entrance of the hall and be told, "Oh, cameras and purses are not allowed. Books are not allowed inside". Oops! You will have to go back to your room and leave them there. Within that time, you may miss *Bhagavan*'s *darshan*. One may feel that a day is lost.

The next day, *Bhagavan* may not come. If you have come there, amongst your busy schedule, for two days, your full programme may get spoiled. Expectation is cut from the root. A big churning! A big shakeup. You may get disappointed. Your ego is thrown down in the trash. However, if you think, "If I see *Bhagavan*, it is fine," or, "If I do not see *Bhagavan*, it is okay for me," if you nullify your ego and just let go, then probably *Bhagavan* may come and touch you, or may even call you for an interview!

So, the biggest gift one can give to a Master is to live his teachings. This is also the best way to understand the Master. Otherwise, a visit one pays to the Master was just a picnic. If you are not living his teachings, nothing has shifted in your consciousness.

Nothing is a tragedy. We cannot pray that *Bhagavan* should remain in his body because this is up to him. He has come for a purpose and He very well knows his purpose. He also knows when to leave. It is selfish of us to ask Bhagavan to stay in the body. When he has achieved his purpose, is it worthwhile to ask him, "Stay in the body for a few weeks more!" We do not know the larger mission. Those who want to understand him will understand him even if they do not meet him also.

Knowledge is useless unless converted into your daily life's experience. If life has not improved due to additional knowledge, it is just another burden in your existence. If the food that you consume gets digested, it helps your health. If it is not digested, it only upsets your stomach, your equilibrium. It is like, how much food can you digest without getting indigestion. If your stomach cannot digest the food, it has no value.

The Consciousness is permanent. It is not situational or conditional. Have faith and intensify faith. Then there is no fear. Faith will give you the tenacity and toughness to get through all situations. Express deep gratitude. Mean it, feel it. Live the teachings of your *Guru*, if you Love him deeply and sincerely.

Expressions and Understandings

A student threw a stone at his teacher. The teacher was hurt and hospitalised. The head of the institution asked the student's parents to present themselves for a discussion on disciplinary action to be taken against the student. The parents appeared on time. The first thing the principal asked the student's father was, "Do you throw stones at your superiors?" The perplexed father said, "Well, of course not." The principal asked again, "If you have that much wisdom, then why is your son behaving in this way?"

The point here is that all of us are individuals. Every being is unique. We all have our own expressions and personal style. We are inimitable in that way. But society is often two-dimensional. When we do something seemingly wrong, irrespective of our reasons for these actions, society will blame our upbringing for that. They will blame our parents, grandparents and even our clan, on some occasions.

Likewise, we have seen or heard many spiritual Masters in our lifetime, both alive and departed. We have also seen or witnessed their followers. Some of them are extremely fanatic and some are moderate, considerate, or more tolerant. Yet, we as a society, look at their expressions and judge their *Guru* – alive or departed . Am I right? Do we not judge a *Guru* based on the expressions of his disciples? Are we right in doing so?

The *Guru* could well be enlightened and might be a total renunciate. His disciple might be a pretender or just another seeker of knowledge carrying big baggage of sundry desires, dreams, and aspirations of making it big in life. He may choose to use the name of a famous *Guru* in order to satisfy his personal desires. Do you think the *Guru* asked him to do that? Do you think he is reflecting the *Guru*'s teaching? Do you think that we can blame the *Guru* for all the actions of his followers? The answer is a big and categorical 'no'.

Just like the father of the student was helpless in the above school example, every *Guru* is helpless in the case of his or her followers. What can a *Guru* do if his disciple chooses to misinterpret or deliberately twist the *Guru*'s teachings for his personal advantage? This is especially so when the mission grows and the *Guru* becomes a public figure. He is even more vulnerable. People approach him with multiple interests. Some come in search of guidance and to seek liberation. They are sincere seekers and a big rarity.

Some come to obtain a *mantra* to achieve instant success, which is more common. Some come to see how he operates, which will help them set up their own shop at some point in time. There are many like this. They are collectors. They are after transferable knowledge and not non-transferable experience from the *Guru*. Some come to test the *Guru*. Some wish to compare one *Guru* with another, and to judge, criticise, or ridicule. Some come because of simple things such as – they like the food in the ashram or because their spouse cannot cook well. Some come to escape from their nagging realities. Some come because the girl or boy they love visits this *Guru*. Likewise, different reasons for different folks!

One famous model or actress said to a famous *Guru*, "Your Holiness, I want to sleep with you." The Saint smiled and said, "Why sleep, my darling? I am trying to wake the sleeping people up!" On this occasion, for the model, it is another feather in her cap, "I have also slept with a holy man!" This could possibly give a morale boost for her public standing and her socio-commercial positioning. She may gain more space in the gossip columns and may attain more press coverage. For the *Guru*, it is usually scandalising. He may get ruined. His reputation may get tarnished. This is especially so if the *Guru* has worked hard to maintain uniformity in his image or cultivated an image of invincibility! For those who do not care about their public image, nothing matters.

How can the *Guru* help all the reasons of his disciples? He can only stay neutral at all times. Terrestrial entanglements are not worth it. Great Saints may have become involved from time to time, but for specific reasons and purposes. For e.g., Vyasa, Vishwamitra etc.

Whatever rises must fall. This is the way earth's gravitational forces work. Nothing can stay in the air for more than a reasonable time. No bird can stay in the air forever. It must rest its wings sometimes. If we expect happiness and upliftment all the time, it cannot happen. We have to go through the dualities of existence until we die. Or, until we are not worried about or bound by terrestrial sensory objects in order to find our fulfilment. If we are self-sufficient, i.e., sufficiently established in the self, we will be established in perpetual happiness.

Do not judge or criticise anyone – let alone a *Guru* or a spiritual teacher, because we do not or cannot know and understand anyone fully, nor do we know their *karmic* configuration, which provokes their thoughts, words, and actions. *Ahimsa* (non-violence) is the best path. Perfect non-violence in thoughts, words, and action. Do not judge a father by looking at his son. Do not judge any *Guru* by looking at his or her disciples. The *Guru* can give only as much as a disciple can carry with him. If the *Guru* is a flowing river and a disciple has the capacity to carry only one glass of water, can we judge the *Guru's* capacity as one glass of water? Here, the disciple can publicly express his *Guru's* stature only within his capacity and understanding, which is only one glass!

Please understand this clearly: the *Guru* is often limitless. Followers usually have tremendous limitations. The *Guru* will indeed try to strengthen them to enhance their capacity. It is like bodybuilding. You cannot lift the weight beyond your initial or actual capacity, even if your instructor asks you to take or try more weight. Your instructor may lift the weight easily because of his experience. You have to work everyday and slowly increase your capacity. You need faith, tenacity, consistency, application, and dedication. Same with spirituality.

You cannot understand the consciousness of a *Guru* overnight. It takes time and it definitely takes patience. *Gurus* exist in a much higher realm and the higher they go, the less street-smart they become. Their operational medium becomes unconditional love. When they cross over to spiritual realms and establish there, they stop depending on their body, mind, and intellect. I am talking about *Sadgurus*, the great Masters. *Acharyas* are doing it for money. That is a differe story. So, do not judge a *Guru* based on the expressions of a ciple who operates with his limited body, mind, and intellec ve and let live.

> ✽ **Question:** Living in the presence of enlightened Masters has been given so much importance in the Dattatreya, Kriya as well as Siddha Tradition. In fact, all the Traditions recommend living near a Master. What is your opinion?

Mohanji: I have split your question into two. Both are good questions and most relevant in today's time. It is true that the presence of a living Master has a purgative, purifying effect in a receptive disciple. If the disciple is not receptive, even if the highest Master is near him, it will not benefit him. Individual receptivity and eligibility or capacity for absorption is the key to gain maximum benefit from the proximity of a *Guru*.

The presence of a true Master is like the fire, keeping the cold of *tamas* away when you sit near the fire. The *tejas* (radiance) of a true Master will keep away *tamas*, or inertia – the most detrimental factor in spiritual progress. This helps the disciple to evolve faster. The proximity of the Master is also a constant reminder to a worthy disciple. In his energy field, situations melt and events flow through life, effortlessly. A true Master can see and understand the constitution of a disciple and delivers only what he can consume. Wastage never happens. The same medicine cannot cure all diseases.

A true *Guru* will only prescribe the medicine the disciple actually needs, irrespective of whether it is sweet or bitter. When the intention is pure, then the medicine works. Unshakeable faith of the disciple in his *Guru* is the key here. Shaking, wavering or shifting faith cannot bring clear results, just like if you keep shaking the glass, milk cannot be poured into it without spillage. So, living with a Saint has its unique value. However, do not imitate the Saint who has already attained enlightenment. Allow him to be himself, and follow only his directions and teachings, without judging his attitude and behaviour. Leave him alone and be yourself. Live and let live.

> ❧ **Question:** People hesitate to feed the poor and hungry, but they shower their riches at the feet of *Gurus* and in some temples. I cannot understand this. Why is God so cruel?

Mohanji: You are talking about people and why do you drag God into this argument? Leave God alone. He is Truth. He is Compassion. He is Benevolence. However, he allows you to choose your character, habits and constitution, and allows you to be natural. Has he ever interfered with the ugliest of your thoughts? So, God is objective and impartial. Now, people give money only for purposes that will benefit them in some way. Every investment has an expectation behind it. They want salvation, redemption from their sins, marriage of their daughter, removal of a damaging partner etc.

They approach *Gurus* and temples for this purpose. They give money there. True *Gurus* and Gods need no money. This is ideally recycled back into society for the benefit of the poor and the hungry. This is the grand collaboration. *Gurus* and Gods collect the money offered at their feet and they deliver it back to the ailing masses, and use it for the betterment of the poor, needy, and hungry, for the birds and animals etc. If this works in this way, it is beautiful. Sometimes though, greed interferes, and the *Gurus* use it for expressing personal pomposity. They fall. When selfishness takes root, people fall, irrespective of their social standing. We have seen it happening all around us, many times over. Hope you have understood this concept clearly.

All you Need is Firm Faith and Conviction

If you have firm faith and conviction in your path, Tradition, or *Guru*, that in itself will lead you and guide you. All you need is firm faith and conviction. When people asked Baba Muktananda how he achieved his spiritual power, he answered, "I never asked my *Guru* (Bhagavan Nityananda)- Why?" He just followed the instructions of Bhagavan without questioning or analysing. His faith in his *Guru* gave him everything. This is the path of Shiva. This is the path of Dattatreya. This is the path of Nath *Gurus*. All you have to do is take the plunge. The river itself takes you to the destination. Sometimes you may feel there is no movement; that nothing is happening. Sometimes, repetition of the same thing may give you boredom.

Patience. Devotion and deep faith. You will be tested for your determination and endurance. The path of Shiva is not an easy path. Dissolution means agony before ecstasy. If you survive with determination, it is the sacred golden path where only Unconditional Love exists. No expectation or binding exists. When you take the plunge, you become the river. Beingness! Total Beingness! There is no duality anymore. Only oneness exists. Natural acts of kindness and compassion truly make us human. It elevates and maintains consciousness at a higher level. It helps endure and erase the emotional terrains of our existence. When kindness and compassion overflow from deep within, man becomes human.

Gurudakshina is an expression of gratitude. Prior to the foreign invasions into India, and commercialisation as well as communalisation of our educational systems, India used to have a system where those who sought knowledge or those who had the eligibility for knowledge were attracted to the abode of teachers, stayed with them, served them and attained knowledge and skills. Education was spontaneous. The teacher delivered to each one according to their nature, level of receptivity or capacity. This was a beautiful system where the bonding between a student and the teacher automatically opened all channels and the eternal wisdom of the Master enriched the seekers. It also gave practical training in life and living.

Before the student left, as an expression of gratitude, *Gurudakshina* was offered to the *Guru*. It used to be whatever was available in the neighbourhood, as the students were not earning money and the teacher's abode was usually in the forest or in remote villages, away from the contamination of city life. *Gurudakshina* also used to be selfless service to the *Guru* and his mission. So, what can the student give to the teacher? A fruit, a plant, or in some cases, a thesis work on what he learned from the *Guru*. The *Guru* never expected anything from his disciples and delivered everything that the disciple could digest without expectations. The *Guru* would be well pleased when his disciples lived his teachings rather than imitated his lifestyle. This was such a pure relationship.

Even great Avatars like Krishna, Rama, or Adi Shaṅkara were students like this. They were the source of all knowledge, what did they have to learn from anyone? Just to establish the *dharma* and faith in this beautiful system, they set examples by committing themselves to it. Remember, the real test of life is in enduring and navigating successfully through the winding roads of *karmic* life itself, and not in the marks you scored in your examination. This needs faith. This needs Grace. Knowledge may not come in handy at all in times of turmoil. If one has deep faith, Grace is always around them. Grace never leaves their hands. They are always protected.

The criteria for admission to such *Gurukuls* were eligibility, receptivity, and never purchasing power. You can understand the depth of degeneration our education system has undergone. Education has systematically become degenerated over the years. Education is another commodity for sale. It is sold and bought, and there is no value system in its true sense. Superior knowledge is used for gaining supremacy over people, institutions, or governments. Education is invoking competition and one-upmanship. Students are forced into studies, which they do not often like, or are opposite to their natural aptitude. They are forced to compete with one another. They are insensitively called a failure, which ruins them for life.

Our system demands that the fish climb the tree and when the fish fails in its attempts, it is branded as a failure! Children suffer like this. It takes away their faith in education and even in their parents who force them. They become tired. They rebel. They find solace in drugs or unholy company which preaches destruction. There is no peace at home. Parents are anxious, often angry and insensitive. They push the children to the edge. Society and teachers do the same. Their inherent anger instilled by the system is nurtured by negative company. They destroy themselves and the world.

Self-destruction is so rampant today. When a person is self-destructive due to bottled up anger within, one destroys society too. Lack of real spiritual grounding, beyond the walls of religions and emotional existence, is the curse of our society today.

Awareness is the key

Children exist in a virtual world of make-believe nowadays. Relationships are virtual for them. All gratifications are virtual. Nothing is real. They are scared of the real. They expect the ease of make-believe in real life and suffer miserably when alternative realities hit between their eyes. They create friends on-screen and create a virtual life on-screen. Sometimes the speed of connectivity also determines the speed of failure in relationships. When constantly in the virtual world, when a child creates its own sunshine and wind, it fails to accept or appreciate the real sun. The real sun becomes too harsh and intolerable and so does nature. These children become misfits in the real world. If any catastrophe happens, they perish. Nobody can prevent the decay. Society is creating them. Society will also destroy them when they are not needed anymore.

Awareness is the key. Nurturing awareness of who you are and instilling it in the children will keep them grounded. You could use any gadget, as long as nothing enslaves you. Intellect provides artificial comfort and a feeling of superiority over others, at least temporarily. When you know things better than the other, you feel better off. This is also bondage. "One who is proud of his intellect is like a prisoner who is proud of his prison cell" – Fr. Antony De Mello. This is the Truth. When knowledge becomes escapism and a means to show off, man binds himself. These are all subtle traps of our existence on Earth, which we should be extremely cautious about.

We cannot ignore the world and stay spiritual. Spirituality is not escapism. Spirituality is being natural, being flexible and spontaneous. We need to be aware of life, living, and the suffering of the new generation. We are constantly creating a restless world that thrives on emotions and emotional outbursts. Parents are destroying their children because of their undue anxiety and total ignorance of *karma*. Every child is a *karmic* being and will go on with its individual *karma* whether you worry about it or not. Society is destroying the children because of its insensitivity and silly judgments such as 'winners' and 'losers'.

Nobody is always a winner, nor can anybody always be a loser. All are relative terms. It depends on many factors. There is no faith, there is no trust. Just sheer competition. Success in life and not in an examination, is real success. This means a life lived with peace and purpose. A life lived in kindness and compassion, satisfaction and acceptance. A purposeful, purpose bound life will be a complete life. An emotional life overflowing with desires and judgment will never give any satisfaction at any point in time.

Guru is primarily a principle. Life is the biggest *Guru*. Nobody can teach you anything better than life itself. Nature is *Guru*. Every event, every moment gives forth some valuable lesson. We can continue to learn from everything around us if we have the eyes to see or entertain average receptivity. Yet, your personal *Guru* is your own soul. All the spiritual guides who ever walked on Earth are reminders of certain eternal truths of existence. Simple truths such as: whatever you learn externally, has to be unlearned and nullified before you transcend to the highest, or before you dissolve completely. Whatever you learn externally must be shed to 'become the knowledge' and merge into it.

Knowledge lies within. Your soul knows everything. You have to transcend the intellect to reach the soul. In order to achieve that, we must systematically detach from the external. Detachment should happen spontaneously, when the requirement for it ceases. Only what drops off by itself drops off forever. Whatever you forcefully shed only gets suppressed and will sprout back at another point in time. When you grow beyond all *gunas*, after nullifying the binding *karmas*, you merge with the Source, the Supreme. The Supreme contains all knowledge. The Supreme is knowledge. When you and your Father (the Supreme) become One, there is nothing for you to know anymore.

Thus, it is through shedding that you evolve, not through the accumulation of knowledge. There is no need to chase knowledge. Too much knowledge does not help you with liberation either. Sufficient knowledge, which would be promptly delivered from time to time by the *Guru* principle, is sufficient for one's spiritual progress. The need for more knowledge than that is the greed of the intellect, for the sake of some intellectual gratification. Just like material greed, that will not help spiritual evolution. It is not in knowing, but in being, that awareness grows.

Seeming illiterate Masters like Jesus, Bhagavan Nityananda, and Akkalkot Maharaj, etc. proved this point with their own lives. The learned men of their time asked, "How can an illiterate carpenter teach the scriptures to educated priests?" It is possible when you are the Source, or when you actually merge with the Source. Acquired knowledge has limitations. When you become knowledge, there are no limitations and you are not bound by the intellect either. They taught simple things and that too, non-verbally, mostly through their own lives. Simplicity is Godlin.... eal spirituality is having access to everything – but not ne.... anything, even knowledge.

Another in.... rtant matter is: Understand yourself and your guide. Shirdi Sai Baba did not even have a name. Mhalsapati called him Sai and others followed. What was the real name of the One whom we call Akkalkot Maharaj? Great Masters never even had a name of their own, while today we see *Gurus* sporting big and long titles. Even a name is binding, just like fame. In the path of dissolution, all names, forms and titles are barriers, one way or the other. When the matter that the *Guru* delivers is profound, no titles are required. In today's spiritual climate, titles are a clear sign of the deep insecurity of the teacher. A sign of doubt within themselves; whether they are recognised and revered or not. Beware of fancy titles which do not confirm any spiritual stature. They may have acquired knowledge and certain *siddhis*. However, that is the minimum you can have in any case. All that glitters is not gold.

This is your individual journey. If my image or what I teach is seemingly blocking your progress, be bold enough to remove me and my teachings and progress further. If history proves that it was a mistake to leave me or the path that I am taking you through, welcome back, my doors are always open. Just do not develop regrets or guilt.

The Path of Shiva

The path of Shiva is the path of dissolution. There are no stops or detours until we become Shiva. There should be no mid-way stops. There are only two possibilities here. Either we are Shiva (The Source or the Conscious) or *shava* (the unconscious, the ignorant, or insignificant, or another brick on the wall).

True *Gurus* need nothing from you. Every seeker should have eyes to see this. Who is a true *Guru*? One who exists beyond gunas, One who is always connected to the Source. The sign of a true *Guru* is usually silence and a reluctance to be visible in public. He will not be bothered about *siddhis* and will usually be matter-of-fact. He would be deeply rooted in non-duality. All the rest are *Acharyas* holding fancy titles. Beware. As Swami Rama said, "Most are chasing *siddhis*, or miracle powers, to earn their sustenance. They make tall claims and if they cannot deliver, they blame the inefficiency of their disciples."

Adi Shankara said the same thing, "For the sake of a square meal, these people are dressing up in weird ways." One truth that Swami Rama categorically expounded makes real sense even today. When a man spent years learning the *siddhi* of spitting fire from his mouth, his *Guru* said, "Oh, that is a sheer waste of time. I would rather buy a matchbox!" The *avadhoota* whom we met at the *Kumbha Mela* said, "When will people drop the cravings for finding aura, chakras, or *kundalini*, and catch God?"

We have indeed been beating around the bush for lifetimes! Craving for smaller *siddhis* wastes our lifetimes. When will we shed the dark, thick wall of our conditioned ego and embrace the overwhelming light? From darkness to Eternal Light! We must develop eyes to see the Truth. A true Master has truly mastered his mind, elevated himself beyond the gunas, and is existing in the eternal bliss state. He lives beyond all barriers. This will be unmistakable, too. Love is the expression, along with perpetual compassion and kindness towards all beings. Keep your inner eyes open, you will see.

Nurturing the Inner Eyes

Inner eyes! That is what you must nurture. The inner eyes always show us the Truth. External eyes are always confronting illusions. Poor guys, they are confused. They cannot see what is real and what is unreal. When they finally decide to focus on the real, the image changes and they get disillusioned again. Trust your inner eyes. They never deceive you. They are always open and focused on the Real. They are married to higher awareness, too.

There are Masters in all planes of existence, not only on Earth. They are the conduit between the gross and the subtle. They are the eternal connectors. They are the promise of higher connectivity. Delusion is mostly on the earthly plane because we use our senses much more than our inner eyes, intuition, or sixth sense. We hardly use our inner eyes consciously. The external eyes follow what glitters. We chase spiritual powers and get stuck with them. We flaunt these and pull ourselves down and away from the path of liberation.

Liberation is the ultimate aim of every soul. Any knowledge or any path that makes it take further detours is its enemy. This is one criterion for knowing the right path. A path that keeps you liberated, unbound, and takes you towards liberation is the right path. All that bind you to rituals or *Gurus* are wrong paths for the soul. Everything should be dissolved before the final exit. The less baggage of habits and demands, the easier the transit! True *Gurus* keep you liberated. *Acharyas* bind you to systems. Systems give solace to the mind because the mind needs consistency. It cannot accept changes.

Change is inevitable. Everything changes. Nothing can remain constant forever. Being flexible is important. Just by watching your thoughts, words, or actions, you can reach the highest. Being aware is the key, not 'doing' many things. Doing keeps you busy and makes you feel fine. But, ask yourself – are you being occupied or are you actually evolving? Has peace settled in? Is your inner space clean? Do you entertain anxieties and worries? Has your awareness shifted? Do the same anxieties and fears still bother you? Think again. Walk away from anything that binds you as this is your individual journey. No *Guru* will carry you on his shoulder.

CHAPTER 4:

Mohanji

Do Not Marry the *Guru*, Marry His Consciousness

🌿 **Question:** Mohanji, who are you really?

Mohanji: I understand your curiosity to know more about me. But tell me, how will that help your spirituality? Do not marry the *Guru*. Marry his Consciousness.

The *Guru* in the physical frame is as perishable as all physical frames are. It is vulnerable to changes. It is affected by time and the seasons. Remember one thing: Every physical being is vulnerable to time and changes. Therefore, do not be too curious about me as a person. If you attach yourself more and more to my physical image, forgetting the simple messages that I deliver from time to time, you will develop expectations. Expectations and reality may not match. Eventually, you will suffer from disillusionment. Anyone can easily create expectations about another. Understand clearly, it cannot work that way. Life may take a different course altogether.

I do not believe that anything is wholly right or wholly wrong, as long as people travel a *karmic* journey. When the mode shifts to dharmic, it is a different story. Kindly refrain from sending me emails about my personal life. Leave it alone. There is nothing for you to imitate or enjoy in it. It is a life filled with work, work, and more work. Do you want to try? Sure. Most welcome. If you like my messages to the world or my meditations, you are welcome to follow that path. Again, it should be because you like the message or the Truth in the message that applies to your life, not because you like my physical frame, voice, or lifestyle. Once again, "Marry the Consciousness, which is permanent and unshakeable. Never marry any *Guru*". They are crazy people. Believe me.

Who am I? Very difficult to say who I am. It is easier to say who I am not. In the ocean of existence, I am all beings. I am all expressions. There is nothing apart from me. In this life, I am called Mohan. A temporary existence. Trying to perform the role of a lamp on the path of liberation. Just one of the many lamps in the path. Limited significance, unlimited existence.

🌿 **Question:** Who is talking through you when you take classes? How do we know?

Mohanji: There is no need to know. It will make no difference to you, whether Mohanji is speaking or Raman if the message is not useful. It does not matter. If the message coming through me is worthwhile – take it, else discard it. The question, "Which Master is talking," is probably arising because of my blog post on Babaji[7]. People want to know who is talking, but this is out of context. Why do we want to know who is talking? What is the big deal about it? Whoever talks, would it make a difference if the message is not worthwhile? It does not matter who is talking if the message is clear and beneficial for you. Further, if you do not implement the message, then the whole time and energy are wasted. We are always looking for divine intervention, while we do nothing to increase our eligibility for receiving it. Isn't this ironic?

How do we know? You do not need to know. For argument's sake – suppose you do know, what will happen? If you know that *Babaji* is talking, then you may want *Babaji* to talk further!

---

[7] The blog post series "Babaji Beyond Definitions" on brahmarishimohanji. wordpress.com

It becomes another reason to feel proud, privileged, and even egoistic. Indeed, this is a mind game. The mind will always remain unsatisfied. Even if I say, "*Babaji* is talking," it is my experience. It is not your experience. If it is not your experience, it is of no value to you. If I say, "*Babaji* is walking here," it is of no value to you as long as it is not your experience. It just remains as Mohanji's words! How do you know that I am not lying, especially if you are not experiencing it?

Abandon such requirements and hold on to your individual present and individual experience. Masters will come to you when you become eligible for them. It could be Lord Shiva himself, Jesus, Buddha, or Krishna. You cannot search outside and find Lord Shiva. You have to surrender within and reach Him. He lives within you. The *Guru* material is within you. The *Guru* lives within you. Do not worry about Mohanji, John, or Habib. Do not worry about *Baba*, *Babaji*, or Buddha. They mean nothing to you until you reach their 'grade'. Ultimately, it is your journey that matters. What you do with your life is what matters. Remember that, always.

It is better not to have thoughts in your mind of who is talking or walking. If the answer is relevant to you, take it, else discard it. For e.g., there is some food on the table that you cannot eat. Will you still eat it? Is it of any help to you? If you eat it because someone forced you, you may have indigestion or vomit it out. It is that simple. You can only eat what you can eat. In the same way, if a message is coming to you, take it if you can digest it. Otherwise, do not take it.

ꙮ **Question:** What is your mission in a nutshell?

Mohanji: In a nutshell, I would say, "It is to introduce you to yourself." My mission is to bring you to your soul. Once you meet your soul, then you do not need me. Your soul is your primary *Guru*. But, because you were wandering outside searching for external *Gurus*, you reached here. So, in a nutshell, I want to take you home. Once you shake hands with your soul, do you need another *Guru*? Your *Guru* is in-built in your system. He is sitting in you. You do not need anybody else.

🌿 **Question:** How long will you keep doing this service to humanity?

Mohanji: This is simple. I will work as long as Divinity needs me and permits me to do it. I will stop when Divinity asks me to stop or pulls me out of this system. If the world does not need it, I will be pulled out. This is how the constitution of the world works. Nature works that way. Words will not reach people if they don't have to. Words will reach people if they have to. What brings you here today is that divine design. You only heard what you were supposed to hear. Otherwise, you would not have been here nor experienced this. The individual does not matter. The story matters. The message matters.

If Mohanji is not here, somebody else will talk! If you have to hear these words, somebody will tell you. We miss a movie probably because we were supposed to miss it. When we are mature enough to understand a particular movie, we will see it, because only then will we understand it better. This happens in life all the time. It does not matter if Mohanji is talking or not. Nature arranges someone to deliver. The story goes on. Nature makes it happen at the right place, at the right time. We feel that we are an integral part of the whole universe. We feel that the world will stop if we are not around. The world does not stop without us. The moon will rise, the sun will shine, clouds will continue to give rain, rivers will flow, and nature will continue.

If we consider the cosmos, we are like ants, utterly micro-entities! If a few people die or the atmosphere changes, the world will go on. Society will exist. New people will come. They will have the same emotions and the same feelings, just like us. Essentially, like animals, they will also go through a clockwork style of life. They will play, study, graduate, get employed, get married, have children, grandchildren, retire, worry about siblings, and then die! This is the continuous, routine process that has been happening in the world for a long time. Except for those who choose to awaken.

❧ **Question:** How long will you work?

Mohanji: I will work as long as I live. I do not want to sit idle, expecting somebody to feed me. It will not suit me. I have always worked. I never sat idle, ever. But what work will I do? I do not know that. I am presently working in an office[8]. Maybe I will not work in the office after a while. I may do farming. I do not know about that now. But I will be working for sure. I consider work to be worship. I am working twenty-four hours a day. If not the office work, I am answering questions, doing blogs, and charity. I never 'sleep'. I always want to deliver spirituality as a gift to society. This is the least I can do as an expression of gratitude towards this existence.

I cannot think of a situation where somebody is giving me food or I am at someone's mercy. They may say, "I will not give you food today because I do not like you!" This can happen when dependency develops. I would instead work to sustain myself and give people what I can give, free of cost. It is a beautiful relationship, isn't it? A relationship without conditions and expectations! Just like the relationship between God and man! I love it. Dependency creates expectations and frictions. I would like to remain liberated and work for a living. I would tell everyone, "Please work hard."

Body, mind, and intellect are given for that. Why should we ever think about sitting idle? Procrastination is always anti-spirituality. Use your time and body to the maximum, as long as you exist. You should have everything with equanimity – suf-

---

[8] This discourse happened before 2012 when Mohanji was still working in a corporate job

ficient sleep, sufficient food, sufficient work, sufficient exercise, sufficient silence, sufficient fun, and so on. This is important for good living. Anything in excess will cause damage, one way or the other.

The *Ashwini devatas*, the Lords of medicine, questioned a famous physician, "Who is a healthy man?" The physician replied, "Those who neither eat too much nor too little; those who neither sleep too much nor too little; those who neither indulge too much nor too little; those who are neither too emotional nor too little. Whoever operates in this plane of perfect equanimity can be called healthy." The Lord was pleased with the answer and blessed him with *siddhis* (spiritual powers) for healing. This is the story of life. This is the Truth of existence.

Procrastination is unhealthy. If you procrastinate, what will you tell the world? What message will you give? You need to lead by example. For most spiritual people, life itself is an example. Shirdi Sai Baba would get so much money everyday. But by evening, he would disperse all the money to poor people. When he slept at night, he had only enough money in his pocket for his burial. He did not want people to carry out his burial for free. No favours on that level too. Such a liberated life! No worries, no anxieties, no fears.

❧ **Question:** Why didn't you call me? Why didn't you wake me up?

Mohanji: I have always called you, since generations. How come you never heard my call? Well, who has listened to my calls? I tried to wake you up many times, but you chose to sleep. I respect your choice. I am available. Using me is at your discretion. I bring light to you. Choosing light or darkness is at your discretion. Your decision does not affect the light, nor does it affect the darkness. Those who witness the light in the darkness remain in the light always.

❧ **Question:** Mohanji, why are you so elusive?

277

Mohanji: Am I elusive? You are talking to me, and I am answering your questions the way I can. I am indeed an introvert who enjoys isolation a lot. Tell me, what will I gain in the marketplace? Most of the things that society offers, especially sensory objects, have little value for me. I have seen it all. I tasted it all, over lifetimes. Only through accomplishing it can we overcome it. We need to taste it to overcome it. Avoidance does not amount to eradication. When we entertain the feeling of lacking something, it will stay rooted as the seed of a wish in our mind until its total fulfilment.

🌿 **Question:** I genuinely believe you when you say you are in isolation. That is why we took so long to meet. You kept postponing.

Mohanji: Well, I wasn't too sure if there was a real purpose for this meeting. Just idling or wasting time discussing sweet nothings or gossiping about other people is not my cup of tea. What do we achieve with all that? Instead, if we could use the time to float in the silence within, that would be much more meaningful. Anyway, what do I have to give you which you do not have already? We are crazy for knowledge. What do we do with that? Do we ever convert that into wisdom and elevate ourselves? Has it delivered inner peace?

Still, we crave more and more food, more emotional entanglements, and more knowledge. Still, we wander in search of the 'right location' to find inner peace. No location can give you inner peace. Inner peace essentially expresses itself when the mind is calmed. It will be obvious and unmistakable. Analysis and comparisons are a waste of time. Accept what you can consume. Reject what you cannot consume. It is as simple as that. None can force anything on anyone, nor should they attempt to do that. This is violence. Violence of all kinds disturbs the collective inner peace.

Also, tons of literature will not help gain inner peace. Reading becomes another kind of escapism, equal to looking for the 'right environment'. Instead, choosing to drop the baggage of compulsive habits and resorting to the silence within will help you much more. You will become self-sufficient. You can already do this. What more can I give you? Why come to see me? See the God Almighty shining in the eyes of the poor and abandoned people, the hungry birds and animals. Make them smile and remain content. That will elevate you. I am telling you this with due respect to you and your good intentions.

❖ **Question:** It makes me wonder, "Are you from Earth or outside Earth?"

Mohanji: It does not matter. Just try to enjoy the food that I prepare. If it is not good for you, throw it away. Nobody is watching you or judging you on this one.

❖ **Question:** Don't you think people will look at you with more respect if they think you are?

Mohanji: People are usually sceptical. They will not believe it anyway. They will look at me as a pretender and a propagandist. People like to believe in scandals more than search for the Truth. They like to gossip rather than evolve and liberate themselves. Ego does not permit apologies! The ego does not even permit beautiful relationships. Everything is seen through the eyes of a potential scandal, thus restricting the walking space of a liberated Saint.

Imagine the *Guru* is an alcoholic and a womaniser. If his teachings are not good for you, it does not matter to you, does it? Discard the *Guru* and his teachings. Now, imagine the *Guru* is an alcoholic and a womaniser, and his teachings are good for your personal growth. It does not matter how your *Guru* is, right? Just accept the teachings and discard the *Guru*. So, it does not matter. Spirituality should never become a handicap for anyone. Spirituality means liberation from mundane bindings. However, it is not a license to cheat and rape innocent devotees.

Are we not the same people who crucified Jesus? Are we not the ones who gave poison to Socrates? We even took the great Master Shirdi Sai Baba to court! We never accepted any Saints when they were in their bodies. We glorified them after they were dead or killed. This is our nature. Hence, our Tradition insists that we respect and treat our parents, teachers, and even our guests as God. We belong to a rich Tradition of acceptance and love. Times have changed. Respect is a rarity. Today relationships are based on usefulness, that too, on mostly commercial usefulness. There are many traps and quagmires in the path of spirituality. We certainly get what we deserve.

It is advisable to accept life as it comes. People can only express their available consciousness, which is varied and differs from person to person. We cannot understand or appreciate another person's dimension fully and completely. This is the Truth of our existence. Then how can one fully understand the consciousness of a Saint? This is why many people considered Akkalakoṭ Maharaj and Shirdi Sai Baba as madmen. They were two of the greatest Masters Earth had ever seen. *Avatars* of Lord Dattatreya!

Who craves respect? Respect created through fear or compulsion has no longevity. Respect should happen by itself. Respect should arise from a clear understanding of the stature of the *Guru*. Then it stays. Just like money and fame earned through bad deeds do not last and often do not come in handy when required the most, emotions have very short longevity. They die as soon as they take birth. So, I do not give much importance to human emotions. They come and go. People love scandals. Even if there are no truths behind the scandal, fertile human minds will weave their own truths.

Awareness is the only medicine or remedy to cure jealousy, hatred, anger, and all other evils. Awareness needs eligibility. Eligibility is attained through *viveka* (discrimination), or the ability or wisdom to segregate Truth from untruth, gossip, and rumour, and staying with the Truth against all odds. I have seen people coming with expectations and leaving with hatred towards me and my path. I lose nothing here. Who knows who will be with us tomorrow?

❧ **Question:** 'B' says that you are as slippery as a fish.

Mohanji: A fish is so supple and fluid. This is a good state to be in, especially in the spiritual path. I hope 'slippery' does not mean escapism. Being unavailable is not a bad idea. Those who need us will reach us – one way or the other. Being too available will also induce situations where you are taken for granted. Also, why should one always be available at all? 'B' does not know me. He swayed when people talked badly about me. He forgot about his experiences with me and chose to marry others' words. When you disown your experiences and choose others' words and circulate them, your spiritual progress ends there. You slip down a lot and it takes lifetimes to climb back to your earlier spiritual stature.

Gossip-mongers may find pleasure while spreading it, but they will suffer a lot to come clean from that *karma*. It is like an acute diabetic choosing to consume ice cream. He will enjoy it while he is at it, yet he will have to endure lots of medicines and treatment to overcome the effects of this paltry pleasure. I have only pity for those who have to resort to these ways. They have no idea what they are doing and what the consequences are. They are doing me a great favour. Those who were on the borderline decided to go away. Those who were connected with me came closer and anyhow, only they will be benefited. Now, imagine whatever they said is true. Just compare their words with your experience and determine which has more weight. Use your intellect, your discriminatory powers wisely.

Now, I may behave like a 'slippery fish' because people try to put me in frames. Frames restrict. I constantly break frames. I am walking the path of liberation. I destroy anything that binds me or owns me. I behave differently from their expectations so that they get disillusioned. This is my style of non-conformity. Those who get disillusioned will drop off. Those who stay will grow with me too. Those who entertain huge expectations from anyone always suffer. This is the law of *karma*.

🌱 **Question:** Will you not get tired?

Mohanji: Being tired is *tamas* (inertia). When you are forced to do what you do not want to do, *tamas* takes over. Tiredness is a sign of *tamas*. I love my mission. I am here to do that. I do not get tired. Once again, abundance is a perpetual state. This is also applicable in terms of energy.

🌱 **Question:** What about giving? Won't you deplete yourself?

Mohanji: A well never depletes itself, even if many buckets of water are taken from it. Fresh water immediately replaces the water removed by the bucket, and the water level is maintained. The well remains constant. It is not the same for the bucket, which depletes itself when water is poured out completely. Depletion depends on your stature. If you are like a well, you will never be depleted. If you are a bucket, you will be. So, now you can decide what is what.

🌱 **Question:** Won't individual consciousness contaminate Superconsciousness?

Mohanji: I like that. Look at the oceans! Many rivers of the continents pour much water into the oceans. The ocean remains the same. Likewise, Consciousness is vast and unfathomable, a trillion times larger than the vast oceans of Earth. Water can get contaminated. Consciousness can never get contaminated. It is just like your soul, which can never get contaminated and always stays neutral, aiding you but not interfering in your lifestyle, whatever your lifestyle is. Individual consciousness, even when it becomes collective, cannot contaminate the vast Superconsciousness.

Eventually, everything is nullified and dissolved in it. Bubbles exist for some time on the water. Then, they dissolve. Likewise, individual consciousness stays afloat for some time and merges into Superconsciousness. Nothing remains forever. Nothing has permanence except the Supreme Consciousness.

⚘ **Question:** That is interesting. What exactly is permanent?

Mohanji: The Supreme Consciousness. Some call it the 'Father'. Everything came out of it, and everything goes back into it. Everything is projected out of the Father, and everything is recalled to Him as well. The Father remains silent forever. The Father silently observes everything. Just like your conscience observes all your thoughts, words, and actions, without interference, the Father watches the plays of life in the vast universe, objectively, unemotionally.

⚘ **Question:** What is good? What is bad?

Mohanji: Nothing is good or bad in the absolute sense. All are just experiences. Just sundry experiences. So, my dear accumulation-oriented man, think again. What exactly are you accumulating? Nothing belongs to you forever.

⚘ **Question:** Do you operate in multiple consciousnesses?

Mohanji: Yes. I do. Simply speaking, in the limited consciousness associated with this body called Mohanji, and in the higher state of Consciousness, which is well beyond this body called Mohanji. All people do. But the difference is most do not know that they do because they lead an unconscious existence. That is why they get surprised when certain revelations or messages eventually come true. Even though I am trying to explain this in simple terms, this aspect has multiple facets.

The distance between the limited and unlimited is sometimes huge and sometimes non-existent. We are simultaneously both. We usually operate in limited consciousness when we are angry, sad, depressed, disheartened, weak, etc. When we tap into the higher realm and source subtle truths of existence, we are operating in the higher Consciousness. I am tangibly explaining this only for understanding's sake. This is a very deep subject.

We can see the expressions of our non-understanding in every area in the form of emotions and expectations, especially education. We fail to see our children's talent and are more interested in moulding them into just another brick in the wall. We are afraid of risks and opt for safe bets. A fish is powerful and comfortable in the water. That is its natural habitat. Our education system tries hard to make it climb a tree and, in the end, calls it a failure! We expect a fish to climb a tree, and, in the bargain, we destroy the fish.

Thus, we are destroying the next generation. Once their talents are crushed, they become insensitive, which is why we see the gross insensitivity all around us. None care. None are happy either. All complain and criticise one another, finding pleasure in pointing fingers at one another rather than connecting to their own inner space and establishing and sharing peace. When we give wind to the wings of our children, they soar confidently. When we trim their wings out of our fear and anxiety, they are crippled forever. We are what we make ourselves to be. We should never forget that.

> **Question:** When did you become aware that you are capable of imparting power or divine energy?

Mohanji: Never. I never existed in the first place. I still do not exist.

❧ **Question:** How do you manage so many things every-day?

Mohanji: I do not manage anything. Everything happens through me. Why do we develop this ego aspect that we are managing matters? Are we managing our respiration? Circulation? Digestion? Conversion of food to energy and waste? Heartbeat? Secretions? When we are not controlling all these vital functions essential to keep our body working, what are we controlling outside? The feeling that we control things is an utter delusion. Just be far away from it. Be clear about that.

No Flowers – No Sweets – A Happy Birthday

Mohanji: My beloveds, I am overwhelmed by the plans you are making to mark my birthday. I sincerely thank you and appreciate your true love towards me and your many expressions of it. At this juncture, I would like to share a few thoughts with you in this regard.

❧ **Question:** What makes you happy?

Mohanji: The only thing that makes me truly happy is your sincere expression of kindness towards the poor, sick and hungry people, the hungry and helpless birds and animals, and the truly selfless trees and plants. If you consistently and honestly express deep compassion to your fellow beings, I feel genuinely happy. The overflowing compassion, kindness, and unconditional love from your heart towards the helpless, forgotten and ignored beings of the world makes me feel rich inside. It makes me proud of you, my dear family members. Nothing else makes me truly happy.

❧ **Question:** Who are you?

Mohanji: I am what you make of me. I am fluid. If you think I am good, I am good. If you think I am bad, I am bad. I am formless. I am a non-entity. I have no birth or death. Birthdays are only milestones in my current physical existence, which has a definite duration. I do not attribute any more value to my birthdays. I am what you think I am. Like water taking the shape of the container that holds it, I take shape and reflect your mind, constitution and consciousness. I reflect you, sincerely and truly, like a good mirror. My only message for humankind is: "*Tat Twam Asi*" (you are That). Know it. Experience it. Live it.

ᛢ **Question:** What is a celebration for you?

Mohanji: Your expression of non-violence in your daily life is a celebration for me. Your spontaneous expression of kindness, compassion, and love towards all beings, without discrimination, is a celebration for me. Your consistent expression of love, compassion, and kindness to all beings, including nature, is indeed a celebration for me. Then my time on Earth becomes truly worthwhile.

I do not believe in blowing out the candle flames on cakes, as I believe in bringing light and brightness into the lives of people, or at least removing some of the darkness from the minds of those that will allow me. I always feel it is ironic to blow out the candles' brightness as part of our celebration. Candles represent complete selflessness – burning themselves while providing light to the world! No cakes attract me. No sweets attract me. No bouquet attracts me. I love to see flowers in the garden, alive in nature. I look at flowers as the 'bliss of nature'. I do not like to pluck them from their mother plant. I feel that to be selfish. I love flowers, especially if they remain in nature. I like to see birds free and flying, not in cages. I do not like to see any being bound and caged. No gifts attract me. What will I do with them?

Remember the Supreme Lord Krishna's words: "I will be satisfied if you offer me a flower or a leaf. But remember, they are all mine anyway." Whatever we offer to the Lord is legitimately His! In the realms of unlimited consciousness, everything exists within you. What can you gain? What can you collect? What can you own? Everything is within you. Everything is already yours. So, please do not send me flowers, cakes, or sweets. Even without all these expressions, I love you, and that is not conditional. Nor will it ever change.

🌺 **Question:** What is communication for you?

Mohanji: Do not spend money on me. Do not spend time on me. I appreciate your time. I appreciate your kindness. The money or time that you will gladly spend on me may kindly be spent on the poor and the needy of the world. If you can do something for the other beings around you, even buy a hot tea for a poor man feeling cold on a winter morning, you have communicated your love for me. This is what I consider to be a true communication of love. I will not be happier, even if you call me, text me, or e-mail me.

I will be happier when you feed a hungry dog or a bird, who represent detachment because they never hoard or store anything. Clothes to the poor and needy, food to the hungry, shelter to the homeless. This is the communication that I like. This makes me feel happy and rich within. When you do such good deeds, please inspire others also. Let this become a movement. Let this become spontaneous. Let hearts swell with love and compassion. 'Me' and 'Mine' should melt and wither away, and become 'Ours' and 'Everybody's'. Selflessness should become your very nature.

Furthermore, do not blame me or be offended if I do not take your call. You must know that I love you, honestly and sincerely, in every situation and time. Our love and relationship should not be conditioned or bound by terrestrial gadgets such as phones or the internet. Faith should replace all such needs. It is better expressed or communicated through your actions, which anyway happen within my Consciousness. You need not tell me anything. Through positive thoughts, words and actions, when you enrich your consciousness, you get closer to the Supreme Consciousness, which makes us inseparably one.

In summary, please do not send me flowers, sweets, or cakes. Please refrain from sending me texts or emails. Use that day, time, and money to stay in my Consciousness and enjoy the feast of unlimitedness. Feel we are one. Express compassion, love, and gratitude towards your existence and fellow beings. Exist in love. Express it fully. Meditate. Shed your skins of conditionings and for once, be yourself. Be yourself. Express yourself. Love everything wholeheartedly, without expectations. Love unconditionally. Nothing else will make me happier. I do not need anything else from you. This is my sincere request.

Yes, I am Shiva

ᘓ **Question:** This question wells up in my mind, "Are You Shiva?" when I look into your eyes.

Mohanji: Yes. I am Shiva.

ᘓ **Question:** And the other beings of the universe? Who are they?

Mohanji: All are Shiva. All are units of Shiva. All are drops of the same ocean.

ᘓ **Question:** Are you sure?

Mohanji: Yes, I am sure. I am witnessing Shiva every moment. All are Shiva.

ᘓ **Question:** Who or what is Shiva?

Mohanji: Shiva is beyond any definition at all. Attempting to define Shiva would be an adventure. A real mission impossible! Shiva can only be experienced and not intellectually understood. A bucket cannot contain the water of the ocean.

Shiva has two distinct identities in human understanding, which become blurred at times – the Supreme *Parabrahma*, and the finite entity married to the Goddess *Parvati*, who has children. As the Supreme *Parabrahma*, Shiva is formless and beyond time and space. He is the indivisible unity. This Shiva has no beginning or end. He is *Parabrahma*. The Shiva *lingam* represents that Shiva. It is multi-dimensional or pan-dimensional. Here, I am talking about Shiva as *Parabrahma*, just as Lord Krishna represents the Supreme in the *Bhagavad Gita*. All identifications of such elevated consciousness are only with the Supreme formless, which is beyond all dimensions.

On the other hand, we also worship Shiva as this finite entity, who is both *kshipra kopi* (easily annoyed and angered) and also *kshipra prasadi* (easily pleased). Shiva as the householder represents human existence, a god with a wife and children, yet supremely, spiritually powerful. He is a householder and a Master at the same time. Master of Masters – Supreme Master and Saint of all Saints – Supreme Saint! He floats with time and is timeless too. Shiva came as a *chandala*[9] with four dogs to give wisdom to Adi Shankara. He came in the form of a tribal hunter to grant his weapon, the *Pashupata*, to Arjuna. Another aspect of Shiva is Dakshinamoorthy, the knowledge incarnate. Hanumanji is also considered as an *amsha* (essence) of Shiva.

❧ **Question:** I consider Hinduism a path, a Tradition and not a religion because there are three hundred and thirty million Gods in the Hindu tradition and there are many castes and sub-castes within the tradition. In the Hindu tradition, Brahma, Vishnu, and Shiva have equal im-

---

9   a man from a 'lower caste' in the Indian caste system

portance. Then, why only Shiva? Pardon me if this question is stupid.

Mohanji: No, the question is relevant. You are right. Hinduism is not a religion. It is a path, a Tradition. There are three hundred and thirty million Gods (deities) because one-third of every being is the God element. The soul element is the God element. Only if you worship the soul element within you, will you merge with the Supreme Soul, *Parabrahma*. Only if you recognise the soul element or God element in every being, will you witness the all-pervading God who dwells in all beings. As long as we see differences, we are in ignorance. When we look around, if we only see God, we are complete. We are one with God. The path to *Parabrahma* is our soul.

Each deity is a representation of the Supreme Unmanifested just like you and me. Each incarnation is a manifestation. Each thought, word, and action is a manifestation. Everything should remind us of the silent yet potent force which manifests through billions of creations. The subtle, unseen and unrecognizable through the senses, is the force that moves the machinery called existence in the universe. Every plant, tree, river, and stone is its manifestation. A part of it is in everything. This is represented by the 330 million deities.

So, how do we worship them all? Simple. We worship the one that is close to us. Our own soul! Our subtlest aspect can only be found when we detach from our gross aspects. When we go deeper and deeper into the subtle aspect of us, we will start feeling its manifestations in a moment-to-moment level. We cannot perceive it through any of our senses and the mind. We can only perceive its manifested forms like you and me. By connecting to the essence behind the manifestations, we will start feeling the essence all the time. Then we will start operating in the essence level – shedding the lure of the gross manifested level. In other words, we will fathom the actual size of the whole iceberg which is huge underwater, much bigger than its manifested aspect above water.

The Source can only be experienced. None of our faculties can understand it, except some aspects of its gross manifestation which are bound by time, space, beings and also situations. They are temporary. They change. Hence, it is very vital to connect to the essence behind the manifestation. This is the reason we consider everything to be a manifestation of God so that we start seeing only God everywhere. This is the preliminary step towards seeing God inside yourself. When we start seeing God in everything outside, we will always stay connected to God and then we will automatically get diverted to the God inside us.

The God within! This is the real you. Then you will know that there is no difference. All are One. Every being is One. All are extensions of the One God, the subtlest Unmanifested form that runs the universe. Then we realize that we ourselves are the universe. There is nothing apart from us because we are the essence and not the sundry perishable manifestations. So, the 330 million Gods represent every flavour of our existence. The types, shapes, forms, characters, emotions, needs, etc. You are free to connect to any of them as per your constitution. When you connect to the manifested form of your constitution outside of you, it serves as a mirror to yourself. In other words, you can only connect to a God that represents your constitution. Only then can you attain unity and fulfillment. The path says that you can see nothing except God in all manifestations. Now it is up to the seeker to get there.

Regarding the second part of your question, Brahma, Vishnu, and Shiva represent three aspects of the Supreme *Parabrahma*. That means creation, maintenance, and dissolution. They have equal importance. They are all the same. All manifestations are formed out of the Supreme Unmanifested. There may be some variety in subtlety, but essentially, they are the same.

The Supreme Unmanifested is raw energy. Thus, all aspects of the Trinity are equal and equally powerful. My mention of Shiva is about Shiva as *Parabrahma*, not as an entity with the limited role of dissolution. In that context, Shiva, Vishnu, and Brahma are the same. There is no Trinity. There is only Unity. There is only *Parabrahma*. One energy behind all manifestations. That is *Parabrahma*. The real source. All forms represent the formless. All forms have materialised from and will dissolve back into the formless.

❧ **Question:** What is Consciousness?

Mohanji: Shiva is Consciousness. Consciousness is Shiva.

❧ **Question:** So, what are we?

Mohanji: Consciousness. Shiva.

❧ **Question:** Is there any degree of variation?

Mohanji: There are no degree variations. Consciousness is full and complete. But there is a degree of variation in awareness. Some experience fully, some partially, some randomly, and some do not experience at all. Those who constantly experience will exist in bliss and silence, and those who seldom experience will keep talking theories, book knowledge, or someone's words.

❧ **Question:** Mohanji, I like your style, clarity, and if I may say so, your straight-to-the-point approach. Tell me, how do we gain that clarity?

Mohanji: Simple. Be me. Be my consciousness. A shift in consciousness brings forth the corresponding clarity. Simply be.

❧ **Question:** What is knowledge?

Mohanji: Just an intellectual requirement.

🌿 **Question:** Does knowledge exist?

Mohanji: Apart from you? No. Apart from you? Yes.

🌿 **Question:** I do not understand.

Mohanji: We are knowledge incarnate. Everything is within us. So, knowledge does not exist apart from us. We are knowledge incarnate, yet our intellect fails to recognise that and seeks knowledge outside of us, using our senses. This is highly limited. One has lots of good quality food at home, yet prefers to eat from the street. The beautiful ocean within us goes unrecognised, but the small pool outside is appreciated. It takes a lot of awareness to recognise what lies within us. Instead, we try to find happiness outside of ourselves. So, in the context of the intellect, it is true that knowledge is outside of us. Ultimately, the very Truth is 'No', as all knowledge is within us. However, in terms of *Maya*, it is 'Yes'.

🌿 **Question:** Understood. So, what exists outside of us?

Mohanji: Nothing.

🌿 **Question:** Then, why this illusion? Why this drama?

Mohanji: Just multiple expressions of *Maya*. *Maya* at work! Multiple expressions of duality. Relativity at work.

🌿 **Question:** I agree. When everything boils down, when all waves subside, the still ocean remains.

Mohanji: Absolutely and the ocean itself is *Maya,* if you are witnessing the ocean from outside. If you recognise that you are the ocean yourself, it would be just a realization – *Aham Brahmasmi*! There is no 'me'. There is nothing apart from me. There is nothing to 'know'.

🌿 **Question:** Ah! Wow! You said it so simply. That is a profound Truth, indeed!

Mohanji: This is the same Truth that all the Saints and *yogis* (spiritual practitioners of *yoga*) have been telling us ever since time began. This information is nothing new.

- **Question:** Mohanji, it has been a week since we communicated. I have been assimilating what you discussed with me so far.

Mohanji: Did you finally realise that it is all a bunch of crap?

- **Question:** On the contrary, I feel this would be useful for the generations to come.

Mohanji: Do not worry about the generations to come. We have no real control over the future. There will be others to guide the generations to come. We have only now to consider. Is it useful now? Yes? Then it is worth it.

- **Question:** My cousin 'L' says she is in love with you. She wants to marry you.

Mohanji: What a joke! Anyways, I am indeed happily married in terrestrial terms! But 'L' is certainly welcome to marry my consciousness. That is the real me. It is worth it, as it is permanent. As a human being, I do not 'exist'. This body is temporary, fragile, and highly perishable. All are welcome to marry my consciousness. Sixteen thousand and eight women married Krishna's consciousness and attained liberation. Consciousness is eternal. Through my consciousness, I can have many 'wives' beyond gender, space and time.

Moreover, terrestrial marriage is usually a deep entanglement and often leads to jealousy and ownership unless higher awareness and lack of expectation are developed from deep within. Marriage should never be based on boredom, escapism, expectation, and infatuation, in terrestrial terms. Marriage should always be purpose-bound, two people coming together for a larger purpose in existence, which leads to the perfect fulfilment of a joint *karmic* agenda. I believe 'L' is at least forty years older than me. So, she needs to marry my consciousness before it is too late!

✤ **Question:** What is marriage for you?

Mohanji: Completion.

✤ **Question:** Completion of?

Mohanji: Journey. Completion in Life. Completion of a *karmic* life, objectively speaking.

✤ **Question:** Mohanji, what is your religion?

Mohanji: Religion of love. All other religions are just barriers, walls. I only believe in unconditional love beyond all human barriers.

✤ **Question:** Mohanji, how do you handle distinctly different planes of existence equally – professional, spiritual, charity, family, socio-commercial – without ever mixing them? Where do you get so much energy from? Don't you get tired?

Mohanji: This is simple. We are everything. We are a father, husband, son, boss, servant, social being, commercial being, and so on. When you operate, be extremely objective. Do not blur the boundary between tasks. Do not procrastinate. Just do it. Work should be considered as sacred – as worship. If we know what we are doing and our mind is firmly fixed on our activity of the moment without oscillation, time is aplenty. Procrastination saps a lot of time from our lives and leaves us tired and inefficient. People think a lot, avoid all actions and later complain that life is not treating them well or is worthless! I fail to understand them.

Lastly, I have never been afraid to walk alone. I do not understand the meaning of the word 'fear'. Fear paralyses us and marries or binds us with forceful inaction.' I believe in truthful action, where fear has no existence. When you love what you do, when your life is purposeful, there will not be any tiredness or boredom. Tedium is a by-product of having to do what you do not enjoy doing. I enjoy what I do. I do not get tired. My path is clear and my life is purpose-bound. I am a passionate man.

> ❧ **Question:** We in Europe are a bit addicted to lineage. Does the lineage of a *Guru* matter?

Mohanji: In the family of a legend, can you expect a similar prodigy in each generation? Most of our past great Masters just happened or appeared from nowhere. They shone brightly just because of their stature. A *Guru* might be of a high calibre. It does not mean that any of his disciples are of his calibre. Likewise, look at the whole Datta Tradition, where individuals became prominent because of their stature.

Spiritual stature has much more value and is more important than status, pedigree, or lineage, which only tells about the path and can perhaps guarantee status but can never guarantee stature. Often people mistake status for stature. Status may get us name, position, and fame. But stature has got to be acquired through lifetimes of spiritual practice. Who cared about the lineage of Adi Shankara, Vyasa, Vasistha, Shirdi Sai Baba? Everyone respected their stature.

> ❧ **Question:** Mohanji, a funny question – Are you real? I often feel that you are not real, that you do not exist.

Mohanji: It is not a funny question. It is a good question. No. I am also an illusion. I do not exist.

> ❧ **Question:** How can there be differences? How can there be high and low?

Mohanji: There are no highs and lows in the absolute sense. There are only variations in vision and awareness. Physical manifestations or representations are only expressions of relativity. How can there be a high without a low? How can relativity be expressed without duality?

🌿 **Question:** Relativity confuses.

Mohanji: The answer lies within the question itself. Go beyond relativity. The confusion ends there.

🌿 **Question:** How long will you work in the highly competitive commercial world, among the pretensions and the heavy gross?

Mohanji: As long as this heart beats, I will work, but perhaps not in the highly competitive commercial world of profits and pretensions. I am proving a point here. If we have the will, we can operate in contradicting worlds with equal ease and effortlessness. If we choose, we can remain pure in all worlds. Escapism is not a solution. Wherever you are, be at home. The environment does not matter. Our deepest determination and will matters. Spirituality is not only for Saints. It is accessible to all. It is inherent in all. Renunciation is a state of mind for which you need not go to the Himalayas.

🌿 **Question:** Mohanji, we cannot have enough of you.

Mohanji: I thought the world was fed up with me. Mohanji is not a person. It is a continuation. It is a constitution or a constellation. It is Consciousness. It will always exist, even after this body goes back to where it came from.

🌿 **Question:** How are you today, Mohanji? You were not well last week.

Mohanji: The Consciousness is the same. The body keeps floating up and down.

✤ **Question:** Mohanji, what do you see in people when you address large gatherings? Their body, soul, or *karma*?

Mohanji: I see Shiva. All are Shiva. All are expressions of myself, just acting out individual *karmas*. No differences between one and the other.

✤ **Question:** Between man and woman too?

Mohanji: What has gender got to do with it? All are the same. What is the gender of the soul? What is the gender of *Parabrahma*, the supreme soul?

✤ **Question:** Then, why does the Hindu religion have Gods and Goddesses? Why does Shiva have a wife? Why do you have a wife too?

Mohanji: Firstly, all things are reflections of *Parabrahma*. All are One. In answer to your second question, duality is the prime expression of relativity. So, there are two. 'One' represents unity. There is nothing apart from One. 'Two' represents relativity – You and I. When you and I unite, we become One – Unity. Shiva is the energy aspect, while Parvati is the material aspect. Expressions become complete when they unite. But essentially, man is an extension of a woman and vice versa. Shiva is also *ArdhaNarishwara*[10]. I have married because this completes this soul's journey too. Womanhood is sacred. Woman is mother-hood. This is why we worship women.

✤ **Question:** Your answers amaze me. So, all Gods and Goddesses are One?

[10] Lord Shiva in the composite forms of the deities Shiva and His consort Parvati, half-male and half-female split down the middle to indicate a synthesis of the masculine and feminine energies of the universe and their inseparability from each other

Mohanji: Essentially One. All *Gurus* are One too. All knowledge is One. You are Unity. When you work through the body you have rented for the time being, you feel divided from the Father. When you return the body to Earth, you unite again with your Father. We have attributed tasks and purposes to Gods and Goddesses. They represent that task. We have created deities based on certain systems, worship methods, and certain mathematical calculations. If there are changes in that, there will be changes in deities too. There are *mula mantras* for each deity – the root *mantra*. The root sustains the deity. The root *mantra* maintains its attributed strength. There is nothing apart from One. Whatever is apart from One is an illusion, *Maya*.

🌱 **Question:** Did you ever fear that people might not understand you?

Mohanji: No, I never had any insecurity and will never have. I do not keep any agenda.

🌱 **Question:** What is fear for you?

Mohanji: Illusion. Fear does not exist.

🌱 **Question:** Do you have any fears?

Mohanji: No.

🌱 **Question:** Even the loss of near and dear ones?

Mohanji: I have already experienced the loss of near and dear ones in this life. I know how it feels.

🌱 **Question:** What is terrestrial life?

Mohanji: Terrestrial life is only about various experiences.

🌱 **Question:** When you look at the world, what do you see?

Mohanji: A divine comedy of errors.

🌀 **Question:** Life is a comedy of errors for you?

Mohanji: Yes, it is a grand joke. I laugh at the seriousness of people. All are grumpy and serious. People are tired and wrinkled. People are afraid to laugh – as if their teeth will fall out! With all that seriousness, they will die and go. What do they gain? I always laugh at life. There is nothing to be serious about here. It is indeed a comedy of errors. There is only this moment at our disposal. We do not even know our tomorrows. So why worry at all?

🌀 **Question:** Why errors?

Mohanji: Errors due to wrong identifications. Such as – people think I am Mohanji. I am Mohanji for this world. I am not just Mohanji. When I die, this body will be called Mohanji's body. People think they are their mind or intellect. Even that is not true. A philosopher once said, "I think; therefore I am." Then, what about him when he does not think – such as in the deep sleep state? Just look around. You can see the wrong identifications all over. People believe they are something else and behave accordingly.

🌀 **Question:** Last questions. What is your real name? Why do you use the reference *Parabrahma?*

Mohanji: My official name is P.K. Mohan. 'P' stands for the family name and 'K' for the name of my grandfather. It is still my official name. Mohanji is the name that is used in the spiritual circle, which a Saint initiated. He was the first to start calling me Mohanji, and everyone followed afterwards. Mohan is the name, and 'Ji' is a suffix used to address someone respectfully. I do not call myself Mohanji.

Moreover, I always sign off as 'M' because the alphabet letter 'M' usually has no value by itself. It needs something more, some more alphabet letters to gain meaning. I am just an alphabet letter, meaningless by itself, transitory, temporary, and momentary. I keep myself as insignificant as I can.

Parabrahma is the mirror that I am showing to the world. *Parabrahma* is unity. The two words *Para* and *Brahma* cannot exist as duality. They must merge into One. It exists as an illusion. It must merge and is always merged as an entity. Secondly, it is a reminder of who you are and where you belong. You are *Parabrahma* and you belong there. *Parabrahma* is the Father from whom all dualities have originated. This might tell you that we are all One, that there is no duality amongst us, and that whatever we see as duality is just a grand illusion. The concept is the same as applying sacred ash on our forehead. Ash is where we came from and ash is where we will return to. We are just a handful of ash in reality. The ash on the forehead is a reminder. It teaches humility. Likewise, I used that name to remind you of who you are and what you think you are now. Two words represent duality, Truth, and illusion. I exist beyond all these.

Stay Connected to My Consciousness

❧ **Question:** How do you connect with us while you are physically so far away?

Mohanji: I connect when you connect. I connect when you do not connect too, just like electricity stays latent at the switchboard on your wall. When you think or talk about me, irrespective of whether it is good or bad, you are connected to my consciousness. I am always with you, whether you see me, feel me or awaken in me. I am not the body. I am the consciousness that this body represents. There is no distance in consciousness.

❧ **Question:** Sometimes, I feel disconnected.

Mohanji: You are never disconnected from me. Your mind is. You are not your mind.

❧ **Question:** I want to be with you always.

Mohanji: Being with my physical body will never ensure proximity to me. If you are one with my consciousness, you are always with me and completely connected with me. This is more permanent, as well. Do not misunderstand that those who are physically close to me are actually 'close' to me. Some of you who are physically far away from me are closer to me (through the unity of Consciousness) than those who are physically near me. So, the desire for being with me should not be about being with me physically.

Furthermore, many of you will not handle my physical proximity because the chances of disillusionment are very high. I may kick your ego from time to time. I will tell you things that you may not like to hear, to shake you up and liberate you from some *samskaric* bindings. You may not like it. So, beware. When you have tremendous maturity to handle whatever is given, you will automatically reach me. This is for sure. Otherwise, it is just infatuation. It has no spiritual value.

Being in physical proximity and at the same time being egoless and in complete surrender, like Shama or Mhalsapati to Shirdi Sai Baba, is real Grace and a blessing. Then the disciple and the *Guru* are one, though in separate bodies. This is possible and achievable if you have consistency in effort and total determination, and a will for the individual ego's annihilation.

❧ **Question:** How can I see you in your real form?

Mohanji: See yourself in your real form. You will see me.

❧ **Question:** How do I know you?

Mohanji: Know yourself; you will know me. What your mind says is not me. What your soul says is me.

❧ **Question:** Where do you exist? In which realm?

Mohanji: In your heart. In the realm of your consciousness. I have no other existence.

The Gross and the Subtle

Do not be disillusioned. No gross form is equal to God if God is formless, colourless, desireless, and omnipresent. Form has limitations. Form has reasons. Form has weaknesses. Forms dissolve and die. A form can represent higher consciousness, which we could call an *Avatar*. Forms represent various degrees of awareness. But forms also represent duality. While owning and operating a form, there is alienation, division, and corresponding disillusionment. Forms that represent certain aspects of the all-encompassing God are considered deities.

All forms on earth have their constitution, which is well beyond generalisation, even though generalisation is possible on the basic level of operation such as hunger, sex, sleep, blood circulation, and the basic general rules of gross existence. When we expect to see complete unity and diversity of God in gross forms, we fail to understand creation, creativity, free will, and uniqueness within the diversity of existence. We fail to appreciate the basic as well as the collective operating levels. We get disappointed and disillusioned.

Uniqueness is the basis of creation. It is no factory product. Creation in the larger sense is always handmade. Understand creation at the cellular level, and then you will understand the Universe!

Let us make one thing clear. This body is called Mohan or, in your words, "Mohanji". Till my last breath, this body will remain under the name of Mohanji. People may confer titles before or after this name. But the name will remain the same. This body is not Rama, Krishna, Shiva, Sai Baba, or Jesus. This body, existing today, is called Mohanji. The consciousness that operates or works through this body is intangible, invisible and often incomprehensible to public eyes. Never be disillusioned. We can only see what we are capable of seeing. Be happy!

All people are connected to something, somebody. This connection is due to their inner compatibility with the object of their connection. One may see the reflection of their object of connection in me. That does not make me that object. There could be resemblances, character similarities, but one is certainly not the other. Be aware of that! No person can be another person. Even when the soul takes a new birth, the incarnation has a different name, form and purpose. Nothing is ever the same. Time and space are different, and so is the purpose on Earth.

Do not be disillusioned. This body is called Mohanji, and it will remain so till this body dies. Do not be affected by or connected to me while imagining or thinking this as someone else's body. That will lead to disillusionment and disappointment.

All incarnations portrayed their unique character and constitution, just as we do. Sai Baba is Sai Baba, Krishna is Krishna, and Jesus is Jesus. These are names of bodies (certain people) of the past. Their consciousness is certainly One, and their consciousness is eternal. Hence, they are eternally available. They all are one. You are one with them too. This is why you are connecting with them or their certain character aspects so effortlessly. There could be many similarities in them and their characters that you recognise in others. There could be consciousness compatibility, which makes you feel that this one is that one. But it is a mirage. Do not be disillusioned.

All bodies have duration and purpose. Purpose is always time-related on Earth. Time changes matter. Requirements change on Earth. Incarnations that could handle such requirements take birth. They may have attributes from the past. But they are in a new body. They have a new name and form. They have a new set of parents, a new language and a mission. They are new. Do not be disillusioned. This body is called Mohanji and will remain so.

A son may resemble the father, but he is not his father. Likewise, each incarnation is unique. Our inflexibility and non-understanding are due to our conditioning and mental pictures, which we have acquired and maintained. Once we become flexible and fluid, clarity takes place spontaneously.

Seven billion people. Seven billion personalities. Seven billion types of expressions. Do not try to change the world outside. Change the world inside. If seven billion do the same, the world outside will be a much better place. The tragedy lies in the fact that we are trying to change the world outside all the time, ignoring or discounting our conditionings, fears, phobias, and prejudices.

When we are always 'against' something, we will fail to see the subtlety and beauty of existence. When you only look outside, all you see are states of duality and disparity.

Unity lies within. The key to a unified existence, oneness with all beings, is kept within us. When we become unified with ourselves, we see the whole world unified with us. The 'way out' lies within.

Section 4:

...SHOWS THE WAY...

~~~~~~~~~

"This world is our real school. Life is the Guru. Soul is the Principal. Waking state is our classroom. Dream state is our homework. Beings of nature are our lessons. Experiences are our learning. Awareness is the method. The mind is the examination. Winning over the mind is mastery."

CHAPTER 1:

Signs of the times

Shifting Times – A Profound Understanding

We have been discussing the shifting times and their impact on our lives for some weeks now. Some have discussed the changes that have already been experienced in life and their approach towards life. Those who operate in the emotional realms have been tested a lot. Those who opted for witness-hood have been rewarded. Very interesting times indeed!

What follows might clarify some of your doubts regarding the current phenomena, time and energies in operation. I shall explain the scenario as lucidly as I can. Yet, understand the complexity of the subject and approach it accordingly. Digest it slowly, according to your capacity.

The energies are shifting, and they have shifted so rapidly in the last few weeks[11]. As I mentioned earlier, those who still chose to operate from the emotional plane have suffered a lot, and those who chose to operate in objective witness-hood and the intellect plane, have taken the changes in their stride comfortably. As we know, we can use our emotional heart and react to each situation, and we can use our intellect and respond to each situation.

The difference is 'reaction' versus 'response'. There are miles of differences between these two. When emotions and ego are at play, suffering is more. When the intellect is in charge, objectivity is more, and it helps understand the situation in a better light. If there is a body, there is change. When one inflicts pain through thoughts, words, or action on another, the one who inflicts suffers for a longer period of time than the victim. This is the law of nature.

Now, in order to understand the changes that are happening in our realms, let us take a close look at the scenario of our own death. At the time of death, when we take the last breath and the soul exits our body, the strongest emotion or the strongest feeling which we have at that moment determines the texture and flavour of our next incarnation. This is why, in our scriptures, it is strongly recommended to chant the names of God and contemplate or meditate on any form or the formless aspect of God as much as possible so that we attain God as we exit our physical body. The lighter we are at the time of our death by marrying love and kindness, the more we will experience a smooth transit. If hatred, greed, fear and jealousy plague us at the time of our death, we may become earthbound due to its heaviness.

Likewise, the soul associated with our life undergoes evolution, shedding off baggage, even through the plane after death and before the next birth. Hence, transition during death is important as a definite means for higher elevation. After the primary transition of a physical death, the soul undergoes a gestation period of clarification about past lives, events, emotions, relationships, as well as the agenda that is forthcoming while preparing to take the next journey in another physical body. During this time, some baggage could be discarded or properly packed as per its relevance or lack of it. Evolution is a continuous process. It happens through death, through gestation and through re-birth.

The advantage during the suspended state between death and birth is that further accumulation does not happen during that state because our operating levels are not the senses and the mind, and the operating platform is not Earth. (Almost all of our agenda is related to the realm of Earth). This is a big relief. We are only sorting out the baggage in hand at that time. The lesser the baggage, the easier the transit. Hence, accumulation while living in this body should also be controlled through awareness. If we follow wherever our mind follows and add more and more things to our shopping list, we will have mountains of unfulfilled desires, and it could transcend into more incarnations. Beware.

Now, we have two interesting time zones at hand, 12.12.12 and 21.12.12. Both are transition points, high in energy and frequency. This will be a transition for each and every soul that walks on Earth. As I mentioned above, just like the time when our soul leaves our body, a big transition happens. During these two days also, a huge shift in consciousness is possible. As I mentioned above, having higher feelings, emotions, desires or thoughts during the time of leaving the body will determine the texture and flavour of our next incarnation. How we handle ourselves, including our thoughts, actions, and feelings during 12.12.12 and 21.12.12, will determine our life in the days ahead.

This is why I recommended that all in our global Mohanji family feed the poor and the needy, do acts of compassion and kindness, do good, feel good, and say good things. Meditate, connect to the Lord that you worship through chanting, prayers or silence. Most importantly, since our mind will keep wandering – which is the nature of our mind, it would be a good idea to indulge wholeheartedly in service activities of whatever nature that is affordable for you. However, inertia and procrastination should be totally wiped off on those days. You should not procrastinate using lame excuses. You cannot cheat yourself. You must shed inertia and run. That will help you in life beyond 12.12.12. Another 12.12.12 will only happen a thousand years later.

I hope you have understood the importance of the time that has been delivered to us by the kind universe. This is the time to express the qualities of our soul and the Father. Unconditional love, care, charity, kindness, compassion, so on and so forth. Refrain from consuming food that increases inertia, such as dead organisms and substances that dull our system, such as alcohol. Consistently, consciously, perform acts of kindness and love. Love your own family members, friends, and colleagues. Forgive everyone as you are elevating yourself into a higher realm. Reduce your baggage consciously so that the journey can be more enjoyable. Transits and transitions can be easier.

Express kindness from the heart. Forgive and forget pains and hurts consciously. Donate for charity and wholeheartedly participate in such acts. Feed the hungry and earn much Grace through such acts. Shed hatred, fear, anxiety, greed, and jealousy. That will reduce your baggage a lot. Fill the space with unconditional love, which is lighter in nature and easier to handle. Engage in discussions and conversations of higher nature (*satsang*). Discuss how we could make things better for the larger benefit of the world we live in, or how we could make our life more meaningful by being worthwhile to the larger world, etc.

Step out of your comfort zone and make a positive difference in the world outside. Use your life positively and constructively for the betterment of the world. Entertain sensitiveness. Do not waste your time with talk about other people, and do not judge them or criticise them. Thought is the first level of creation. Thoughts conglomerated could become events! Let your thoughts be of higher nature. Words and actions will automatically follow.

Also, this is a good time for souls who are transcending, meaning those who are very sick or in critical condition. If they choose to stay in a body and go through the shifting times, allow them to. During such a time, the best thing to do is chanting, such as *sahasranama* (1008 names of a Saint or deity) or Sai *mantras*. One cannot and should not interfere in another being's *karma*. Deliver your love through chanting, prayers and service to other beings such as food, clothing, shelter and healthcare support to the helpless in the name of your dear ones.

This is the time of subtlety. All subtle expressions will gain more impact during such times, similar to *Brahma Muhurta* time, where prayers, chanting, or meditation have a higher impact on the consciousness because of the clarity of the environment. Consider this time as similar. Remember, this is the best time of your life for spiritual elevation and evolution. Use it wisely. Always remember that we are lucky to be alive during this time to enjoy and experience the transition. This is the time of lightness and brightness. Use it to elevate yourself.

Just like death and rebirth, consider that you are going through a similar transition while you are in your body! This is the miracle of this time. Shed your ego and start a new life. This opportunity will never recur. Instead, if you hold on to your heavy baggage of regrets, hatred, enmity and guilt, you will miss the bus. Or at least, you will not get the possible benefits of this God given transition.

Do not fear that 2012 is the end of the world. It could very well be the end of our heaviness. It could very well be the end of our wrong identifications. The body will exist, but with a different consciousness package, a new software. Shed your limited mind and look beyond. You will know that life is far more important and interesting than our silly ego, that our limited mind made us believe.

The Shift

✤ **Question:** Why is the shift taking place now?

Mohanji: Well, the shift is not taking place now. It is a gradual process; it has evolved into this kind of situation. According to me, the shift started much earlier, at least in the last fifty years. It started becoming evident in the mid-1980s. Then, it started triggering, and it evolved almost in tune with the technological era, the technological revolution. It may more or less coincide that way. The momentum has increased slowly, slowly, slowly, and in 2012 the spinning of Earth changed, and it also coincided with the earthquake and tsunami that happened in Japan. That was a very major shake-up. Then there were five eclipses last year. These are all various aspects that change the structure of things on Earth.

Thus, the shift is basically the shift of consciousness. The shift is in consciousness. All other things, the environment, the mindset, the speed of time, all these things aid the shift of consciousness. Those who cannot cope with the shift of consciousness fall into depression. They become more mind-oriented; they become more suffocated. You can say the shift is shifting from the mind to awareness, to consciousness. If you are still stuck with the mind, then it is very likely that you will suffer a lot (the emotions, the problems, the situations). Everything will squeeze you.

But the moment you rise above the mind, you will start experiencing freedom in such a situation. You will start feeling freedom, liberation. All these things happen when you are in the mode beyond the mind, beyond the intellect, beyond the restrictions of the body. Restriction means the space called the body, mind, ego, intellect, all these things attached. Once you break free and you are able to go beyond it, then it is a free flow. Then you will flow through time, flow through situations, whether they are good or bad, it does not matter; you will have a smooth journey.

The shift has happened well before, and it is a continuation. I would say that even now, after 2012, it is continuing and probably into the mid-2010s, probably 2016-2018, you will still see major shifts happening. This is a process. By 2022-2023, things will have settled down. Upheaval is happening, and to see the smooth flow, it will take further time. Now things are changing. Once the eruption happens and things are moving, then it settles down over a period of time. The sky will be full of ash and smoke. You won't be able to see what is going on. But it is worth the journey.

What helps this transit is faith. You say, "Ok, beyond the smoke and ash, there is life." Once we know that, we can move ahead; with faith, life is smooth. During this time, the main thing to hold onto is faith, and act. Keep moving.

> ✤ **Question:** Thank you. Is there any specific spiritual or physical practice to help us be in tune with the shift?

Mohanji: Being in the now. Being in the present. That is perpetual meditation. When the path is slippery, and you are walking through slippery grounds, what do you do? You hold on to something so that you are steady and you are moving. In this way, hold on to faith, and be in the present. This is the biggest and the best *sadhana* you can do during times of transition.

> ✤ **Question:** How to know that we are in tune with the shift?

Mohanji: You will know that whatever is happening outside, it is not affecting you inside. It is a clear sign of your progress. To achieve that kind of state, you have to be objective. Extremely objective, "Things are happening. Fine. Let me handle it." It is not like being emotional about it, crying over it, and blaming other people. All this should stop. Just stay focused. Just be.

Just be in the present. Keep looking, "Hey, who is suffocated now? The situation is here. Who is getting affected?" If it is the mind, go beyond the mind. If it is the ego, go beyond the ego. But be aware.

Be aware of all this process, all that is happening in you and outside you. Just be aware. Just be aware all the time. "Things are happening, things are flowing, this person is giving me pain, this person is giving me pleasure, both are fine. Both are different flavours of life. This person is taking me to higher realms; another person is trying to pull me down." Avoid the person who is pulling you down. Embrace the person who is taking you higher. If you move objectively like this, that is it. That is the practice you need to do. Be in the present. Accept reality. Move on.

Question: What is happening in 2012?

Mohanji: The earth is already shifting. In Serbia, I was asked about the recent tsunami in Japan and what I felt when the earthquake happened. I said, "From a distance, it was just like a hiccup." From a cosmic perspective, this is not a tragedy. But what is happening to Japan is serious. The earthquake hit right in the middle or stem of Japan – which is a coral formation – and the country tilted and shifted to the east.

Another quite interesting aspect is that Japan is the only country that still practices whale hunting. They say they do it for 'scientific' reasons. Last year, according to some statistics I saw, they killed about 550 pregnant whales for 'scientific' research. In a daily newspaper, I have read that three big whaling ships were thrown onto the shore by the tsunami, and a big whaling factory was completely destroyed in Ayukawa. Also, a temple dedicated to the souls of killed whales was completely destroyed. The dead whales don't care about the temple!

When creation happened, the natural energy was pure – wind, water, sun – were sufficient and did not cause pollution.

The oil that was still under the earth worked like the shock-absorbers in our cars. This was creating a balance between the continents on the whole Earth. This has all gone. Over time, we took all the oil from the shock-absorbers and replaced it with water. Will that work?

Whales and dolphins are very special creatures. They are the only creatures that are still energizing Earth. Their songs have soothed and nourished Earth.

The shift is also about the process of rebuilding. If you have a house you cannot repair anymore, you have to destroy it and rebuild it from scratch. Let us not worry about it. If you want to use the time to elevate yourself, then the best you can do is shift to your spine. When a baby forms in the womb of a mother, the spine is the first part created. Every existence is based on the spine. The spine is the stairway to heaven.

To go back on the topic of time, as I said, energies are changing very rapidly on Earth now, with a lot of calamities expected from now to 2022. You can see the effect of it on people. The mind is restless and controlling. Connecting to higher frequencies and meditation have become difficult. Thus today, chanting has greater value than meditation, and it can lead to meditation.

Time is shifting. From 2012 to almost 2017, time is denser and darker in nature. My calculation is that until December 2017, the speed of the journey or hurdles will be more or less similar. It will not be much different from now. It is from December 2012 to December 2017, i.e., five years. But now is a very good time to plant the seeds for what you want to do in the future; it is time to start doing it. Before December 2017, you can set everything in order and then it will be a smooth, hurdle-free journey. From 2018 to 2022, time would be of a lighter, softer, subtler nature. This is what is expected.

You can see that the basic instinct or basic aspect of people's character has been enhanced in the last few years. People who are oriented to spirituality, meditation, to exploring themselves have intensified it. Because at this time, Earth is spinning faster. A little effort from you helps much more. One year is almost equal to fifty years. If you invest in awareness now, it will help you to achieve your goal much faster.

This year, 2014, is important as the year of creation because of the moon. Moon means water; water means new life. It is a new creation. It is a good time for starting things anew. This year, there is a ninety five per cent for any new effort, towards something very specific, to happen. If you are taking one message from here, this should be the message. Nurture positivity now, or positive aspects now, or clear purpose: "This is what I want to be or achieve in the years to come" or "I want to be liberated in the years to come." That kind of powerful decision, powerful purpose, if you sow the seeds now, it will grow beautifully in the years to come.

This is very important to remember in these ten years between 2012 and 2022. It would be a good idea for that seed to be 'liberation' because we are stuck with so many things created by the mind. We are dividing more than uniting. We are all related, but our mind does not accept it. The mind likes to keep differences and divisions rather than unification and unity. All we need is love.

Evolution

☙ **Question:** Is evolution linked to awareness?

Mohanji: Spiritual evolution is indeed linked with awareness. Awareness is expandable. In the path of evolution, it may take lifetimes of cleansing to experience the subtler. The mind gives you many options for enjoyment. When senses get attracted, the body follows. We existed for many lifetimes like this. One day we feel, "Let all this be enough." Voluntarily, few things are dropped from the heart. The process takes time. How difficult it is to drop those impressions of many lives which you carried to create this character!

You must recognise and understand each aspect of yours that built this character, and then unwind it. This can happen only through recognition, contemplation, and meditation on yourself. When you are with higher consciousness, the lower automatically drops. A doll which was important when you were a child is no longer important when you get a bicycle! Thus, evolution occurs. Some at a lower level of consciousness cannot see the higher consciousness. It may take them lifetimes to realise, but eventually, it will be realised. From the spiritual point of view, let it be!

Time is speeding up. Twenty-four hours just go like that! You have only two choices: either operate at the level of emotions or at the level of awareness. We had more time and space ten years ago. Today, the weeks go so fast! While operating through emotions, one cascade will lead to another, and eventually, it will crash somewhere. Those who can catch the higher awareness will catch it now. Those who are at the borderline may fall into the emotional side. This is the way things are happening. This is a very interesting time. Just watch global happenings and you will understand the changing time.

Nature is responding. Things will get better. If someone is travelling at a speed of 20kmph, how far can you follow him by walking? You will need another mode of transport to catch him. Similarly, choices are to be made now. Earlier, procrastination was allowed. Now no more! Either play the game or get out of the field.

You Are What You EAT!

❧ **Question:** There is so much information available today on just about every topic imaginable. Sometimes my 'analysis' of it all leads to 'paralysis'. How do I know what I need for my spiritual quest?

Mohanji: We are eternal consumers. We consume everything; we keep eating all the time. Most of our discussions are about food of some kind, such as food for the stomach, food for our mind, or food for our intellect. We either fill our stomachs with a variety of food, fill our minds with a variety of emotions, or cram our intellect with a variety of information or ideas.

Most of these 'consumables' end up going to waste since their quantity is usually greater than our capacity to process them. Overeating leads to various types of illnesses. All of us are 'crammers' with respect to one or more of these aspects of our existence. Those who do not have any dependency on any of these three aspects are definitely considered as liberated.

Most of the food that the stomach gets to operate on is wasted, or stored as fat for future consumption. Most of the emotions that we carefully, and sometimes even gratefully consume, only tilt the equilibrium of our daily life. We are constantly making webs with our own emotions and we trap ourselves in them. With these emotions, we either become constipated, or we suffer from diarrhoea! Most of the food that the intellect consumes is also unused. It is either forgotten or is converted into ego.

Furthermore, we live a self-centred existence as far as food is concerned. We are usually in competition with others. We are in a hurry to cram more. We are proud of our capacities. We are proud of our 'vault' (storage).

The choice is indeed yours. Who are you? What is your choice of expression? Is this the life you have been looking for?

When you meet your friends or relatives, what do you normally talk about? Is it about the cuisine in various restaurants, tasty food or the best of wines? Is it about the emotions related to soap operas, about the fight that your neighbours are engaging in/enjoying, or is it about the books that you have read recently, the courses that you attended, some intellectual talk or some *Guru*'s gospel?

Ultimately though, only you can see where you stand. You are your own *Guru*. If you know where you stand and what your destination is, then the journey is easy. However, if you think that you don't know, that you don't understand, or if you pretend to be someone or something, then you are feeding your own ego and your journey will not be easy. Hence, you must see where you stand. That is the exact point (the only point) from where you can start walking. You cannot walk from a different point unless someone else carries you there. Then, it is not your free will.

If you are always thinking and talking about food and restaurants, then you are very much on the terrestrial plane. You are relatively gross in nature. Yes, you could become a 'connoisseur' of food. No problem. But still, it is obvious that your operating plane is relatively gross.

If you are operating on the emotional plane, even if you are into social service, you are still operating in the denser mode unless there is detachment. It is relatively better than the physical gross plane of a consumer of food. However, unless there is detachment in emotions, there cannot be liberation. Tears should well in the eyes but not overflow.

If you are operating in the intellectual plane, it is another story. Usually, you are craving an opportunity to vomit your knowledge from books or other people. This certainly binds you. You cannot detach from this dire need to talk a lot. Arguments and debates happen. Ego shoots up. Enmity and competition take shape. Man suffers. Those unfortunate people who are destined to suffer from your verbal diarrhoea will pray to God that this seed of His be removed from Earth! As knowledge gets converted into ego, man alienates himself from God.

Then, there is another one. A rare species. He is not bound by any of the above cravings. He is happy if all these types of food are provided, he is also happy in the absence of all these kinds of food. His existence does not depend on gross food, emotional food, or intellectual food. All three faculties are kept relatively empty. He never suffers from indigestion of any kind. He has the capacity to say 'no' and walk away; he does not suffer fools gladly. He feels and helps without expectations. He is self-sufficient. 'Self'-sufficient.

He loves unconditionally. He never operates on the plane of gross ego, remains unassuming, and many times undemonstrative. His watchdog is conscious awareness. He is objective towards life. He is always aware of who he is and what he is here for. He does not become fascinated by any glitter on this Earth. He sees through everything. He has no dos and don'ts. He is never too bound by any habits. Like water, he remains fluid, flexible.

He is liberated. He will have no regrets at the time of death. He craves for nothing. He will leave peacefully, without leaving anything pending. No wishes, no dreams, no desires. Pure and simple existence.

Eat Less and Digest All

The level of our personal evolution determines the depth of our understanding. Most people just see the words but will not grasp them. Some read and forget, which is a waste of time. Some swallow without tasting and understanding as they believe in quantity and accumulation; yet boast about its experience, which eventually causes indigestion. That food was not useful for their body at all. Some read and digest at their natural pace, which gives them further energy and elevation.

You are digesting and progressing. Eat less and digest everything. That will ensure sustained growth and peaceful, well-balanced progress in spirituality. It is not in doing more that you earn more. It is in doing the right thing and being with the action that we achieve the optimum. I wish you great times ahead.

Obesity Matters

Once again, some more food for thought. I was answering some queries of our Madhuban restaurant (*a sattvic* vegetarian restaurant in India) team on food. I thought I should share with you the gist of the discussion, which may provoke some thoughts in you, too.

Since everything that goes into our system can be considered a food of some order, it happens on all three levels – body, mind and intellect. The food that we consume each day is mainly of three kinds – food for the body, food for the mind, and food for the intellect. All our intakes are bound to have some effect on us. Therefore, what we consume has a lot of say about what we are today!

We do consume food everyday. We should, to keep the body alive. The body is the temple of our soul. We must take care of our body. Tangible food is helpful to sustain the body. It is meant for that. But sometimes food becomes recreation, or we eat because we are bored, restless or insecure, or just because we have nothing better to do. If we eat more than the body needs, it could cause an imbalance in our system. It could result in indigestion, and if we over-eat continuously, accumulation will happen in the body and the visible sign of that accumulation will be obesity.

If we feed our mind with too much data, emotions, feelings, and information, clutter will happen; and either constipation (gloom, depressive moods, etc.) or loose motion (outbursts of every kind) will happen. The staple diet for the mind is emotions. If emotions are not happening on their own in your life, the mind will find ways to create them for the mind to survive! We can see spontaneous quarrels over paltry, insignificant matters all around us. We can see people picking up arguments for nothing. We can also see people using intoxicants to 'open up' a quarrel or to 'make a point', which leads to continuous emotional outbursts over a period of time.

The same happens with intellect. If we overload the intellect with knowledge, it becomes inactive. They often become theoreticians, or they become impractical in the regular world. Sometimes, the more degrees you accumulate, the less practical you become; the bigger the clutter, the lesser the flexibility. An obese mind and an obese intellect are much more harmful to the person than an obese body.

The body has intelligence. It obeys its own order and it has nothing to do with the conscious mind. The bodily functions are auto-run by the subconscious mind. Thank God! The conscious mind usually only creates problems for the body by indiscriminate inputs. It either becomes over-cautious and starves the body, or eats emotionally and abuses the body.

The body has its system of detoxing. It segregates, digests, uses the essentials and discards the waste. It runs this machinery without fault only if the mind does not interfere. Every anxiety and every fear the mind experiences affect our digestive system, too. This is beyond the faculty of our subconscious mind to prevent. These are sporadic and unplanned changes affecting the system. How can the poor, programmed subconscious mind beat it?

The mind also has its own way of cooling its system. Sleep is one. Total shutdown is another. Some people just collapse and shut themselves down when they are overloaded with emotions. The mind also diverts its attention to something not-so-important – just to escape. The mind loves escapism. It hates facing bitter realities. This is why people usually do things that they 'like to do' rather than what they 'have to do'. It is a challenge that all those who want to liberate themselves must consciously observe.

Are you doing things that you like to do, due to whatever reason, or that you have to? If everyone only did what they had to do, life would be simpler; the world would be better. When we only do what we have to do, we will also allow others to do what they have to do. A live and let live situation! Beautiful! But– alas! We love to do what others do and also do only what we like to do, even if it is escapism from our immediate reality. When things go wrong due to our escapism, we blame others and try to escape further. How can we run this way? What can we run away from? Obesity is increasing in the mind, and soon we will fall.

Forgetfulness or memory loss is one of the ways that the intellect detoxes. It even takes it a step further and deletes the memory completely, or leaves insufficient fragments that never provide the subject matter's effect or intensity. We may even completely forget the emotion or feeling related to the event, person or knowledge. Even if we consider the mind and intellect as two sides of the same coin, forgetfulness and memory lapses can be seen spreading beyond the boundaries or walls of these. It is difficult to draw a clear line between these two.

Obesity makes us inflexible. It makes us heavy. It limits our mobility – physical mobility, mental mobility, and intellectual mobility. In these three levels, we should be flexible and mobile. If you consider this well, physical obesity is probably not as bad as the other two. Mental obesity and intellectual obesity are really troublesome for healthy living. An intellectually or mentally inflexible person will fall many times in life. Whatever toxins make these two obese have to be carefully removed. Physical obesity is the only one immediately tangible and visible to the senses. However, mental and intellectual obesity reflects all through our character as well as daily life. When the ego is high, we are heavy. The ego makes us heavier.

Sometimes we also see people carrying themselves with borrowed feathers. Just like a crow that stuck peacock feathers over its own and pretended to be a peacock and fell flat when the real test happened, many people pretend to be what they actually are not and try to get away with it. This is a clear expression of insecurity or emotional obesity. Falsehood is definitely an obesity of the mind. Anything unnatural in character adds to obesity. It means this person is definitely prone to disease or a total shut-down. There are many people who are not-so-rich but pretend to be and move in the rich circle. When they fail to live up to their image, they borrow to continue their pretension, and their whole family suffers various calamities in the bargain.

Selfishness is also an obesity of the mind. Anger, fear, jealousy, selfishness, treachery, deceit, recklessness, etc., are all expressions of obesity. Hence, as I said, an obese body is much better compared to a crippled or obese mind or intellect. Physical obesity could be reduced through physical training and medicines. Mental and intellectual obesity is much more difficult because you cannot see it in front of your eyes. You can only feel it in the character. By default, we either glorify it or tend to ignore it as insignificant.

Overdose of knowledge makes people obese in their intellect. Ego is the result. Ego alienates. It makes them more and more rigid and inflexible. The discriminatory facility of the brain is a blessing if used wisely. It tells you that touching fire is not a good idea as it burns. It tells you not to tease a snake or a tiger. Such guidance keeps us in good shape and health. However, when the discriminatory faculty is used for comparisons between two people, or to get the upper hand over another, or to cheat or kill another, it is a sign of disease.

This is invisible obesity. It kills; it violates. It kills and violates character and destiny. It makes a mess of our lives. This is why most soap operas and movies that portray cunning, violent, and treacherous people as their characters, serve as poison to our minds and take the viewers away from purity in thoughts, words, and action. It destroys our inherent innocence and goodness.

I think this is sufficient food for thought for the time being. We can explain this for hours. However, the bottom line is, beware of obesity, especially the obesity of the mind and intellect. This is very harmful to our existence. The 'lean state' of mind and intellect is being simple, straight, pure, and unaffected. Most of the physically obese are very good at heart. Those who are physically obese could be physically inflexible but are not as disease-prone as the mentally and intellectually obese. We should be careful about our inputs in all three levels – body, mind and intellect. This means that we should operate from the present, in the present at all times, during our waking state. We should gather sufficient strength to discard trash food in all three levels and embrace healthy food. Reduce compulsive input and stay healthy.

The Right Management

⚘ **Question:** You managed several companies as a General Manager. Can you tell me what management is?

Mohanji: Management cannot be defined in one statement. It is situational. The best management that I have ever seen is the management of our own vital systems. How synchronized and perfect it is! Our brain is the best manager ever! The one who created the brain is the best scientist! When we manipulate or distort our own natural system, how sick we feel! What are we doing to our own system, apart from abusing it? Still, it is adjusted and managed well. Only when the abuse becomes intolerable, the body reacts. Just think for a few minutes about it. You will be amazed. Think of it everyday; it will help you tremendously.

Coming back to your question, I would like to say, "Start with self–management." Management has to begin with self-management. The internal management must precede the external. If you cannot manage yourself, you cannot manage other people. It is very easy to tell others, "Do this or do that," but very difficult to tell ourselves, "Do this."

Management has to begin from within oneself. This is because creation always starts from within. First, thought happens inside; it then becomes word and culminates in action. This is the fundamental process. Usually, what happens is that we tell others to do the work, and the work does not get done. This could also be because you cannot do it yourself. According to me, if management is to become successful, the manager has to manage himself or herself first.

The other important thing is clarity. You need to have clarity for yourself; then you can express or share with clarity to the other person. One should be clear about all aspects of any situation; then only can that situation be expressed to another person. Otherwise, it is called gossip or speculation. Decisions made from partial information will go haywire and/or collapse.

Every situation has a past, present, and future. Something triggered the event in the past, hence we experience the results now! That means there has been a past. If you do not know the past of an event, you cannot make a decision in the present and the future will also be equally affected. To be a successful manager, you should have a clear understanding of the past, present, and future of every situation. Along with this knowledge, experience is also important to hold the position of a manager.

If I had to sum up management in one sentence, I would say, "Managing yourself is real management and the rest follows naturally."

❧ **Question:** If every situation has a past, present, and future, then how to remain in the present?

Mohanji: The present is your only possibility for taking decisions, even if the decision is pertaining to a future event, such as forecasting or planning. Remain in the present, do whatever is the best possible in the present. You know there is a future, and there are days ahead. If you make a management plan for the next year, you have to think of all the pros and cons possible in that one year. This is not being anxious about the future. It is living in the present fully, analysing the possibilities of the future and making plans and alternatives accordingly.

Being always futuristic, and ignoring the present, usually means having anxiety about the future. This is negative. Planning well for the future is a positive aspect. In the given present time, you are making plans. This adds to your clarity. Using the available resources and the intellect, a strategic plan made today, will generally produce positive results in the days ahead.

Whatever you are doing today, you will do in the present, whether it is an analysis of the past or plans for the future. Both should be done today as a part of your job. Do it as worship. Do it with surrender to existence – in other words, without ego. Avoiding this is procrastination and could become a problem. You are creating potential room for anxiety with such avoidance. You cannot say that I exist today, so I manage the company only today! As a manager, you have to forecast and plan too.

In a company, you have to look at everybody as a manager. It could be the person who makes the tea. He should manage the kitchen. Everybody in effect is a manager; only the portfolios are different. Responsibility levels are different. If tea arrives late, we will not die! However, if a senior management person fails, the company will die/collapse, and many will lose their jobs. This is serious. This is why such positions attract higher remunerations.

Being anxious about the future is not a good idea. However, being clear about the future with positive and realistic alternatives is good. Having an idea but not being attached to it is the best situation. You are flexible and always open to changes. Changes are for sure in everyone's life. Life itself is filled with changes. Adaptability keeps us afloat.

Straight Talk

✤ **Question:** I am confused.

Mohanji: Good. You are perfectly living the duality of existence. When you know that you are confused, when you are aware of your confused state, your diagnosis is complete. The remedy lies in the state itself– clarity. In order to understand what clarity is, there should be confusion. Sound is essential to know silence. Silence is essential to know the sound. One complements the other. So, be relaxed. When the clouds of your mind leave, the sun will shine bright.

✤ **Question:** Life and death

Mohanji: Life and death are not contradictory, but they are complementary. Life takes one to death and death takes one to life. It keeps happening. Time and space change. Destiny and destination change. However, they are essentially complementary. We need to have life to know death and death to know life. One cannot exist without the other. Both are two sides of the same coin called terrestrial existence.

❦ Question: Hunger.

Mohanji: This body has consumed kilos of food and litres of water. Still, it craves for more. How can we appease this craving? By going beyond the mind. By connecting to our eternal soul that has no needs or cravings. When we shed our dependency on food and water, we proceed in our path of liberation. Hunger is more of an emotion than a necessity in today's world. We have wasted large quantities of food with great indifference. Fine food adds to the ego. Presentation of food – ego. Dinners – ego. We live a complex life. Where is the escape? Simplicity and purity. Hunger will never control you. You will control hunger.

❦ Question: What is bad?

Mohanji: Bad is an aspect of terrestrial duality. The other side of the coin of which one side is called 'good'.

❦ Question: If a person constantly lives with dreams of the future, what happens to his present?

Mohanji: There is no present for him. He only lives in the future. Since he is not handling his present, his future will become chaotic. Those who always dwell in the future are usually escapists. They are lazy and *tamasic*. They kill their future by ignoring their present.

❦ Question: What do you think about competition?

Mohanji: I only look at it as an aspect of duality – *Maya*. If we compete in life, we are fools. Doing our very best is all we can and should do. If we compete with another *karmic* being, we are absolutely silly.

❦ Question: What about sex?

Mohanji: A good question. Without that, you would not have been here to ask this question. What I do not understand is – why do people give over-emphasis to sex? According to me, its importance is similar to eating or sleeping. It is just another necessity to keep the species alive. I feel that our near-impotent society made sex a taboo or a big deal. We are blindly following that notion. Why can't we just let sex be, just like our breath, heartbeat, hunger, or any kind of strong emotion? What a shame if we give it over-emphasis and brood over it!

Question: Do you think I am selfish?

Mohanji: Yes. All are selfish. All embodied beings are selfish; there are very few enlightened ones. Look at yourself; observe yourself and your thoughts. You will know what I mean.

Question: Why can't they understand me?

Mohanji: There is a huge variety in levels of consciousness. Each one is in his own sphere, in that context. Those who bother us are those who cannot reach or understand our level of consciousness. Forgive them and love them. Soon enough, they will see what we see. It can also be the other way – we may not have the capacity to see their realm of existence. Then, we tend to disagree with them. We fail to understand them. Nobody is perfect. We are all walking the same wide Earth seeking varied experiences. We are all trying to understand this existence, using our faculties, through the senses and mind. We are all enveloped in different levels of consciousness.

Question: How to choose a field?

Mohanji: The field is provided; Earth is the field. The field had to happen as per your *karma* and eligibility. It is not your choice. That is why I was talking about destiny. Certain activities and certain thoughts, words, and actions have created the field for you. You are given the field. You are given the consciousness to operate in that field. You also have been given the right understanding to perform. How you perform in the field with the surrounding is up to you. Once you decide to lift one leg, another cannot be lifted in the same moment! That is the field of free will. Free will is limited after birth until death. It stops when one action is done.

We have free will till we decide. Once you decide to lift one leg, you cannot reverse. Your free will is dissolved. You have to wait for another situation!

❧ **Question:** What is the root cause of our suffering?

Mohanji: Ignorance. The depth of our identification with that which is impermanent. When our identification is with our soul, there is no suffering.

❧ **Question:** What is spirituality?

Mohanji: Simplicity and unconditionality. Faith and patience. Liberation from everything, including name, form and *karma*.

❧ **Question:** What is the reason for excessive stress in life?

Mohanji: Ownership and doer-ship. Non-understanding or non-realisation that 'everything passes away', both situations and people. When this understanding takes deep roots in one's mind, life becomes an every moment game and each moment would be pleasurable and stress-free.

❧ **Question:** Can you give me some simple advice?

Mohanji: Love all, serve all. I am borrowing these words from the great Master Sathya Sai Baba. Also, remember this every moment – we reap only what we sow, in many folds.

CHAPTER 2:

Spiritual practice

Kundalini

Kundalini is the Shakti energy existing in every human. Man's potential to experience and merge with the ultimate Truth. It is the very potential in every human to realise the supreme. It is depicted in the shape of a serpent lying dormant in three and a half coils. As it moves up through the *Sushumna* to attain Shiva, various changes happen in human consciousness. As it touches and merges with the supreme subtlety beyond our s*ahasrara* (crown *chakra*), enlightenment happens.

The ultimate aim of Shakti is to merge with Shiva. Sooner or later, it should happen – whether in one lifetime or more. To achieve Shiva, it must cross a series of hurdles, such as *brahmagranthi, muladhara* (earth), *svadhishthana* (water), *manipura* (fire), *vishnugranthi, vishuddha (air), anahata (ether), ajna, rudragranthi* and leaps to *sahasrara.* This movement becomes easier if *samskaras* are less. Actually speaking, we have to go beyond even the images of *kundalini* and *chakras.* We have to nullify identifications of any kind. In the path of *kundalini,* everything – all sorts of attachments, even if they are subtle images, are indeed obstacles or hurdles. The image of the motion of a serpent is good only as a comparison for the sake of intellectual understanding. Remember what Osho said, "It is yes, no or wow."

Stones and gems

✤ **Question:** I would like to ask about precious stones. People advise wearing stones as they have some favourable effects on us.

Mohanji: Please understand that our system or configuration is made up of five elements: earth, water, fire, air and space. These five elements have come together to create our body. When we experience elemental imbalance, or when some elements are losing powers, i.e., do not have sufficient powers, then you add them through other concentrated sources. Stones are a concentration of certain aspects of some of the elements which constitute our body. The idea is, when we wear the right stones, they enhance or boost our system, or they balance the missing elemental intensity.

All in all, we are made up of elements, and if the power or potency of certain elements in our system is lacking, we compensate by wearing the right stones. Our *chakras* have a certain vibratory level. Stones and gems also have certain vibratory levels which may suit the *chakras*. When you wear the right stones, they enhance the operation of the *chakras*. *Chakras* are like transformers. They distribute the energy into our system.

This is all scientific. But, if the stones/gems are not prescribed well, they can also harm us. For example – if you have an excess of the fire element in your constitution and somebody advises you to wear a stone that will further enhance the fire element, you will become extremely agitated. You may fight with people and do things that are quite detrimental.

Also, please note, from your birth till death, no *chakras* will ever remain constant. Your energy levels do not remain constant. The levels of prana will fluctuate high and low! Your constituition will remain the same, but the levels will change.

Accepting those levels and moving on with faith is the best solution.

Masters usually do not wear stones. Some Masters used to, but then, they would have had their own reason. Usually, regular people who are insecure go for such things because they think it will help them! If you are inclined to wear a gemstone, make sure a true authority prescribes it. Take it from a person who is genuine and not just interested in selling it to you. It also becomes an addiction. You may feel more insecure when you do not wear it. This creates dependency.

There is a science behind all this; nothing is wasted on Earth. Everything is used. However, our aim is liberation. Thus, avoid dependency! Stones are from Earth. But because of their vibratory level, they enhance any related *chakras*. It could be air, water, fire, space or earth! It is up to you whether you go for it.

In the path of Shiva, dependency on any element is binding. We can understand that this is our constitution. As long as we are on Earth, we have to stick to this constitution. When the fire leaves the body, we all regard that body as a dead body. When *prana* leaves, it is also a dead body. We have to live with the constitution that we came with. We certainly need this *annamaya kosha* (food sheath), *pranamaya kosha* (pranic sheath), *manomaya kosha* (mind sheath) and all the other *koshas* (sheaths) – we need all of them to operate.

However, everything is binding on the path of Shiva. Eventually, everything must be eliminated. At one point, everything gets automatically eliminated, and then you merge. Their assistance in this process is required only on Earth. Souls are also operating in other planes, but they do not have dependency on the same systems that we have, for e.g., our body cannot stand the heat of a hundred degrees. This programmed set-up is earthbound. There are souls meditating underwater in the sea. They have a different vibratory level.

I met a man who was taught by a Master who lives under the sea! This Master does not come out of the water much, nor does he have a body like us. He appears on the surface, taking some form of a body, slightly transparent. If you put a hand through that body, it goes through. You see the body, but it is not concrete or solid enough, like ours. This Master taught this man how to align elements within the body to remove all imbalances and maintain good health during earthly life. Stones also align the elements. There are mudras (hand gestures) to align elements. When you do that or wear a stone, it brings some equilibrium. So, it is up to you whether to go for it or not.

🌸 **Question:** What does *rudraksha* indicate?

Mohanji: Renunciation. Shiva.

Chakras

🌸 **Question:** Sometimes, people say that one's *chakras* should be open. How do we know that they are open?

Mohanji: No need to know. This kind of inquisitiveness is connected with one's intellect. Intellect never leaves one alone. It binds to Earth, disallowing free evolution and spiritual elevation by posing questions. Knowing is a game of the intellect. It is definitely an obstacle, and you may get stuck there. *Chakras* will open at the right time. No need to think or worry about it. No use too.

🌸 **Question:** What is the meaning of *chakras* open or closed?

Mohanji: *Chakras* are open means your receptivity has increased. *Chakras* are closed means you are Earth-bound. Closed *chakras* mean you are dense; open *chakras* mean you are lighter, and you are connected with higher energies. This will automatically happen when you are eligible. Even if I deliberately open your *chakras*, you cannot make use of it! Even if I open all *the chakras*, you may not be able to take that energy, and *the chakras* will become closed again. When you are actually ready, they will never close as you are operating with them. If I do not use my hand, the muscles will become weak!

Chakras, naadis, kundalini,... forget about it now. It will all happen in its own time. Just walk the path with complete gratitude and surrender to the supreme Lord Almighty, the Father of all.

The Astral Plane

When you are in the astral plane, you are in your hometown, because you go there after every death. There are no comparisons there because all are in the energy plane: all are energy bodies. There is no discrimination; how much you earn, how much I earn... it does not matter. There is an immense level of peacefulness and a beauty of existence on that plane. But when you come to the gross plane, there are 'n' number of comparisons.

Before you took birth and came to Earth, you had a definite plan, you chose your parents, you knew you were going to take birth to experience and express these things, and planned this whole life. The same way, when consciousness shifts, you will also decide to leave the body, and you will be able to leave the body at will.

I don't know how many of you have seen the picture on top of the Himalayas, with a pool full of bodies inside. Those are Saints who left their body at will. It is at an altitude above eight thousand metres. When they are meditating, they get a command that the time has come to leave since they have finished their purpose here. Then they withdraw their soul from the toes upwards and they exit. That is why they go to the pool, because nobody is there to bury them. It is cold, it is ice, so the body is preserved. They enter the pool, they withdraw and they leave the body at will, just like we took birth. This is absolute power. Absolute control. This is the real control, not controlling others. This is all within us, we can achieve all this.

I think some of you have already met me in the astral plane. We can definitely meet when you connect to my eyes and discuss various things. When you connect to my consciousness, we definitely meet. This is why I tell people to connect to my eyes, because through the eyes you reach my consciousness. You can see what I see. You cannot look at both eyes together, it automatically shifts to the third eye. Don't look at the third eye first, because it will not work.

You will know when we are connected because you will get the brightest of the answers rather than thoughts that happen all the time. If I appear in your dream, it usually isn't the unconscious mind, but an astral experience. When you wake up, you will think it is a dream. You say, "I met Mohanji in my dream and he gave me this answer." But how do you know the difference between a dream and an astral experience? The clarity.

So What?

My father is a medical doctor. He is an orthopaedic surgeon. I never interacted with him qualitatively when I was a child. He was always busy. However, sooner or later, I realised that he is a benevolent man, and people were respecting him because of his truthfulness, honesty and sincerity. Once, I overheard him saying this to a patient's relative: "I have done (surgery on the patient) the best any doctor could possibly do. I have done my best. Now, leave the rest to God Almighty. Pray for a speedy recovery." I thought, "Why can't he promise a cure? Is he not confident enough?" Later on, I realised that it is actually divinity that heals. We can only do our best under the given circumstances.

Nature takes care of creation, maintenance and dissolution. We feel we are doing everything. We feel that it is through our actions and words that everything takes place. Actually speaking, we are being used by nature in aiding this grand process called life. All of us are tools and part of the divine design. It is a grand collaboration. Many pieces dancing to one tune and yet, actually creating the effect of many!

As children, we pick up impressions from our elders and continue to do so as we grow. Hence, it is important to 'behave ourselves' as adults, as children are constantly watching and collecting impressions.

Once we grow up, we start taking everything too seriously, clinging to our expectations. We are constantly getting frustrated when our expectations do not bear fruit, right? So, it is important to keep asking, "So what?". Let me explain.

Say I tried my best in performing a particular task, yet, it was not good enough. Should I blame myself, or consider myself inferior to others? No way. I tell myself "My best was not good enough. So what? There is always a next time. I shall try to do better next time. If another opportunity does not appear, so what? There will be something else more interesting." This is how life works. We all are functioning within our limitations, whether we know it or not. Likewise, anytime you end up blaming yourself or adding guilt to your existence, just ask yourself, "So what?" Never allow guilt to take root. Keep asking, at all points, "So what?"

The same applies to our ego and doer-ship. When others praise us, and we see our ego getting bloated, ask "So what?" Everything is changing every moment. Maintaining equanimity during changing times is important. Expectations get beaten time after time. Keep asking, "So what?" Once we make this a habit, we will be travelling light, without the burden of guilt and fear.

Now, please do not think that we can do everything good, bad or ugly and say, "So what?" and feel perfectly fine. No. Negative actions, words and thoughts are not at all good for spiritual evolution. Non-violence in thoughts, words and actions are essential. There are no two ways about it.

Asking ourselves, "So what?" is only to confirm that our best effort needs to be accepted by our conscious mind. We can also use this question to fight guilt if there is any. Being benevolent is important. Being compassionate is important too. Having these qualities intact within us, if we could not perform up to our expectation, just destroy the guilt with the question "So what?"

Japa Yoga

Question: How does mantra chanting fit in this whole story? What is its use? Is it good or not?

Mohanji: When various factors of our existence challenge the inner and outer world, meditation is difficult. One can still meditate if he or she is well established and well settled within the world inside (inner world), and dependency on the external world is minimal. When an individual uses his senses purposefully, and if the mind is not affected by the most enchanting of sense objects the world can offer, he can always bring his senses under control and detach from them at will. We are living in a world of fancy. There are many things that glitter around us to hook ourselves, sometimes consciously and mostly unconsciously.

Inertia is easy to sell. Television and the internet sell it well. Most of the objects that we experience using our eyes, sell inertia. At the same time, in moderation, everything has value. They are part of our life. We cannot ignore them all and be part of society as well because human existence is oriented in relationships, which is the tangible extension of relativity - the basic substratum of creation. This is also because there is an underlying flavour of emotions spicing up our relationships. Do remember, anything in excess is bad.

The sale of *tamas* is rampant. *Tamas* means inertia. When we become couch potatoes, it is a clear sign that we have swallowed a lot of *tamas*; we have already bought ourselves into it. When inertia is at its peak, one cannot even handle the slightest of turbulence in life. People blame others for their situation, which they themselves consciously or unconsciously created.

They resort to excessive food, alcohol, sex or drugs to maintain their comfort levels. They watch sob stories such as soap operas and enjoy the sadistic pleasure of watching others suffer with an inner glee that they are relatively better off than those characters in the film! However, they do not understand the most important point: they are accumulating similar *karma* in their lives by gathering and storing such emotions.

The data of suffering is unconsciously entered into their system. Since they are emotionally participating in those stories, they are living it or experiencing it. Those impressions are stored in their mind. This will become the realities or ingredients of their next incarnation. Some people never have a clue about their suffering. They do not know why they are suffering in life, despite the many good deeds they might have accomplished in this existence. It is simple. Whatever data is entered into our system or whatever is consumed through thoughts, words or action, or whatever food we consume through our body, mind and intellect, becomes the ingredient and basis for our further existence, this and the next.

Remember, inertia sells well because its buyers are many. Food for the senses is always sold well. If a new book is released with the title, 'Tantric sex for you', or 'A hundred new ways of making love', it will sell well, and such authors who do this for money will be well respected by society. Meanwhile, people will avoid a true *satsang* or the company of an enlightened Master because "Ah, the same boring lecture about the soul which nobody has seen", or "This man brings forth my worst hidden fears into the light". People will rather choose to keep their fears and not let them go and pretend that they do not exist.

Society consists of people. When society is filled with *tamasic* people, they either convert the not-so-*tamasic* to their group or destroy them. That means a *tamasic* community makes people in their own image, or they destroy them. If we dig a little into history, we can see that we have consistently destroyed, either killed or silenced, all those who speak eternal truths. If we could not do that, we ran away from them and their teachings. Human existence!

We can see heavily *tamasic* and greedy people sitting in places of power, which is actually a big tragedy. They dish out 'believable' excuses for not performing any positive action. They have 'impossibility' pasted on their forehead loud and clear. Then again, they have come out of the same society that we belong to. Society created them. People will only get the rulers they deserve. Hence it is important to shed *tamas* from the grass-roots level to create a better world. Transformation should positively happen in every part of society.

When time creates restlessness, it tests the talent of even the most consistent spiritual seeker. This is natural. Meditations and practices (*sadhana*) will become difficult. On the one side, the looming cloud of *tamas* constantly pushes one to 'sleep a little while longer', and on the other side, there is the lack of environmental support. The mind really sways. Many give up. Many become disillusioned. Many change their *Gurus*, imagining that it is because of their *Guru* that they are suffering!

During such times, the best recommended practice is *japa* yoga, or the yoga of chants (chanting of the Lord's name).

Lord Krishna and almost all of the great Masters who walked on Earth have acknowledged the importance of *japa* yoga. "Among the various types of *yajna* (a ritual or sacrifice into the fire, which consists of *mantras* and materials), I am the *yajna* of *japa*" – said the Avatar Krishna in the Bhagavad Gita.

The Gita also emphasizes the importance of chanting which destroys all afflictions, sins and sufferings. Patanjali instructs that *japa* must be done for prolonged periods without interruption so that we become one with the chant, and this should be done with deep reverence and respect. Japa is the very form of God. Perfection can be attained by chanting the divine name. In this context, I remember the great Saint Valmiki – the transformation of the hunter Ratnakara to Sage Valmiki! He attained the highest possible state of spiritual elevation and total transformation (metamorphosis) just by chanting the name of Lord Rama and thus becoming one with the name.

Constitutional change can happen when we become one with the name of the Lord. God is the subtlest of the subtlest. In that context, even the name is gross. But, the name itself can be considered as the form of God, where the sound is the form. The sound 'Om' can be considered the form of God because God is formless or all forms.

Jagad Guru Adi Shankaracharya says, "Control the self, restrain the breath, and sift out the transient from the true. Repeat the holy name of the Lord and still the restless mind within. To this universal rule, apply your heart and soul." Zarathustra says that *japa* (name of the divine) cures all ills. *Guru* Nanak said that holy communion with the *naam* (the Lord's name) is the only means to have oneness with the Lord Supreme. The great Saint Kabir Das says, "Without sincerity, thought or chant of the Lord's name is not possible. If one imbibes (is one with) just one particle of naam, no-half a particle, all one's sins will be reduced to ashes".

Khwaja Moinuddin Chishti said, "If you rub the mirror of your heart with the name of God, you will see God's effulgence reflected on it". Beautiful! Ramana Maharishi said, "*Mantra* is a channel of shifting current of thoughts. *Mantra* is a bund or dam put up to divert the water where it is needed. Japa is clinging to one thought to the exclusion of all other thoughts; that is the purpose of japa. It leads to dhyana which ends in self-realisation."

Bhagavan Nityananda of Ganeshpuri says "*Japa* is a means. Very easy as well as highly efficacious. Through *japa sadhana*, vibration is created that cleanses the body and makes the mind pure and divine. Continuous *japa* will result in *nada-upasana*, and such a state will help to reach the state of self-realisation". Here, *Bhagavan* talks about cellular level purification due to the vibration created by chanting. Since body and mind are integrally connected, cleansing happening in the body also cleanses the mind, so on and so forth. Sincere japa with a steady mind on the sound and the Lord will ensure all-round cleansing. This is the most effective practice possible in turbulent times.

Saint Teresa of Avila found completeness when each breath began to say the name of the Lord silently. Eknath said, "Remembrance is liberation. Forgetfulness is regression. The utterance of the name is essential devotion."

Shirdi Sai Baba said, "God's name is eternal, *Allah Malik!*" Baba also implies that God has no name. He is beyond names and forms. However, for us, a name or form will be helpful to transcend to the formless. We should catch the rope of the name and climb to the highest possibility of our existence while we can.

Tukaram said, "The Lord's name is eternal. Do *japa* of '*Rama Krishna Hari*', and he will always save you. This is my last request and advice!"

This is profound indeed; chant from deep within. Be one with the chant. Keep your spine erect, and chant in your spine, if you can. Chanting just from the throat is of no use. That will just be an addition to the already existing sound pollution. Going within while chanting is important, and being one with the name you chant is also equally important.

The scriptures have given a few road signs or guidelines for chanting, especially on its results. Some of them are as follows:

1. This is the era or *Yuga* (*Kali Yuga*) where people can achieve the same results that one might achieve through penance, rigorous practices or rituals, through the chanting of the Lord's name.

2. In this era, even *mantra* recitation needs a systematic approach while chanting the Lord's name anybody can do it anytime, without any restrictions. Hence the best practice to follow in this era is chanting of the Lord's name.

3. The only requirement that any devotee needs is absolute *bhakti* (devotion or faith) towards the deity of worship.

4. The Lord's name has the power of fire which burns hard *karmas*.

5. One who consistently and with absolute surrender and dedication chants God's name will become as powerful as a *yogi* who has done years of penance. He will be as purified as one who has done penance on fire.

6. One who chants more than 30 million times the name of God will even change his hard destiny. The lines of his hand will change for good. Diseases and afflictions will leave him.

7. Those who chant more than 40 million times the name of God will never suffer poverty and will be rich inside and outside.

8. Those who chant more than 50 million times the name of God will have awareness as that of great Masters. Their

stature will grow beyond limits. The more they chant, the more they will become pure inside. Nothing that belongs to Earth will affect them ever again.

I shall leave you now to contemplate on these thoughts. When we cannot meditate, chanting helps. Even when we can meditate, chanting can lead to deeper meditation. The name of the Lord, the sound, the breath, the vibration, everything helps silence of the mind. Chant the name, contemplate on the name of your chosen God or *Guru* and merge with that constitution, which would be the state of oneness. I wish you that.

Finally, let us sincerely chant 'Lokah Samastah Sukhino Bhavanthu'. May all the beings of all the worlds including the worlds themselves, be happy and peaceful. All are one: one consciousness – or various expressions of one consciousness.

🌿 **Question:** What is the easiest and most powerful *mantra* that you could recommend for daily chanting?

Mohanji: *Aum Namah Shivaya, Aum Namo Bhagavate Vasudevaya* or *Aum Sai Ram*. These are all powerful *mantras*. It helps one in detachment.

Each *mantra* is a configuration that helps some part of your constitution. Sometimes it is to rejuvenate; sometimes it is to calm. Each *mantra* has a purpose. Normally a *Guru* gives a *mantra* to the disciple upon looking at the disciple's constitution. That is like prescribed medicine.

There are *mantras* like 'Aum Namah Shivaya'. People say this *mantra* is enough; no other *mantra* is needed, which is true. It is very, very powerful. I've previously explained each syllable. That constitutes every aspect of our existence such as the five elements that constitute the body, the five types of air that circulate in the body, and the five types of fire, five types of existence, and so on. Every aspect is covered in this five-syllable *mantra*.

The same fire can be used to cook the food and burn the house. It is up to us to decide what we need from the fire. People like to have powers. Hence, they configure *mantras* to give that effect. Similarly, there are *mantras* for protection, like a sheath. The Gayatri *mantra* has the power of protection and also the power of elevation.

Every *mantra* has a reason and power. However, if you connect to the white *mantras*, like '*Aum Namah Shivaya*', etc. no harm will happen to you in any way. As for other *mantras*, power-oriented ones, you should be careful. They can help us, and they can also hurt us.

✹ **Question:** How to know which one may be dangerous?

Mohanji: The most recognised, the most approved and pleasant chants are from the white. Because they enhance your protection, your energy, and your wellbeing, they are fine. Or you can check with your *Gurus* who understand, and they will recommend one for you. We can also individualize *mantras*. With a certain *mantra*, you will have a particular effect if you use it, yet another person will have a different effect. Thus, *mantras* cannot be generalised all the time.

These present times are good for chanting. When you chant, chant from the stomach centre, not from the throat, the stomach is the seat of fire. When you enhance the fire, it burns the stored emotions. When you keep chanting a positive *mantra* in the stomach centre for a period of time, the scriptures say that you can even change the weather, climate or even destiny.

✹ **Question:** Is it important to calm your mind while chanting?

Mohanji: Calmness happens to the mind when you are connected to the *mantra*.

✹ **Question:** It does not matter if the mind wanders around?

Mohanji: The mind will wander anyway. You cannot control the mind and start the show. It never works. Please understand that the mind is the most restless factor in your system. It is never stable. Don't think that you can attack your mind directly. It is impossible. The mind will catch you every time. Also, the mind will manipulate you. That is why I say if you depend on the mind, the mind will keep you the same and help you change the *Guru*.

The mind is filled with concepts from society, from education, from parents, from every aspect of our existence. We have collected the concepts and filled our minds. Our life is equal to that which concepts allow us to experience, not reality. We are not experiencing the world in reality. We are just trying to sound it off with our concepts. The more concepts we have, the more inflexible we are.

Has everybody heard of Sathya Sai Baba? A boy was staying with Baba for many years to do service. It was going on well for a few years; he was serving Baba, he was happy, Baba was happy. One day, he decided to leave Baba. People said, "Are you crazy? A lot of people are waiting to serve him, and you are with him! Why are you missing this opportunity?" Then he said, "I saw Baba shaving. How can God shave?"

He forgot that when you are in the human body, you have everything related to the human body, including the growth of hair. What was the problem? He had a concept that Baba as God should be like this, in a particular way. When he realised that this concept does not fit the man, he was completely affected. He couldn't accept it. Thus, he missed the big chance. He could have reached the highest if he was not bound by concepts. All of us are like this. We have limitations. We buy the frame in advance; then we cut the picture inside. We never buy a frame for the picture. The frame is equal to a concept, and a picture is equal to reality. We cut the picture (reality) for the concept.

🌿 **Question:** Is it important how we pronounce a *mantra,* or is it all right if we pronounce it as we feel?

Mohanji: Most *mantras* are in Sanskrit, and the diction and writing are more or less the same. Pronounce every word. Don't swallow words. There are numerous languages spoken by people in the world. I do not think there is ever a hundred per cent accuracy in anybody's chanting. However, the nearest possible should be ok, because that's the best you can achieve.

Stay rooted in your spine

Nullification of our individual identities through increased awareness is the key. When personal identities dissolve, we become that. When we, as conditioned individuals, do not exist, we start moving into the higher consciousness. Connecting and operating from the spine on a perpetual level is a good way of becoming one with the supreme. Your spine is the path. Connect to your spine more as general awareness. You will see the difference.

When we shift our operating platform to the spine, we will still express our emotions but will not be participating. You are free to express ego, anger or frustration. But, do not be involved in it. Just express for the sake of conveying a message. When you become involved, you become weak and helpless. When you express objectively, you are in control. This can happen with practice. Thus, your inside will remain calm and cool like the deep blue sea. You will never be affected by the waves of emotions. You will not own them or judge them. They will come and go. You will remain tranquil, eternally. This loosens up your *karma* as well as attachments.

Do not lose track of reality ever. Keep remembering who you really are, beyond your waking, dream and deep sleep states. Keep remembering who your real father (*Parabrahma*) is. Stay rooted in your spine at all times and be a witness to your own daily life. Do everything perfectly well, but objectively. Do not run away from anything. Whenever a problem is born, a solution is also born. So, hold on to supreme faith and keep walking with supreme objectivity and love.

You can do four things. First, connect to my eyes for two minutes before you go to bed. You can do it everyday. The second thing is that whenever you lie down, lie down connecting to your spine. Nothing will stay there; whatever has to go will go. When you are lying down, feel the spine and start breathing through the spine. When you are breathing, feel the spine as if your breath is massaging your spine from inside. Thirdly, whenever you handle people, do not be emotional about it. You have to do it objectively, without any emotions, just like a doctor with a patient. Fourth, you can take rock salt or sea salt and put it in every corner of your house, or at least in the room you work in. Don't worry, and I'll take care.

> ☘ **Question:** This is a preliminary question: "You said that we need to concentrate on the spinal cord and, at the same time, concentrate on breathing in and out. I was trying to do that, but I could do only one thing at a time. I do not think I am able to give justice to both processes simultaneously."

Mohanji: It is very simple. When you start learning how to drive, it is very difficult to remember to keep a watch on steering, breaks, gear, clutch and mirror, all at the same time. It is difficult to coordinate all at a time. You also have to follow the traffic lights, etc. You find it so difficult to achieve this before you actually learn the art of driving and get a driving license. After that, driving becomes automatic. It becomes mechanical.

Are you doing all that together consciously? Doesn't it all just fall into place? Don't you drive smoothly there after? Of course, your subconscious takes over whatever you repeat.

There is a difference here – in meditation since all our other aspects are quiet, our consciousness will shift. It is kind of a partnership with your conscious mind and the subconscious. When, through repeated activity, your awareness shifts to your third eye, you can see everything from above. Then, you will be in perfect synchronicity: consistency and patience.

How does it happen? You need to concentrate. This is because we are front oriented. We usually operate only at 120 degrees. We do not see the remaining 240 degrees behind us. Are we fully aware of our back side until something happens at the back? This remaining 240 degrees definitely exists, but we do not notice that. Being spine oriented is a big shift. It is like playing back-foot in cricket. We are naturally tuned to play the front foot. When we shift to the back foot, time and space change and are different for playing the ball.

Life changes when one becomes spine oriented. One needs to catch that thread of being spine oriented. Then elevation is automatic. When you chant *Aum*, you move to the spine. When you move to the spine, eyes concentrate on the third eye automatically. Try to close your eyes and visualize your spine. Automatically, your concentration goes on to the third eye. It is all effortless. The system is built like that. Later on, it becomes natural.

I suggest people concentrate on my eyes to receive the energy. Many say, "We do not need any pictures! The moment we close our eyes, we see you." Many people are saying that. They are so tuned to my energy and physical form that it happens instantaneously. Someone told me the other day, "When I look at Babaji's picture, I see you. When I look at your picture, it shifts to Babaji's photos". Understand that Masters play such a game to remove attachment to any physical frame. All physical frames have validity, duration and a sure disintegration.

Human nature is such that we like to visit a house that receives us with warmth and love. We do not like to visit a place where we are unwanted. When a higher source is good and reliable, we automatically get attracted to it. We get connected with it. You will connect with the source which is good for you. You do not have to think about it consciously. Also, even if you want to, you cannot find it consciously. But you will automatically get connected to the right source. Whatever your elevation level is, you will get lessons of that kind. If you are spine oriented, you will get that kind of connectivity. In the third-grade, I cannot give the syllabus for the Master's degree. Even if I do give it, you will not be able to use it.

How do we synchronize so many things? First, concentrate at the physical level. Concentrate on mind and body. Mind is active all the time, and you know it. The body you can feel. Senses are always active as otherwise you cannot hear or see! Senses with the mind give us the experience. Then you shift to the breath. When you shift to the breath, you are subtler. From breath, we should shift to *naada*, the sound. On reaching *naada*, the first *naada* that you will hear is the sound of your own heart. This is a basic rhythm you are born with. Heart beats are like the *damaru* (an small drum used to give rhythm) in Lord Shiva's hand. The heartbeat signifies waking up in life and also the rhythm of life and existence. With the damaru, Shiva wakes you up. What is waking up? He wakes you to reality! The reality of who you are – *Tatwamasi*. The dance of Shiva is the rhythm of existence.

So, you have moved from body to mind to breath to sound. The final sound is ....mmmmm... in the *Aum*.

To chant *Aum*, the tongue is not required. A person without a tongue can also say *Aum*. It is a universal sound. When one reaches *Aum*, he/she also reaches the *Sushumna naadi*. Reaching *Aum* is also merging with the *kundalini*. Reaching *Aum* is reaching Shiva. Shiva exists in *naada*. The *Aum* is a conglomerate of many bindus. Bindu or naad-bindu is a minute particle of sound. It is a perfect merging. It is subtle, subtler, and subtlest. It brings about the merging with the eternal silence.

🌱 **Question:** How do we reach Jesus' consciousness?

Mohanji: Through your spine. If you want to reach anybody, you first reach your own soul. To reach your soul, to understand your own nature, you have to go beyond your mind. Find unity in all the three stages I explained to you before – waking state, dream state and deep sleep. First, we reach our soul; then we reach other souls. Then we will become one with the supreme consciousness.

What is the difference between you and me, soul-wise? We are children of the same father. The Dalai Lama says it beautifully: "Remove my clothes, remove my skin, you and I are one." It is true. We are creating barriers based on our identities in this life. We only live 70-80 years. Such a short life! But we are hanging on to that saying "I am Indian, I am German, I am British. etc".

Another thing: The sun has been around all along since Earth began. It is a witness, and we are not even able to connect to the sun! Once you start connecting with the energy of the sun, you will see the same energy and brightness existing within you. No difference. Sun uses the same energy and the heat that you use to digest food. It is all interconnected. How did we disconnect from all that?

🌱 **Question:** You said we could connect to Jesus' consciousness through the spine; what about the heart?

Mohanji: Heart automatically reflects. When you connect to your spine and Jesus' Consciousness, love is the only experience you will have. Jesus' main teaching was: "Love your enemy as you love your friend." You cannot differentiate. You go through the spine, and it is coming back to your heart.

Connectivity to anything higher has to happen beyond your senses, through the third eye. The third eye is linked to your spine, and the expression happens through your heart. It is all interlinked. If you connect with the heart, the heart cannot always stand the whole intensity. An expression can happen, no problem. Like your hands, you can use them to do a job, but they are not running the show.

Look, eighty per cent of your vital functions are controlled by your subconscious mind, like breathing, digestion, blood circulation. Just imagine if you gave the responsibility of the eighty per cent to the conscious mind-one day you might forget to breathe!

But coming back to the point, how do you think those great Masters function? Do you think their subconscious was controlling their vital functions? When in the path of liberation, slowly everything is taken over by the conscious mind, then the conscious mind is aware of every heartbeat because you are completely centred with it. You can travel through your body with every drop of your blood, consciousness-wise.

When I say shift to your spine, you will not experience that moment as an external entity. The experience and the experiencer become one in the spine because you will not be separate from the experience; you will merge with the spine. Then, no heartbeat happens without your knowledge. Perpetually you are in a meditative state, a *samadhi* state. Then you can control the whole body. Dimensions of existence are amazing. But people are only concerned about what to have for breakfast!

🌿 **Question:** How can I ensure my spiritual progress?

Mohanji: Strive to be always in 360-degree awareness. Watch your limited mind and ego. Be always detached from them. Be steadfast in your devotion as well as conviction. Do not only listen to others. Listen to your own soul and understand your own experiences. Understand and grow into yourself. Grow within. Be rich within. All external expressions should be expressions of your inner richness and not your limited mind. As Gandhiji said, "Be the change that you want to see in the world outside." Be unconditional love.

Taking the next step

🌿 **Question:** Meditation is more intense with many people.

Mohanji: Yes. Meditation is like a passport. It is just used to be united. But more than meditation, what is happening is consciousness is getting connected. You can say meditation is a tool to bring everybody together, but more than meditation, what is happening is the marriage of consciousness. This has more value. You can think of meditation as a boat to cross the river, but the consciousness is continuing. The mind can never understand this. The moment we start analysing, we fail. But the soul understands, and the connection is from the soul level. That is why we will not leave. We are connected, not only from this life, but we will continue in that mode. We can say that the thread continues. Whatever happens, it does not matter, but we are united in consciousness.

The moment we analyse, we fail to understand. This is why people get confused. I sometimes get messages which are crazy, and I don't even reply. I say, take your time, talk to yourself. Get back to me once you have a proper question. I say, "I will not wash your clothes. You wash yours". The ego plays a major role. When people come to me and say, "Oh, I've done this course, I've done that course..." I say, "Please continue." Because what will I do? What we have done in life has no value apart from what we are.

The more courses we do, the more the ego gets pampered and stronger. Then, it is very difficult to cross over. It is like the gate is small and the person is very fat. Intellectually you can also get very, very fat. Today, a person, I think from the Netherlands, sent me a message saying, "Mohanji, I follow you, and so many changes have happened. But not the final un-caging. The lion is ready to go out but cannot break the cage. How?" I said, "The only blockage you have-the cage, is your mind. The lion is ready to leave any day. But what keeps the lion inside the cage is the mind. The more solid the cage, the more difficult it is to break. We need to dilute ourselves and to empty ourselves so that the cage itself falls down." I said it symbolically, but this is the point.

<ul>
<li>Question: Only observing the thoughts and not paying attention to them, not energising them is the trick, and not dealing with the mind at all?</li>
</ul>

Mohanji: Correct. Just less energising of the mind will decay the cage. Also, one more thing we must understand clearly. The mind has a tendency to project a situation that may not be real. For e.g., a man said, "I am deeply connected to you; I look at your picture twenty four hours a day." But it need not be; it is the mind confusing you. It is not your connecting to the picture or not but whether you are feeling me? Are you being me? This is the point. I receive a lot of emails in which people ask me, "I'm deeply connected to you. Are you feeling me?" I say, "Don't worry whether I am feeling you, but are you feeling me?"

I'll give you one example. There is a doctor in Dubai. She connects to me and gives answers to people. She has no idea how the answers come. She has never read anything, but she does that. In 2004 or 2005, when I met her, I said, "One day, you will be representing me." She is married and has children. At that time, she did not know it but later on, she started saying things that surprised her: "How do I know this?" Answers are real. Because people who receive the answer say, "Thank you, I've got the answer, or the problem is solved". She used to call me saying, "Mohanji, this is working wonderfully! How is it happening?" I said, "Stop calling me now. Feel me now. Do not talk to me on the phone or use anything. Connect to me."

Because then you have to take the next step. Once this is happening, go to the next step saying with a hundred per cent conviction that we are connected and act on it, feel it and move it. Then eventually, we are connected a hundred per cent, full time, and you are operating in that plane. So, consciousness is one. How we use it is the most important thing. The moment you feel Mohanji is separate from me, or the consciousness is separate, the wall is the mind. Mind projects that you are very well connected to me because there is a picture on the wall. That is nothing. Many times it is like that.

Consciousness is important at this time because most of us are beating around the bush. We are practising something; it does not matter what we practice; which *Guru* we follow is also ok; which God we connect to is fine, but are we connecting to the consciousness? This is the most important point here.

One example of the connection is a three-year-old boy. We came back from Belgrade at night. My wife Devi was not there. Our hosts forgot to put the blanket on the bed, so I was feeling cold. The boy woke up his mother in New Delhi and said, "Mohanji is feeling cold", took my picture and put it under the blanket. If you ask him what I'm doing now, he will tell you. He is deeply connected to my consciousness. The reason I'm giving this example is that this is a state you can achieve. We should be so deeply engraved in consciousness that you will not feel different from me.

Another aspect is, the moment you start evolving in consciousness, many people will get attracted to you. There are two ways they will come. Sometimes a person of negative nature will come to you to take the energy, like they want help. It is up to you how much time you want to spend with them. This is for sure. The second is that like-minded people will come to you. People who are evolving will come and hold your hand. This will become a beautiful family. I always tell people, if there is a problem in a relationship, evolve yourself, and then the relationship that comes to you will stay because they are not judgmental. Otherwise, usual relationships are based on expectation and judgment. You keep judging a person based on whatever awareness you have, with expectations.

Whenever a relationship is based on expectations, and it moves in a kind of judgmental way, "If you do this, I like you, if you don't do this, I don't," there will be conflicts all the time. But the moment the consciousness grows, the relationship shifts to purpose, "We are together because there is a higher purpose to achieve." This is beautiful. Then, there is no conflict because there is no room for conflict. There is nothing to fight for. This is to be understood clearly. Whenever there is a blockage in a relationship, evolve and catch the higher. Then the whole thing comes up. Only such people will meet you. The rest will leave you because you are useless to those people.

It is extremely important to cultivate awareness. Normally, we do not see the consciousness and say, "This man looks good; I want him." He might be carrying so much baggage. Man or woman, it does not matter; we fall for the looks, the senses take you to the looks, and then we suffer. It is not easy. How do you know? It is important that you raise yourself so that you attract that kind of personality into your life. This is not only in marriage; but also in any relationship in life.

ॐ **Question:** Don't look for a perfect person, be a perfect person.

Mohanji: Yes, be the perfect person; there is no need to look anywhere. That comes to you. Only then it stays. Otherwise, every relationship is based on expectation and emotion. Respect happens with higher consciousness. Respect comes to you. Respect has to be earned. You can probably get a status, e.g. somebody tells you, "You are the president of this place." But stature has to happen through maturity, through approach, through higher awareness. Only then it stays. Otherwise, you see many people attaining a position and falling down. One person asked me, "How can we keep you here longer?" I said, "I never leave this place. If you are able to see, you will see." Physically, it is very difficult because there is only one body. But otherwise, I'm here.

🌿 **Question:** You are everywhere.

Mohanji: Yes.

Sharing Enhances, Hoarding Diminishes

Maintain your inner space tidy and clean by being kind, unpretentious, gossip free, soap-opera-free, living acts of kindness, being spontaneously compassionate, unconditionally loving, non-violent in thoughts, words and actions, and travelling inward much more than the outer world. Be happy and peaceful with what you have been provided with, and learn to share rather than hoard. Sharing enhances you. Hoarding diminishes you. Share the inner and outer wealth with others. Share experiences, share joy. These would take you a long way in spiritual elevation, much more than hours of spiritual practices and visits to places of worship, guaranteed!

Q&A on Spirituality

❧ **Question:** What makes people wander in the spiritual journey?

Mohanji: Unsatiated mind that creates expectations, falls for sensory glitter, nurtures concepts and non-understanding and makes one believe that peace is always elsewhere.

❧ **Question:** What is celibacy?

Mohanji: It is a state of mind. It is a level of awareness. It is detachment in action.

❧ **Question:** What is the least I can do to remain spiritual?

Mohanji: Love unconditionally. Serve unconditionally. Let all your relationships be beyond conditions and expectations.

❧ **Question:** What is right and what is wrong in spirituality?

Mohanji: Nothing. Everything just is.

❧ **Question:** In simple terms, what is higher and lower consciousness?

Mohanji: One, who perpetually operates from the realms of unconditional love, possesses higher consciousness. He is selfless, kind, truthful and unattached to his actions. One who perpetually operates in the realms of selfishness, 'I' ness, possessiveness, ownership, greed, fear, etc., operates from the lower consciousness. The operating levels declare the stature of the being.

❧ **Question:** I cannot concentrate.

Mohanji: Do not concentrate. Be aware of this aspect of yourself and accept yourself with this aspect wholeheartedly.

Never resist. Just be aware of your own breath pattern and then your heartbeat. You will surprise yourself.

❧ **Question:** Can you help me?

Mohanji: Do you really need help? You are all-powerful. If you feel otherwise, hold on to me until you find yourself. I will help you. You need crutches only until your own legs become strong enough to carry you.

❧ **Question:** I cannot sleep.

Mohanji: Good. Practice awareness. It is better than sleep.

❧ **Question:** Why do we wander?

Mohanji: Because you follow the mind. Mind always remains dissatisfied. It drags the body along. It delivers fears and alienations. It keeps you running after one thing or the other, through disillusionment and non-understanding.

❧ **Question:** Man's quest for knowledge.

Mohanji: Waste of time, unless it helps his shedding.

❧ **Question:** What is worth pursuing?

Mohanji: Silence.

❧ **Question:** What is worth investing in?

Mohanji: Awareness

❧ **Question:** Siddhis?

Mohanji: Candies.

❧ **Question:** Why?

Mohanji: It wastes time. It maintains duality. It could nurture a stronger ego. It forces detours. It alienates man from unity.

❧ **Question:** Ultimate destination of man?

Mohanji: Narayana, the destination of man.

❧ **Question:** Is it Lord Vishnu?

Mohanji: *Parabrahma*, the supreme formless God. The one who generates, operates and dissolves. All forms are formed out of him and dissolve in him.

❧ **Question:** Why do we visit holy places?

Mohanji: The urge to bathe in higher energies.

❧ **Question:** What do we carry from there?

Mohanji: Depends on your stature. It is ideal to carry higher awareness and silence of mind if you could. Usually, you only carry some photographs of your own form against some divine backdrop! This only tells you that you were indeed there and makes you feel the worth of money well spent. The ability to experience gets enhanced with surrender and silence. Silence brings you more awareness than any book knowledge. Expectation kills the fragrance of every experience.

❧ **Question:** I am confused!

Mohanji: You are not confused. Your mind is. Understand the mind and detach from it. Let it be confused, but you are not your mind. Be what you really are, and there is no confusion.

❧ **Question:** How can I achieve a fundamental shift in character, habits and such bindings in this lifetime?

Mohanji: Choose to energise positivity in life. Discard everything negative in nature. Energise merits, ignore demerits. Cherish what you have in life. Ignore what you do not have. Be in the present and do your best right now. Keep reinventing yourself every moment with the question – "What else can I do for the world?" Explore yourself more. Be positive against all odds of life. A good life is a choice. A good life is an attitude. This is an attitude that is worth it. This is the secret.

❧ **Question:** Who makes dos and don'ts?

Mohanji: Limited minds.

❧ **Question:** What creates *samskaras*?

Mohanji: Habits. Usually, habits are emotional in nature. Repetitive action creates attachment to action.

❧ **Question:** What is ego?

Mohanji: Doer-ship. The feeling that you are the 'doer'.

❧ **Question:** What creates attachment?

Mohanji: Everything. Any thought, word, action, along with emotion, creates binding and attachment.

The Soul is the ultimate guide

Spirituality is the path of the soul. True spirituality leads one to his own soul. Adi Shankaracharya said, "Some walk with a shaven head, some with matted hair, some with a switch at the back of their head, some wear saffron, some wear nothing. Please understand, O ignorant beings, they are doing all these just for their own stomach's sake." Centuries ago, Adi Shaṅkara uttered this eternal Truth. It remains true even today.

When man handles his terrestrial existence through his senses, he falls prey to such visual appeals. When the soul is guiding, he automatically gets guided to the right *Guru*. In order for the soul to guide, one must bring the senses inward. He should watch his thoughts and calm his mind through observation of thoughts as a witness. Shirdi Sai Baba is one of the greatest Masters who ever walked on Earth and continues to walk with his subtle body. If Baba is guiding, then there is no need to doubt. He will protect you from all mishaps. He will only guide you to the information or *Guru* that is right for you. Just do not doubt or analyse. Surrender everything to Sai and walk the path.

CHAPTER 3:

Meditation

The Power of Purity Meditation

The Power of Purity is meant for internal cleansing. When you are being cleansed, various feelings will emerge. Some will be good, and some will be bad. Allow yourself to be cleansed through consistent practice. We have stored tons of *samskaras* in our system. What is being removed is that which is hindering your progress in the path of liberation. You could also chant '*Aum Parabrahmane Namah*' while also concentrating on your spine. Do not be afraid. This meditation will not harm you. It will release many hidden, suppressed emotions or feelings from lifetimes.

    ❦ **Question:** This meditation cleanses one's body, mind or both?

Mohanji: The body is cleansed when we take a bath. The body is gross. It is made out of five elements – fire, water, earth, air and space. Elements are gross. What is cleansed with this meditation is the inner space. Inner space is fully made up of emotions/impressions of various degrees from various lifetimes. This can be cleansed. This is what we are trying to do in this meditation. A purified inner space makes us feel lighter. *Shaktipat* is like a trigger. Gross *karma* provoked you to take birth. *Shaktipat* penetrates through these gross *karmas*, eliminates chaff and makes further progress easier.

Be clear about one thing – whatever you wanted to achieve in this life with this birth, you have brought enough fuel to achieve that. Things will happen as per the master plan of this life, whether you like it or not. This is called destiny. The fuel is not sufficient for any additions. Your destiny made you come here and sit. You may not know me. Maybe you have never heard these words before. These words are provoked by your destiny because you were supposed to hear them today. You could not have been elsewhere today. This is what we called the time-space junction point. You can only be at a particular space at a particular time with a particular constitution. It is impossible for you to get to a different place and time at this moment.

What you do not know in your conscious mind is what provoked this birth. After you are born, your's is a kind of unconscious existence. You knew exactly what you wanted to do before getting into the human womb. After birth, social and other conditionings made you forget what provoked this birth. You continue to exist, thinking, "I am doing the right thing!"

You do not control eighty per cent of your vital functions. Your heartbeat, circulation, respiration, digestion, and so on are not controlled by you! The brain is not controlled by your conscious mind. Thr limitations are so heavy that what we control is nothing compared to what we do not or what we are, in totality. With this understanding, you can do one thing: to allow fewer things to go within your mind structure and thus create less *karma*. Be in the present and avoid resistance of all kinds because you created your situations subconsciously.

✤ **Question:** Can you explain the background music – the sound of water and the recurring wave-like music?

Mohanji: Interesting question. In three years, nobody has ever asked that question. Nobody thought about this. It is an old friend's composition. Our constitution is always peaceful. The mind is like a wave – and the music is exactly like that. The music is teasing in that way. But it is not contradictory; it is complementary to the program.

> ꙮ **Question:** Is there an energy difference whether I sit on the floor or on a chair during the meditation?

Mohanji: In our meditation, the most important thing is that you should be comfortable and able to sit without moving for an hour. This is a cleansing meditation – when things are moving out of your system, the mind tries to manipulate the body in a way that you want to move, shift, or do something.

> ꙮ **Question:** In response to a mobile phone which rang just at the completion of the meditation session.

In any meditation class, your mobile should be switched off. This is because you are going deep within. External sound gives a sudden jerk to the body. It is very bad for your system. How would you feel if someone poured water on you while you were in a deep sleep? You would be shocked and jerked from sleep. It would not be a welcome experience. The loud sound of a mobile shakes not only you but also others. It is not good. This is general guidance for everyone.

Experiences During Meditation

> ꙮ **Question:** During the Power of Purity meditation, my eyes rotated by themselves to about sixty degrees upwards, so that I almost had to open my eyes. I don't know what happened.

Mohanji: When you connect to the third eye, and your eyes rotate to the third eye, that means you are in the mood of forgiveness, you are forgiving, you are letting go. On the normal eye level, we always attract, collect and store, but the moment it shifts to the third eye, we start letting go, we release. This is the sign that you were ready to release. We are, by nature, collection oriented. Through our eyes, nose, ears and all our faculties, we attract information, experiences, and a lot of things. We store it all.

The more we store, the heavier we become. It is natural. So what happens is the experience also starts getting repeated. It is called *purva samskara*, which means past impressions. We collect impressions, and we repeat them in life. It is important to let go, to release because every second is fresh, every moment is fresh. If we bring something from the past and put it in the present, we miss the fragrance of the present, or the flavour of the right moment, this moment. What happens is we are usually superimposing, e.g., "I knew this before, or I've known this person before, I've known this situation before, I've been to this place before," but every moment is changing, just like our body. Change is part of life. Change is part of earthly existence. We must look at life afresh. Then we start enjoying life, and then we are in the present.

In the meditation that we've just practised, we are asking people to connect to the spine. When you are connected to the spine, your eyes automatically close, and you shift to the third eye. Then you are ready to release. Otherwise, you will not release. Even normally, when we sit down and close our eyes, we do not release. We are just trying to manipulate our stored impressions. That is one of the points.

Normally, we meet a person and say, "I've met him." What you are meeting is the physical form and the expressions of the person. But there is a deep inherent consciousness that is expressed through the person. For example, if you say, "I know Mohanji," that means you know this physical form and my way of expression. That's about it. But it is not possible for you to know where it is coming from. To know that, you must be operating more from the third eye. That way, when you meet a person, you actually understand him. Otherwise, all we are doing is meeting the physical form and collecting the expressions and judging a person. This is very wrong. This is not the way. That is why we have conflicts. Normally, when we meet a person, we see the differences. But when we operate from the third eye, we see unity.

The simplest technique for operating from the third eye is connecting to your own spine. I'm not saying meditate, but connect. When I say to connect, it means to feel the spine when you are walking, when you are sitting down, even for five or ten minutes. It is not that you feel the spine all the time. Eventually, with every activity, if you start feeling your spine, you start operating from the spine or from the third eye. Even if you close your eyes and feel the spine, you will automatically know that you are operating from the third eye. When you start operating from your spine, the difference will be fewer emotions and more awareness. As awareness grows, you will increase in strength and become stronger. This is very simple.

You do not have to go to any *Guru* or any particular place to do this. As you lead your life, you can connect to your spine. You can be peaceful and will also enjoy the silence as the mind gets stiller and stiller. Thus, when you establish yourself in awareness, you will be detaching from your mind and your body, yet at the same time, you will be functioning very well. Here, you are not controlled by the mind or the body.

❧ **Question:** As we discussed yesterday, one may feel heavy, lazy or groggy after meditation. One does not feel like moving, etc. If my understanding is correct, this is because of intense cleansing and relaxation – however, most of the patients I see also come with similar complaints. We treat them as physical symptoms! How am I, as a medical doctor, to differentiate the cause behind these similar symptoms? I feel symptoms after meditation would stay for a short time, and later on, one will be very energetic. However, those who have physical symptoms will always have those complaints.

Mohanji: As we evolve in meditation, depending on the individual constitution, experiences will vary. The initial phase is a tremendous urge to open our eyes and shift our position. The body involuntarily revolts. Mind wanders. Thoughts attack from the left and the right. As we progress, the mind accepts. The body stays still. Thoughts will not affect us much. Then, as silence deepens, the mindless states are experienced. We become aware of energy movements. Thus, from the gross, we slowly start shifting to the subtle. The more subtle we become, the more we start to enjoy our meditation. At the same time, our dependency on external objects also decreases. We become happy in our introversion. Once again, according to our individual constitution, changes happen. Those who are visually oriented – see things. Those who are hearing oriented – hear mystic sounds. Those who are feeling oriented – experience the presence of their protecting angels or higher spiritual Masters.

Everyone has a higher self. Everyone has a protecting angel. Usually, we confuse our higher self with the protecting angel. We could listen to them and communicate with them. They also play a role in directing us to Masters. They are never angry or unhappy however many detours we take and deviate from our path of spiritual progress.

Anyways, your understanding is correct. In the presence of higher Masters, it is human to be like a sponge and suck in energy; we get tempted to do that. When we subconsciously try to absorb more energy than we can digest, we may feel dizzy or heavy. This feeling erodes and balances within hours. This is not harmful if the guide is a true Master and the student is undergoing a natural evolution. The hazard is only when we try to run before we learn to walk; or try to eat more than we can digest. In the presence of a good Master, this is taken care of. No harm will happen to you as you are his responsibility. Intense cleansing leads to relaxation on a cellular level. You want to take it easy and let go. This is a symptom of perfect unwinding and stresslessness.

Disease is acquired. Diseases are external expressions of wrong notions nurtured inside over lifetimes. They are formed over the years under pressure, within one's subconscious mind. An internal shift could possibly, or rather theoretically, dismiss a disease with ease. It does not happen because this wrong notion is also a part of man's total constitution. With this disease, the man is complete. Or in other words, he chose his character, including this disease. For example, one man used to constantly repeat: "Oh God, what a headache this is". By headache, he meant problems. Eventually, he developed a chronic headache because his subconscious took his words literally and nurtured that reality for him.

So, every thought, word or action that we produce can never go wasted. Its results appear in some form or the other, at the appointed time or in the right environment. Such things are hard to cleanse unless we go back to their root and clean them from there. We have to fry the seed at the causal layer. We should remove its capacity to germinate.

So, the best way for the patients is to allow them to flow with a guided meditation to replace their thought process from that of a patient to that of a seeker. Even if the situation remains the same, their agony will be less. This will make them optimistic. This will help to heal. Medicines should be administered, but any symptomatic treatment is actually short-sighted. The root is elsewhere. Symptoms are only on the surface. If the root remains, it can germinate anytime in the future. Therefore, eradication from the subconscious level and removal of the seeds from the causal layer are the best ways to ensure the total cure.

❧ **Question:** I have seen bright golden and white light during meditation. It comes suddenly like a flash, fills me, gives bliss and a jerk, and vanishes. What is this?

What is the understanding? I know I must go beyond these experiences, but I am curious to know.

Mohanji: They are various energy bodies merging with your system. Colours signify certain levels of elevation too. It is true that we must drop the need for analysis. At the same time, being aware helps. Especially in the presence of Masters, each one gets what he/she needs. One's deficiencies get nullified. This is usually experienced in the form of coloured energy forms. Just accept them with gratitude and allow them to work.

- **Question:** What is yawning? We still do not know the reason for yawning in medicine. Yawning happens during meditation. What is its significance? We also yawn otherwise!

Mohanji: When the mind is relaxed, you yawn. Meditation also relaxes. Yawning leads to sleep. Yawning is like a warning of fatigue and the need to sleep. The mind hates meditation because meditation is aimed at arresting the wandering mind. Who wants to forsake his freedom? Mind the least. So, the mind plays many games to take your attention away. It brings forth many fond memories, tasty food, body pains, and even yawning. This deviates your concentration. Thus, the mind wins.

Yawning is also a natural mechanism to add more oxygen to the body. Sometimes during intense exercising and sweating, an urge for yawning can suddenly come. This means that the body (especially the brain) requires more oxygen, but since our breathing is too shallow, yawning is prompted as a natural remedy.

- **Question:** During the meditation, I felt like I was moving in this merry-go-round and also had glimpses of people I did not know.

Mohanji: Yes. All those are glimpses from a realm which you are otherwise unable to tap into. These are all collectors as well. It means you have to meet them – shake hands and depart. Or it could be something which was exiting you.

In this meditation, tremendous cleansing happens. You get relieved from a lot of stuff, which passes through your mind. Some entities, which may or may not have a body, pass through your mind and exit; you will feel something has left you and/or that you have met somebody. The mind will try to contemplate, but consciousness cannot understand because this probably is related to another life. So it can only be felt. It can never be perceived exactly. In such cases, what you have to do is – watch it like a movie and do not get attached.

Sometimes the traumas are tremendous. It really gives you the squeeze, and your emotions will overflow. At that time also, just watch it like a movie and let it go. The more you hold it, the more the agony. The lesser you hold it, the lesser is the attachment or agony. We have to be very objective about all these experiences. Just watch, say, "Ok, fine. I had this experience. No problem." and move on.

The more you root in your spine, the more your stability will increase. Your strength happens when your subtlety increases. At the gross level, you are weak as you operate through the senses. For example, it is like when you go to, let us say, a bakery. You see a lot of pastries there for sale. Automatically half of your strength has gone there because senses have pulled you already. Then, your mind is already weak since your senses say, "I want to taste this". Then, you are just going through the process of paying for it, buying and consuming it.

The more you get to the spine and exist in your spine, the less the push or pull of the senses will be. That becomes your strength so that you will not be easily swayed by what is visible outside! This is why Saints sometimes operate in jungles. They do not even want to get exposed to sensory objects, including people. Sometimes someone comes to you with glass, ornaments and things of the sort, which you might get attached to.

ॐ **Question:** While I was in deep meditation, my inner sight was extremely focused, so, let us say, I was in a thoughtless state for a longer time. At that moment, I felt a strong heartbeat, as if I had a heart attack. My heart was pumping, pumping, pumping, and I did not know what to think or feel. It was like my heart was going to explode. Could you tell me what happened?

Mohanji: These are always phases when energy shifts within. Sometimes when you meditate, especially when the mind goes blank, when the mind empties completely, suddenly there will be a surge of energy in the veins, through the meridians. Then it can conglomerate in some places, especially in the head, heart or stomach centre. It usually moves up and down. This is natural. Just allow it to happen and, at that time, surrender more. Your mind would have completely emptied itself, so you just have to focus on that thing and keep breathing. In this case, I understand that you may feel panic, but it is also important to connect to me at that time. If you connect to me at that time, you will automatically feel that the energy is normalizing. Try that.

ॐ **Question:** I do not feel anything during meditation!

Mohanji: If you do not feel anything, it is ok. We are used to the gross body, mind and intellect. Subtlety is not easy. In this world, we mainly operate with the gross. We do not think of the subtle throughout the day. Do we think of our soul during the day? We do not think about our soul till death! By that time, it is too late. It takes time to feel the subtle. But once you feel it, it makes you powerful. Nothing outside will affect you. Internally, you become so strong that nothing can shake you. This is not easy. The same mind, which always goes out for a stroll with the senses, should be tuned back – same vehicle, different purpose.

ॐ **Question:** How can I interpret the various colours that I see during the meditation?

Mohanji: There are different types of people. Some are vision-oriented. They talk about how something looks. Some are sound-oriented, and they say how nice something sounds. Some are feeling-oriented. Depending on your orientation, you may see, hear or feel vibrations. In this way, our meditation gives different effects to different people. Of course, you can also shift from seeing to feeling orientation as you progress spiritually. Colours signify the movements of energy and energy shifts. Energy is never constant.

Throughout your life, your aura and your chakras will keep changing depending on situations. It does not mean that chakras disappear and come back, but that the intensity of the energy in the chakras change. If you experience a situation of deep fear, for example, your heart shrinks. When the heart shrinks, it cannot give full love. Sometimes you feel deep love for the whole universe without reason. This can also be the presence of a higher entity within you, like an angel. These things happen in life. Colours are basically a confirmation of an energy shift. But I always tell people to ignore it because the colours do change quite often. So why should we hold on to some colours?

❧ **Question:** What about the colour white?

Mohanji: The chakras have the same colours as the rainbow. The colours show the state of elevation. White is the place where you originate from, where all colours come together and nullify. All colours come out of white, and all colours merge into white. Similarly, all souls merge into the supreme soul, and all souls come from the supreme soul. White is like a motherly light. That light is soothing, rejuvenating and nourishing. However, every meditation is different, and it all depends on the constitution of the day. Many people ask me about their visions and what I think. I always answer – nothing!

In this context, I hear more and more about aura readings. I am not against you experimenting, but please be careful; it is your life. Prevention is better than cure. If you are reasonably confident about yourself, you don't need any aura or chakras readings. Hence, I insist you go to the spine more and more because insecurities are linked to the conscious mind. You have no insecurities when you are in a deep sleep and dream state. Likewise, almost all these issues are related to our conscious mind and the problems we create.

⚘ **Question:** I had an intense experience with colours during the meditation. Is that the mind or reality?

Mohanji: Colours are usually expressions of our constitution. Because we are a collection of various factors, there is love, anxiety, fear, goodness... a mixture sitting in you. This gets reflected in colours. But it is a good idea because once you see them, they are probably leaving you as well.

⚘ **Question:** After yesterday's meditation, I dreamt a lot.

Mohanji: If we cut the strings of various emotions, sometimes this goes through your dreams. You will notice that in your dreams and also when you are awake. Some people tell me that their stomach was churning, or they had a lot of hunger, or sometimes diarrhoea, sometimes feeling anger and agitation. These things have to go through you, through your systems. Various things can happen, just accept it and don't hold on to it. We are used to carrying the weight, and until it is gone, we do not even realise that we were carrying something.

Sometimes our ego does not allow us to get rid of the baggage. Pain is also associated with the ego. Some people like to say that they are suffering. It is so important to them. The dream state has more room for action because it is not bound by time and space, so cleansing can happen faster. While you are sitting here, you have limitations. Dare to dream!

Whatever you cannot handle, pass it on to a higher level or surrender it to God or your Guru. At work or in the office, if there is something we cannot deal with or beyond our handling capacity, we usually consult or pass it on to our superiors, right? Let your Guru do his job. You can say, "Please take it over; I surrender this pain or experience to you." In Shirdi Sai Baba's case, many people asked him to take over, and it worked. Baba always said that once you leave it and hand it over, don't look back. That means faith is very important. If you have no faith, it is as if you planted a seed and checked it everyday to see if it is sprouting, then it will never grow. Surrender and faith are important. Faith is like a big protection shield. If you surrender with faith, it will work immediately. But when you just mentally say "I surrender", it won't work.

The more subtle you go, the more powerful you become. If you are operating on the body level, you will just have physical power. If you are operating on your mental level, you have a different type of power. On the intellectual level, it is different again. When you are operating on the pranic level, like breathing, it is again different. But finally, when you reach your soul level, you have the power of God.

For example, in the case of the Master Lahiri Mahasaya, many times when people took a photo of him, he was not visible in the picture. When you are operating on the soul level, you become very, very subtle. Even your physical body becomes quite subtle. You will have a shape, but it is more or less transparent. On that level, you can command when the wind should stop; you can control the elements because the soul is above elements. But let us understand; those great Masters were able to heal because they were not really worried about their bodies. The body was just a tool of expression, and they never cared because the body has a beginning and an end anyway.

We give unnecessary importance to the body based on our identifications, and sometimes we suffer because of that. They say we should treat our body like a temple, and that means it should be pure. The god in the temple is the soul. So don't pay too much attention to the body, but pay attention to the soul! Furthermore, you do not need any priest or Guru to bring you to your soul. Everything is given to us; we just have to see our own potential.

In the case of Jesus, he was a hundred per cent purpose bound. There was no confusion. He went ahead with his mission in a razor-sharp way. He had a very clear picture that people would destroy his body someday. Do you know what he was attacking mostly? Inertia, tamas. Inertia is what? Complacency, laziness, interest in negative things, overeating, jealousy, anger and greed. During the time when Jesus was around, the community was well established in inertia because there were comfortably placed priests who controlled people, and the life pattern was set. What do priests normally do? They control people through fear of punishment. Jesus wanted to liberate the people. He told the people: you have the potential to reach the Father. Everything is within you. Your soul is the channel.

When Jesus was attacking inertia or *tamas*, the people fought back. Because who really wants to leave their bed early in the morning when it is still dark and cold outside. Of course, I am not talking about actual sleep here, but life in general. Jesus was trying to wake people up and told them to get up and start running. Do you think people liked that? And if society does not like something, they find every reason to eliminate the very cause of their dislike.

When the Truth is spoken, it can sometimes be very frightening. We do not like the Truth, we don't like to hear it, and we like to postpone the inevitable. That's our nature. When someone tells us the stark Truth, we either prevent him or annihilate him. Socrates told the Truth, and we gave him poison. Jesus was only telling the Truth, and we crucified him. That's human nature. We like to kill those people and then put their pictures on the wall and say they were good. I'm not criticising anything, but let us recognise the reality.

One thing about the Truth is important: when you hear the Truth, your whole consciousness responds. It is not the mind responding with "Oh, this is interesting, it could be true", but your whole being will react and say, "Yes! This is correct." This happens when the Truth is clearly stated.

On Easter Sunday, we celebrate Jesus' resurrection, using the occasion to have a drink. But do we use the day to connect to his consciousness? Use the day to connect to his consciousness! Jesus' body has left us, but his consciousness has never left us; it is available. If you are able to connect to his consciousness, you will be able to heal people, for example.

✤ **Question:** I had super sensations during the meditation this time, really. I saw my hand with my eyes closed with beautiful white light, and I couldn't believe it. I just moved my hand in front of my face. This was the first time I saw this.

Mohanji: This is normal. These are stages of evolution when you come to a subtler level where gross is not blocking you. The body is very gross; the mind is gross, intellect is gross, and ego is gross. You're going beyond it to your real form, which is very soft and subtle, which is bright. The moment you touch that, you can see all the gross. Maybe you have seen my pictures where my hands are transparent. Actually, it is true. It is not imagination. When you connect to very subtle energy, and you are conveying it, you become like that – the whole constitution changes.

✤ **Question:** During the meditation, I felt I was in some state between dream and sleep. I cannot define it, nor did I want to analyse it. I felt I was radiating from the third eye and solar plexus chakras, and my hand was as if some beam was coming out of me. When we finished, I saw a white belt around you and people next to the wall, looking like a cloak. It wasn't a play of shadows. It was a reflection of light.

Mohanji: Firstly, there are various energies in the plane of existence, not just here, but everywhere. They are all looking for redemption; they are all looking for elevation. Many of them also get redemption in our process. Secondly, you reached a state of altered consciousness, which means connecting more to the soul; that is exactly what we are trying to do in our meditation. We are bringing you from the gross to the subtle, and then you reach a state of altered consciousness, where you can see much more than you can normally see with your senses and eyes.

That is why I said to connect to my consciousness; that is why we keep our eyes on the card. States change very rapidly provided we allow it. Your receptivity is very high; it is normal that you can see much more because you can move into the consciousness. The mind is the blocking factor here. Mind confuses between the superficial, like the body and expression, and the real. It says, "I know Mohanji, he is like this, or this is how he talks", But it is nothing. The moment you connect to consciousness, it is a completely different world.

🌿 **Question:** When some people started crying, my heart was aching tremendously, like I was crying too.

Mohanji: This is because it becomes one consciousness, like my extended consciousness, and I take out things. When this meditation happens, it works the same way, even when I'm not here. That is why this meditation is becoming so popular all over the world. Actually speaking, we are all related, which is why we met. We can call ourselves soulmates. A soulmate is not just the husband or wife. They are a set of souls who decided to meet on this plane. We took this decision well before. Thus, we decided to come here to experience life and interact on some level at some points in time. Some of us will connect for some time and then go off on our own, while some will be connected for a longer period of time. The timespan of connection has no value here. We are connected. That has value.

Sharing the experiences

The effort of sharing experiences is perhaps only for the sake of explaining the dimensions that you experienced and could actually operate from, for the sake of oneself (one's own doubting mind) and for the understanding of others who might want to know. Nothing more. I consider that there is nothing special about me as a person. This facility, the electricity that we spoke of above, is accessible to all. When you share experiences, first of all, you recognise the existence of different dimensions which are indeed accessible to you and others but unused or ignored by most of us primarily due to lack of awareness. Suddenly, we realise and through us, the readers realise that as well, that there is much more potential that we could actually use and experience in our everyday life.

Our Tradition is that of selflessness and unconditionality. Keep walking the path, beyond images into the consciousness. You will 'find' yourself there. You will find everyone there. We all truly possess the abundance of the state of Shiva. *Shivoham*!

When we share our experience, we reconsider it once again in our mind and our conscious mind reconciles with it. Otherwise, others' words or book knowledge will overlap our actual experience and dissolve it in the course of time. We have to begin and continue our journey primarily through our experiences. External knowledge has no further value than situational guidance. Accepting and sharing experiences reinforces our stature, understanding levels and even tackles the ever-doubting conscious mind. It also helps others to understand their own experiences, in the light of yours. They will sooner or later start to own experiences and grow with it. Hence, this is a great *seva* too.

Owning one's own experience is important. That's where you start your journey.

Meditation Technique

🌿 **Question:** I connected with you, Mohanji, that's how I saved myself!

Mohanji: Yes, I know. I can give you another technique. For a few minutes, sit quietly and go through the breath entering your system, and *prana* going through the body. It may take some time, but just focus on your breath entering through the nose, and reaching every cell of your body. Totally internal. Only breath and you. Just start feeling. When you concentrate on the breath, on the air going in, you will start going through the breath, to the energy particles of the breath, which are actually nourishing the cells through the meridians. Just feel the energy flowing through your body, through the veins, through every meridian, as it reaches all the parts of the body.

Just be with the energy flow. When you flow through that energy, you can reach every cell of your body, every part of your body, every organ of your body inside, so that it touches everywhere. When you are aware of that, slowly you will be aware of the sounds of your body. First the sound inside the body, the heartbeat, then the blood circulation, the secretion of juices in the stomach, and so on. All these sounds will occupy you. Thus, when you go through the breath, the next is sound. Once you go through the sound, when you become the sound, automatically with the sound there is vibration. You will become the vibration of the sound.

When you become the vibration of the sound, slowly, slowly you will start feeling the brightness of every cell because every cell has an aura. You start feeling that aura. It is light, very, very, very thin, but it is brightness. You will start feeling the brightness. When you start feeling the brightness, you will also start feeling the lightness of the body. The body becomes very light. When the body becomes lightness, or when you start feeling the light, you will start feeling the light of the soul, the energy that operates your body. Once you start feeling the energy that operates the body, once you start feeling the soul, at that time you will have completely merged with the consciousness.

Thus, the first and the only effort you need to take is to stay with the breath and that breath will take you to every other stage, that of sound, that of light, and that of brightness, and dissolution. You'll go to all the stages automatically; you don't have to do anything. Just be with the breath in the first stage. That is the only determination you need. You can practice this on your own and will see the difference. Nowhere will the energy be blocked. Before you start, please connect to my eyes for two minutes, then start. It may take some time, from the breath to the brightness.

It may take one year, two years... but it is worth it. Because in a couple of years, you will completely become brightness. You do not need to do anything more. This is very, very, very powerful. It is worth trying and you don't need any Master, or anybody to guide you. You can do it yourself, at your own speed.

Meditating in a Group or Alone

🌿 **Question:** How do you decide to come out of meditation?

Mohanji: It depends on where you are meditating and how you tune the mind. Are you meditating in a group or alone? Group energy works. It is like a herd– cows automatically follow each other. When in a group, it cannot be our 'will' to come out of the meditation. The collective consciousness of the group works on you.It is different when you are meditating alone. It depends on how you tune the mind. You may sit longer then. You will be restless if the mind is not tuned well. The job of the mind is to be restless. It also depends on the day and the surroundings. Sometimes, when you go far away from home, you meditate well. A different environment makes the situation conducive to meditation. Sometimes it is also good at home. It all depends. It is difficult to generalise.

Deep meditation works well on your system. We do internal cleansing here. We have carried garbage through lifetimes and have never bothered to clean it or leave it! How do we know we never left the garbage? Look at the child and its character. We may say, 'This child has so many traits of the grandfather!' But it is not true. Every child is unique and comes with a distinct character. A child may be born to parents who are doctors or lawyers, but he wants to be a pilot! There is no one in the family who flies an aircraft, but the child has a distinct character. Where has it come from? It comes from the pattern that one has carried over lifetimes. It is in the subconscious and that collectively works on the destiny of the child, and parents have nothing to do with it. The child has its own *karma*.

Everyone is unique and has a distinct character. Conflicts are created when we do not understand it. We take ownership of our son or daughter. We also feel that they should listen to what we say. But we do not understand that they are operating their *karma* and not ours. We come together when *karmas* are together. At night, everyone is operating at their *karma* level. We forget our name, gender, qualification, time, and space at night. Everything comes back when we get up, but we attribute a lot to the waking state and identify ourselves, "This is me."

We try to express the same to the world and the world may not accept it. The conflict starts then. Internally we have expectations that my husband, son, or daughter will behave this way. When they do not, the conflict begins. In society, we behave the same. We expect certain things here as well – like, people will be kind to me, they will love me... When it does not happen, conflicts start with society, nature etc. Restlessness gets expressed in society. We see calamities taking shape, growing and destroying the very fabric of existence.

Our rich Tradition is our bank balance. The Tradition where we welcome everyone, we never harm anyone and we always provide to the whole world. Which Master was taking-oriented? All the past Masters always gave everything they had, without any expectation, unconditionally.

Meditation for Children

Meditation is good for teenagers and other children (let us say, above seven years). This is the impressionistic time. They grasp thoughts, images, ideas, and many such things. Usually, television and commercial media fill them up with desires of various kinds. They encourage extroversion, which leads to dissatisfaction and emotional chaos. It also leads to comparisons and disappointments, so meditation is a good way to detach the mind from senses and sense objects and bring it inwards, into self-exploration. It helps them to find their way within and explore the brightness behind their closed eyes. It will give them a taste of peace through detachment from the senses. At the least, it will make their mind stable at least for a few minutes, so it is good.

Any child who comes for meditation is not there due to co-incidence. Understand that there is a definite background that brings them there. The soul is of the same size and capacity in both child and adult, so take care of the children and treat them as equals to adults who meditate. Please remember – it is not only meditation that happens in the Power of Purity meditation. A definite shift in consciousness happens. A software change happens. This is the same for everyone, so all will certainly be benefited.

Along with this, there is *satsang,* or the positivity of good company. This helps neutralise negativities. Through divine company, indifference/detachment towards sense objects happens. Through indifference to sense objects, desires reduce drastically. With the lack of desires, the mind becomes still and unwavering. When the mind becomes still and unwavering, liberation happens.

Meditation may not be suitable for very young children. This is also because children always exist in the present. Their minds do not dwell in the past or future for too long. Adults however are usually either in the past or the future. This causes fatigue and confusion. Actually speaking, if we can always be in the present, we do not need to meditate.

People are sent by the Masters

ᴥ **Question:** Should we ask people to come for meditation?

Mohanji: I usually do not ask people to come for meditation. When this whole thing happened to me, I told all the Masters, "I am an introverted person. I cannot invite people and deliver talks." Masters said, "That is not your problem. We will bring people to you." So, I always believe that those who are attending my sessions or the Mohanji Foundation group meditations, all over the world, are sent by the Masters. I deliver whatever I can in one go and within their capacity or whatever they can effortlessly carry. Even if we do not meet again in life, I have delivered what I could today.

Tomorrow if they bring a bigger bucket, I will fill it up too. Today they have received according to their capacity. What people get out of this class depends upon what sort of utensil they bring. If someone is inspired by them to attend this class, it is because their *karma* drives them here. Their eligibility brings them here. We have a lot of desires which do not get fulfilled. Whatever we deserve – we will surely get. This is the fundamental principle of life. If something has not come to us, it means we were not eligible for it, but our ego does not allow us to understand and accept this. We can tell people that we had a good experience. I always encourage people to write about their experiences. Tomorrow our mind may say, "Oh, that was my imagination."

You can only start walking from where you are standing right now. Similarly, in spirituality, start walking from the position where you are standing. If you are in grade I, start from there and go to grade II, grade III, ... Your mind may ask you to jump to grade VI or grade VII; there is no shortcut, you must pass from grade I to grade VII, going through all the intermediate grades in between. This can happen through lifetimes, not only in this life. You have done what you could in this life. You may continue in the next life. Let it be. What is the big deal? Start walking from where you stand. *The Guru* is holding your hand. You are walking. *The Guru* cannot walk on your behalf. *The Guru* can secure your walk. He will not allow you to fall. He is just a road sign. He gives directions. You have to do the walking and travelling.

Similarly for your friends, tell them that it helped you. It suited you. They can try if they like. Take it if it suits you. Discard it if it does not suit you. If you approach with equanimity and objectivity, it will stay, but what happens, in reality is, we say, "Oh, my *Guru* is the best and the perfect one!" We sell the *Guru*. Then others get bored and probably suspicious. Friends may turn away thinking you are mad.

Perpetual Meditation

Most of the time, while doing an activity, the mind is elsewhere. I thought to share this important understanding. Cleansing is happening with every Power of Purity meditation. But when you go into the world outside, contamination happens again. If you want to maintain the purity achieved during this meditation, be aware of every thought, word, and action. Whatever you carry within should be pure stuff. What is pure stuff? Something which is not selfish; something which is absolutely selfless. No rituals can bring that purity which you can cultivate from within. Selfless actions elevate man to the highest.

Any kind of *mantras* or *pujas* cannot eradicate *karma* beyond a certain extent. In fact, it can only dilute it a little bit, if at all, but presence of mind in every thought, word, and action can eradicate *karma* or at least nullify its effects. It can liberate you. Rituals can bind you. Certain *pujas* you are stuck with can bind you. Rituals are experiential in the beginning but soon become habits. Though you start a ritual with experience, later on, when it becomes a habit, you cannot live without it! Thus, it binds you. Any habit, whether extremely good or bad, is ultimately a habit because it binds you. How can liberation be possible when you are bound?

Defining *Shaktipat*

🌿 **Question:** Important question: What is *Shaktipat*?

Mohanji: Important answer: Read my earlier book, 'The Power of Purity'.

🌿 **Question:** Seriously Mohanji, I would like a precise answer from you. I have read what you have said earlier. I want to give something more precise to the world. You could do that through me?

Mohanji: Whatever I gave is precise. *Shaktipat* is the infusion of a higher energy into the often-static lower energy planes in existence. The higher energy activates everything that is dormant. It brightens up the cells and rejuvenates the existence. It removes blockages and also changes or upgrades the frequency of the receiver.

🌿 **Question:** What about *Pranapat* and *Shivapat*?

Mohanji: Theory is the same. Intensity is different and effect is different. How does a stone become a deity? When the *prana* or the power of the deity is infused into the stone in a ritualistic manner, the stone becomes God. Likewise, we are stones of existence or at least stone-like, often insensitive and unresponsive. Please do not take me wrong; no arguments, please. Just understand the context, the example, in its light. I am not calling men stones. So, when matter gets life, it becomes an entity. Likewise, through *Shaktipat* we rejuvenate and revitalise the life force, which elevates the receivers. It takes them to higher dimensions. It changes their inner software.

There are different *mantras* and methods for installing different deities, right? Likewise, there are differences in the energy levels and capacities of each person. Each person gets only what he/she can handle. What happens when a twenty-watt bulb gets a thousand-watt infusion? Just for argument's sake, what happens when a normal human womb receives the soul of an *Avatar*? (It is highly unlikely.) The womb will not be able to hold that soul for long. The womb will burst. Of course, an *Avatar* always chooses the right mother to deliver it; the entity that is powerful enough to bring forth an *Avatar*.

I am describing this only for understanding's sake. The natural frequency of an individual is never violated when *Shaktipat* is delivered. This is why outstanding results are recorded all around the world.

All of us have our set of blockages, just as we have our levels of awareness. *Shaktipat* shifts the level of consciousness in an individual, burning the *karmas* that are blocking the way and removing blockages in multiple levels such as physical, emotional, intellectual, spiritual, so on and so forth. Who will be benefited the most from *Shaktipat*? Those who are open and receptive. Receptivity makes all the difference. Some people come with a closed mind and complain that they felt nothing. Such people blame me as ineffective and will never accept that they were not open to receiving the *Shaktipat*. Human nature!

> ❧ **Question:** It is well known that most of the Masters from the *Vedanta* Tradition use *mantras* for initiation. As far as I know, you do not do that, at least not in that way, but you do use *Shaktipat*. Does *Shaktipat* play a similar role or is it somewhat deeper and more direct than that? Can you say a little more about *Shaktipat*?

Shaktipat involves cutting down whatever is stored which you do not need, that which is acquired and stored. This is what we are burning through *Shaktipat*. We are dissolving through *Shaktipat* what you cannot take out yourself or would take a long time for you to clear. This is what *Shaktipat* is all about. The original idea is that *shakti* energy, which is already in human beings, is enhanced and allowed to evolve from the lowest to the top of the head, the highest.

When you enhance *shakti* energy, it burns down so many things which are not wanted. It should not be enhanced when the *karmic* push is strong. When *karma* is strong, that means you have already created an agenda for life. In our path, the *Guru* never ever interferes with one's free will. No manipulation, no forcing. It should be spontaneous. If a person comes to you surrendered, in the sense of, "Please help me," or, "I'm ready," that's the only time the *Guru* helps.

Shivapat involves transferring the same energy or the same power of the *Guru* to the disciple. This is very, very rare because the person has to develop to that level to receive it. A *Guru* also has to be very lucky to get such a disciple because it is very rare and difficult. An African American came and met me in Virginia, USA. I was surprised when he asked me, "Can you deliver *Shivapat* to me?" I said, "I can give you *Shivapat*, but can you take it?"

When it comes to *Shaktipat*, there is no scientific proof and honestly, I am not really bothered about that either. Science is for the brain or intellect. We have to go beyond intellect and logic to understand and experience spirituality. Logic is for the mind. However, spirituality can only be experienced, not known.

Intellectual understanding is a great binding too. It leads to comparisons and conclusions. Spirituality is beyond everything. Science has limitations. The limitations of our brain. Spirituality has no limitations. It cannot have limitations because spiritual experiences are well beyond our brain. They belong to the realm of absolute awareness.

Can mind or intellect understand infinity? Never. Unless we touch the cosmic consciousness, we can never understand infinity. This is the Truth. Let us live that Truth.

In the past Masters used to allow students to walk their path towards enlightenment, giving them subtle guidance. Guidance was limited to 'Not that'. No explanations or descriptions. The disciples searched and searched and would at one point finally reach the Truth. The Truth always remains elusive unless possessed. Once possessed, it never leaves you. This is self-realisation.

In the current scenario, out of deep compassion, we are giving experience instead of guidance. This experience is also a shift in the consciousness of the seeker or disciple. This shift is not a simple thing to give. First of all the Master should be capable of delivering and empowering his disciples. He should be well established in the Truth to deliver experiences of that nature. Secondly, the disciple also should have optimal purity to receive and transfer this priceless treasure.

The shift is for sure. The shift depends on where one stands at that point. The shift has to happen from the present position. The shift allows better understanding and awareness and thus slowly pushes the disciple to complete cleansing and eventual liberation. It may take a few days or years, depending on his/ her *karmic* backlog.

Shaktipat is an expression of deep compassion. The compassion that overflows the consciousness of the Master and his deep urge to deliver experience to his disciples to make them see what he always sees. *Shaktipat* has been practiced from time immemorial. This is a *Shaivic* path. The ascended Masters used to touch the disciple to give them the big shift. This was used only rarely. Now with the big Earth consciousness shift around the corner, Masters are speeding up the process. *Shaktipat* has no side effects because the giver knows exactly how much the taker can receive. This is not an intellectual understanding, but a spiritual awareness. The greatest blockages in the capacity to transfer are ego and intellect

The biggest advantage for the giver is the significant speeding up of his own spiritual evolution because Masters operate through him. Elevation is spontaneous. *Shaktipat* therefore, is no joke. It is a big responsibility. It is a great gift. A priceless gift. People do tons of spiritual practice (*sadhana*) to be able to attain the capacity to deliver *Shaktipat*. Still, without Grace, the *Shaktipat* will erode the hard-earned spiritual strength of the one who delivers it. *Shaktipat* does not work without Grace. Period.

This is why many Saints never allow people to touch their feet or deliver *Shaktipat*. They are afraid that they will lose their own hard-earned powers. This is true. Why are all of our family members of the mission who are empowered to deliver *Shaktipat* only progressing? Grace. That's why.

I am with everyone. I am personally protecting everyone. When I empower someone, a part of me is implanted in them. This helps them to grow and deliver without attachments. This is precious. Without stature, if one delivers *Shaktipat*, he will become empty and dry.

Software Change

ᴥ **Question:** I talk to my colleagues and friends about spirituality. But I get negative answers from them, most of the time. Why is this?

Mohanji: You cannot force anybody. If you are here today, that means you have that particular *vasana* and *karma* in you that brought you here else you could have been watching a movie at the cinema. What made you come here may not be the same as for another person. Constitutions are different. That person may not understand what you are talking about. Do not force anyone. Tell them once, twice, and no more. If they are interested, they will come to you, asking more questions. If not, they are not interested and leave them alone.

My path is a no-nonsense path. This is a path of annihilation. This is not a 'feel good' path. This is the simplest possible path. The reason is that this path is like a child monkey clinging onto the mother monkey. One does not do anything apart from cling to the mother. The mother is the one climbing the tree. *Shaktipat* is the power that is changing you, not only this meditation. This meditation is just words and will work if your mind stays within you and you follow it, without wandering off. If words could really change someone, then everybody would be changing.

The software change that happens within you is also through the *Shaktipat*. The *Shaktipat* burns the unwanted chaff or debris of *karmas*. This clears your path. This works at the physical, mental, intellectual, emotional, spiritual, and all other levels. It works in various planes. Each *Shaktipat* has the potential to make distinct changes in the receiver. It is life-changing. It is a very serious thing. All the people who are empowered to give *Shaktipat* have taken on big responsibilities.

In answer to your question, if somebody does not come, it does not matter. If somebody comes it does matter, because there is a reason for their coming here. We deliver with utmost purity and dedication with no other agenda.

Speeding up the Spiritual Process

ᴥ **Question:** A question about the *Shaktipat* process – is it to correct a deficiency in the body or to transfer energy for the purpose of healing?

Mohanji: The Tradition of *Shaktipat* serves to speed up spiritual process. You can do *sadhana* and achieve. *Shaktipat* aligns the system to receive the energy. The one who gives *Shaktipat* is able to handle much higher energy than a receiver. The bulb is only twenty watts but the electricity line carries much higher energy. The bulb is only tuned to receive twenty watts. When it is transferred, you receive the quantity that you can handle. That way you are not burnt!

It operates at the physical level because it has healing powers. It operates at the emotional level to heal emotions. It also operates at the intellectual level so that you think clearly and your awareness can grow. It shifts your consciousness to a plane of spiritual progress. Your awareness is shifting, which you will know in the days to come. The *Shaktipat* energy works over a period of time, the cleansing is continuously happening, you are evolving. Tomorrow your capacity will change. You will be given *Shaktipat* or will receive *Shaktipat* according to your capacity.

To be capable of giving *Shaktipat*, one needs initiation. The main criteria are that the person should be operating from the level of purity, not from the level of desire (desire to become a *Guru*, desire to have money, etc.). It has to come to you. If you decide, that desire becomes your blockage. When you are pure, the perfection of transfer happens. Receiver and giver are in perfect synchronicity. The receiver will get what he or she deserves.

> ❧ **Question:** I would like to know the most effective method of *Shaktipat*? Who can give *Shaktipat*? What are the criteria? I have also read that one of the signs of a true Datta Master is his ability to change one's consciousness through the delivery of *Shaktipat*. Am I right?

Mohanji: You are right. The most effective *Shaktipat* happens in the presence of a real *Guru*. Many spiritual paths and Masters use the technique of direct transfer of consciousness or at least energy. This not only pertains to the Datta Tradition. Great *Shaktipat* happens in the presence and energy field of a true Master. Introversion, silence of mind, and surrender are a must in a disciple to attain it. An agitated and questioning mind, ego, analysis etc., will close the doors of your receptivity. Just the Master's presence, a look, or even eye contact, let alone touch will deliver what the disciple needs. It is like water flowing spontaneously from a hill to lower land. In the presence of a true Master, *Shaktipat* happens constantly.

There is no need to get stuck with the word '*Shaktipat*'. Call it merger of consciousness, energy transfer, cleansing energy or whatever you like. Words have lesser meaning in this context. The effect is more important. Indeed, the Datta Tradition believes in *Shaktipat* or purification by a Master. A True Master can deliver *Shaktipat* and all those whom he has empowered can also deliver *Shaktipat*. When those initiated take it lightly, lose their purity or misuse and even scandalise it, the *Siddhi* comes back to the Master. Initiation into *Shaktipat* is just like reproducing one's self in another. The initiated has to become the initiator to perform while delivering it. As I said, purity is very important and experimenting and mixing it with other methods does not help. It even takes away the effect of *Shaktipat*.

A true Master can deliver *Shaktipat* wherever the disciples are, irrespective of their physical proximity. *Shaktipat* can be delivered by a true Master through his third eye, a look or touch. In some paths, there are also instances where *Shaktipat*, energy transfers or initiations are done in waist-deep water, near fire or even naked in burial grounds. In another method, depending on the level of blockage of a disciple, Masters deliver *Shaktipat* straight to the *muladhara chakra* or the space between the scrotum and anus to jumpstart the dormant energy. All these can only be done by true Masters, who know exactly what they are doing.

Otherwise, the blockage will get transferred to the one who performs it, which could be quite traumatic and binding. There are many methods. It is only for academic interest that I have mentioned them here. Misuse of such power will take it away from the user. Extreme internal purity is needed to deliver it with perfection. In the Datta Tradition, the compassionate Masters remove many *karmic* blockages from those who approach them through a mere glance, by applying sacred ash on their third eye, by blessing or through touch. It does change the consciousness of the receiver. It removes the blockages, which have existed in their system for lifetimes.

CHAPTER 4:

Selfless service

What is Happiness Worth?

We wake up and run each day, to catch up with life. Precious moments are passing by. Stress is building up. We learn to hate more than we remember to love. We blame others for our own follies and create endless lists of enemies in our lifetime. Truth is often misunderstood while masks are respected. We keep building relationships with masked faces. Time after time, we get disillusioned, as the masks prove false with time.

We wake up and sleep in ignorance. We sleep inside our concepts, fears, phobias, words, and opinions. We wake up every morning, but never wake up in life. Our problems originated within us and not with others, even though we conveniently blame others. This is sheer ignorance. Where are we going wrong? Perhaps it is time to ask yourself this question, "What is real and what is fake? Am I faking at all? What in me is real?" These questions may help you in the days ahead.

We are waking up and running after achievements, compelling commitments, and seeming responsibilities, which are often acquired more out of ignorance than an inherent inevitability. This is especially so in our relationships. Everything in life is relative. Everything is temporary. Everything changes. Our relative responsibility should definitely be based on our actual capacity and not as per the positioning of the mind, based on external comparisons (usually with others, which adds to stress).

Perhaps a few thoughts in this area might help you to streamline your life ahead: Am I overdoing it? Am I truly possessive about people, places and materials? Am I doing what I have to do or what I love to do? What am I chasing? Am I realistic? Am I just emotional and boring to other people? Am I just being judgmental when it is actually none of my business? Am I clear-headed or is my mind embalmed with emotions? Is my expectation becoming taller than Mount Everest, in terms of life and relationships? Am I binding people with expectations? Am I free?

We wake up and enter the 'pre-cast' stables of our own existence. The walking space is predetermined by our own minds. We elbow each other for more space, but the world is a mirror; it only gives you what you chose initially. Then our minds blame others for lesser space within oneself. Ignorance! Non-understanding! We created our own stables. We created our own existence. We created ourselves.

"Am I free?": this is the billion-dollar question. When entering this life, you were. When exiting from this life, you could be. Are you free now? Why? Why not? This is a question or a provocation for self-enquiry. This is a very important one too. One tip which may help your thoughts ahead – If your existence is relative, if your level of external dependency is high, if you do not have an absolute existence, you are not free, irrespective of whether you are spiritual or not, according to you!

What is happiness worth? Happiness is a state of mind. If happiness means inconvenience to others, if our happiness depends on others' possessions, materials or even love, can we be really happy? If our happiness means the torture or death of our fellow beings or species on Earth? If it means denial of something to others? If it means selfish pursuits? If it means ignorance, possessiveness and controlling others for our pleasure?

Does our happiness include self-torture, mind-induced isolation, blame games and depression?

Are you really free from yourself? What is happiness worth? Even if you conquer something on Earth, how long can you hold it? Does true happiness lie in giving unconditionally? Can we actually own anything on Earth? Then what are we chasing all the time from birth till death? What actually makes us happy? Is it our underlying and hidden character traits such as greed, sadism, cruelty, pessimism, insensitivity, etc.? Is it love and compassion and a rich heart?

You need not answer me. Rather, ponder over it and fine-tune yourself. This needs introspection, contemplation, and positive action. It would be worth it if you could make a conscious search within yourself and feel how it is working in your own life! Selfishness, greed, suspicion, doubts, insecurities, and hatred reduce us, our walking space, our peace of mind and even a good peaceful sleep at night. It contaminates our inner space and breeds diseases. It eventually makes us miserable.

Some Food for Thought

It might be worth countering each negative thought with a positive action. When anger happens, do an act of kindness. When hatred happens, get involved in compulsive acts of kindness. When insecurities happen, feed the poor. Take care of children from the streets. When doubts and dilemmas take place in your inner space, feed birds and animals, rescue and rehabilitate them from butchers or cruel owners. When anger is uncontrollable, indulge more and more in supporting forestation, plant trees, nurture them and help them grow. As they grow, your patience will also grow. Compulsive acts of kindness have far-reaching effects.

When you identify a set of people with negative thoughts, words, and actions, collectively buy a space and start a sanctuary for poor, abandoned and rescued animals and birds. Feed them, treat them and nurture them. Play soothing, loving, melodious music to animals, birds, plants and listen to it with them. Feel the unconditional energies of the birds, animals, plants, and nature. Nurture positivity. Remember, hatred binds while love liberates. We may not understand the constitution of another. We need not understand too. Yet, love can certainly work as a bridge between constitutions. Love is the remedy. Love heals. Love nurtures. Love protects. Love rejuvenates. Love expands. Love is all we need.

I am just showing an objective mirror. I am just showing you some road signs. Your choice and freedom to witness or ignore are well respected.

Ammucare

Ammucare was started in 2003 even though the thoughts behind Ammucare began in 2001. I had no plan to set up any charity organisations. This was not part of my conscious agenda. Nature made it happen. Nature nourished it. Nature keeps it alive.

It was one lazy evening. I was sitting on the banks of Ganga in the Himalayas, along with *Swami* Govindananda. We were silent, lost in our world. Suddenly, *Swamiji's* words jerked me back into the present, "What do you do for a living?" As I was enjoying my silence and non-compulsion for any speech, I almost brushed off that question with minimal words. I said, "Business." He was staring into my eyes. He said, "You will be successful in whatever you do, but do something for the children of Mother Earth. You will have eternal peace."

Now I was fully in the present. Those words hooked into me just like the hook pierces the inside of the fish. It was like a thorn that got stuck into my flesh as a task. It ached. It was unclear to me. In fact, everything was unclear. What am I supposed to do? What can I actually do at all? As night fell, we parted. While walking back to the ashram, the words 'children of Mother Earth' kept ringing in my mind.

Ammu passed away on August 23rd, 2000, leaving a big vacuum in my life. As soon as I came back to Dubai after this incident, I lost my job. I got another one and relocated to Oman. I was still under the influence of the deep sorrow and vacuum which Ammu had left behind. I kept pondering... 'children of Mother Earth'... There are many organisations doing so many things for children. Many in the world. The world does not need another one. Should I associate with an existing organisation and do something for children? Nothing seemed complete. There was something missing. I could not find what I was looking for. What exactly was I looking for?

I started communicating about these aspects with my close friends, through a Yahoo group called Mohan's Friends. Many suggested forming a new one. I was wondering how to go about it. I did not have much money in hand. Existence was more or less hand-to-mouth. I did not have enough support to start a new setup. All my friends were working people, like me. Our time was limited. What could we do?

At that time, two realisations happened to me. One was that 'children of Mother Earth' meant all the beings that Mother Earth delivers and nurtures, and human beings are just one species among them. We should take care of all the plants, birds, animals, humans, and the environment. All that is moving and not moving is part of Mother Earth. They are all her children. This was a big eye-opener. The second realisation was that most organisations have vested interests. They amass huge funds and use them for private causes. Some are bound by religions and some are bound by powerful people of society. In both cases, it is not unconditional. I realised that charity that creates dependency is not charity at all.

We should aim to liberate people. Our efforts should nullify guilt and fear in people and eradicate dependency. My thoughts and aim started becoming clear and loud. I decided to form an organisation that needed no membership fees and no compulsory payments of any kind. We decided that nothing should bind anyone to anything. We are born free. We should not allow our minds to imprison us. Thus, Ammucare was launched on the day of *Diwali* in 2003. Many well-wishers said that without any payments, it would not survive. It survived.

Ammucare worked as a platform for expressing compassion. Many people benefited, many people came forward and used this platform. Yet, none were bound to it. Ammucare survived many storms over the years. Many people came and left, as is common with any organisation. Many stayed. All were benefited. Everyone took home fond memories. Everyone's life got enhanced, one way or the other. Ammucare elevated all.

Every year, we distributed blankets to the poor and the old in the slums and suburbs of New Delhi. The joy of giving was felt and inhaled by men, women and children. The joy of purity of action was also inhaled deeply by all. Thus, Ammucare became a global family.

In 2003, ACT Foundation was also registered in Dubai. From providing aid to a burned-down labour camp to the Lebanon war, ACT was one of the most organised and effective charity platforms that ever existed in Dubai. The recession and associated relocation of many people reduced its activity to a minimum level. This was also because all of the ACT members were serving voluntarily. There were no paid staff to run the show.

Today, ACT Foundation has gone global. Everything that ACT does is free of cost. Everything is charity. From the meditations to elevate people's consciousness to physical assistance to the poor and helpless, every act is completely selfless. ACT is operating on various levels. It is touching many souls positively. We say, "At least one positive ACT a day," will help cleanse our accumulated *karma* and make us lighter.

We do not believe in caste, creed, country barriers, community barriers, colour barriers, and any other man-made barriers. We believe in the children of Mother Earth and stand to help the helpless. We are visitors on Earth. Earth is a temporary home for us. We are liable to pay the rent. The only rent possible is the sincere expression of compassion and love and through helping the helpless children of Mother Earth. Unless we pay the rent, a smooth exit from here is impossible.

The soul behind ACT is Ammu, the kind soul that walked the earth for only a few months short of five years. The potential and power of a soul can only be recognised after it leaves its original body, continues to exist, serve and elevate the children of Mother Earth, through many other bodies. Ammu continues to express tangible love and compassion through all the activities of ACT. This is the sure sign of a highly elevated soul.

ACT will grow because you will grow and evolve. ACT has to grow. The world needs ACT. The world needs each one of you. You are ACT. ACT is you. There is no difference. ACT is the external expression of your inherent compassion. ACT is love. You are love. Understand that our true nature is unconditional love. We cannot hurt anyone. Hurting anyone is not our true nature. Our very nature is that of delivering spontaneous assistance without expectations. This is you and this is ACT. ACT your true nature – you will attain everlasting peace.

ACT is not an organisation. It is the third level in the chronology of creation – thought, word, and action. You cannot live without action. Lack of action is equal to death. All living beings ACT. Thus, ACT out compassion. ACT out unconditional love. Do more for the children of Mother Earth. With the support of an organisation or without, be spontaneously kind and compassionate. Express yourself fully and completely. You are expressions of the Lord Almighty, and you are embodiments of kindness and love.

Let us ACT...at least one positive ACT a day. Do it for yourself, not for anyone else. No ACT of compassion is sufficient in today's world. Do more. You will reach the highest bliss state.

The Art of Giving

There is nothing more beautiful than giving. especially, if the giving is totally unconditional. When we give wholeheartedly, our whole heart expands. Our life becomes more meaningful, worthwhile. When we take from someone, we may perhaps be happy for a few minutes or hours, then the happiness erodes and more wants and desires replace that space which was occupied by the momentary happiness a few minutes earlier.

Giving, however, keeps you liberated. Giving keeps you free and abundant. Abundance fills our hearts and it shows. It shines forth in our expressions. Fresh water fills into the well when the bucket removes a quantity of water from it. When we give, Grace fills in. Giving also has its degree variations. When we give the most precious possession for a higher cause, it becomes a challenge to our existence. If we survive that challenge and if we perform the act of giving, our consciousness shifts. Our awareness level changes. We achieve beautiful states of existence.

Many people have good hearts and the attitude of service in them. Spiritual liberation depends on how one expresses that in daily life. Some spontaneously give money for a good cause and forget it. This is a passive good man. He is reasonably indifferent. Some collect materials or money and help the needy. This man is further evolved. Some people stay through until the problem is solved. They are still higher in their evolution of selflessness. Some take another step by preventing a recurrence of the same calamity in the victim's life. These are still closer to liberation.

So, it would be a good idea to look at yourself and understand your method of operation in such situations. Look within. Only you can change yourself.

Now, consider also one important point: When you crave to express your kindness, such as feeding the poor, it becomes the responsibility of nature to provide you with the poor and hungry. Look at it from another angle – In order to satisfy our wish, or to achieve our happiness, we need an object that suffers. So, those who walk the path of *karma* yoga (selfless service) should understand this concept very well. We should help the helpless, no doubt.

However, an act of kindness should be a bridge to liberation for both the giver and receiver. This means, an act of charity should be aimed at creating self-sufficiency in the receiver. The more self-sufficient the receiver is, the more liberated you are from him. The one who gives and the ones who receive are interdependent. One does not exist without the other.

So, our aim, our prayer should be, "*Lokah Samastah Sukhino Bhavanthu*. Let everyone be self-sufficient. With my act of charity, may the receiver be empowered to lead his life on his own. Let me not create dependency in those to whom we give. Let me stay liberated and let those who receive from me stay liberated. Each act of charity may attain completion this way. Let my life be complete, too."

This is the art of giving. Giving should lead to completion and liberation. Giving should automatically lead us to shedding and liberation. Liberation is the ultimate aim. Giving without awareness breeds dependency. We create takers. We create dependents. This binds us. This binds them to us. So, whenever you give, do it with awareness. Do give, but, give only with awareness. Never create dependency.

Lastly, I am very happy to see the world responding to my call for giving food to the poor and hungry. The purpose is to feel the bliss of giving.

This means, as far as possible, do it yourself along with your family. Giving money away to orphanages or poor homes is secondary. Do it that way, if you cannot do it yourself. The first preference should be to do it yourself. This can help create a shift in awareness. The bliss of giving that you will experience yourself, when you serve wholeheartedly, can make a constitutional shift within. If you prepare food yourself and give, it is even more blissful. If you chant *mantras* while cooking, the food becomes an offering to the Lord Almighty. You can create higher and higher dimensions to your art of giving.

Let children also enjoy the bliss of giving. Tell them that the receiver is extending us a favour by taking food from us. The receivers are helping us to attain the bliss of giving. They are also an integral part of our existence. They are also representing the eternal *Guru* principle. They are helping us experience bliss and this is a first-hand experience for yourself. Bless them, have gratitude towards them for that.

Support Need Not Greed

❧ **Question:** If we are too kind and compassionate, we will lose ourselves. Yet, we are supposed to be selfless. Where is the ideal line between serving others and pursuing one's own goals?

Mohanji: It is very simple. Firstly, you have to take care of yourself. Because you have taken birth to enjoy this existence. By denying everything you cannot move forward. But while living, if you have an attitude of kindness, an attitude of compassion, that is selflessness. It is not denying any of the things which you would probably want. Like food, clothing, your house, whatever you want to enjoy. Not as per the greed, but as per the need. The world does not expect you to starve and feed another person. Like they say in the aeroplane, "Please put the [oxygen] mask on your face, before helping other people." Similarly, you should be happy first because you can help other people only when you are happy.

You should not expand your conditions for happiness, For e.g. "I need one million dollars more than what I already have to be happy," etc. Then, it will be difficult to serve other people. While being satisfied with what you have, if you enjoy life and at the same time express compassion and kindness, and not hurt anybody through thought, word, or action, you are selfless.

Charity or selflessness is not just about spending money on somebody. For e.g., if a child is crying and you put your arm around the child and say, "Don't worry, I'm with you.", that is a selfless expression of compassion. It is the opposite of indifference. Or, you've had a good meal, you are very happy; you see a very old, poor woman who has had no food for the last two days and you buy that person a piece of bread. That is selflessness. It is the attitude that you will exist in a hundred per cent state of non-violence – in thought, word, and action. If you do that, you will automatically raise your consciousness to the higher level. There cannot be any greed. Greed or selfishness cannot happen.

Wake Up, Get Up and ACT NOW!

Yesterday afternoon, I was speaking at a function organised by 'Stop Acid Attacks' to bring awareness to the tragedy of acid attacks which are endured mostly by women.

I spoke about the importance of higher awareness, beyond our sundry emotions and differences. Emotions are momentary. They wreak havoc, and then pass. The resulting devastations and wounds are difficult to heal. Society needs higher awareness. These victims do not need any sympathy from anyone. They just need a helping hand to feel oneness with society. Nobody is a victim if they choose not to be one. Nobody is below anyone. There are none higher or lower in this world.

When an act of aggression takes place that creates inconvenience to society, a laser-sharp judiciary system should ensure prompt justice. A corresponding support system should ensure rehabilitation. The rest will be managed by itself.

Consider this, my beloveds. We are living in a society of extreme dualities. Many kinds and types of cruelty take place here each moment – against people, animals, birds and the environment. We should feel. There is no point in feeling and forgetting. Also, it is sheer escapism to be indifferent. When we have the strength and ability to do so, we should do something about it, and we can.

At the time of our death, who will care to consider how many parties and pompous dinners we attended, which required the massacre of hundreds of animals for our paltry sensory pleasures? We are often living a life of utter insensitivity and abandon. We are taking our own life and all that it has offered to us for granted. What are we giving back to Mother Earth? It is time to consider. Especially now, when time has accelerated. Time has become faster and more precious. We are racing against time. Can you look at those who suffer? Are you able to see these boys and girls who have suffered because of the emotions of another human being?

Anger is clearly a weakness. Anger hurts oneself and others. Those who are angry must be considered ill. Treat them with the balm of love. Help them to understand their weaknesses. When the momentary rage wanes off, most of them regret, and often live in regret their whole lives. Rage should be countered by awareness. Rage happens out of emotions, non-understanding of higher Truth and often unfulfilled expectations. It is important to bring society to the operational level of clean awareness, which arises from intellect and beyond. When rage happens, intellect is shut down. Regrets essentially take place.

I met the parents of the young girl (whom the press called *Nirbhaya*) who was raped and killed in New Delhi. She was torn to pieces by five drunken men in a running bus. Later, they were arrested, put behind bars and are expecting their final court verdict soon.[12] The girl's parents have not recovered as yet. They are still mourning. Nothing can replace their loss. I told them that I do understand the pain of losing our dear ones. I have experienced it myself and I am with them.

This is a wake-up call. Wake up before pain hits you. Wake up before insensitivity and *tamas* lure society like cancer. We should get up and ACT. ACT now. Never be disconnected. Don't hide inside your comfort zones and believe that everything is alright. A life of inertia always meets up with compelling tragedies. Beware.

I sincerely suggest to all those who are in India, to kindly support the various causes taken up by Ammucare. Those living in other countries may support the various causes taken up

---

[12] Editor's note: This was written on 27th October 2013

by ACT Foundation. Of course, you are definitely free to act upon any causes that are closer to your location too. If you wish to involve Ammucare or ACT in any of those, please connect with their respective officials.

We shall make good use of our opportunities to voice our opinions and speak out as best as we can. Even if our voice gets drowned in the roar of the drunken parties of society's negative elements that make everyone feel that everything is fine, we shall certainly keep trying our very best. If we can bring a smile to the faces of a few people, we will. We shall not miss any opportunity. This is our elevation too.

When we leave this body, we can smile and leave, with the belief that the days we spent here benefited many. We lived our life well. We were not selfish or self-centred. We made friends and united kindhearted people over noble causes. The days that we spent here were well worth it. We used all our time and energy to make the space around us a better place for the people, birds, and animals.

It does not matter how much we were able to do. What matters is whether we did our very best or not. Pleasure is in giving. Pleasure is in seeing the smile on many faces. Pleasure is in selflessness. The beauty of life gets enhanced when we spread the fragrance of hope and kindness to a thousand more souls around us. We are the world. Only we can bring about change within us and outside of us.

Help the helpless. Feed the poor and the hungry. It will make you rich inside. True richness is our inner richness which transcends time and space. It will make your life and beyond worthwhile. Do not hesitate. This is an opportunity. This is a good chance to elevate your consciousness. ACT is you. You are ACT.

Section 5:

...TO YOURSELF – THE SHIVA WITHIN YOU

~~~~~~~~

"There is no Right or Wrong.
There is no Good or Bad.
There is no High or Low.
There is no Night or Day.
There is no Happiness or Sorrow.
There is no Activity.
There is no Duality.
There is no Beginning.
There is no End.
There is Shiva."

CHAPTER 1:

Back to Basics

L ook at yourself. Are you taking your life more seriously than you should? Are you becoming more and more rigid and inflexible as time flows? Is it worth it? Have you missed some of life's most important experiences because of your fears and phobias, your binding and conditionings, or even others' words based on their set of fears and phobias? Are you a slave of your mind or habits? Is constant postponement bothering you, destroying you from within, and eroding your self-esteem?

Just remember, you have very limited time on Earth. It is only a matter of time before you too exit from this scene on Earth, at least temporarily. Irrespective of whether you believe in reincarnation or not, death is for sure – sooner or later. Even if you re-enter this drama at some other point in time and space, you may not remember the previous role you played at all, in the way that you are currently ignorant about the lives you lived in the past. So, once again, is this over-acted seriousness worth it? Is this anger, anxiety, fear, hatred, inflexibility, and insecurity worth it? It is high time you contemplate this. It is high time you looked at yourself, considered yourself, loved yourself, and cared too.

When was the last time you laughed whole-heartedly, sincerely? It is time! Have you lost your childhood or the wonder-fuelled child in you? Have you lost your laughter? When was the last time you sincerely and guiltlessly appreciated a thing of beauty? When was the last time you sincerely complimented your spouse or children? When was the last time you consciously decided to abandon your nagging guilt as a useless emotion and get on with life, honestly speaking? When was the last time you chose to be yourself?

Do you feel that you control or can control others' lives? If yes, first try controlling yourself– your mind– before you attempt to control others. Is your guilt based on sexuality? Yes? Why? Isn't sexuality an integral part of the life of every species? Sexuality is an instinct provided to sustain the species. Why should you be guilty about sex at all? Have you considered this thought ever? Guilt binds man as much as any other habits and conditionings do. Awareness and understanding truly liberate man from all kinds of bindings.

Are fears of any kind necessary at all? Why? What is there to be afraid of? Are you afraid of yourself? Are you afraid of society, name, fame, money, and position? Are you rebelling? Against whom? Are your expressions constant acts of ignorance or helplessness? Can't you choose to grow beyond it? Do you consider food and sex as recreation, getaway, or escape? Do any addictions bind you at all, however innocent they may seem to be? Are you a slave to anything? Does it help at all? I believe it is time we considered our lives differently, as time does not stand still for anyone.

Are you passively accepting or suffering the company of negative people, who instil fears, phobias, and hatred in you? Do they influence your thought process and make you ridicule, criticise and condemn Gods, *Gurus*, and even your parents? Are you afraid to leave the company of such people? Are you mechanically, almost helplessly acting on their command, suggestion, or manipulations? Why? It is time to think. You have the full right to choose good friends, those who bring brightness, sunshine, and love into your life. You have the right to choose love and freedom, as much as you have the right to choose hatred and further bondage. Remember, you are creating your realities and your inevitable destiny.

Have you ever considered contributing something creatively for the less privileged children of Mother Earth? Have you consciously decided to make your existence on Earth more meaningful than the clockwork life comparable to that of animals or a life bound by compelling habits?

Have you ever considered that war and peace happen in our minds first, before they get manifested in the world outside? Have you ever considered with gratefulness that you have three square meals a day and numerous snacks in-between, and have you ever really thought about the hungry, dying, and deprived children elsewhere before you waste precious food and water? Have you ever considered that the grains that you wasted had the potential to become a plant and produce many more grains of its kind? If not, it is time to consider. Better late than never.

We usually lead an unconscious existence. We live mechanically; just a clockwork life. We repeat our inherited constitution quite mechanically and even become proud of it. We boast upon others' words, wealth, or 'borrowed feathers'! We boast about our inherited character or conditionings. Is it worth it? What are we proud of? Is there anything to be proud of at all, which is not temporary in our life? It is time we think about ourselves before we think negatively about others. Is it because of others that we are suffering, or is it something (a negative trait or tragic flaw) in us, which repeatedly brings such people and situations into our lives, that we are tired of? It is time to consider this carefully.

When was the last time that you experienced and expressed sincere and wholehearted faith towards yourself, your *Guru*, and ultimately God? What is the use of entertaining conditional faith at all? Are you not wasting the precious moments of our existence on Earth by being unreal? Time to think! When was the last time you broke your patterns consciously? When did you consider yourself as infinite – at least potential-wise? When was the last time you explored yourself and reinvented yourself? When was the last time you stopped complaining about something and decided that you had the courage, power, and strength to change that matter that was bothering you?

When was the last time you consciously realised that we are eternal creation machines and create our destiny? When was the last time you paid attention to who or what is running this body, fuelling our thoughts, and making us experience various thoughts, words, situations, and events? It is time. I strongly feel that it is time we started looking at ourselves. Let us judge others only after we have understood ourself fully. If we have not understood ourselves fully, how can we understand another at all? How can we ever decide the walking space of others at all? We have no right to put others in frames, nor do we have any right to treat another being – not just human – with contempt.

I am sure we have always been discontented with life in general or at least many things in life. We have not been happy about others either. We constantly complain. This is because we usually compare our situation with others. When was the last time you counted your merits rather than your defects? When was the last time you considered, with gratefulness, that your conscious mind does not control most of your vital functions such as your heartbeat, circulation, digestion, and secretions? When was the last time you considered, with gratefulness, that your conscious mind does not, thankfully, control the most critical functions of your own body? Did you ever consider not abusing your body? It is time to think.

When was the last time you recognised, with gratitude, that this was the precious body of a live animal or bird, which sacrificed itself to give you sensory satisfaction before you devoured its flesh? When was the last time you decided not to postpone a vital action, breaking the cage of your conditioned mind? When was the last time you kept your promises? Primarily, you are not answerable to anyone except your own conscience. When was the last time you broke your pattern of delaying actions? When was the last time you ever considered that your mind is blocking your progress and nobody else can be blamed for it?

When was the last time you dared to act and you believed in what you did, irrespective of the fear of possible consequences, others' words, and further actions? When was the last time you trusted your own experience rather than others' words and felt proud about it? Why are you afraid to leave your comfort zones? Isn't the whole world your arena? Why are you locking, confining yourself to one space at all? Why are you so afraid to confront your fears? What exactly is there to lose, as death is inevitable in everyone's existence?

Have you ever considered that none else but you yourself are blocking your path towards a successful existence? Isn't your ego getting in our way? Why are you disappointed? Why are you depressed? Why are you angry? Why do you hate and abuse yourself and others? Why do you lie, cheat and contaminate your own inner space? Why do you make yourself helpless? Do you believe or feel that your own inner space is the temple of your God? It is time to contemplate that. Can you contaminate your own inner space, the temple where God resides?

When was the last time when instead of asking, requesting, or begging for something from God or *Guru*, you just uttered from deep within, "Thank you for everything"? When was the last time you asked God or the *Guru*, "What can I do for you?" instead of "What are you going to give me?" A true *Guru* or God will need nothing from you. When was the last time you honestly said, "I am happy"? When was the last time you decided to be real and not pretend to be what you are not? When was the last time that you discarded ownership of your actions, but acted sincerely and said with conviction, "Lord, let your will be done. Not mine," and whole-heartedly embraced the fruits of action, whether good or bad? When was the last time you whole-heartedly accepted the realities of life without resistance?

When was the last time you looked at yourself in the mirror and uttered with absolute sincerity, "I love you," and "You are truly wonderful"? When was the last time you felt grateful to be alive? When was the last time you touched the 'skin' of Mother Earth and gratefully uttered, "Thank you"? When was the last time you touched the leaves of the plants in your house and uttered with deep love, "I love you; we are closely related"? When was the last time you consciously discarded negative thoughts and swapped them with overwhelming optimism and love?

When was the last time you truly loved someone without expecting love in return? When was the last time you could bring a smile and hope to a stranger's face? When was the last time you looked into the eyes of your teacher, *Guru,* and said, "I am not separate from you, you and I are one"? When was the last time you embraced honesty and selflessness wholeheartedly? When was the last time you considered, "How many more years will this body walk the Earth"?

Did you consider, "These people around me will also disappear sooner or later, forever"? Did you also consider, "Now is the only time to express unconditional love, whole-heartedly, sincerely, and gratefully"? Did you ever consider that you came empty-handed and will leave empty-handed? Did you consider that all that you need is a bit of shelter, clothes, and food? What else can you use?

What is permanent? We own nothing on Earth! Everything will pass away. Have you considered it? It is time. It is time! Even this one will pass away. I own nothing. All I have, I give you. I keep nothing for myself. I am fluid. I represent the Consciousness that you came from. My love for you is complete. I embrace you as myself. I am indivisible. I am Yourself. I love myself, and myself is you.

CHAPTER 2:

Beingness

Be Here, Now

Whenever you go anywhere, start feeling it. Feel the place, feel the location, feel the whole programme. That is the way to remove things from your system. Secondly, however deep you are able to let go, that much will go. We are talking about lifetimes of storage. We are talking about centuries of stored data, not just from this lifetime. So don't underestimate with, "Oh, I did so many things in the last forty years, it will all go." It is not so. Because whatever you have carried forward, that is what's manifesting now. Whatever you could not fulfil before, that is manifesting now.

We are addressing something very deep, so maintain that seriousness. Do things with application, with the intent of letting go, "Let this go out of my system", and becoming empty and pure. If that is not possible, it will be a wasted exercise. Your result will depend on how much you are able to let go. If you are not able to let go, forget this lifetime. Even the character traits, some kind of anger, some like and dislike, all this matter will stay if you are not able to let it go. It will continue through lifetimes. That is why we carry character traits through lifetimes.

Be here now. 'Be' means, be yourself. Be what you are. Be the essence, not what you see physically. If they ask you who you are, you may say your name or say this is my place or these are my parents, or this is my qualification. These are all external, and some of them also change with time. People get married, then one person becomes a husband and another person becomes a wife. When one person leaves, they again become an individual. Likewise, there are various combinations happening in our lives at every point in time.

That is not being, that is not being what you are. That is not your essence. Your essence is your naked entity, your basic entity which is totally, completely detached from the whole exercise, the whole drama. That is what you are. 'Being-ness' is being one with that entity that is permanent. Understand that clearly. Being one with the entity which is permanent in your system. Not your changing emotions, not your changing mindset, character, anything which is changing, and which is not you. This is part of the doing. So 'Be' means 'Be that which is permanent'. This is your essence. Be one with the essence. Be one with permanence.

To be, you need to feel. If you want to understand what being-ness is, or how to be, you need to feel. Again, 'feeling' is introversion. You should introspect. To feel, you need to feel within. You can feel an external thing, but again, the feeling is happening inside you. You may feel the wind, but how do you know the wind? The translation of that feeling happens inside you. Feel everything. Feel life. It is a huge difference.

Today I wrote 'Romance life, it is worth it'. Why did I say that? If you romance another person and they go away, you will be sad. But if you romance life, your whole life will be full of romance. This is the point. For that, you need to feel. Feeling is very important. So, this is 'be'. Silence is an aspect of being-ness. Automatically you will become silent. Because when you start feeling, you may even close your eyes, you will feel and you will be silent. Silence is part of the process. Silence is a spontaneous expression when you start feeling. The more you feel, the more silent you become. Not physical silence – silence because you don't have any physical expression. Silence because you are not pushed into talking.

That is the beauty of silence. That is real silence. Otherwise, if you are just silent for the sake of silence of the mouth, it is probably good for other people, but it does not make much difference in your psyche. If you keep quiet, other people are happy but it may not change anything within you. Things should change within you. If things change within you, then you need to be silent within, empty within. This is all part of 'be'. This is very important to remember, be here, now. These three words are the core of this process. It needs a hundred per cent total application to make a difference in your life, and you can make it happen. This is in your control. This you can be.

Otherwise, you are always pushing ahead. We are sitting here, but we are thinking about the future. We want to be something else. You cannot be something or somebody else. All the other people are already taken. You can only be you. Now you have to take another birth to be somebody else. Again, the ingredients are all the same. It is like global brands that change the box from time to time, to bring freshness. In this way, you are changing your life. You are bringing a new life for freshness, but the ingredient is the same! Otherwise, you wouldn't buy, right? This is the process.

So, 'be' is very important, then 'here'. 'Here' means there is a location for your expression. You need to have a location, you need to have a space, and that space is important. While here, if your mind is elsewhere, it is a useless exercise. When you are here, at this location, be here in this place Not ninety nine per cent, it is not good enough. Be here a hundred per cent. This location, this place, this is your only reality right now. There is another location outside this place, but that is not your reality. It is somebody else's reality. Maybe somebody else is there. But as far as you are concerned, this is your only reality. So be here, this location, this space.

Then the time, now. What is now? This moment. This moment is your only reality. The next moment we have not seen, we do not know. The next hour we do not know. The next day we do not know. We are anticipating, yesterday was like this, so tomorrow might be like this. But on the whole, like if there is more rain, it can change things. It is as simple as that. We are trying to predict and we are trying to control the factors which are not in our control. It gives pain. So we have to go with the flow. We have to flow with time.

Time is very important. Now is important, this time is your real time. Use it well. How do you use it well? When you are objective. When you are clear. When you have clarity, when you have objectivity, you are using the time well. If you are subjective, if you do not have clarity, life will be murky. How do you gain clarity? When you detach. When you see from the outside, you have a clear picture. When you are inside, you do not know what is happening. This is the difference between clarity and lack of clarity.

Involvement removes clarity sometimes. But application is not involvement. If you are deeply involved in something with full concentration, when you are in the now, this is ok. But involving emotionally in something removes the clarity. When the clarity is removed, life is purposeless. Thus goes life. Most people who work or live do not have a clear purpose. Why? Because they live a routine life. They live through life. So be here, now. 'Be' means this is you; be in this space, in this time.

Use this time to introspect, to ask yourself, "Is this me? Am I anxiety, is this anxiety me? I'm having fears. Are these fears me or have I acquired them?" You are having jealousy, hatred, or suspicion, doubt, "Are all these me? Or mine?" Mine is also not a good idea. The more you own, the heavier you become. So, "Is this me or is this mine?" If you ask this question clearly, you will understand that either you have acquired all these from outside, or you have created them out of illusion or non-understanding. You created a mountain through non-understanding, and also through lack of clarity.

Many, many incidents happen because we respond or react emotionally, impulsively. But the moment we think and respond, the problem will not be there. Speculation is the reason for many problems. If we don't know something, we speculate. For example, I did not get a call from X. I was expecting a call, she did not call me. Then, what do I feel? Something is not right. Then again I start imagining. If the call does not come the next day as well, it becomes more. Sometimes my ego will not permit a call back to check if everything is in order. So, the third day the call does not happen, then I may start creating gossip. Then, from the mind, distanching happens.

This is how we are creating life. This is also how we are creating destiny. The more emotions we create, the more intense destiny becomes. The more lives we will take. Therefore, allow life to flow, without many emotions. This is very simple. Those who do not use emotions casually are safe.

Live Today, Love Today!

❧ **Question:** It feels like time is rushing past, like I'm always on the go. I have too much to do and so much on my mind. I am also witnessing a wide array of emotions– up, down, up, down, like a rollercoaster. What does it mean really to live fully in the present?

Mohanji: Today. This moment. That is all we have. This moment is our property. We are custodians of this moment. We cannot own anything. We can only use this moment. We can live this moment using our intellect or our emotions. If we use our intellect, we save ourselves from further agonies. If we use this moment emotionally, we invite further agonies associated with emotions. We do not know our tomorrows. What will happen? Who knows? We assume that everything will be fine. We assume that all the people whom we love will be with us. We assume everything. Does our assumption prove right all the time?

So, live today. Love today. Live this moment to the fullest. Live this moment without guilt, fear or anxiety. Live this moment fully, with the clear understanding that we do not own our morrows. The sun is shining today. The dewdrops are glittering. nature is beautiful. Enjoy it today. Do not sit inside the walls of your own mind, nurturing your fears, anxieties and sad thoughts. Get out of your cage and enjoy nature today, just like an innocent child. Inhale the fragrance of the flowers in the garden. Sing with the birds. Relish the love and protection of the mighty trees. Feel the grandeur of the mountains. Adopt the persistence of the waves of the oceans. Enjoy the soothing love of the caressing moonlight. Be blissful with Nature and feel your blessings. Divinity is in its full regalia, all around you. Look around. Feel. Live today and love today.

Maybe what we did today hurt someone unintentionally. We are human. We make mistakes. Correct it, apologise and move on. Whether the other person accepted your apology at that point in time or not, does not matter. You apologise sincerely and you move on. Others will understand you and follow your sincere love sooner or later. Expectation leads to sorrow. Never expect. Never mind. Do not postpone a word or an action. Live today and love today.

Maybe my moves were all wrong today. I could not perform well today. It does not matter. When you understand and recognise the wrong moves you made, you also recognise what is right. Understanding is important. Corrective steps are spontaneous. Remember, life is all about the experiences. Everything is about experiences. Nothing else but experiences. Enjoy each experience without guilt.

425

Never blame yourself. You are a human being. Human beings tend to err. A child falls many times before it learns to walk. It must keep trying, ignoring the falls, otherwise, it will never walk. A child is ignorant that society considers falls as failures. It is blissfully unaware of that. A small child fortunately, remains unconditioned by society till it reaches a few years on Earth. If we ignore consciously, or if we are unconsciously ignorant that the failures of life are unacceptable to society, life is smooth. Ignoring failures with full awareness is a beautiful state indeed.

Success and failure are part of our existence. Accept your mistakes gracefully and walk boldly towards the next opportunity to test your mettle once again. Nobody is ever a failure. The other side of success is failure. Failure leads to success, just like pride over success, and the associated ego, definitely leads to failure. So, live your failure and success with ease today, love it today.

Maybe I feel sick today. I will be fine tomorrow. Maybe I overindulged in food today. No problem, be careful tomorrow. Accept today as it is. Do not judge or criticise.

Live today, Love today. We never know about our tomorrows.

Soul as the Witness

♣ **Question:** How to let the past go?

Mohanji: Through objective awareness. Be aware of the present which should have nothing to do with the past. The past will leave its impressions on the present. Be aware of that too. When you become constantly aware of your present thoughts, words and actions and handle the present objectively, you are always in a meditative state. This will release the past from the present.

🌿 **Question:** Is the soul a perpetual witness?

Mohanji: Only in the human context, we can consider this so. This is because we have many other layers of witness-hood to consider. The mind, ego, intellect etc. In that context, we can consider the soul as the final witness. But, in the absolute sense, the soul has nothing to witness. Soul is everything. The witness, the witnessed and the object. Neither is the soul anything. The soul has no agenda. The soul is always free.

Operating in Witness Mode

Soul is the petrol of your car. It has no particular preferences of destination. The soul's sole aim is perhaps only to get back home at the earliest. The soul's home is the Supreme Soul, the father or ParaBrahma. The soul aids all experiences. It aids each thought, word and action (the three levels of creation) and remains neutral everywhere. It never interferes in any of our transactions. The mind along with senses weaves dreams and wishes. The soul helps it. Our character is carried over through many lives. It has evolved over time and space. We do not know that or understand that fully from our current level because we cannot see our past lives and future lives. We are actually present-oriented. All the traits that man displays have been brought forward. Experiences are also chosen subconsciously. So, we cannot blame another for what is happening to us, even though we conveniently, ignorantly do that. The soul can never be contaminated. It is part of the Supreme Soul, ever pure and ever glowing. The soul carries the big bag of our *samskaras* and *karmas*, life after life. People behave as per their level of consciousness. The broad pattern is mentioned above. From the base barbaric to the level of an Avatar – the entire humankind lies somewhere in-between.

We are always responsible. Our mind is responsible. Every thought, word and action is responsible. We create our own destiny. Emotions can be checked by shifting to the witness mode. By witnessing ourselves getting angry, sad, anxious etc., we successfully detach from that emotion. This liberates us. Anger, hatred, ego, etc. can be effectively brought into control by witnessing. We see ourselves getting angry etc. This also makes us familiar with using our intellect more than emotions. This gives us a good deal of immunity from our regular sorrow and happiness. Thus, being in witness mode and surrendering all ownership to Masters or God will deliver and free you from many afflictions, affectations or despair.

The intellectual approach is balanced and unemotional. For example, someone scolds you and your emotional reaction almost always brings forth regrets in the future. Doubts are also part of the insecurities that we carry. Some are rooted in past experiences, or the impressions of past experiences that we carry. The more we use our intellect for tackling situations, the more we always maintain our poise and balance. Postponement is *tamas* (inertia). Not having the energy to act upon what we believe in is also *tamas*. Even when emotions overflow, if we can observe it as an outside entity, it is intellect at work. We could call it the witness state. This helps us to stay away from the emotional baggage of any situation.

Accept and Observe Yourself

Accept yourself the way you are. Do not try to change anything. We are fine the way we are. Do not compare with another. There is no problem in treating God as your friend. God is your soul. You can say anything to your soul. As long as you do not entertain guilt or anxiety, it is fine. Understand that all situations of life are created by ourselves, in the past. Our *karma* is our driving force. *Karma* is created through thought, word, and action, attached to emotions. So, we create our own happiness and suffering. Just accept that. Talk to God as a God within yourself. Talk to yourself. Observe yourself. To get rid of anything, the best way is to watch it like an outsider. Sooner or later, it will fall off.

Watch, observe your conditionings. Be a constant witness. Never censor or judge yourself. Watch. Detach. You will liberate yourself for sure. It is a process. Patience is the key.

Do Not Worry

Phases of confusion happen in everybody's life. This is not permanent. Turbulence brings forth calmness. So, watch everything that is happening in your inner space. Do not participate in it. Just witness as if you have nothing to do with it. Inner space or mind should be protected. Negativities grow like weeds without your nurturing them. So, like a good gardener, keep your inner garden clean and tidy. When confusion happens, accept it. Say, "So what? This is also part of my constitution." Thus, when you start accepting the good and the bad, it (the emotions, anxieties, fears etc.) will all start to get cleansed by itself.

Observe Yourself

Blockages will evaporate by themselves when subtlety increases. When we move from the gross body, gross mind, gross intellect and gross ego to the *pranic* layer itself, shifts happen. When we move from the pranic layer to subtler layers, further releases happen. In order to know what your blockages are, it is very simple. Just look at what irritates you. Just look at your own daily expectations and anxieties. Just watch yourself. Observe yourself. You will know. Observing one's own thoughts, words and action releases most of the blockages, because we come to terms with ourselves. You can take care of anger and ego in the same way too. Observing yourself as a witness keeps your conscious mind firmly in the present. This is the best possible meditation.

Shaking Hands With Our Reality

Our reality is absolutely perfect for us. First is shaking hands with our reality. It is not a coincidence that you are at a place at a particular time, at a particular juncture, with the particular intellect and the particular body. This is not coincidence and it was all supposed to happen. Everything is pre-decided. So now what you do with that system, infrastructure and the available incidents is what is more important. Do you get the point? It is nothing to be scared about. It is just to operate in the present.

Firstly, acceptance, as I said before. Secondly, non-resistance to a situation, i.e., if some food you never ordered has come to you, just accept it as it is. This is not passive acceptance, it is not being a doormat. There is a difference. Being a doormat is more the feeling of being a victim. Non-resistance is like, "This is the situation today. Let me go through it, so that I get empowered." There is no friction or resistance within. This empowers you. You are stronger when the dissipation of energy is less and resistance is less. We are a body. The body has a constitution and the consciousness. Accept that.

Whatever it is, it is fine. Never compare. Somebody else has a better body. Arnold [Schwarzenegger- Ed] may have more muscles and a better body than me. We can never be satisfied if we compare like this. We always look at somebody who is better than us, in our mind. We never look at somebody lower than us and say, "I am better than him! When we stop comparing and accept ourselves as we are, there begins liberation. Less friction and resistance leads to liberation. Feeling that I did not get what I deserve is wrong, because again, we are comparing. The *Dharma* of existence is that everyone gets what they deserve and not what they desire."

Increasing Awareness is the Solution

⚜ **Question:** Mohanji, I know that you have not accumulated wealth in this life and that you prefer to spend it in support of the poor and helpless. Is there anything worth nurturing in this life, apart from spirituality?

Mohanji: Nothing is worth nurturing in this life apart from awareness. Even spirituality is not worth nurturing. Spirituality is a state, which is natural and is also an ingredient of our existence. If spirituality becomes repetitive and ritualistic, it loses its purpose. Spirituality usually intensifies and dilutes as per the circumstances and necessity. Spirituality happens to all, sooner or later, because it is related to spirit, the same energy that runs our life! Whether we nurture it or not, it will happen.

Usually, people access spirituality only when helplessness is at its peak. When there is nowhere else to go, we turn to God. This is human nature. There is nothing worth nurturing external to us. We will have to leave everything behind when we depart, including wealth and relationships.

Awareness is the only aspect within us that is worth nurturing. The awareness that we nurture grows with us, through lifetimes. It is worth nurturing. Awareness is our connectivity into consciousness, the ability to 'plug in' at will. Just like we grew as students from grade to grade, year by year, we grow in aware-ness through life times. As awareness grows, higher conscious-ness becomes accessible. It has always been available, but until we have the faculty to access the higher consciousness, we can-not enjoy it.

Awareness is the path that helps us reach higher realms of consciousness. In order to cross the mighty ocean of duality and reach the realm of non-dual consciousness, we need the help of higher awareness. It is worth investing in. It is the only thing worth investing in and it is purely an internal matter. Nothing external. Even your external *Guru* can only direct you to your internal *Guru*. *Guru* helps to remove your ignorance or *Maya*, by showing the light of wisdom. But, it is your increased awareness that makes you realise who you actually are!

꽃 **Question:** What practice helps develop higher aware-ness?

Mohanji: Witness-hood (*sakshi bhav*). Being in the now.

Connect to my eyes. Also, watch yourself consciously. When we are totally external, looking at the outside world for peace and happiness within, when we are too dependent on the out-side world, pain and disappointment take place. Watch your-self. Until you watch yourself consciously, you cannot start receiving through watching my eyes too. Have faith. Be opti-mistic. Keep connecting to yourself, without judging and criti-cising yourself. Life is a process. It is never stagnant if you allow it to flow. Only the mind has the tendency to become stagnant. Be aware of that.

Increasing your awareness is the solution. Watch your thoughts, words and actions consciously and be aware of your strengths and weaknesses. Do practice the Power of Purity meditation everyday and thus do cleansing in the deeper lev-els. See how it works. Remember, only you can change yourself. Your life is based on your free will.

✺ **Question:** What is real wealth?

Mohanji: That which can be carried with you when you die. That wealth is awareness. Only awareness. This is why meditation is important. Contemplation on Truth is important. Right understanding is important. Death cannot remove awareness from you. Awareness travels with the soul along with other *samskaras* and unfulfilled desires, when it sheds the body. Death snatches everything else away from an existence. So, the only thing that is worth striving for, is awareness.

Awareness happens from within. Money and wealth always exist outside of you. It is certainly good for terrestrial existence. However, at the time of death, you can take only what is within you. That means, only what is close to the soul can be taken by the soul. Body and everything outside of the body must be left behind. We must be aware of this truth always.

✺ **Question:** How do we know that awareness is growing in us?

Mohanji: The usual expression of higher awareness is decreased dependency on everything outside of us. We will automatically distance ourselves from greed, selfishness, anger, dissatisfaction with what we have and craving for what we do not have, perpetual sadness, jealousy, competition with one another, comparisons, inertia and accumulation orientation, etc.; and we spontaneously shift to selflessness, kindness, compassion, unconditional love. Self-sufficiency and happiness with or without a thing, (it could be anything), is a clear sign of increased awareness. Having everything and not needing anything is real richness. Real richness is a state of mind. That is when nothing outward attracts us anymore.

Of course, even as our awareness increases, our *samskaras* that are built-in by nature still continue to come forth. But our dependency level will change. We start to lead a liberated existence. In such an existence, a particular ritual, meditation, *mantra*, chanting or anything that usually makes us feel happy or comfortable will not be a necessity anymore. We will not be bound by anything. No habit binds us. We stay liberated from within. Such a person can walk any path, do anything – but nothing will touch him, nor will he become dependent on it. If these aspects of higher awareness are practised consciously, awareness will grow automatically. Reversal also works! That is, when we consciously practice the visible terrestrial signs of higher awareness, it will eventually lead to higher awareness.

Silence is our nature

Question: Why do we keep the picture of the eyes in the card?

Mohanji: When you connect to the eyes, you connect to the consciousness. That's why. Eyes are like gateways. Through the eyes, you connect to the consciousness. So when you connect deeply, that is the consciousness working on. So you are able to see through. That is why people are coming to me.

❧ **Question:** But I did not even try connecting!

Mohanji: No need to try. The moment you try, the mind comes into the picture. When you don't try, the mind is sleeping.

❧ **Question:** That is a tricky thing.

Mohanji: That is the point. Most people connect only to the gross, terrestrial, "Why is this happening, why is that happening...can you do this, can you do that..." These are all immaterial. What you can be is material. This is what is more important. You can be absolutely powerful when you are absolutely subtle. The moment you connect to the gross, the aches, and pains, and changes are there. You cannot avoid it, and if you have noticed, the subtler you become, the more you want to detach from people. The more you want to be silent. Even small sounds might not be good for you. Do you know why? Because our nature is silence. Sound is not our nature.

So, once we transcend over, we start loving silence. Silence is not even somebody not speaking. Even silence from inside will be beautiful. So, we will be more connected to the silence and we will detach from sound. We may even detach from people. Like one person from Belgrade wrote to me today, "I just want to sit next to you because I have never felt so much silence with anybody in life. I met you for a few minutes and I became silent and this feeling hasn't gone yet, after two or three days. I just want to come and sit near you. Don't talk to me. Don't even answer my questions. Just let me be near you."

Why is this happening? Because this is your nature. When you find your nature, you will not leave it. Otherwise, you will keep checking, searching. The search will go on. The moment you find your nature, your true nature, you will never leave it. Another thing in the same context, the more you are checking why this is so, why that is so, or is this real, you are entertaining the mind. We are energising the mind. Mind is the storehouse of questions. So the more we search why, why, why, we are just making sounds in our mind. The more we entertain the mind, the longer the mind will stay. When the mind stays, you can never connect to the Truth.

❧ **Question:** Very simple and yet, very hard at the same time!

Mohanji: The diagnosis is more difficult than the cure. So, diagnosis is done. The cause of the problem is the mind. Now the cure is easy. The medicine is simple. Do not energise your mind. Don't think it is difficult, because thoughts come without our calling. But don't entertain them. Feel them, leave them. Always feel your thoughts, feel your actions, feel life. This in itself will be great. Rather see, and listen and feel. Feel life. The moment you start feeling, it is not normal senses which are working. You are internalising it. You are touching and feeling life... children do that, you've seen. Children feel materials, they are more feeling-oriented until we tell them, "Look here..."

In our path we only tell people where to look, we never tell people what to see. Because you already know what to see and you will only see what you need to see. When you start feeling life, feel the sun, feel the moon, feel the cold, feel the heat, what happens is that there ends the desire for feeling. You will not postpone it. Feeling need not be from the mind. The mind can be used to feel, but the mind is not the only faculty that can feel. When you read a book, you feel something. It is reality for you. That is not from the mind. It is from the intellect. You operate in multiple levels, but the moment you start feeling from inside, the desire ends there. There are no more desires.

For e.g., you have a coffee. You feel the coffee. Then you have no more desire for a new coffee. But if you are watching the television and having the coffee, half an hour later you want another coffee. Why is it so? The feeling is not registered inside. You were not here while you were drinking the coffee. In this way, repetition happens, if your mind is not present, or you are not feeling. Thus, feel more than you see, or hear, or think. When you start feeling yourself, most of the questions end. Because you connect to your own nature.

The only reality for you is your own nature. Each person has a different nature. You are born with it. That's the nature which you have to connect to, for being real in this world, for being successful in life.

Seek Nothing... You are That!

❧ **Question:** Mohanji, an average human 'seeks' something his whole life. Why?

Mohanji: He does not know exactly what he is seeking. He runs after the glitter of life. He seeks externally, eternally. He does not know that what he seeks lies within himself. He does not know that there is nothing to seek. We seek something that we do not have, right? What do we lack at all? Seeking something, not knowing what is sought, literally takes lifetimes away. This eternal seeking continues over generations.

Seek nothing! All that you seek is within you. We seek knowledge, pleasures, possessions and even enlightenment as if it were a commodity! Whatever we seek eludes us constantly. We get frustrated. We miss the whole point. We go after books, *Gurus*, ideas, various types of spiritual practices, relationships, money, love, food, sex... and? There you go. Nothing works. Finally, at last, wisdom arises. Then, we start to unlearn and shed our skins of accumulations, one by one.

First, we insanely accumulate and then we struggle to give up. Just like when we cram food into our stomachs, we overeat and then we sweat and struggle to shed weight. Many fears arise while shedding and they often wreak havoc. Finally, finally, when we become totally naked and empty, elevation in consciousness takes place. We become ready to dissolve. The path lies within us. The destination lies within us. There is nothing to seek outside. This eternal Truth is difficult to comprehend and even more difficult to apply in life.

❧ **Question:** So, (visibly confused) what do we seek?

Mohanji: Seek nothing. You are That. Instead of seeking, watch yourself, watch everything. Observe everything. Things are happening through us. We are not doing anything. Everything is within us. When we keenly observe ourselves with child-like wonder, all duality will disappear. Expectations will disappear. We will start feeling the subtle power of supreme consciousness that runs through all beings like a thread joining beads, and you will find the perfect symmetry of life in its large canvas.

We travel miles and miles in search of peace, while peace really lies within us. We seek external *Gurus*, while the *Guru* Principle is already within us, built into our own consciousness. When seeking becomes too external, peace eludes us. Action replaces silence. We wander away from our true home and sometimes even lose our way. Then, it takes lifetimes to get back 'home'. Do you understand me?

   Question: Well. I guess so... When will we truly reach this understanding?

Mohanji: When eligibility is right. Conscious, consistent effort is essential.

   Question: What could be a potential deterrent?

Mohanji: Inertia. Inertia is like cancer. It deters our determination. It wastes lives. It wastes lifetimes.

   Question: 'Seek nothing' bothers me. I feel as if there is nothing to live for.

Mohanji: This is because we are slaves of our mind and senses. They exist to seek everything. When you shift from your senses and your mind to intellect, you will feel the difference. When you shift from intellect and ego to your soul, you will seek nothing anymore. The seeker becomes the sought. They are one. You are that.

CHAPTER 3:

The road ahead

Reducing the Baggage

Your body-inside, is like a house that is dirty. I have found this in almost everybody, because we are not only carrying the baggage of our life, but also that of our family tradition and that of our country. This is also the reason why we sometimes do not understand why certain things are happening to us. If you look at your own past, it is easy to understand, but what about your environment and the conditioning around you? An example: you read today's newspaper, some information caught your emotion and you got attached to it. This experience sticks to you as a memory. Just as with a computer, sometimes if there is too much data, the computer crashes. In this way, we also sometimes go through those crashes.

I have just had several big group sessions in Serbia, and I have seen again how most people try to analyse their experiences. Once we stop analysing, we are free. To analyse, we use our intellect and we continue churning the experiences. When we drop this and just accept the experience we are liberated.

What we are here for is liberation, reducing the baggage. We are all carrying excess baggage, this is why we cannot enjoy every situation, we are not in the present.

Be Aware and Let Go

We keep a lot of stuff inside. We are collecting various things every moment and keeping them inside. We cannot know how much we have stored and eventually, this makes us heavier and heavier in life. Every event, every day, leaves an impression in our system. Unless we let go of it, we cannot evolve. Not only spiritually or terrestrially, we cannot change anything, even in our daily life. We have accumulated so much and unless we let go or leave them, we cannot be light. Why do we have to meditate at all? Actually, we do not need meditation if our mind is completely with us – but our mind is so scattered all around us.

We suffer because we cannot bring ourselves to ourselves. All of us are complete by ourselves. Nobody is higher or lower. The only difference is how much weight we carry. What is this weight that we carry? It is the weight of stored data such as things that happened in the past, emotions attached to people, situations and every aspect of life. This becomes very heavy. If you look at your own life, you can see that it is repetition over time. One thing repeats again and again over time.

Our daily life is equal to past impressions (*purva samskara*). What we collected in the past gets repeated as our reality, in the present as well as the future. What we are today is a bundle of our past impressions. You can see this very clearly in relationships. Sometimes we attract wrong partnerships. Many people suffer because of that. This is because the impression is continuing through time and it just goes on and on. So, how do we sort it out? How do we release it?

The first step is to be aware. Be aware that things are getting repeated through time. Be aware and if you don't energise them and let go, they will go away. The second step is to let go. Let go of time, people, places, incidents, as dead things of the past and detach from it. The third step is to be in the present. Once you are clear about your thinking, talking, your own life, you start detaching from it. That is why I say, spend some time with yourself. It is not even meditation. Try to understand yourself. What makes you angry? What makes you sad? What makes you agitated? What makes you hate people or hate a particular place or thing? Understand yourself. You must spend time with yourself.

Let me tell you something. You may feel you are weak, but you are not weak ever in your life. What makes you weak is the mind which is filled with concepts, collected from the past. I have not seen any meditation more powerful than observing yourself. That is more powerful than any meditation in your life. If you decide to spend time with yourself, just watch your thoughts, words, actions and understand yourself more and more. Explore yourself more, introspect. Especially when you become angry, when you become sad, or when you feel you are being ignored, when insecurities happen to you, just watch yourself. Keep watching. What is going on? Situations can be very bad, but you can still be powerful if you are with yourself.

I'm not talking about theories here. I'm talking from my own experience. When things were going wrong, everything was going wrong. At exactly that point in time, if we choose to be with ourselves, and if we choose to weather all storms, then we are successful. Success happens inside first. Richness is inside first before it becomes outside richness. If you are confident with yourself, in yourself, and if you are confident that you are one with yourself, doors get opened at every level.

It is the job of the mind to wander and be restless. But you are not the mind. So, minus the mind, you are very powerful. The more you entertain your mind, the more you become weak and tired, because the mind keeps you moving. The mind does not allow stillness, and stillness is the nature of the soul.

🌿 **Question:** How do we get rid of the baggage?

Mohanji: I will tell you. First, you have to start today. You cannot move back into your past. Today you can choose to be in the present, consciously and be with every thought. Let the mind be present with your thoughts. How do we do that? Imagine you have, let us say, four or five children and some are very naughty and you are just like a loving mother watching them play. Let them play. Our thoughts are like our children. Just watch them play, just observe, without doing anything. No scolding, no criticising, no judging, no censoring. Then you will be fine with your thought process. When you do that for one hour everyday, play with your children, then you will be in the present with your thoughts.

You don't know what I am going to say next, right? Likewise, you do not know what you are going to think next. It is only after the thought is born that you understand it. You have better control over your words. Before you talk or while you talk you can be with your words. Likewise with action: have control over your actions. Thus, you can work on three levels of creation – thought, word and action, and you are accumulating something on those three levels. Again, it is like with your computer and the internet – thinking is like surfing the internet, one thing leads to another, one site leads to another and so on.

Next are words, here you are actually doing something, you're talking, but when your mind is present with every word, then there is no guilt about the past or anxiety for the future; you're in control of the words. Then there is action. We have many thoughts, fewer words, and still fewer actions!

Now, how do you detach from all that? If there are no emotions with any thoughts, words or actions, you are on the path of liberation, because emotions are the glue that attaches every word, every thought and every action to your system.

When the mind is with the past it is very difficult not to have any emotions. For e.g., you saw a beautiful car and wanted to buy it. You went home, checked your bank balance and found that the money you have is just not enough to buy it, but the mind is not happy until you buy that car. Then, after you bought the car, your mind actually does not care anymore. Then the mind wants a better car, but until you bought that car, that was the most important thing. That's how our mind operates, it can never be satisfied.

What you can do is: watch the mind like a mother and watch how it operates. You just stand there, watch the thoughts and slowly they will start becoming conscious of you watching them. No need to tell them anything. When you are just watching, they will come and start giving you excuses. They will stop by themselves, we don't have to tell them anything. Watching and observing is much more powerful than talking. This is one way of detachment. The best way of detachment is meditation, meditating on your own thoughts and mind.

Now imagine a small window and thousands of people want to go through that window to the other side. Everybody is pushing and fighting as only two or three people at a time fit through that window. Our thoughts are like that. Now, when you start observing this like a policeman, they will stop fighting and stand in line. Likewise, when you start observing your thoughts, the intensity of your thought movements will reduce. Slowly gaps will open up between the thoughts.

Over a period of time, the gaps between the thoughts will increase. What will be in this gap? Silence. Nothing else but silence. When you do this continuously, you will not fear silence anymore. You will fall in love with silence. The pressure of thoughts is gone, and the space is filled with silence. So where is the baggage? There is emptiness. A beautiful feeling. Bliss! You don't have to do anything else.

What are we doing everyday? Look at the world out there. People are trying to fill their inner space with activities. They are afraid of any vacuum. They go from one pub to another or do one action after the other, in order not to feel the vacuum.

One person asked me the other day, "Don't you get bored when you are alone?" I answered that I get real when I'm alone. I am not afraid of being alone. It is not depressing loneliness. It is self-sufficiency, which means you are content and complete within yourself.

When the senses are driving, you will always have to do something, otherwise, the result is depression. Then, self-worth will be so low. When senses are driving you, you continuously have to do something and you will not understand the value of silence. Silence is much more valuable than anything else in this life. The only conquest which is worthwhile, in this lifetime, is the conquest of your own mind.

 ❧ **Question:** How can you detach from the mind?

Mohanji: This is what we just practised during the meditation – we shift our awareness to the spine. Usually, we are driven by our senses, which are oriented towards the front in just 120 degrees. When we shift our consciousness to our spine, by breathing through our spine, we start operating in 360 degrees and this way the push of the senses is getting less. We won't be pressured for action anymore. No 'pressure for pleasure' anymore!

Actually, the intellectual side of our mind is a much better friend for us, but whenever we become angry or emotional, the mind immediately puts the intellect into a locker. So that emotions are in total control. When the emotional wave is over, then our mind unlocks the intellect and it can come out again and then we regret, because we had a fight and we are sorry. When you shift to your spine, when your consciousness is in your spine, then intellect will be in charge and then you will have space between your thoughts, words, and actions. You will not be pressured for something and when you are not pressured for anything, the success rate will be very high.

Whenever we operate emotionally, success and failure rates will always fluctuate, like a swing – sometimes success, sometimes failure, most times worry. This is one way of reducing the baggage. If you practice the Power of Purity meditation, most of your stored emotions will come up. If you operate more and more from your spine, pressure will be less, anxiety is getting less and intellect is in control. Accumulation will be less.

We have various ways to reduce our baggage. Social service is very good. There is a saying, "Hands that serve are holier than lips that pray". If you can buy a poor man a tea, it will liberate you more than going to church or a temple. If you help someone you will have a much more expanded heart. I always recommend that. Do something beautiful. Not just with money, and don't think that you need a lot of money to do social service. For example, you can teach a child something or help someone to get a job. Some activity that is unselfish will liberate you.

Gratitude Matters

Gratitude will indeed help in spiritual growth. However, people forget fast as they are using their conscious mind for their daily life. They go after glitter and other's opinions instead of their own experience. Jesus healed many leprosy patients. There was no cure for leprosy during those days. Leprosy patients were locked and sealed in caves and left to die! They walked with a bell around their neck to warn people. Yet, once they were healed, they dissolved into society without even a glance of gratitude for the healer. Their ego did not permit them to declare in society that they were leprosy patients in the past.

Jesus did not expect any gratitude, though. It would have been a great evolution for the consciousness of the patients, if they had stood up and thanked the healer; nor did they come to his assistance when Pilate asked the question if Jesus should be pardoned. All those who benefited from Jesus never gave anything back to him. This is the nature of our society. Gratitude is good for the seeker. The real *Guru* wants nothing.

Conviction & Passion

Conviction is all it takes. Conviction breaks all mental barriers. When a man performs out of conviction, he does not wait for approval, nor will he care to prove to others about his mission or reason for a particular action. His action will never depend on others' opinions and applause. He will be supremely self-sufficient. Man's clarity and confidence depend on his conviction. Conviction leaves no room for indifference. Conviction travels in a chariot drawn by confidence.

A man who is unsure will remain unsure, and will almost always blame others for his follies. Those who gossip or blame others all the time are usually people who are unsure about their own existence, path and destination. Those who try to change others into their own image or character are also insecure and ignorant. They need company. They are afraid to walk alone.

All great Masters lived their life with conviction. Jesus was very much sure of what his purpose of existence was. He never looked back to see if anyone was indeed following him. Nor did he look ahead in anxiety, hoping that he would eventually fulfil his tasks at hand. He was immune to both anxiety and dilemma. He was immune to others' opinions about him and his mission. He behaved very much like the 'son of man' all the while holding the Divine in its full glory, in his heart. Conviction was unshakeable.

Time was scarce, but that never bothered him. He was not bothered whether everyone understood him all the time. He never cared if anyone became too frustrated with his profound teachings and left him to ease his/her confused mind. Some went and came back. Some got caught up in regular existence which demanded no particular eligibilities and criteria to exist in society. Knowledge and ignorance are both approved. "Everyone has their place in society. So why follow an unknown language and make oneself insane? Let Jesus have his peace, and us ours". This is the way some thought and spoke.

Some said similar things to Jesus' mother. She would never answer such questions. She knew that her son had conviction, he was purpose-bound, and that whatever he said was apt and accurate for the existing society. There was not a grain more nor a grain less. This was the exact medicine for a society of chosen men, reeling in gross inertia. If society failed to measure the quality of the grain, how could a son of man be blamed for that? The mother's smile was deep and pregnant.

To a neighbour who kept nagging her about the obscurity of Jesus' words, she said, "Serve the helpless, mother, and you will understand him. The only God a hungry man can understand is food. The only God for a thirsty man is water. Mother, listen to him. He is only telling these truths which you already know". The mother of Jesus never interfered nor interpreted what her son taught. That would have been nonsensical. That would have been inappropriate.

A man of firm conviction is walking the earth, talking his subject. If there was more clarity needed, he would have arranged that himself. Why do we need another interpreter existing as a contemporary? The future may need interpreters, as the subject matter will get distorted with time. It happens all the time. Men adapt truths the way it suits them. The real Truth has nothing to do with the adapted truths.

447

Society is filled with cowards. Brave hearts have always been a rarity. Even those who approved of his thoughts and words, seldom expressed it and were too cautious. Some of those who were truly convinced, expressed and dared discrimination. Those who opposed him and thought about him as a menace to society, always voiced their concerns. Negative matters definitely find tongues. Positive and benevolent thoughts often do not find tongues at the appropriate time and invariably suffer a premature death. Society has always been brimming with cowards who could never stay with their understanding and conviction. This kind of passive society only expresses stoic indifference. They are good for nothing.

Jesus was equally indifferent about death. The mother knew that her son was walking a tightrope. He was always treading into danger zones. This was part of his mission. Dare the storms and prove your point. The storms might knock you down. Still, dare the storms. The whole world will have to pay heed. That was essential to shake the world from induced slumber. Those who needed power created fear, and through fear absolute control over passive people. Sleep was thus induced for convenience's sake.

It needed a lion's heart to shake the unshakeable slumber. Someone had to wake up and roar. Society needed this shake-up. The danger had always been the complete annihilation of thoughts, words and action; ethnic cleansing. There was no choice. Either accept the available opportunity to sleep or fight against the sleep of generations and wake them up at the cost of one's life. Jesus braved death. Finally, to ward off the slumber and create a new light, he embraced crucifixion. This was also part of his agenda.

The mother knew it. She had learned to accept anything and everything. Whether it was thorns or roses, it never mattered to the mother. She knew that, after the bloodshed, compassion would prevail. Compassion must prevail. How much more could hearts shrink with pain and hatred? How much more could generations grow in suffocation and lack of expression? How much longer? Everything was worth it, even the sacrifice of her beloved son, for the sake of a larger good: Liberation!

Liberation it was. Jesus liberated himself and showed the path to those who had just woken up. The expressionless people looked at the whole episode in awe and disbelief. Those who cared deeply about possessions, relationships and greedily safeguarded their physical bodies could never digest the message of imminent perishability that Jesus so blatantly demonstrated. Also, it was quite intangible to believe that he could or would actually 're-create' the body in a short while just three days! All this was bizarre and inconceivable.

However, the son of man did prove his point. He had conviction that was well beyond self-annihilation. He was not afraid of anyone. He was truly That. The divine within. The father element. The Father. "I and my Father are One," he roared with absolute conviction.

The Power Within You...

Tamas or inertia is like the seasons. Seasons express themselves explicitly in time. Just like we say summer, winter, rainy season etc., our states or flavours are called *tamas, rajas* and *sattva*. These are our operating levels. A person operating on the *tamasic* plane will express inertia, lethargy etc. and will tend to blame others for his predicament. He will often blame the situation for his inaction. Such a person suffers due to delays and a lack of conviction in action. A *rajasic* person may perform an action quickly and is definitely superior to the lethargic individual in state, however, his action could also be based on emotion or ego.

A *sattvic* person usually performs from the intellect and will stay beyond all excesses. His operating level will be increasingly based on purity. A person based in the state beyond the waking, dream and deep sleep, the fourth state or turiya state, will operate on the plane of perpetual silence which is beyond compulsive thoughts, words, and actions. In other words, his operating level will be that of *dharma* or pure duty which is beyond selfishness and expectation.

Every person has a variety of expressions. One fundamentally expresses his inherent constitution at all times. This could be *tamasic, rajasic* or *sattvic*. Each thought, word, and action – if they are combined with emotion, should leave a residue within your system. We are entering and storing such data into our subconscious or our personal hard drive at every moment of our waking state. Sometimes we store data consciously, but often unconsciously. The deeper or grosser the residue, the deeper will be its impression in one's character.

This could also be an external impression, such as a feature film that influenced, a tragedy that one watched on the television, or even a strong opinion about a person or an incident elsewhere. All these can stay as silent residue within. Likewise, if trauma of any kind has happened and its residue stays hidden in the folds of one's character, blockages in energy flow happen because of it. Clutter of residue leads to blockages. The blockages will produce mental and physical inconveniences, phobias, fears and sickness. So, as we accumulate residue, all the more reason to clean ourselves, too.

As I said earlier, forgiving and repenting does help. This is the basis of our Power of Purity meditation. Unhooking from past events is very important. A bad experience of the past could sting us time and again. It should be replaced with higher awareness and higher purpose of life. Otherwise, the same event will come back again and again in life.

The residue of past lives exists in every being. That is the basis of our unique constitution. This is more or less unchangeable, unless a conscious effort is taken to understand oneself and shed it from the root. Fears created out of this residue produce such realities in life, which re-confirm the inherent fear. It will bring situations and reasons to enjoy the state of fear. Love is the same. Hatred and enmity bring forth such realities. Sometimes people become possessive and cruel too, because of their inherent insecurities. These are the external expressions or in other words, the gross manifestation of the inherent residue.

When residue leaves, lightness happens, clarity and flexibility happen and finally, enlightenment happens. Those who lead a confused existence accumulate residue much more than the ones who have clarity in action. Those who are emotional by nature also accumulate much residue. Those who crave sympathy or applause, those who constantly blame situations or other people for their seeming failures in carrying out responsibilities, those who constantly blame injustice in society without doing anything about it, are filling themselves up with deep residue at each moment.

Where does the residue stay? Mostly in the lower region of our body. The lower part of the Shiva *lingam*. Shiva *lingam* means our body minus legs, hands, neck and head. When energy moves through the body, vertically and horizontally, in alternate waves, the residue of thoughts, words and actions, combined with emotions are dropped to the bottom. It gets accumulated or stuck at various locations of our system, of which the tangible gross is our body, and intangible are the subtle meridians.

It accumulates mostly around the *muladhara* and the *svadhishthana chakras* and these get clogged over a period of time. This prevents the *kundalini* from moving anywhere. This is also why it is said that pushing *kundalini* forcefully, through *mantras* and practices could lead to lifetimes of agony. The removal of residue will automatically clear the path and will allow *the kundalini* to rise to where it belongs or where it came from, effortlessly and without any artificial stimulus.

The clogging at the lower part of our system stays when conscious unhooking does not take place. Forgiveness, repentance, feeding the poor, sharing of wealth with the needy and under-privileged, spontaneous acts of kindness and every aspect of truth and compassion reduce the residue. This is why such acts of kindness are well recommended in most paths of the world. *Bhakti yoga* and *karma yoga* are powerful tools that reduce the residue.

What happens when residue leaves through *sadhana* or by the Grace of the Master? Usually, all the hidden fears, anxieties and traumas will surface first. Sleeplessness, confusion and many such emotions can surface. Only a person who is strong enough to handle unknown fears and hidden traumas can actually make use of this *sadhana*. Some tend to suppress the residue back into themselves out of overwhelming fear and confusion. Some prefer to change the *Guru*! It takes an expert guide to take you through this time. This is quite a vulnerable time and the practitioner should be extremely objective, patient and kind.

When we embrace silence through practising witness-hood, the same happens. The first that comes out from us are negative emotions such as fears and anxieties. We have to allow them to surface and go. We must sincerely let go. Many cannot. Some cannot even release their own illnesses. They hold on to everything and the whole exercise becomes futile. In some paths, there are practices such as talking nonsense to themself, or shouting at the wall for minutes. This is to expel the hidden residue.

However, understand that nature also has the same power to hold. There is scientific proof that if you scold or show anger to water, it forms a different pattern within than when you speak words of love to it. Nature holds the residue of events. This is why accidents happen almost always at the same place. Accident-prone areas or death prone areas tell this story. Just like we always attract similar realities. We are indeed a part of nature, or nature is integrated into us.

Watch yourself, watch through your emotions, use intellect more, try to bring up all the lower emotions through the breath to the higher parts of the body. Remember yourself as a Shiva *lingam*. Breathe from the back to the front and breathe from the front to the back, alternatively, in a gap of five minutes. This could bring forth the hidden residue from lower to higher, and release it from the system. When this movement becomes fine and smooth, perfect distribution of energy takes place. Equanimity and balance happen in life.

I could go on and on. But, the fundamental truth of accumulation and release always remains. What you earn should be spent. What stagnates, decays. Residue slows us down and prevents us from being fluid in life. It makes us stiff. The earth and water elements of our system, namely the *muladhara* and *svadhishthana chakras*, suffer the most. Instability happens if earth is not stable. Contamination happens, if water is unstable or stagnant. Do not worry too much about the fire, which is the stomach centre. If the lower ones are contaminated, the 'black smoke' of unburned residue will contaminate the air and space, the higher *chakras*, and obscure the heavens which are *ajna* and *sahasrara*.

You are the world. You are the universe. Thus, a conscious practice in cleansing yourself is the most important thing in everyday spiritual practice. Likewise, if the guide is not confident, do not experiment. Leave *kundalini* alone. Instead, concentrate on the removal of residue. This is important. Make a conscious choice. Understand yourself and the reasons for your actions.

Are you after spiritual elevation or sensations? Any practice can give you some sensations.

Only shedding or emptying will give you spiritual elevation. You are like a balloon tied to a stone. When the stone is removed, the balloon will float up in the air. When we are heavy and caged, limitations are experienced. Unlimitedness means freedom. This is the aim of true spirituality. Rituals of an unconscious nature or running after sensations cannot deliver that.

Does the *Guru* take on the residue of their disciples? It depends on the receptivity and surrender of the disciple. Yes. Some do. Not all do. Many do not even allow people to touch their feet because of this reason. True *Gurus* often take many blockages onto themselves. They relieve the devotee from pain by taking it on to their own body. Some even shed their body due to this. Remember, Shirdi Sai Baba shed his body in lieu of the son of Baija Maa. A true *Guru* always protects, ignoring himself, unconditionally. Jesus only asked for faith from the people who needed his help. *Babaji* exists in multiple realms as a personification of unconditionality.

What Can I Do?

There is another plane being developed to accommodate denser energies. Here on Earth, however, consciousness is falling more and more. Good people are getting sucked in. We should be extremely vigilant to stay in the path of White (path of *dharma*). It is a desperate attempt of the dark to dominate. It is very heavy. They will do all that is possible to keep us away from the Source. All Masters are working hard to keep and maintain the good, to contain the bad. However, usually what the mind fancies is the dark. What is not too palatable is the white.

To stay in the path which is for elevation, we need to be extraordinarily careful. The mind will put forth all sorts of blockages. All sorts of different ideas and thoughts will be generated by the mind. Oh! Why do we not just try this way or that way? No problem, experimentation is part of spirituality. But if the experimentation is taking you one step further, deeper into the whirlpool, what is its use? You lose your soul. Identifying the path of great Masters is difficult. It is very easy to get out of the path. Do not consider this message as a threat.

Consider this as a message to be vigilant. We should sharpen our faculties of discrimination. We should sharpen our senses. All sorts of objects, confusions and lures will be kept in front of you, to suck you in. It will create conflict within people. It will also create conflict within you. It will create a lot of discomfort within you. It will create inner conflict. It will say – "Why are you bothered? Here is your comforter and pillow. Just relax." Then, you think that this is your path. But once you are sucked in, you cannot escape. This is binding. It is just the opposite of our plan of liberation. Comfort zones are created to bind. Comfort zones are created to lure wandering souls into the path of captivity.

There are entities that thrive only on the consciousness of people. Consciousness is their food! Please be aware of that. All Masters are doing extraordinary, extra hours of tedious work to safeguard people. But Masters never impose, just as your soul never imposes anything on you. You choose it. Any true Master, or any path, is just like your soul, guiding you to yourself. The negative path has an enormous variety of lures and attractions. It is a treacherous path. At one point, we may say and feel that we are fine, and we will divert and choose the way which we feel is comfortable.

Many of the new generation spiritual teachers who are using the white symbols are not from the path of liberation. They are using the symbols of the positive path to lure, attract and bind unsuspecting seekers into the ritualistic dark path.

It depends on how long you will prolong, keep patience, and entertain tenacity to be on the positive path. You are sitting on a tree and the tree is being shaken constantly. If you have the tenacity to cling to the tree you will survive. If not, at some point in time, you will get frustrated and you will drop your hands and leave the tree. You will fall. Then, to climb up again will take time! Not just time or this life. It may take several lifetimes to reach where you were, or to climb again!

You may ask then, what is the role of the True Masters? Why are they not protecting us? They are protecting. However, if you choose another path, they will not object because it is your free will. Just like your soul never objected to whatever you wanted to do. It only helped you. If you wanted to sit here today, your soul aided you. Your mind decided to come here today. Soul never asked you to come here, but your mind decided to come.

I would like you to take these words seriously. This is because times are moving faster. This is the time to hold on. If you hold on, you save yourself. Then you do not have to worry. You are firmly established in the path of liberation. You will not take many more bodies. You will be fine. If you fall, how many more lifetimes will you have to take? Difficult to say! It could be quite a lot!

I want you to chew on this message. How much is our mind making us crazy? How many sensory or sensual lures are put forth everyday? We shift from one Master to another, and the body and mind keep moving, achieving nothing!

Another important thing is *tamas*. *Tamas* is the sword of the dark. *Tamas* is the nectar or lure of the dark. Being *sattvic*, or even *rajasic* to some extent, can lead to liberation. *Tamas* can only lead to binding. *Tamas* is given to you and you enjoy it: "Oh, I am fine today or I am lazy today. I may try tomorrow!" In this way, *tamas* works at every point. Laziness, inertia, greed, anxiety, fears, anger... all of these vices are given by *tamas*.

Let me make money today, I will try to help somebody tomorrow. We will never think, let me share what I have today. We think, let me make one million. Once I have one million, then I will start charity. One million can never be enough, however, because your lifestyle has changed. You need more to stay with the same lifestyle or improve on it. You will never be satisfied. If we have one million, we look forward to two million to be happy. This is how it goes all the time. Our mind will never be satisfied with any material. It will ask for more.

The most important message that I want you to be aware of is this: The present time is like a sword which has two edges. If you hold on to the path of White, then nothing can stop you. You are automatically lifted up. At the same time, if you fall from this path, you will take lifetimes to reach here. This shift in awareness and understanding is important. The awareness is provided to you in such a way that this awareness itself automatically takes you higher. Time is automatically taking you higher. All you have to do is 'just be' in the path of *dharma*. Just keep inner purity and deep faith with zero expectation. Just be fluid and just flow with absolute spontaneity.

Watch yourself. Watch how your mind functions. Is it creating greed, anxiety, fear and doubts? If this is the case, ask the mind again— "Is that necessary?" or "Is this the real me?" At the same time, the mind could be creating benevolence against all odds. For e.g., if I have one dollar to spare, let me share it with someone who does not have that. It is not that you don't eat or enjoy the fruits of life. You do eat, but you also share. First, feed your family. Safeguard yourself and then help others. This way you will exist in perpetual consciousness all the time. Otherwise, you may say, let me make one million and then I will start charity. That one million will never be enough. One million will need to be two, three and then four. It goes on.

Similarly, we often ask the question– "Why do I have to do this? Why can't someone else do this?" This is *tamas*. *Tamas* is the weapon of darkness. Tamas is darkness. *Tamas* makes you tired, it gives you inertia. It tells you– It is okay for today, let us see tomorrow. *Tamas* leads you to the trap. Through inertia, one loses life. Once you marry darkness, you lose your life. You lose your soul. Existing in tamas will make you lose your soul. Greed happens. So many emotions happen. This is the reality of existence and we should be clear about it.

I would like you to contemplate on it for the next two-three weeks. Watch your thoughts and watch yourself very closely. Introspect! What are my ingredients? What am I consisting of? What is making me work? What is the provocation behind every action or reaction? Is it selflessness or selfishness?

Existence itself is bliss. However, it depends upon your mind, whether your mind will accept it or not. The mind may not accept it. Otherwise, every moment is bliss. If you are able to accept today, right now, without resistance, it is bliss. Accepting your reality in a different mode is not bliss. It is frustration.

Are you confused by what I am saying? If you live this Truth, then it is bliss. I am seeing people getting sucked in. I encounter too many of them each day. When you get sucked in, there will be an inclination to come out of that. It is like quicksand or a whirlpool. You are working very hard to get out of the whirlpool, but the whirlpool itself sucks you in. It throws you into a zone where there is no map in your hand or compass for directions. You cannot find the way out. You may know the destination, but not the way. Then you may get stranded for lifetimes.

3 a.m. to 6 a.m. is *sattvic* time. If you commit a crime during *sattvic* time, it has much more impact than when you commit a crime during *rajasic* or *tamasic* time. This is because the whole atmosphere is in a prayerful subtlety. Whatever you do at *sattvic* time reverberates all over the universe in a much larger way with much deeper intensity. One will carry heaviness much

more if a crime is committed at that time. I am not saying that committing a crime at times other than *sattvic* is better, however, the impact is different. Non-violence is the path for spiritual elevation.

Please understand that this period of time, through the shift, is *sattvic*. Predominantly *sattvic*! I am not saying one hundred per cent *sattvic*. That is why those who have an inclination to evolve are coming together. They have been given guidance. Thus, you have the choice. Nobody is forcing anything on you. You have the choice to stay on this path and move.

Introspection is extremely important to stay in the path. You have to keep watching yourself and your thoughts. Ask yourself, "Am I getting more *tamasic*?" There is only one medicine for being *tamasic*, and that is to become *rajasic*. Action beats *tamas*. Get on and get moving. When *rajas* becomes extreme, it shifts to *sattva* by itself. This is the difference between *tamas* and *rajas*. It takes effort to move from tamas and go into *rajas*. Keep moving, take action! The transition from *rajas* to *sattva*, however, is beautiful and automatic. One cannot make efforts to become *sattvic*.

If you put in the effort, sometimes, you slip back into *tamas*, because those efforts often carry expectations as well as the corresponding frustrations. If you think – "I am not feeling good, let me sit and meditate". This is procrastination. Meditation becomes escapism here. You need to address the issue that provokes *tamas* in you. Meditate because you love to meditate, not because of any other reason. Please understand what I mean. At such times, the best way to beat *tamas* is to be hyperactive. Extreme action leads to inaction in *sattvic* mode. The *sattvic* mode in existence, over a period of time, may slip back to *tamas*. A person works hard and comes to the shape of *sattva* and then to the mode of *sattva*.

From here, you can slip back into *tamas*. Again, you need to rejuvenate into extreme action. When you feel inertia, think about this. Switch to extreme action. Change the gear and beat it! Swami Vivekananda said, "Go and play football". He did not say, "Go and meditate". Tire yourself and then sleep. This sleep is not *tamasic* sleep. The body is tired, you want to rest and this is ok! The other way round, when we are tired and lazy and do not want to get out of bed, it is *tamas* and definitely not good.

Do you really understand what I am saying? This is very important and I want you to chew on this. Digest it as much as possible.

In reality, nobody needs a *Guru*. The *Guru* principle itself will guide you. You do not need anyone to come and tell you to do it this way or that way! This is a fundamental truth of life and fundamental truth of existence. It is simple yet really effective.

When people say, "Let me meditate and I will talk to you later", is that meditation, or are you trying to escape because you do not like some situations? I am not too 'pro' visiting temples that are far away. However, if you take the trouble of visiting them, it is still better. This is because it is an action, and not *tamas*. It takes great effort to walk all the way to the shrine of *Sabarimala* or the *Vaishno Devi* temple. What moves you? *Bhakti* or devotion moves you. Your inclination for that activity as well as surrender moves you.

In this way, it is good since it is not *tamas*. That is why temples are sometimes built far away, high up on hilltops, and may not be easily accessible. You must shed your *tamas* and take the trouble of reaching there. Then one reaches *sattva*. You reach the temple, you pray, you melt, you become one with God, you feel connected to God and you feel good. You can feel the inner vibrations are changing. Vibrations go from your third eye to the Deity's third eye, from its *anahata chakra* to yours. The circular motion happens between you and the Deity. This is individualistic. Nobody can give this to you.

You do not need a *pujari* (the priest who performs rituals in the temple) between the deity and you! Why do you need anyone? It is individualistic – you, your soul and your connection. I can only give the message. The walking of the path is for you to do. I want you to chew on this for the next three weeks. This is very important. Otherwise, what happens? "I am coming for the meditation". Good enough, very nice, but what about evolution? Evolution is a big question mark. Evolution is important. Whether one sits here or not, many people are still connecting with us. No location matters. Location has no value; attitude has value.

We are the kind of people who do not forgive ourselves, who forget to forgive others too! We judge ourselves and create more and more walls everyday. Finally, we are unable to get out. There are some varieties of spiders, which build webs but get themselves caught up in those very webs and die!

I do not know if I have conveyed the message clearly, but I would like to tell you that this is a very serious message and I want you to take it seriously.

Life is very short. We think we are here forever. Sorry, we are only here for a few years. The entire story lasts more or less eighty years perhaps? Out of that, you are unable to do anything for some parts of your life, like your childhood years and then beyond the age of fifty-five to sixty years. One is helpless in these times. The body does not support you. Out of eighty years of life, more than forty per cent is spent in a helpless state. The body deteriorates. You often need to go to the garage to repair it.

The only constant thing is ego. Ego remains strong and that keeps us going. Mind, body, and emotions are all changing; the only constant thing is ego. Nothing else is constant. This is a reality of existence. Please understand, this is not to scare you, but to make you more aware. No need to be scared of anything. What is there to be scared of? We should, however, be aware.

So, in another plane, spaces have been created to accommodate the denser souls while Masters clean up the earth. But on this plane, darkness is trying to catch us as much as possible. The water is kept murky with human confusion. Catch as many fish as possible, because the fish cannot see through murky water. This is what is happening. Why is the water murky? Because it is a transition. There is always some kind of uncertainty during transition. One can get sucked in fast while in uncertainty. Without your knowledge, you are pulled into a different net. Who allows that? Your mind. If you are on the path of White, hold on to the feet of the Tradition. Do not leave the feet of the great Masters. This is a one hundred per cent ensured way.

In the path of *Avadhoota*, there is no give and take. There are no conditions, or conditioning, or even concepts. It is a straight deal. If the mind is continuously blocking, just remember that more lives have to be expected to clear the backlog; maybe in another plane, with all sorts of things like greed, jealousy, anger, one-upmanship and fights.

I hope I am not scaring you. If you do not understand this message, travelling further will be difficult. My intention is that you should understand this aspect. It is not to scare anybody. I want you to digest this message well. You need this message to move ahead. Forget about *Gurus*. Now, talk about yourself. Think about your mind, how it functions. How caught up are you? How liberated are you? Instead of asking the question – "Why should I do it?" Ask the question – "How can I do it? What else can I do?" Your first question should be, just like in customer service, "Can I help you?" Beat inertia. Your next question should be, "Can I help you further? What else can I do?"

ACKNOWLEDGEMENTS

I thank all the seekers whose inquiry and discussions have revealed the questions and answers that are communicated through this book. Though the answers may have come from me, the wisdom and knowledge is eternal and belongs to the Tradition. I consider myself as a projection of the Tradition and a mere channel to communicate its teachings and messages. Many have come before me and spoken these truths, many are speaking at this time and many more will come and speak in the future. Our mission is to awaken the generations to realise their highest human potential, become active, effectively responsible and benevolent in the world, and always ensure their adherence to purpose.

To our global family working towards that noble end, I express my deepest and most sincere gratitude, especially Mohanji International Foundation, Mohanji Global Management Team, the respective country leadership and teams, Mohanji *Acharyas*, Mai-Tri practitioners and all Mohanji Foundation volunteers, as well as the leadership, volunteers and members working for Ammucare, ACT foundation, ACT 4 Hunger, Early Birds Club, World Consciousness Alliance, the Himalayan schools (yoga, dance and language), Mohanji Youth Club, Invest in Awareness, Fruit Tree Plantation Drive, and countless other inspired initiatives and activities, who are unassumingly, silently and effectively adding value to the world in every way, by serving, helping and empowering all beings. With inherent purity and perfect awareness of the path and the mission, their dedication and silent thoughts, words and actions have helped spread the mission and its value far and wide.

I thank my parents; Dr. P. K. Namboothiri and Mrs. Sreedevi; my wife Devi and my daughter Mila and express gratitude for their contribution in my existence on Earth. My heartfelt gratitude to my late daughter Ammu (Sreedevi Mohan), who despite her short tenure on Earth, was my greatest teacher and showered immeasurable love and wisdom on all who came in touch with her. Her legacy lives on through Ammucare and the ACT Foundations that continue to let her benevolence uplift countless lives.

My deepest respects and gratitude and humble prostrations at the feet of Shri Shri Vittalananda Saraswati Maharaj (Vittal Babaji), Baba Ganeshananda Giri Maharaj, Avadhoota Nadananda, Devi Amma, Vasudevan Swami, Gopal Baba (Shri Prabhudananda Saraswati Maharaj), Mata Devi Vanamali, who have always stood by me and unconditionally supported me through all my activities.

Last but not the least, I humbly surrender all that I did and will ever do at the lotus feet of the Divine Mother who has always guided and protected me, Lord Dattatreya and the Dattatreya Tradition, Shirdi Sai Baba, Sathya Sai Baba, Bhagavan Nityananda, Akkalkot Maharaj and the great Masters of the *Avadhoota* Tradition, Mahavatar Babaji and the great Masters of the Kriya yoga Tradition, Sage Agastya, Sage Boganathar, Shiva Prabhakar Siddha Yogi and the great Masters of the Siddha Tradition, Adinath, Balaknath, Gorakshanath, the Navnath Saints and all the great Masters of the Nath Tradition, Ramana Maharshi, the grand Tradition of Lord Dakshinamoorthy, the great Naga Devatas, Lord Jesus and all the great and selfless Masters who ever walked the earth and will ever do so.

I prostrate in complete faith and surrender at the feet-less feet of Lord Krishna and Lord Shiva, a representation of the formless Supreme Consciousness – Parabrahma, the Supreme Father, who manifests through every being, through time and space, eternally.

I do not exist. Only He exists.

My sincere hope that this book reaches all those who need it, guides them to understand the various aspects of their existence and inspires them to walk the path of pathlessness. Thank you for your presence. May you attain the highest liberation in this life.

Remain blessed.

Yours,

Mohanji

GLOSSARY

Acharya: A teacher or highly learned person with expert subject matter knowledge, generally religious.

Adharma: Unrighteousness. In other words, selfish existence resulting in/from evil thoughts, words and actions.

Adi Nath: The primordial Lord. The first *Nath* (Lord) Shiva, whose state was used by Lord Dattatreya as the basis upon which to model the *Nath* Tradition.

Adi Shankaracharya/Adi Shankara: An Hindu philosopher and theologian from India, believed to be an incarnation of Lord Shiva. He consolidated the doctrine of *Advaita* Vedanta philosophy and is considered the reviver of modern Hinduism. He is also considered the *Yugacharya* for *Kali Yuga*

Advaita: Non-duality.

Agastya/Agastya Rishi/Agastya: One of the *Saptarishis* of the *Satya Yuga* in the *Vedic* texts and is respected as a Tamil *Siddha*, who invented an early grammar of the Tamil language, (*Agattiyam*.) He also played a pioneering role in developing spirituality at *Shaiva* centres in Sri Lanka and South India. Sage *Agastya* composed many verses of *Rig Veda*, and also composed the *Lalitha Sahasranama*.

Aghori: Ascetic *Shaiva sadhus* who often reside in burial grounds, engage in post-mortem rituals, and smear cremation ashes on their bodies.

Aham Brahmasmi: A Sanskrit phrase originating from ancient Hindu philosophy, which means 'I am Brahman' or 'I am the ultimate energy'.

Ahankaar: Ego or having excessive pride.

Ahimsa: Non-Violence.

Ajna/Ajna chakra: The third eye energy center, situated in the space between the eyebrows, related to perception, intuition and consciousness.

Akkalkot: A town and a municipal council in the Solapur district in the western state of Maharashtra in India. It is widely known for its association with Swami Samarth, a.k.a. Akkalkot Maharaj.

Akkalkot Maharaj/Swami Samarth: A highly revered Indian spiritual Master, popularly known as Swami Samarth, who lived at Akkalkot, India and is believed to be the third incarnation of Lord Dattatreya

Allah: God, as named in Islam.

Allah Malik: A phrase meaning 'God is king', or 'God is the lord of all.'

Amba: In the Hindu epic *Mahabharata*, *Amba* is the eldest daughter of *Kashya*, the king of *Kashi* (modern-day Varanasi) and the sister of *Ambika* and *Ambalika*. *Amba* was abducted by Kuru prince *Bhishma* and held him responsible for her misfortune. Her sole goal in life became his destruction, to fulfil which she was reborn as *Shikhandini*, the daughter of king *Drupada* and the sister of the epic's female protagonist *Draupadi*.

Ambalika: Along with her sisters, *Amba* and *Ambika*, *Ambalika* was taken by force by *Bhishma* from their *Swayamvara*, the latter having challenged and defeated *the* assembled royalty. He presented them to Satyavati for marriage to *Vichitravirya*. Ambalika and her sister spent seven years in their husband's company. *Vichitravirya* was affected by phthisis.

Ambika: Along with her sisters, *Amba* and *Ambalika*, *Ambika* was taken by force by *Bhishma* from their *Swayamvara*, While *Amba* expressed her desire not to marry him as she was in love with a king named *Salwa*, *Ambika* and *Ambalika* married *Vichitravirya* and spent seven years in their husband's company.

Amrit: Ambrosia, the celestial nectar which grants immortality when consumed.

Amsha: An essence, fragment or a part of.

Anahata/Anahata Chakra: The energy centre (*vayu* or air element), situated at the centre of the chest, related to unconditional love, compassion, empathy and joy.

Ananda: Bliss or eternal happiness.

Ananta: Endless, limitless, eternal, infinite. Also, refers to *Sheshanaga*, the celestial snake, on which Lord *Vishnu* reclines.

Ananta Shayana: Sleeping or resting on infinity. Established in limitlessness.

Annamaya Kosha: First and outermost of the five *koshas,* composed of and maintained by food.

Ardha Narishwara: Lord Shiva in the composite forms of the deities Shiva and His consort *Parvati*, half-male and half-female split down the middle to indicate a synthesis of the masculine and feminine energies of the universe and their inseparability from each other.

Arjuna: One of the five *Pandava* brothers, who are the heroes of the Indian epic *Mahabharata*.

Ashwini Devatas: The twin Gods associated with medicine, health, dawn and sciences according to Hinduism.

Ashram: Spiritual hermitage or monastery. A place dedicated to spiritual practice.

Ashtavakra: Literally 'eight bends', reflecting the eight physical handicaps he was born with. Great Saint and *Guru* of King *Janaka*.

Ashtavakra Gita: A dialogue between King *Janaka* and Sage *Ashtavakra*, on the nature of soul, reality and bondage and through this dialogue the King *Janaka* attained enlightenment.

Asura: Demon or selfish being of lower consciousness.

Atithi Devo Bhava: Sanskrit phrase equating guests to God.

Autobiography of a Yogi: An autobiography of *Paramahansa Yogananda* which was first published in 1946, chronicling his experiences as a spiritual seeker and various encounters with highly spiritually evolved people.

Avadhoota: A liberated being who is beyond egoic-consciousness, duality and common worldly concerns and acts without consideration for standard social etiquette, and who gives his insight to others about his realisation of the true nature of the ultimate reality.

Avadhoota Gita: A sacred Sanskrit text of Hinduism attributed to Lord Dattatreya in which he expounds upon the nature and state of an *Avadhoota* and ultimate truths of existence.

Avatar: An earthly manifestation of a deity, aspect of existence, or previously liberated soul in bodily form. A strictly purpose-oriented incarnation, usually with a specific mission.

Ayodhya: Ancient city in Northern India. Home of *Rama*, from which he was exiled for fourteen years.

Ayukawa: A whaling port in Miyagi prefecture of Japan.

Mahavatar Babaji/Babaji: A renowned Master or the great *Yogi* of the *Kriya Yoga* Tradition who manifested Himself about 5000 years ago and who has promised to remain incarnated in physical until the end of *Kali Yuga*. Known in the Dattatreya Tradition as *Mahatapa*.

Baija Maa: Famous devotee of Shirdi Sai Baba.

Barsana: A historical town and nagar panchayat in the Mathura district of the state of Uttar Pradesh, India. Barsana is believed to be the home of the Hindu goddess Radha, the consort of Krishna. It is in the Braj region.

Bhagavad Gita/Gita: Also known as the Song of God, it is a 701-verse Hindu scripture that is part of the epic *Mahabharata* during a colloquy between Lord Krishna and *Arjuna* during the *Kurukshetra War*, on the battlefield. The philosophies and insights of *Bhagavad Gita* are intended to reach beyond the scope of religion and to humanity as a whole, and are often referred to as the 'manual for mankind'.

Bhagavan: The Supreme God or Absolute Truth, as a personality Who has divine qualities.

Bhagavan Nityananda: A highly revered Indian spiritual Master, who lived in *Ganeshpuri*, India and was believed to be the sixth incarnation of Lord Dattatreya

Bhagavan Sathya Sai Baba/Sathya Sai: A highly revered Indian spiritual Master of the *Dattatreya* Tradition and philanthropist whose life was his message and he inspired millions of people world-wide with his universal teachings.

Bhakta: A spiritual devotee who has deep devotion, affection and love towards God or Guru.

Bhakti: Devotion.

Bhakti Yoga: Devotion as the path of spirituality.

Bhoomi: Earth, place, location or arena.

Bindu: Point or dot.

Brahma/Lord Brahma: Creator of the universe. The aspect of Supreme Consciouness or of the trinity of *Brahma*, *Vishnu* and Shiva, which is responsible for creation.

Brahmagranthi: The 'knot of Brahma' situated in the *muladhara chakra*, is the first energetic constriction preventing the free flow of *kundalini* energy in the body and symbolises attachment to the material world and is connected with *tamas.*

Brahma Muhurta: The hours between approximately 3 a.m. to 6 a.m. Considered to the subtlest time of day, when *sattva guna* is predominant and most conducive to spiritual practice and evolution.

Biryani: Mixed rice dish originating among the Muslims of the Indian subcontinent. It is made with Indian spices, rice and vegetables

Buddha: A revered philosopher, meditator, enlightened spiritual teacher, and religious leader who is respected as the founder of Buddhism. He left the comforts of royal life as a prince to become a monk and attain enlightenment.

Buddhi: Intellect

Chandala: A man from a 'lower caste' or untouchable in the Indian caste system who deals with the disposal of corpses.

Chakras: Literally 'wheel'. Subtle energy points or centres in the body. They act as transformers through which energy is channelled to nourish various parts of the body (both gross and subtle). Minor chakras are located all throughout the body at various points. There are seven major chakras, considered to be of prime importance, which are located along a central channel, the *sushumna naadi*, which runs parallel to the spine.

Shankaracharya Chandrashekhar Saraswati/Shankaracharya of Kanchi: A revered philosopher and spiritual leader who was the 68th successor to the lineage originated by Adi Shankaracharya.

Charles Darwin: An English naturalist, geologist and biologist who was best known for his contributions to the science of evolution.

Chidakasha Gita: A book documenting the teachings of Bhagavan Nityananda.

Chitta: State of mind or consciousness. 'Mind stuff'. In *Yoga*, thoughts are considered as movements or whirlpools within chitta.

Crore: Ten million.

Dakshina: Offering (usually in form of money or other material)

Dakshinamoorthy: Shiva as the supreme Guru. Shiva as the supreme and all-encompassing knowledge. An aspect of supreme Consciousness of wisdom of Creation.

Dalai Lama: His Holiness the 14th Dalai Lama, Tenzin Gyatso is the spiritual leader of Tibetan Buddhism who has spent his life dedicated to benefiting humanity.

Damaru: A small drum associated with Lord Shiva which symbolises the sound that originates creation and perpetuates the universe.

Darshan: Literally 'sight', or, 'seeing'. The auspicious and most importantly, transformative, 'seeing' of a deity, divine being, or a sacred object.

Dattatreya/Datta: All-encompassing incarnation of the Divine Trinity (*Brahma, Vishnu* and Shiva). Considered to be the first or primordial Guru. *Yugacharya* of *Dwapara Yuga*. Codifier of the *Nath* Tradition.

Dharma: The eternal principles of existence, cosmic law underlying right behaviour and social order, righteousness or one's righteous duty.

Dhyana: Meditation.

Diwali: The festival of lights and one of the major festivals celebrated by Hindus, Jains, Sikhs and some Buddhists. Associated with the return of *Rama* to his home in *Ayodhya* after his fourteen-year exile and defeat of *Ravana* in battle.

Dosa: A thin pancake or crepe, originating from South India, made from a fermented batter predominantly consisting of lentils and rice.

Duryodhana: The eldest of the *Kauravas*, the main antagonist in the Hindu epic *Mahabharata*.

Dushasana: A *Kaurava* prince.

Eknath: Indian Hindu Saint, philosopher and poet who was a devotee of Lord Krishna.

Fakir: A Muslim religious ascetic living on alms.

Fr. Antony De Mello: An Indian teacher, public speaker, Jesuit priest and author of '1 minute wisdom' among many other books.

Ganga: The second largest river in the Indian subcontinent, revered as sacred and for its power of purification, and deeply beloved by countless spiritual seekers and Masters for thousands of years.

Ganeshpuri: Place of pilgrimage about 70km outside of Mumbai, in India. It is where Bhagavan Nityananda lived most of his life.

Gayatri: Highly revered and widely chanted mantra.

Gehenna: Thought to be a small valley in Jerusalem. In the Hebrew Bible, Gehenna was initially where some of the kings of Judah sacrificed their children by fire. Thereafter, it was deemed to be cursed.

Grihastha: The 'householder' stage of life. Second of the four life stages through human beings must progress in order to fully develop spiritually according to Hinduism. In this stage the person is occupied with family life, working, maintaining their home and raising a family.

Gunas: The three (*tamas, rajas, sattva*) fundamental qualities, or flavours of creation. All aspects of existence, all material objects, and all beings in existence are a combination of these three in varying ratios.

Guru Nanak/Baba Nanak: An Indian spiritual Master, known as one of the greatest religious innovators and founder of Sikhism. He is the first of the ten Sikh Gurus.

Gurudakshina: An expression of respect and gratitude or traditional repayment given to a teacher or Guru from a scholar at the completion of learning from that teacher or Guru.

Gurukul: A residential school system where scholars live as part of the Guru's family and serve and learn directly from the Guru.

Guru Tattwa: The Guru principle.

Habib: also known as Habib the Carpenter, or Habib Al-Najjar, according to the belief of some Muslims, he was a martyr who lived in Antioch at the time of Jesus Christ.

Hanumanji: Hanumanji is the incarnation of Lord Shiva and most capable devoted servant of Lord *Rama*. He is also one of the heroes of the Hindu Epic, *Ramayana*. Considered as the epitome and exemplifier of devotion.

Hatha Yoga: Form of spiritual practices primarily concerned with physical training and purification of energy channels within the body.

Himalayas: Mountain range in Northern India, Nepal and Tibet. Considered a place of holy isolation and practise.

Hiranyakashipu: An *adharmic* being, An *asura* and king of the race of demons known as the *daityas* from the ancient scriptures of Hinduism.

Iccha/Iccha Shakti: Will or will power.

Jagadguru/Jagad Guru: Guru of the world/universe.

Japa/Japa Sadhana/Japa Yoga: Repetitive singing of a verse or mantra, sometimes counted with the help of a rosary or mala. The spiritual practice of chanting the name or names of God.

Janaka/King Janaka: King of the *Mithila* region in Northern India. Father *Rama's* wife *Sita*. Janaka is revered as being an ideal example of non-attachment to material possessions.

Jesus: Also referred to as Christ and Jesus of Nazareth. According to Christian Gospels, He was the Messiah, the Son of God who was crucified for the sins of humanity before rising from the dead. His teachings revolved around love, forgiveness, peace and attaining the kingdom of God.

Jnana: Knowledge. Generally used in the context of spiritual knowledge or knowledge pertaining to the deeper truths of reality.

Jnana Yogi: One whose primary spiritual practice is the pursuit of divinity through knowledge.

Jnaneshwar: 13th-century Indian *Saint*, poet, philosopher and yogi of the *Nath* Tradition.

John: also known as John the Apostle, was one of the Twelve Apostles (disciple) of Jesus.

John the Baptist: John the Baptist was a Jewish itinerant preacher in the early 1st century A.D. Other titles for John include John the Forerunner in Eastern Christianity, John the Immerser in some Baptist traditions, and the prophet John in Islam.

Kabir Das: A 15th-century Indian mystic poet and Saint, whose writings influenced Hinduism's Bhakti movement and his verses are found in Sikhism's scripture Guru Granth Sahib.

Kali Yuga: The fourth *yuga* or age in the *yuga* cycles which we currently living in that spans 432,000 years as described in Hinduism, and is also known as the dark age of chaos, quarrel and confusion.

Kamsa: The tyrant ruler of the kingdom which had its capital at Mathura (a city in Northern India). After a heavenly voice prophesied that Krishna would slay him, *Kamsa* imprisoned Lord Krishna's birth parents, *Devaki* and *Vasudeva* and then cruelly murdered their infant children, however as prophesied, *Krishna*, the eighth son of *Devaki* defeated *Kamsa*.

Karl Marx: A German philosopher, economist, historian, sociologist, political theorist, journalist and socialist revolutionary who was famous for his theories about capitalism and communism.

Karma: A cycle of cause and effect rooted in thought, word, or action with attached emotions that get stored as imprints in the subconscious which provokes taking birth and the associated experiences of life, taking birth for the fulfilment of unfulfilled desires.

Karma Bhoomi: Land where the prevailing culture aids and supports a spiritual seeker in neutralising, completing, or fulfilling his/her *karma* through ritual, service, and penance.

Karma Yoga: Spiritual practice of selfless action or service, whereby in detaching oneself from the fruits of actions and offering them up to God, one learns to sublimate and dissolve the ego.

Kaurava: Royal dynasty of mainly, but not entirely, *adharmic* kings and princes. Chief antagonists to the *dharmic Pandavas* in the Hindu epic *Mahabharata*.

Khwaja Moinuddin Chishti: An Islamic Sufi Saint who established the Chisti order in South Asia and was known as Garib Nawaz (benefactor of the poor).

Koshas: The Five sheaths or layers which cover, or are worn by the soul. The grossest and furthest from the soul being the *annamaya kosha* (food sheath) and the subtlest and nearest the soul being the *anandamaya kosha* (bliss sheath).

Krishna/Shri Krishna: *Avatar* of *Vishnu* and Supreme Lord who was the key character of the epic *Mahabharata* and exponent of *Bhagavad Gita*.

Kriya/Kriya Yoga: Literally 'action', 'deed', or 'effort'. A system of spiritual practice that consists, among other things, of breathing, postural control, and visualisation, based on techniques intended to rapidly accelerate spiritual development and engender a profound state of tranquillity and God-communion.

Kshatriya: One of the four social orders of Hindu society, associated with warriorhood, bravery or being a warrior, soldier or protector.

Kshipra Kopi: Easily annoyed and angered.

Kshipra Prasadi: Easily pleased or propitiated.

Kumbha Mela: One of the largest human congregations of faith, involving pilgrimage to one of four holy towns (*Prayagraj*,

Nasik, Ujjain, Haridwar) in India. Initiated by *Adi Shankaracharya* partially as a way for solitary Masters and spiritual seekers to periodically interact with society and share their blessings and the hard-won spiritual energy they have accumulated from intense penance.

Kundalini: Divine, latent feminine energy or *Shakti*, believed to be coiled at the base of the spine, in the *muladhara chakra*. As *kundalini* moves up through the *Sushumna naadi* on its way to the *sahasrara chakra* (energy centre located at the top of the head), various profound changes happen in human consciousness. When it reaches its destination, one can be said to have attained the state of Shiva.

Kurukshetra War: Central battle between the *Pandava* and *Kaurava* dynasties in the Hindu Epic *Mahabharata*.

Ladoos: Spherical shaped sweets originating from India.

Lahiri Mahasaya: A highly respected Indian yogi, Guru and a devoted disciple of Kriya Yoga Master Mahavatar Babaji who initiated Lahiri Mahasaya in the science of Kriya Yoga and then instructed him to bestow the sacred technique on all sincere seekers.

Lakshmi/Mother Lakshmi: The Hindu Goddess or Divine energy representing wealth, fortune, power, purity, luxury, beauty, fertility, abundance, auspiciousness, fulfilment and contentment. She forms part of the divine feminine trinity (*Saraswati*, *Lakshmi* and *Parvati*) and is the consort of *Vishnu*.

Lalitha Sahasranama: The thousand names of the Hindu feminine deity *Lalita*.

Leela: Divine play, or all reality, including the cosmos, as the outcome of creative play by the divine absolute. Also, the arrangement of events and people as ordained by divinity to express, experience, or demonstrate an aspect or Truth of existence.

Lingam/Linga/Shiva Linga/Shiva Lingam: A symbol of divine generative energy or an abstract representation of the Hindu Deity Lord Shiva. Representative of the egg, or womb from which all existence is born.

Loka: World or realm of existence

Lokah Samastah Sukhino Bhavanthu: A Sanskrit mantra or prayer which in simple translation means 'May all Beings in all the worlds be happy, joyous and free from suffering.'

Mahabharata: One of the major Sanskrit epics of ancient India, which narrates the struggle between two groups of cousins, the *adharmic Kaurava* and *dharmic Pandava* princes and their successors. The central conflict of which is the *Kurukshetra* War. It has been described as the longest epic poem consisting of over 100,000 - 200,000 individual lines.

Shivaratri: Annual confluence of energies and celestial bodies such that the frequencies of supreme consciousness and perfect detachment are easily accessible on Earth. A time which is considered to be conducive to the attainment of the state of Shiva.

Mahatma Gandhi/Gandhiji: An Indian lawyer, anti-colonial nationalist, and political ethicist, who employed non-violent resistance (*satyagraha*) for India's independence from British rule and he drew international attention to the plight of Indians in South Africa to help them. Lovingly known as the Father of the Indian Nation.

Maharajas: Great kings of ancient India.

Mahavira: Also known as Vardhamana. A great Saint of Jainism who was born a prince but renounced his royal life at the age of 30 and became an ascetic. A contemporary of *Buddha*.

Mahishasura: A powerful and deceitful buffalo demon as depicted in Hinduism who had the ability to shapeshift and due to his intense tapasya, he gained the boon from Lord *Brahma* that no man of any species could kill him. He was eventually defeated in battle by the divine feminine deity *Durga*.

Manipura/Manipura Chakra: The energy centre (*agni* or fire element) located at or near the navel region, related to self-esteem and self-confidence.

Manomaya Kosha: Third of the five koshas or sheaths, known as the mind sheath which involves processing thoughts and emotions.

Mantra: A Sanskrit word, sound or phrase repeated often during praying or chanting.

Matthew: One of the Twelve Apostles (disciples) of Jesus.

Maya: Illusion. That which is not eternal.

Menaka: One of the most beautiful *apsaras* (celestial fairy) who emerged during the churning of the ocean.

Mhalsapati: Close devotee Shirdi Sai Baba and priest of a local temple in Shirdi.

Moksha: Complete liberation or freedom from the cycle of birth and death.

Mudras: Symbolic hand gestures or yogic postures which can be done during meditation or spiritual practice to manipulate or direct energy throughout the body.

Muktananda/Baba Muktananda: Disciple of Bhagavan Nityananda.

Mukti: Complete liberation or freedom from the cycle of birth and death.

Mula mantras: The root mantra to invoke the presence of a specific Deity or subtle aspect of existence.

Muladhara Chakra: The root energy centre (*prithvi* or earth element) situated at the base of the spine, related to grounding and stability.

Naadis: Meridians or energy channels that are part of the subtle energy body.

Naada: Primal sound or first vibration from which all creation has originated.

Naada-upasana: A deep concentration practice or meditation focused on sound within.

Naam: Name.

Nagas: Divine beings who reside in the netherworld. Considered to be the earliest teachers of humankind who taught us about various aspects of creation, sustenance, and dissolution. Often incarnated as snakes in order to preserve their solitude, but also in human form for a specific purpose.

Naga Sadhus: Ash-covered, unclothed ascetics who have renounced worldly life and material pleasures, they are followers of Lord Shiva and live in the *Himalayas* but they come out in plain sight during the *Kumbha Mela*.

Narasimha Saraswati: An Indian Guru of Dattatreya Tradition and the second *avatar* of Lord *Dattareya* in *Kali Yuga*.

Narayana: The destination of man.. Lord *Narayana* or *Vishnu*, The Supreme Father in a state of yogic sleep reclining on the celestial snake *Ananta*. A representation of supreme consciousness.

Nath Guru: A spiritual Master or Guru stemming from an ancient lineage traditionally ascribed to Lord *Dattatreya* who codified the *Nath* Tradition based on the state of Lord Shiva. The purpose of the *Nath* Tradition is liberation, where one can be in everything but at the same time not bound by anything.

Nirbhaya: Fearless.

Nisargadatta Maharaj: An Indian Guru of nondualism, belonging to the Inchagiri Sampradaya, a lineage of teachers from the *Nath* Tradition.

Osho: An Indian enlightened Master, mystic and founder of the Rajneesh movement.

Parabrahma: supreme formless God who Generates, Operates and Dissolves. All forms are formed out of Him and dissolve in Him.

ParamahansaYogananda: Indian Saint famous as the author of 'Autobiography of a Yogi', and populariser of *Kriya Yoga* in and outside of India in the early to mid-twentieth century.

Parvati/Mother Parvati: Also known as *Uma, Durga* or *Shakti*. The Hindu Goddess or Divine energy representing fertility, love, beauty, harmony, marriage, children, devotion, divine strength and power. She forms part of the divine feminine trinity (*Saraswati, Lakshmi,* and *Parvati*) and is the consort of Lord Shiva.

Pashupatastra/Pashupata: The most destructive and powerful weapon of Lord Shiva, which can be discharged by the mind, eyes, words, or with a bow. Never to be used against lesser enemies or by lesser warriors, the *Pashupatastra* is capable of destroying creation and vanquishing all beings.

Patanjali: A sage in ancient India commonly known as the 'Father of *Yoga*' who wrote the *Yoga Sutras*, a classical *yoga* text dating to 200 BCE – 200 CE.

Path of White: The path of dharma

Peetham: Chair or seat.

Pol Pot: A Cambodian revolutionary and politician who governed Cambodia as the Prime Minister of Democratic Kampuchea between 1975 and 1979.

Prana: Lifeforce.

Pranayama: A Sanskrit word meaning 'extension of *prana* or breath' or, more accurately, 'extension of the life force'. The word is composed of two Sanskrit words – 'prana', life force or vital energy, particularly, the breath; and 'ayama', to extend or draw out.

Pranaams: Greetings someone with reverence and respect usually with palms placed together in front of the chest or heart centre in Namaste position.

Pranamaya Kosha: Second of the five koshas known as the prana sheath dealing with vital energy, breath, or life force.

Pranapat: When life force or prana is infused into the spinal cord of recipients which enters the subtle energetic system and can unblock the meridians to clear the pathway for the *Kundalini* to awaken.

Prarabdha Karma: A collection of past karmas, which are ready to be experienced through the present body.

Puja: An act of worship or devotional ritual.

Pujari: A priest or one who performs devotional rituals in Hindu temples.

Purva samskara: past impressions.

Puttaparthi: Town located on the banks of the river Chitravati in India. Widely associated with Sathya Sai Baba.

Radha: Devotee and consort of Krishna.

Radhakrishnamayi: Famous devotee of Shirdi Sai Baba.

Raja: King.

Rajas/Rajasic: One of the three basic qualities of nature (*gunas*) which drives motion, energy, activity and passion and is associated with higher levels of heat energy and movement.

Raja Yoga: System of spiritual practice with the aim of attaining the state of Shiva by dissolving into and merging with supreme consciousness, as codified by the great Saint *Patanjali* in the *Yoga Sutra*.

Ramachandra/Rama/Shri Rama: Seventh *avatar* of Lord Vishnu and the central figure in the epic *Ramayana*.

Rama Krishna Hari: Mantra wherein the names of Rama and Krishna are chanted.

Ramana Maharshi/Bhagavan Ramana Maharshi: A revered Hindu Saint and liberated Being of the *Nath* Tradition who spent His life at the holy mountain *Arunachala*, in South India.

Ratnakara: The hunter who transformed into the great sage Valmiki (also see Valmiki)

Ravana: The demon king of Sri Lanka and primary antagonist in the great epic Ramayana. Ravana was described as a 'ten headed' devout disciple of Lord Shiva, a great scholar possessing a thorough knowledge of many subjects, including ceremony, warfare, and music.

Rig Veda: Oldest among the *Vedas.* (Oldest and canonical Hindu texts)

Rishis/Maharishis: Enlightened beings, great yogis or sages who realised the supreme Truth and eternal knowledge after intense meditation or practice.

Rudragranthi: The 'knot of Rudra' situated in the *ajna chakra*, is the third energetic constriction preventing the free flow of *kundalini* energy in the body and symbolises attachment to the spiritual world and is connected with *sattva.*

Rudraksha: Seed bearing fruit of the elaeocarpus ganitrus roxb tree. The fruits are dried and strung together to form a rosary and these seeds are believed to be the tears of Lord Shiva.

Rukmini: The first queen consort of *Krishna.*

Sadashiva: Omnipotent, subtle, luminous absolute. The highest manifestation of the almighty.

Sadashiva Brahmendra: An eighteenth-century yogi, *Advaita* philosopher and composer of Carnatic music who lived near *Kumbakonam* in Southern India.

Sadashiva Samaarambha: Everything started from Lord Shiva.

Sadguru: A 'true Guru', complete Guru, highest of the Gurus. The One who has reached the highest realm of spiritual attainment, is selfless, compassionate, perpetually exists beyond *gunas* and elevates the consciousness of disciples through His thought, words and actions at all times.

Sadhaka: Spiritual seeker.

Sadhana: Spiritual practice.

Sadhu: Wandering monk.

Sahasranama: A Sanskrit word meaning a 'thousand names' usually of a Deity or a Saint.

Sahasrara/Sahasrara Chakra: The energy centre located at the crown of the head, also referred to as the thousand-petalled lotus, which is related to spiritual connection, higher awareness and transformation.

Sai Satcharita: A hagiography based on the true-life stories of Sai Baba of Shirdi.

Saint Teresa of Avila: A Spanish Carmelite nun, mystic and author of spiritual writings and poems, who lived in the sixteenth century. She founded numerous convents throughout Spain and was the originator of the Carmelite Reform.

Sabarimala: A temple complex located in the Sabarimala hill, in Kerala, India, dedicated to the deity Ayyappa, a personification of self-control.

Sakshi bhava: Being in witness mode and having higher awareness of the terrestrial world.

Samadhi: The stage of union with the Divine, the highest bliss. State of inner stillness.

Samskara: Impression or psychological imprints. Seeds of karmic impressions. Repeated actions form habits, repeated habits form *samskaras*.

Samudra: Ocean, sea or confluence of waters.

Sanatana Dharma: Signifies the 'eternal law', 'eternal way of righteousness' or absolute set of righteous duties performed according to one's spiritual constitution. Also denotes the ancient name for Hinduism or a way of life dealing with ancient sciences, liberation and spirituality.

Saptarishi: The seven highly venerated and illustrious sages of Hinduism. Considered to be pioneers in spirituality and originators of many hymns, *mantras*, and practices.

Saraswati/Mother Saraswati: The Hindu Goddess or Divine energy representing knowledge, music, art, speech, wisdom, and learning. She forms part of the divine feminine trinity (*Saraswati, Lakshmi,* and *Parvati*) and is the consort of Lord *Brahma.*

Satchitananda: Absolute bliss of unity in consciousness.

Satsang: Spiritual gathering or get-together. Company which is conducive to spiritual elevation.

Sattva/Sattvic: One of the three basic qualities of nature (*gunas*) which means existing in purity, harmony and balance.

Satya: Truth.

Satyam, Shivam, Sundaram: Truth, bliss, beauty.

Seva: Selfless service.

Shaivic: Of or relating to Shiva or the path of Shiva.

Shakti: A vital force. The great feminine energy, sacred force or empowerment; the primordial cosmic energy and representative of the dynamic forces that are thought to move through the entire universe in Hinduism. Shakti is the concept, or personification, of divine feminine creative power, sometimes referred to as 'The Great Divine Mother' in Hinduism.

Shaktipat: Conferring of spiritual 'energy' upon one person by another. It can be transmitted with a sacred word or mantra, or by a look, thought or touch—the last usually to the third eye (*ajna chakra*) of the recipient. It is considered an act of Grace (anugraha) on the part of the Guru or the Divine. Absolute faith opens the recipient during *shaktipat.* It shifts the recipient's consciousness.

Shakuni: The prince of the *Gandhara* Kingdom in North-Western Pakistan, who is believed to be the mastermind and orchestrator of *Kurukshetra* war in the Hindu Epic *Mahabharata*.

Shama: A great devotee of Shirdi Sai Baba. Acted as Baba's personal secretary.

Shankar Maharaj: Indian Saint of the *Nath* Tradition who lived a few kilometres outside of the Indian city of Pune.

Shanti: Peace.

Shava: A corpse. As it relates to the path of Shiva, it means a state of inertia and unconsciousness.

Sheshanaga: The celestial snake, on which Lord *Vishnu* reclines.

Shirdi: A village located in the Indian state of *Maharashtra*. Famous as the place where Sai Baba spent most of his life.

Shirdi Sai Baba/Sai Baba/Baba: A great and highly respected sadguru who is an incarnation of Dattatreya and part of the *Nath* Tradition. Baba lived in *Shirdi* and His teachings were focused on love, faith, patience, forgiveness, helping others, charity, contentment, inner peace and devotion.

Shivapat: A spiritual Master shares his own enlightenment, energy or spiritual power with disciples to elevate them to newer dimensions of awakening and awareness.

Shivoham: I am Shiva

Siddha: One who has accomplished a high degree of perfection or enlightenment or one who has achieved his ultimate objective.

Siddhis: Spiritual powers or special abilities.

Sigmund Freud: An Austrian neurologist and founding father of psychoanalysis, a clinical method for treating psychopathology through dialogue between a patient and a psychoanalyst. He believed that events in one's childhood have a great influence on their adult lives and on shaping their personality.

Socrates: A Greek philosopher from Athens who is credited as one of the founders of Western philosophy.

Sushumna/Sushumna Naadi: The central energy channel in the subtle body. Considered to be of prime importance to the spiritual seeker.

Svadhishthana/Svadhishthana Chakra: The sacral energy centre (water element) situated in the pelvic region, related to creativity, flexibility, desire and confidence.

Swami Rama: Indian yogi and Guru, who started several ashrams and institutes in India and America.

Swami Vivekananda: An Indian Hindu Sadguru who was the foremost disciple of Ramakrishna Paramahamsa, an influential philosopher and key spokesman in introducing Indian philosophies of *Vedanta* and *Yoga* to the western world.

Tamas/Tamasic: One of the three basic qualities of nature (*gunas*), which relates to inertia, inactivity, dullness, or lethargy. Generally associated with darkness, destructive or chaotic traits.

Tattva: Principle, or aspect of existence.

Tat Twam Asi: Sanskrit phrase meaning 'you are That' which expresses the relationship between the individual and the Absolute. One of the great Mahavakyas (great statements) of the Upanishads.

Tejas: Radiance or brightness.

Tukaram: A 17th-century Saint of the Varkari sampradaya in Maharashtra and a Marathi poet.

Turiya: The fourth state of consciousness which persists through and transcends, the three states of waking, dreaming, and deep sleep.

Upasni Maharaj: A Hindu *Guru* who lived in a small village called *Sakori* in *Maharashtra*, India and after coming to the Indian Saint Sai Baba of Shirdi, and staying in his care for three years as Shirdi Sai *Baba's* discipline, *Upasni Maharaj* is said to have become a sadguru.

Vaishno Devi: Place of pilgrimage in northern India, dedicated to *Vaishno Devi*, a manifestation of the Hindu mother goddess.

Valmiki: A highly revered Sage who lived in ancient India during the lifetime of *Rama* during *Treta Yuga* and was the composer of the first Sanskrit poem known worldwide as the epic *Ramayana* (story of Rama).

Vasanas: Natural inclinations, inherent traits with attached emotions and terrestrial bindings or behavioural tendency which influences the present behaviour of a person. Related to *karmic* imprints.

Vasishta: One of the *Saptarishis*.

Vedanta: Thesis work of great saints towards the path of enlightenment. It also means beyond the *Vedas* or beyond the state of doing.

Vedas: Collection of the oldest of Sanskrit literature and canonical scriptures of Hinduism originating in ancient India consisting of the *Rig Veda*, *Sama Veda*, *Yajur Veda* and *Atharva Veda* which were composed in *Vedic* Sanskrit and codifies the ideas and practices of Hinduism.

Vidura: Son of sage *Vyasa* and one of the central characters in the *Mahabharata*.

Vibhooti: Sacred ash

Vishnu/Mahavishnu: The 'Maintainer or Preserver' among the Hindu Trinity of the primary aspects of the Divine.

Vishnu Granthi/Vishnugranthi: 'Knot of Vishnu' situated between *manipura* and *anahata chakra*s, is the second energetic constriction preventing the free flow of energy in the body and symbolises emotional attachment. It is connected with rajas.

Vishwamitra: One of the *saptarishis*.

Vishuddha/Vishuddha Chakra: The energy centre (*akasha* or ether element) situated in the throat region, related to communication, self-expression and speaking one's Truth.

Viveka: Discrimination

Vrindavan: A holy town in Northern India. The Hindu deity Krishna is said to have spent his childhood here.

Vyasa/Vedavyasa: A Revered *Rishi* of ancient India who was the traditional author of the epic *Mahabharata*.

Yajna: Fire ceremony or ritual.

Yoga: State of unity with one's self and the divine. Also, the various paths and practices which are conducive to attaining that state.

Yoga Nidra: Yogic sleep. Sometimes referred to as the state between waking and sleeping.

Yogi: A practitioner of yoga.

Yudhisthira: The first among the five Pandava brothers.

Yuga: Epoch or era. Time is divided into repeating cycles of four *yugas* ie. *Satya Yuga, Treta Yuga, Dwapara Yuga* and *Kali Yuga* respectively. *Satya Yuga* is considered the golden age, wherein all beings are established in supreme consciousness. Consciousness gradually declines from there until it reaches its lowest point in *Kali Yuga*

Yugacharya: Primary Guru of a specific era.

Zarathustra/Zoroaster: An ancient Iranian prophet who founded what is now known as Zoroastrianism.